The Myth of Liberal Ascendancy

The Myth of Liberal Ascendancy

Corporate Dominance from the Great Depression
to the Great Recession

G. William Domhoff

Paradigm Publishers
Boulder • London

Copyright © 2013 by Paradigm Publishers

Published in the United States by Paradigm Publishers, 5589 Arapahoe Avenue, Boulder, CO 80303 USA.

Paradigm Publishers is the trade name of Birkenkamp & Company, LLC,
Dean Birkenkamp, President and Publisher.

Library of Congress Cataloging-in-Publication Data

Domhoff, G. William.
  The myth of liberal ascendancy : corporate dominance from the Great Depression to the great recession / G. William Domhoff.
      p. cm.
  Includes bibliographical references and index.
  ISBN 978-1-61205-256-4 (pbk. : alk. paper)
1. Corporations—United States—History. 2. Elite (Social sciences)—United States—History.
3. Liberalism—United States—History. I. Title.
  HD2785.D663 2013
  338.7′40973—dc23

                                                                            2012041702

Printed and bound in the United States of America on acid-free paper that meets the standards of the American National Standard for Permanence of Paper for Printed Library Materials. Designed and Typeset by Straight Creek Bookmakers.

17 16 15 14 13   1 2 3 4 5

Contents

Preface

This project started out as an attempt to understand the conservative turn in American public policy that apparently began in the mid-1970s. But research for the background chapters gradually led to the conclusion that American public policy has been moving rightward since 1939, with slight interruptions due to World War II, the Korean War, and the civil rights movement and the movements it inspired. For those of us over age fifty, the book ends up as the story of everything that was going on in the higher circles while we were too busy living our own lives to notice. For those under age fifty, it is the story of how the United States came to be, by 1984, almost exactly what it is today, with no major turning points in the distribution of power since that time, just increasing corporate domination.

The book draws upon my interviews with business leaders and policy experts who were active in the 1970s, and my subsequent research in historical archives, but it owes more to the brilliant detailed work by a wide range of experts that have dealt with an array of specific issues in dozens of studies over the past fifty years. It is therefore a work of synthesis as much as it is a presentation of new research. I hope I have been able to do justice to the many original studies I reply upon, and I apologize in advance to their authors for any sins of misunderstanding or omission. Although the book makes an empirical case for corporate dominance from the 1930s to 2012 based on their work and mine, it does not use this conclusion to try to support any general theory.

I am indebted to many people who helped make it possible to complete this project, which actually began in the late 1980s and was postponed several times to complete other work. I never could have finished this book without being able to draw upon the colleagueship of these wonderful members of the scholarly network, who saved me scores of hours in the library and on the Internet. The collective impact of their responses on the quality of the book and the time it took to complete it was enormous from my point of view as an interloper into many areas in which I previously had little or no knowledge.

I thank my longtime coauthor, Richard L. Zweigenhaft, for his many editorial suggestions that made the manuscript much more succinct and readable. It is always reassuring to have a friend who is comfortable pointing out mistakes, inconsistencies, redundancies, poor word choices, and awkward phrases. I also want to thank John Manley for very helpful comments based on his careful reading of the entire manuscript, and Kevin Boyle, Michael K. Brown, Alec Campbell, Jennifer Delton, James A. Gross, Howard Kimeldorf, Allen Matusow, Harvey Molotch, Thomas F. Pettigrew, Jill Quadagno, Brian Waddell, Michael J. Webber, and Charles Whitham for commenting on chapters or sections of chapters in which I was drawing in good part on their expertise and original research for an understanding of the topic under discussion.

I am grateful to Sol Hurwitz for correcting many mistakes and misunderstandings in relation to the work of the Committee for Economic Development, the business group I use as my primary vantage point on power conflicts, in which he was an important figure for over three decades in the late twentieth century. I was deeply informed by a stunning background memorandum that Richard Wilbur, a key staff aide to Republican leaders in the House of Representatives in the 1960s and 1970s, wrote on the legislative struggle over the Family Assistance Plan in 1969–1970. He also furthered my understanding of both moderate and ultraconservative Republicans in Congress. I thank Mark A. Smith for providing a copy of his detailed findings on the stance taken by the US Chamber of Commerce on important pieces of legislation that passed Congress and became law during several decades of the postwar era.

I am also grateful to Patrick Akard, Steven Bank, Thomas Bethell, Sarah Blinder, W. Elliot Brownlee, Alec Campbell, Robert M. Collins, David Golland, Sanford Jacoby, David Cay Johnston, Wojciech Kopczuk, Jeff Manza, Mark Mizruchi, Nick Paretsky, Jill Quadagno, Alejandro Reuss, Benjamin W. Smith, and Peter Swenson for providing information and sources in their areas of expertise in answer to my specific questions to them. I thank Clifford Staples for information and sources related to the Business Roundtable. I thank my research assistants of twenty-five years ago, Robert Bulman and Bristow Hardin, now well established in their own careers, for the work they did on lobbying and campaign donations by members of the Committee for Economic Development.

In closing, I want to pay special thanks to Dean Birkenkamp of Paradigm Publishers for his support and friendship over the years, and especially for his many excellent editorial suggestions throughout this project.

Introduction

THE MYTH OF A POSTWAR
LIBERAL-LABOR ASCENDANCY

Once upon a fairly recent time, according to a widely known American fairy tale, the United States was a liberal nation, thanks to the New Deal that emerged from the Great Depression and the Kennedy and Johnson administrations in the 1960s. But somewhere along the line, things began to go the other way, to the right. Did it all start with tensions within the liberal-labor alliance over the demands of the civil rights movement for the integration of neighborhoods, schools, and workplaces, as used to be thought? Or did the downfall happen in the second half of the 1970s, when corporations decided to flex their muscles, which is the new conventional wisdom? Or was it primarily a product of the Reagan administration and its merry band of tax cutters, as other recent analysts claim?

WISTFUL ROMANTICISM

Although rival analysts disagree on when things started to move rightward in the United States, almost all of them agree that the United States was led toward greater equality by a New Deal coalition for most of the years before and after World War II. This coalition within the Democratic Party was all the more impressive because it depended upon an unlikely voting alliance of southern whites, workers who belonged to unions, white ethnic Americans who lived in big cities, African Americans outside the South, and the small minority of people of any race, creed, color, or social class who for unknown reasons became liberals. The impact of this complex coalition seems obvious in retrospect if the focus is on party labels and numbers. After all, the Democratic Party controlled the presidency in thirty-two of the forty-eight years between 1933 and 1980 and held majorities in both the House and Senate during that period, except for brief Republican interludes in 1947–1948 and 1953–1954.

Thanks in part to the development of a liberal-labor alliance during the New Deal, corporations were not as powerful during this golden age as they were before the New

1

Deal coalition arrived and would be after it was defeated. They were not well organized and did not wield the power they did retain very effectively (e.g., Vogel 1989). Instead of mounting a coordinated lobbying effort, individual corporations or business sectors tended to look out for their own narrow interests, so they naturally lost on a large number of general issues, especially those having to do with consumers, labor unions, government social insurance, and environmental protection. In the version of the new romanticism that places the "unseen revolution" carried out by corporations in the post-Watergate era, the business community was "getting its clock cleaned" during the first Nixon administration (Hacker and Pierson 2010, pp. 95, 97, 117). In another version, which finds "little reason to romanticize postwar liberalism," it is nonetheless the case that "a great transformation of American politics began during the years that Ronald Reagan was in the White House," including the beginning of a "prolonged decline" in the labor movement (Phillips-Fein 2009, pp. 262–263, 269).

Either way, things began to change in the corporate world. In the scenario that has attracted the most attention, the biggest corporations, fed up with the new regulatory demands and expenses foisted on them by consumer activists and the environmental movement, finally began to pull themselves together politically in the mid-1970s and the Carter years; in the process of organizing to defeat their new adversaries, the corporate leaders also began an attack on organized labor (e.g., Hacker and Pierson 2010, chapter 4). In the version that locates the turning point in the Reagan years, the infrastructure that ultraconservatives on the fringes of the corporate community had been building since the late 1930s finally broke through the liberal-labor alliance. This infrastructure, a series of new think tanks and a refurbished US Chamber of Commerce, was aided by funding from a few wealthy families and their foundations, along with sage advice from lobbyists and a highly conservative corporate lawyer (e.g., Phillips-Fein 2009, chapter 7).

In both versions, the new corporate mobilization was epitomized by the formation of the fearsome Business Roundtable in 1972, the equivalent of a "domestic version of Shock and Awe"; in addition, the corporate leaders, urged on by their hired lobbyists, created a more united, active, and sophisticated lobbying effort with which they could "flood Washington with letters and phone calls" (Hacker and Pierson 2010, pp. 118, 121). The result was a level of pressure on astonished legislators that had never been dreamed of in the past. Just to be sure they would emerge triumphant, the sleeping giants of the corporate world also increased their influence in politics through large campaign donations to political action committees (PACs), a new avenue for them to fund political candidates made possible by changes in campaign finance laws in the mid-1970s (Phillips-Fein 2009, p. 188).

But these accounts of the right turn are wrong in all their factual assertions. The large corporations—united into a *corporate community* through overlapping ownership, shared directors, and a common desire to limit unionization and reduce progressive taxation—were well organized from the late 1930s through the 1960s, and they were politically mobilized. This fact is overlooked amid the twenty-first-century nostalgia about the New Deal and the postwar era because there were some differences of opinion between moderates and ultraconservatives within the corporate world. As a result, the most effective corporate mobilization was not in terms of political ultraconservatism but in a moderate centrism that made use of some Keynesian ideas during and after World War II, even while the corporate community as a whole successfully fought to limit union power, minimize government power over wages and prices, and reduce taxes on the corporate rich.

The corporate moderates also decided to respond to the turmoil in the inner cities in the 1960s with ameliorative programs, including several spending initiatives. They did not think it was sensible to rely on a heavier dose of law and order, as advocated by their ultraconservative colleagues in the National Association of Manufacturers and the US Chamber of Commerce, whose frequent defeats on a wide range of issues are used as evidence for the weakness of the corporate community when faced with strong and mobilized public opinion (Smith 2000). Some of the new romanticists even inaccurately state the origins of the Business Roundtable (e.g., Phillips-Fein 2009, pp. 190–192). Its roots actually go back to the mid-1960s, not the early 1970s, and it was grounded in attempts to fight inflation in construction costs and change the laws governing labor unions, not in conflicts with consumer activists, environmentalists, or regulatory agencies. Additionally, the wistful thinkers are wrong because the corporate community was extremely active and well-coordinated in its lobbying efforts in the 1950s and 1960s (Hall 1969; Melone 1977; Ross 1967).

Moreover, wealthy owners and corporate executives always spent large sums on political campaigns through personal donations in the postwar era, far more than unions and liberal interest groups. In 1968, for example, "at least one half, and perhaps more, of [Hubert] Humphrey's general election campaign expenses were paid for through contributions and loans from about fifty individuals" (Alexander 1971, p. 152). In 1972, some 51,000 people gave $500 or more (the equivalent of $2,750 in 2012 dollars) to one or another campaign, with the 1,254 who gave $10,000 or more providing $51.3 million to national-level candidates, six times more than the $8.5 million that organized labor donated to presidential and congressional candidates (Alexander 1976, pp. 71, 106). As for the explosive growth of corporate PACs after 1975, most of the new corporate PACs were not activated or well-funded until 1980 (Alexander 1979, chapter 10).

The only observers at the time who were alleging the impotence of the corporate community were corporate lobbyists, who thereby provide the "evidence" cited by those who overstate the influence of the New Deal coalition (e.g., Vogel 1989, chapter 8). The new nostalgia is also off base because ultraconservative think tanks came of age in the second half of the 1970s, too late to have a causal role in the rightward trend that was already picking up speed by the early 1970s. Their impact came primarily through their efforts to identify and energize new electoral activists, although it's true that they may have had a hand in winning over some white middle-income voters and centrists in Congress by repackaging age-old ultraconservative verities.

Although the romantic revisionists rightly note the importance of unions in securing good wages for their employees through collective bargaining, along with their provision of important political support for pro-labor Democrats, they overstate the labor movement's postwar political power. They also wrongly claim that its decline came much later, during the second half of the 1970s, than it actually did (Hacker and Pierson 2010, pp. 56–61, 127–132). Unions not only lost most of the legislative battles in which they engaged between 1939 and 1968, with the important exception of Medicare in 1965, but also splintered over racial integration between 1965 and 1968. They then went downhill as a legislative and lobbying force, even though many large unions in construction and heavy industry continued to win wage gains for the next few years. Strikingly, the turmoil and division both within the unions and in their alliance with liberals are downplayed by some of the new revisionists. They do so by noting that the 1968 and 1972 elections happened "smack in the middle of the great 'bulge' of government activism that runs from, roughly, 1964 to 1977," a sure sign to them that the liberal-labor alliance was still on the march despite its internal problems (Hacker and Pierson 2010, p. 96). They thereby position themselves as the iconoclasts that dismiss the "colorful, easy to tell, and superficially appealing" narrative about a white backlash in the 1960s because it "misses the real story" (Hacker and Pierson 2010, pp. 95, 96).

Nor is the new version of the recent American past accurate in explaining corporate successes in the 1970s and beyond. The defeat of legislation of which corporations did not approve in that decade was due to the continuing existence of the same conservative coalition of Republicans and Southern Democrats that dominated every session of Congress from 1939 onward, not to the corporate community's allegedly new lobbying power. The only temporary exception to that generalization occurred in 1965–1966, when the conservative coalition's potential of 240 votes in the House was seldom realized. But even in that fabled session of Congress, conservatives had the power to moderate or block far-reaching legislation through their control of important committees in both houses and through filibusters in the Senate. (For further discussion concerning these and other misunderstandings about power in the United States, see Domhoff 2013, chapter 9.)

In contrast to the myth of a liberal-labor ascendancy that lost to a newly energized corporate counterattack, which seems to gain strength in proportion to the rising inequality of recent decades, there has been increasing corporate dominance of the United States since 1939 on every important economic and social-welfare issue that came before Congress. The corporate community exercised this power by crafting new policies from within organizations of its own creation, by lobbying successfully for its preferences in Congress, and by providing campaign donations and other forms of support to political candidates who agreed with its policy positions. At the same time, the moderate and ultraconservative factions within the corporate community were in constant disagreement over a wide range of issues, even while working together to fend off, water down, or turn to their own advantage every new proposal that was put forth by the liberal-labor alliance. Those are strong statements, but all of them will be documented in detail in the chapters that follow.

WHAT EXPLAINS DECLINING POSTWAR INCOME INEQUALITY?

Why, then, if corporations were winning all of the key legislative battles, were many of the years in the middle decades of the twentieth century (but not all of them) a time of declining income inequality? It is mainly because it took the corporate community thirty to thirty-five years to roll back or eliminate the changes during the New Deal and World War II that made greater equality possible in the midst of growing prosperity. The world war itself, the unions that were bolstered by that war, increased postwar government spending on a wide range of programs, and the budget deficits created by spending for the Korean and Vietnam wars were the primary reasons for the greater postwar equality.

To begin with, the conversion to military production starting in 1940 created an economic boom and reduced unemployment dramatically. Just as important in the longer run, the need for all-out war production forced the federal government to limit corporate resistance to a new union upsurge in order to guarantee the harmony needed to produce the weapons to fight two wars without slowdowns and strikes. The combination of militant labor organizing and government restraints on corporate efforts to crush unions made it possible for the number of unionized workers to grow from nine to fifteen million between 1941 and 1945, a 67 percent increase, thereby providing a larger and more solid base for the liberal-labor electorate. At the same time, the gradual growth in financial support for the elderly beginning in 1940 (through both means-tested old-age assistance payments and Social Security pensions) put a modest floor under consumer spending by retirees and relieved their grown children from having to spend part of their incomes taking care of them.

The increased federal revenues resulting from higher taxes and the war effort also sustained greater income equality because they were spent on many new government programs, all heartily endorsed by the corporate moderates, starting with the GI Bill, which increased consumer spending and pumped up the economy. Although the GI Bill, which was supported by many ultraconservatives as well, is most often thought of in recent years in terms of financial support for technical training and university education right after the war, it also provided many other benefits for the 40 to 48 percent of American adult males who were veterans between 1960 and 1980, such as free medical care and low-interest loans (Campbell 2004).

More generally, the federal government's increased tax revenues made possible a number of other spending programs, such as highway construction, urban renewal, unemployment benefits, Medicare, and foreign aid (much of which was spent in the United States for supplies to rebuild and rearm Europe). Taken together, these varied programs gave government a larger role in the economy. As a result of high progressive income taxes during and after the war, increased government spending, and strong unions in the largest industrial sectors, there was a significant decline in income inequality between 1938 and 1953. This decline was reversed during the Eisenhower years, then resumed between 1961 and 1968, only to be reversed once and for all in 1969 as part of the return to levels of income inequality that had not been seen since the late 1930s.

Although the percentage of wage and salary employees in unions reached its high point of 35.5 percent in 1945 and sank to under 20 percent by 1985, most of the large private-sector unions held steady in membership for most of the years between 1945 and 1965. They were therefore able to help defend the new social spending programs despite corporate successes in limiting the spread of unions and relentless efforts to undercut those that existed. Unions also could provide just enough financial and volunteer support to reelect pro-labor Democrats, who resisted the ultraconservatives' attempts to reduce steeply progressive tax rates on high incomes. The liberal-labor alliance also was aided in its defense of progressive taxation and high corporate taxes by the government's need to raise taxes to pay for the large military costs of the Korean War, the Cold War, and the Vietnam War, all of which injected government spending into the economy to varying degrees, with strong support from corporate moderates.

The image of a liberal-labor ascendancy also was nurtured by the emergence of a more confrontational civil rights movement in the early 1960s. The power of this movement was expressed through the use of strategic nonviolence in a wide variety of unexpected settings, all of which strained the budgets of local and state governments, caused fear in the hearts of many white citizens, and hurt the bottom line for some companies (especially downtown retailers). The violent reactions to the civil rights movement generated further problems through negative stories and photographs in the national media, which made it difficult for federal officials to ignore the activists and their goals. They not only won many of their demands through the Civil Rights Act of 1964 and the Voting Rights Act of 1965 but also instigated a challenge to the entire power structure by inspiring disruptive feminist, anti-war, and environmental movements, and later a gay-lesbian movement.

By challenging established racial, gender, and sexuality hierarchies, these movements created greater opportunities for many individuals who had previously been excluded. They also led a majority of Americans to adopt more tolerant and accepting attitudes on a variety of issues, resulting in a decline in racial prejudice, more acceptance of women in educational and work settings, and a decrease in the persecution of homosexuals (Page and Shapiro 1992). However, these successes, won against great odds and in the face of frequent threats and violence, do not support the idea of a liberal-labor ascendancy.

Instead, the victories for the civil rights movement were first and foremost the product of the social solidarity of African Americans themselves, sometimes with the support of white college students, who usually defined themselves as radicals or leftists, not liberals. They also had the aid of a small handful of religious, left-liberal, and leftist post-college whites, perhaps most importantly as Freedom Riders into the South in 1961 and as participants in marches in Washington in 1963 and Selma, Alabama, in 1965 (Arsenault 2006; McAdam 1982). As for the liberal-labor alliance, most of its leaders, with the exception of the United Automobile Workers, the American Federation of Teachers, and two or three others, provided only quiet verbal support and modest amounts of financial backing at best.

Even the civil rights movement's most visible union supporters often counseled it to be more cautious because they feared that the tremendously contentious issues of union, workplace, neighborhood, and school integration might alienate the white union members and urban dwellers whose votes were critical. In the case of the United Automobile Workers (UAW), the most liberal of all large industrial unions, it was never able to integrate its Southern locals. By 1967 it faced great hostility on racial issues from at least half of its Northern white members and had only 531 African Americans among its 15,000 skilled members. The result was a growing divide between the liberal union leaders and the civil rights activists. This divide was exacerbated by the stance union leaders took toward the burgeoning anti-war movement, with liberal union leaders often remaining silent and the more conservative union leaders actively opposing it, in part because of their desire to maintain their ties with the Democratic Party and the White House (Boyle 1995, pp. 164–167, 220, and chapter 9).

As for the anti-war, feminist, and gay-lesbian movements, they were primarily the creation of young leftists in university settings and former left-wing labor activists from the 1940s and 1950s who had turned their attention to these issues. These new movements generated negative reactions from enough liberals and union members to create further divisions in the traditional liberal-labor alliance.

WHY THE ACCELERATING RIGHTWARD TREND IN THE 1970s?

Although the elegiac narrative about the decline of the liberal-labor alliance is off base on all its key points, it is true that there was acceleration in the rightward trend in the 1970s, which culminated in the Reagan administration and the reorientation of American politics. But it did not happen for the reasons put forward by the advocates of wishful romanticism. Instead, the accelerated corporate gains on their anti-tax and anti-union agenda were made possible by changes at other levels of American society that were beyond the anticipation or control of either moderates or ultraconservatives in the corporate community.

These changes unexpectedly began with the confrontational strategies and strong demands by the civil rights movement and the movements that followed in its train, which triggered increasing resentment, anger, and fear among a significant minority of middle-level white Americans in all parts of the country. These negative reactions were first seen in the early 1960s in the refusal by most craft unions to integrate their apprenticeship programs. They then led to a surprisingly large vote in Democratic Party primaries in Midwestern and border South states in 1964 for the segregationist governor of Alabama, George Wallace, who captured 30 percent of the vote in Indiana, 34 percent in Wisconsin, and 47 percent in the former slave state of Maryland, where he won sixteen of twenty-three counties, the state capital, and the "ethnic" neighborhoods of Baltimore (Carter 2000, p. 215). The Republicans suffered major losses in the 1964 elections due to presidential hopeful Barry Goldwater's extreme positions on a wide range of issues, but ultraconservatives doubled down by putting even greater emphasis on racial issues in the 1966 congressional elections and experienced major gains, including House victories in a few traditionally Democratic Southern states. By the early 1970s the growing resentment of African American demands for further integration by a significant minority of whites played a part in the reconfiguration of grassroots right-wing efforts, which provided numerous activists for electoral campaigns, most visibly in the South, but in the North as well (Sugrue 2001, 2008).

The nationwide white turn to the Republicans in the face of African American demands for integration, which was first documented in many excellent academic and journalistic analyses, made it possible to create a reorganized corporate-conservative political alliance that began to take over the Republican Party (Carmines and Stimson 1989; Edsall and Edsall 1992; Himmelstein 1990). This alliance pushed out the moderate Republicans, who came to be known by the derisive term "RINOs" (Republicans in Name Only). The corporate-conservative alliance then took advantage of the Southern Democrats' long-standing support for ultraconservative racial, religious, and anti-union policies to fortify the conservative majority in Congress, mount a strong attack on unions, and block the few remaining legislative initiatives put forth by the liberal-labor alliance.

By this reckoning, the major change in the 1970s was not that the corporate community became politically mobilized, as claimed by the commentators who overstate its prowess (e.g., Hacker and Pierson 2010). Instead, it became unified and mobilized in a rightward direction just as disruption subsided and after a growing minority of white Americans (interchangeably called "the Silent Majority" and "Middle Americans" by President Richard M. Nixon) turned to the Republicans of their own volition, based on their resistance to one or more of the changes advocated by the civil rights, anti-war, feminist, environmental, and gay-lesbian movements.

Ironically, the increasing white vote for the Republicans, which included many white trade unionists, strengthened the anti-union forces within the Republican Party. These anti-union forces then proceeded in the early 1970s to overturn union-friendly rulings by the 1960s incarnation of the National Labor Relations Board and to ignore the corporate leaders' rising use of illegal tactics against union organizers and sympathizers. By deserting the Democratic Party over issues concerning race, gender, and sexual orientation, Middle American whites inadvertently undermined the unions that were a key basis for their prosperity, whether they were directly involved in a union or not (Jacobs and Dixon 2006, 2010). Put another way, it is only by combining the new Republican electoral coalition with changing circumstances and views within the corporate community that the stronger push to the right on anti-inflation, labor, and tax policies in the 1970s and 1980s can be explained. The corporate complaints about pro-consumer, environmental, and regulatory policies that are stressed by the new romanticists only emerged after the inner cities were quiet and the labor unions were on the defensive, and they were secondary to corporate concerns about union power and government attempts to tame inflation through wage-price guidelines.

The myth of a postwar liberal-labor ascendency and then a rapid and unexpected liberal-labor decline in the 1970s (or after 1980) has been useful to all those involved in political battles since that time, which is the major reason it persists. For liberals and labor, stories about the New Deal and "the Sixties" provide the inspiration to continue the battle against conservatives and recruit new activists from younger generations. For the social conservatives, who thrive by stirring up feelings of resentment, fear, and victimization in as many white Americans as they can, the idea that an allegedly leftist-environmentalist-feminist-homosexual coalition, led by labor bosses and people of color, is given unfair advantages and undermines American values has been essential to their successful efforts at electoral mobilization. In the case of the corporate community, its endless exaggerations about a leftist-liberal-labor ascendency are useful because they help provide it with a reliable coalition partner in the alarmed Middle American moderates and conservatives, thereby creating numerous opportunities for corporate leaders to realize their own goals by blaming the Democrats and the federal government for the changes forced on Congress by insurgent social movements.

It is now time to explain how I will go about backing up these challenges to the purveyors of the current conventional wisdom. In spite of what they claim, the liberal-labor alliance gradually lost out throughout the postwar era, with the tumultuous events during the Kennedy, Johnson, and early Nixon years accelerating its undoing. Neither 1978 nor 1980 was a major turning point in American politics, and the "Reagan Revolution," carried out against seemingly powerful resistance, was like taking candy from a baby.

Chapter One

Demonstrating Corporate Dominance

To demonstrate the increasing corporate dominance that characterizes the United States after 1939, the chapters that follow link several vantage points that are not usually considered together. The first and foremost of these vantage points comes from a series of policy statements by corporate leaders who were members of the Committee for Economic Development, a moderate policy-discussion group established in the early years of World War II. Its evolving policy views and the actions of dozens of its trustees serve as the touchstone from which postwar conflicts are assessed. A second vantage point is provided by a study of the preferences of the ultraconservative US Chamber of Commerce on 107 pieces of legislation signed into law between 1953 and 1984. A third draws on research by historians and political scientists that examines many of the same legislative issues that concerned the corporate community, but from the perspective of the liberal-labor alliance, with a special focus on labor law, minimum wages, unemployment insurance, health insurance, and pensions.

Fourth, numerous excellent case studies of how particular pieces of major legislation were enacted or defeated, usually based on interviews and archival records, make it possible to show the degree to which the policy preferences of the corporate moderates, corporate ultraconservatives, or the liberal-labor alliance prevailed on a wide range of issues. Finally, several studies of congressional voting patterns on thousands of bills between 1939 and 1984 reveal coalitions of elected officials that tended to work together on different types of policy issues, thereby providing a general framework within which to contextualize the case studies of the major issues. The result of this synthesis is a demonstration of how corporate dominance operated—and increased—during the postwar era, despite the continuing and concerted efforts of the liberal-labor alliance in the face of repeated defeats and only occasional minor legislative victories.

As the previous paragraphs imply, many of the policy conflicts discussed in later chapters are between the owners of large income-producing properties and their conservative political allies on the one side and the employees of these income-producing properties and their liberal political allies on the other. On one hand, the corporate-conservative alliance tries to maximize its power and profits by calling for wage restraint, low taxes, and minimal government support for social services for wage earners. On the other hand, the liberal-labor alliance wants higher taxes on large incomes and great wealth, along with firmer government regulation of the economy, as well as greater support for a wide range of government social insurance programs. The liberal-labor alliance also wants government to support and enforce the right to unionize, an idea that is anathema to all but a very few corporate owners and executives. Taken together, these points add up to the essence of class conflict as it manifests itself within the American political framework.

However, there is also a cluster of issues involving government subsidies and spending that generates cross-class alliances involving some groups within the ownership class and representatives of the liberal-labor alliance. It is these issues that provide the fodder for the fanciful notion that corporations do not dominate the United States. Several of the case studies in later chapters and the rationales that created the spending coalition provide the basis for dispelling the claims of those who deny corporate dominance.

A WINDOW INTO THE MIND-SET OF CORPORATE MODERATES

The Committee for Economic Development, usually called the CED, is the most accessible, research-oriented, and transparent of several moderate policy-discussion organizations. The organization's published policy statements, along with its letters and memos in archives, as supplemented by interviews with several of its trustees and employees from the 1970s, serve as a window into how corporate moderates dealt with ultraconservatives, the liberal-labor alliance, and government officials. The CED's official policy statements are especially revealing because they include memoranda of comment, reservation, or outright dissent that are crafted by individual trustees, and then sometimes joined by other trustees, which makes it possible to ascertain the nature and size of dissident coalitions within the moderate camp on specific issues.

CED statements can be useful in five other ways as well. First, it is sometimes possible to show that they influenced specific pieces of legislation. Second, they may provide rationales and signals for political candidates and elected officials who want to put together plans that they have reason to believe might be accepted by at least some members of the corporate community (Swenson 2002). Third, there are instances in which CED policy statements reveal the corporate moderates' retrospective acceptance of a new policy direction by elected officials. Fourth, some CED policy statements express clear disapproval of new or ongoing government policies, signaling that there will be future conflicts over the issue in question. Finally, due to the CED's major interest in building an international corporate economy, its statements serve as a set of blueprints on the gradual and halting way in which the step-by-step construction of an international ("globalized") economy unfolded in the postwar era.

The CED is also an ideal window into the corporate moderates' collective mind-set because it was at the center of a corporate-financed *policy-planning network* during this time period. More specifically, the CED trustees, who grew in number from a few dozen to two hundred over the decades, shared the central point in the network with the sixty-member Business Advisory Council, a less structured group that met informally with government officials several times a year. These two policy-discussion groups, in turn, had director and financial links to the foundations, think tanks, and more specialized discussion groups within the policy-planning network. Several sophisticated network studies using new methodologies and large databases demonstrate the existence of an interlocking corporate community, an interlocking policy-planning network, and the large overlap between these two networks (see Domhoff 1998, chapters 3, 4, and 7 for summaries of this extensive body of work).[1]

In addition, the most conservative members of the CED and the Business Council (as the Business Advisory Council renamed itself in 1962, for reasons explained in Chapter 5) played the key role in the corporate community's accelerated turn to the right in the mid-1970s. They did so by establishing the smaller and more top-down Business Roundtable, which built on three ad hoc groups that members of the CED and Business Council had created in the late 1960s and early 1970s as part of a renewed offensive against organized labor. From 1972 onward the Business Roundtable, the Business Council, and several trustees within the CED were at the center of the corporate moderates' attack on labor and government. The change was being made at full speed by 1975, well before Ronald Reagan came to office to carry out policies that for the most part accorded extremely well with the new Business Roundtable/Business Council vision. By following the arguments over specific policy issues, especially in CED statements, it can be shown why the same corporate moderates who helped fashion compromise solutions from the 1940s to the early 1970s decided to go in a more conservative direction, due to changes in the economy and a desire to limit further government involvement in the private realms of business.

Using the CED as a starting point for understanding corporate power also provides an ideal angle for considering another issue that separates my analysis from those of the wistful revisionists, namely, the degree to which experts have an independent role in devising and carrying out new policies. New ideas can matter in the face of new problems, and experts sometimes have an important contribution to make, but subsequent chapters show that the experts who have an impact are carefully selected by corporate policy-discussion organizations and then criticized, ignored, or excluded when the goals and policy preferences of the corporate community change. Independent experts who are not connected with the corporate community have little or no influence on anything but scientific, technological, and medical issues, except to the degree that they are part of the liberal-labor alliance.

There is one final advantage to examining the policy landscape from the viewpoint of the CED. By comparing its policy preferences with those of the National Association of Manufacturers (NAM) and the US Chamber of Commerce, on the one side, and the liberal-labor alliance on the other, it becomes possible to determine which issues trigger class solidarity and which ones sometimes lead to cross-class collaborations between the corporate moderates and the liberal-labor alliance.

VOTING COALITIONS IN CONGRESS

Several different analyses of congressional voting patterns make it possible to determine the relative success of the corporate community and the liberal-labor alliance in the legislative arena. These studies reveal two main coalitions of legislators: the conservative coalition and the spending coalition. The first of these coalitions is based strictly on class-based issues, the second on issues that can lead to cross-class collaborations.

The Conservative Coalition

The conservative coalition is typically defined for the purposes of detailed quantitative studies as a majority of Republicans voting with a majority of Democrats from thirteen southern states (Alabama, Arkansas, Florida, Georgia, Kentucky, Louisiana, Mississippi, North Carolina, Oklahoma, South Carolina, Tennessee, Texas, and Virginia) in opposition to a majority of Democrats from non-southern states. This definition tends to err on the side of caution in that it does not include four former slave states that still required segregated schooling until it was outlawed by the Supreme Court in 1954: Delaware, Maryland, Missouri, and West Virginia (which was part of Virginia when the Civil War broke out). However, their exclusion makes partial sense because urban areas within some of these states became more "Northern" after World War II. Then, too, the fact that the northeastern part of Virginia and the southern half of Florida increasingly were populated by non-Southerners also led to a decline in the size of the traditional Southern Democratic delegation. (For the main studies of the conservative coalition between 1939 and 1981, see Brady and Bullock 1980; Katznelson, Geiger, and Kryder 1993; Manley 1973; Shelley 1983.)

In gauging the effectiveness of the conservative coalition in any specific year, it is necessary to determine its approximate "operational size," that is, the number of members of the House or Senate who agree with "the position adopted by the conservative coalition on a majority of votes on which the coalition appears in a given session" (Shelley 1983, p. 150). This more specific quantitative definition captures most of the Democrats from outside the narrow geographic definition of the South that is used in the formal definition, along with a handful of urban and rural Democrats from states that never legislated school segregation. Some of them came from the Southern congressional districts in Ohio, Indiana, and Illinois, but they also included Democrats representing rural districts far afield from the South, whose major agricultural constituents shared many policy concerns with the plantation owners of the South.

The general analyses of the relative success and failure of the conservative coalition concentrate on all votes in which at least 10 percent of those voting disagreed with the majority, so they provide a big-picture view that encompasses many relatively minor issues. For these reasons, they are best seen as a general overview that provides impressive evidence that the conservative coalition seldom lost except in a handful of cases during a few sessions of Congress. Its role inside congressional committees and on major pieces of legislation makes it possible to provide further detail on its power.

To supplement the formal definition of the coalition with a substantive one, the conservative coalition is best understood as "an informal, bipartisan bloc of conservatives whose leaders occasionally engage in joint discussions of strategy and lining up votes" (Shelley 1983, p. 15). This definition is supported empirically by testaments to the existence of this policy coalition after their retirements by two of its founding leaders in the House, one a Southern Democrat, the other a Republican. According to Howard Smith, a leader of the Southern Democrats from the late 1930s to mid-1960s, "Our group—we called it our 'group' for want of a better term—was fighting appropriations. We did not meet publicly. The meetings were not formal. Our group met in one building and the conservative Republicans in another, on different issues" (Manley 1973, p. 231).

At that point Smith or one of the other Southern Democratic leaders would go to see the Republican leaders, or else visit with them on the floor of the House. As Smith's counterpart on the Republican side, Joseph W. Martin of Massachusetts, explained, "In any case when an issue of spending or other new powers for the President came along, I would go see Representative Howard W. Smith of Virginia, for example, and say, 'Howard, see if you can't get me a few Democratic votes here.' Or I would seek out Representative Eugene Cox of Georgia, and ask, 'Gene, why don't you and John Rankin [D-Mississippi] and some of your men get me some votes on this.'" Martin's seemingly vague point about asking Cox to "get me some votes on this" is actually an accurate analysis because there was variation in which Southern Democrats provided the necessary votes so they would not be exposed to criticism or challenge in their home states or districts through negative votes on locally sensitive issues (Manley 1973, p. 232).

When it came to formal voting on the Senate or House floor, the coalition formed on anywhere from 15 to 40 percent of the non-unanimous votes that were taken in any given two-year session of Congress between 1939 and 1984, at which time the growing number of Southern Republicans in Congress made the cross-party coalition somewhat less important. It came together to block any liberal-labor legislation concerning union rights, civil rights for African Americans, the regulation of business, or progressive taxation, which are precisely the issues that defined class conflict for most of the postwar era. Civil rights for African Americans are a dimension of class conflict because they are intertwined with challenges to the coercive control of the low-wage African American workforce. Thus, corporate domination of the United States throughout the postwar era and beyond was in good part dependent upon the corporate community's close ties to the conservative coalition in Congress (see Brady and Bullock 1980; Katznelson, Geiger, and Kryder 1993; Manley 1973; and Shelley 1983, chapter 3, for excellent analyses of the issues of concern to the conservative coalition).

Based on this analysis, the fact that Democrats formally controlled Congress during most of the years between 1939 and 1994 is largely irrelevant in terms of understanding the corporate community's domination of crucial government policies. Instead, the essential point is that a conservative majority had predominant power in Congress on issues related to class throughout most of these years, including on most labor issues in the two most liberal sessions of Congress in American history, 1965–1966 and 1975–1976. Most striking, the only time during the postwar era that the conservative coalition did not stay together on a labor issue critical to employers, in this case Southern employers, occurred when the Northern Republicans finally withdrew support for the Southern Democrats' filibuster of the Civil Rights Act of 1964.

Moreover, the disagreements over unions and civil rights between Southern Democrats and their crucial Northern allies, the machine Democrats from major urban areas, were not as divisive for the party until the 1960s as they might seem to be based on the differences in their voting records on these issues. Machine Democrats, who were regularly returned to the House in those decades, and thereby attained considerable seniority, backed the Southern Democrats on issues of party leadership and the retention of the seniority system, which made it possible for the Southerners to use congressional committees to delay or modify legislation that they did not support.

At the same time, the Northern Democrats were able to maintain liberal voting records by supporting the tepid labor, civil rights, and social welfare legislation that did come up for a vote, thereby satisfying their labor and liberal constituencies. "By voting right," concluded a reporter who covered Congress for the *Wall Street Journal* in the 1960s, "they satisfied liberal opinion at home; by doing nothing effective, they satisfied their Southern allies in the House" (Miller 1970, p. 71). This reporter's observations are supported by a systematic quantitative study based on all committee roll call votes from 1970 to 1980. The conservative coalition formed on 908 of the 4,219 substantive committee votes, about the same as on the floor, and it was successful 8 percent more of the time than on floor votes. Southern committee chairs sided with the conservative coalition within the committee 66.9 percent of the time, as might be expected. But Northern chairs also did so on 32.6 percent of the roll call votes, which led to success for the conservatives on 66.7 percent of those votes within committees (Unekis 1993, pp. 96–97).

The Spending Coalition

Based on analyses that search for issue-focused patterns of voting regardless of region, political scientists have identified a large cluster of legislators who were willing to support most government spending initiatives, which is best understood as a "spending coalition." For the most part, the spending coalition consisted of a majority of Southern and non-Southern Democrats, who were interested in providing subsidies and benefits for their main constituents, namely, planters, ranchers, and agribusiness interests in the South, Midwest, and California, and urban real estate interests across the country (see Clausen 1973; Sinclair 1982, for the studies of issue coalitions that lead to the concept of a spending coalition).

The nature of the bargain between the Southern and non-Southern Democrats in forging this coalition was very explicit. A majority of the non-Southern Democrats supported agricultural subsidies and price supports that greatly benefited plantation owners and other agribusinesses. The Southerners in turn were willing to support government spending programs for roads, urban redevelopment, public housing, hospital construction, school lunches, and even public assistance. Although some of these spending programs are thought of as simply "liberal," in fact many of them benefited the urban real estate interests that financed the urban Democratic political machines in the North and were used to the benefit of Southern Democrats as well. Almost as important, the construction unions that are dependent upon urban growth for their livelihoods were highly supportive of these programs as well, thereby supporting the spending coalition as part of a cross-class alliance (Logan and Molotch 1987/2007).

However, Southern support for the spending sought by urban Democrats, growth coalitions, and construction unions was conditional, based on the acceptance of three provisos. The spending programs would contain no attacks on segregation, they would be locally controlled so the Southerners could minimize benefits for African Americans to means-tested programs, and they would differentially benefit Southern states, even on such matters as hospital spending and urban renewal funds (Brown 1999, pp. 182–200). In other words, the spending coalition that is at the heart of the New Deal coalition was premised on excluding African Americans from many of its policy benefits, which is one reason why the civil rights movement in the North took to the streets between 1963 and 1967 to force government agencies staffed by New Deal sympathizers to change their traditional rules and open up patronage networks related to jobs, housing, and education (Quadagno 1994).

The basic core in this spending coalition was the approximately ninety to one hundred Democrats from the thirteen Southern states and the roughly fifty to sixty machine Democrats from major urban areas outside the South that together controlled the House and Senate committees of concern to them through their seniority and shared interest in government spending and in fending off rule by Republican bankers and industrialists. However, this core coalition had to be augmented by some of the one hundred liberal non-Southern Democrats who were supportive of government spending programs as well as liberal and labor issues. For the most part, the liberal Democrats received nothing in return on two of their most important issues: unions and civil rights. Instead, they had to settle for incremental improvements on economic and welfare issues crucial to the lives of average Americans, which they were often able to win when they could attract the support of machine and Southern Democrats. These victories included increases in the minimum wage and old-age pensions, the addition of disability insurance to the Social Security Act, and increases in unemployment and welfare payments, food stamps, and rent subsidies. However, even these successes were severely circumscribed by the conservative coalition's capacity to block attempts to provide uniform unemployment insurance at the national level, and they sometimes depended on support from corporate moderates.

The spending coalition in the House was managed, for most of the forty-five years that are the main focus of this book, by Southern Democrats from districts on the northern Texas-southern Oklahoma border, in conjunction with machine Democrats from the Boston area. The three leaders of this "Austin-Boston Alliance" (the Speaker of the House, the House majority leader, and the majority whip) both shared an interest in bringing government spending projects to their districts as well as a low percentage of black constituents. They also shared a moderate or centrist stance compared to their more conservative colleagues, in the case of the Southerners, and their more liberal colleagues, in the case of the Bostonians. The one exception to the Austin-Boston leadership regime was a moderate Southern Democrat from New Orleans, Hale Boggs, the majority whip from 1962 through 1970, and then the majority leader during 1971 and most of 1972, when he died in a plane crash (Champagne, Harris, Riddlesperger, and Nelson 2009).

THE PIVOTAL ROLE OF SOUTHERN DEMOCRATS

Based on this analysis of the two main congressional voting coalitions, the Southern Democrats were clearly the pivotal voting group in Congress. If they sided with the Republicans on an issue, which meant that the representatives of major employers in the South and North were united, then the conservative coalition triumphed on a great majority of its appearances in most sessions of Congress. The coalition mostly played a defensive role between 1939 and 1977, eliminating New Deal agencies and spending programs, or else cutting back or blocking new liberal-labor proposals. However, in 1946–1947 and 1953–1954, when Republicans temporarily controlled both houses of Congress, and after 1978, it showed it could play an initiatory role as well, passing or reshaping legislation that was useful to it.

As for the Republicans, they rarely had enough representatives until the 1980s to block government spending programs, which they almost uniformly opposed, if they did not have help from Southern Democrats. Furthermore, when it came to agricultural subsidies, Republicans from Midwestern states often supported the agricultural payments that were considered essential by their wealthiest constituents, namely, the agribusinesses and well-off individual farmers that were gathered into a strong pressure group through the National Farm Bureau Federation (in turn a close ally of ultraconservative business groups by the 1940s).

For the most part, then, the corporate community's primary losses in Congress were to urban real estate or agribusiness interests, both of which need government spending and subsidies, and only rarely to the activists and elected officials in the liberal-labor alliance, which all employers view as their enemies.

However, this does not mean the corporate moderates never sided with the urban real estate or agricultural segments of the ownership class. Based on CED policy statements, it is safe to say that moderates supported downtown developers in promoting growth and protecting real estate values in the cities in which they had their corporate headquarters. More generally, they supported federal money for land clearance, cultural and arts facilities, and inner-city welfare and educational programs aimed at easing urban tensions, especially through programs that were funded by the family and corporate foundations of which they were directors.

Corporate moderates' relationship with agribusiness was somewhat more antagonistic. They wanted to limit agricultural production and avoid below-cost exporting of surpluses, as did the major Southern plantation owners and large-scale wheat and corn/hog farmers outside the South. But corporate moderates also hoped to reduce and phase out the subsidies and price supports that their predecessors had advocated at the outset of the New Deal, which did not sit well with the plantation overlords and Midwestern farmers. At best, agribusiness leaders wanted to phase out price supports only after they knew there would be no surpluses to pull down prices (which never happened). Moreover, small-town real estate owners and downtown merchants worried that the increasing concentration of agriculture would hollow out rural farming towns. As one small-town Texas newspaper put it, "Our farms would be depopulated, our towns turned into ghost towns" (Schriftgiesser 1967, p. 155).

HOW ULTRACONSERVATIVES DIFFER FROM MODERATES

Although the corporate moderates sometimes sided with urban growth coalitions and even on occasion with agricultural interests, the ultraconservatives usually did not. Ultraconservatives' opposition to other segments of the ownership class explains many of the fifty-six defeats the US Chamber of Commerce suffered on the 107 successful pieces of legislation on which it took a stand between 1953 and 1984, some of which involved relatively minor matters in terms of power (Smith 2000). The ultraconservatives often lost to the growth coalitions on issues concerning subsidies for housing or downtown interests. They lost to agribusiness interests on votes for the agricultural subsidies that were vital to plantation owners and other large agribusiness interests. They lost to corporate moderates and the liberal-labor alliance four times—1958, 1963, 1965, and 1972—on programs that provided federal aid to public schools in depressed areas and to universities to support graduate students and basic research in science and engineering. They were defeated on government regulations that in any way interfered with business discretion, including equal pay for women in 1963 and outlawing age discrimination in the workplace in 1967.

Finally, the ultraconservatives were unsuccessful in their opposition to several types of legislation for low-income and elderly people, which were mentioned earlier as victories for the liberal-labor alliance. This legislation concerned such matters as raising the minimum wage, extending or increasing unemployment benefits, providing rent support, and aiding the homeless. The ultraconservatives also lost on several votes that involved changes in the Social Security program, such as increased benefit payments, the inclusion of more occupational categories, and adding disability benefits.

Based on this overview, it can be seen that the approximately 0.5 percent of the population that makes up the wealthy ownership class—the corporate rich; the plantation, ranching, and agribusiness owners; and the major urban land owners and developers—seldom if ever lost to the liberal and pro-labor representatives of the vastly larger class of non-owners, that is, the 85 to 90 percent of people who work in office buildings, factories, and fields for a monthly salary or hourly wage. The few seeming exceptions to my claim, such as the Employment Act of 1946, the Housing Act of 1949, and an education act passed in the mid-1960s, are examined in later chapters.[2]

HOW DO CONSERVATIVES WIN ELECTIONS?

The importance of the conservative coalition as the legislative arm of the nationwide ownership class leads to the question of how it was possible for pro-corporate Republicans and pro-agribusiness Southern Democrats to attract enough votes from members of the non-owning classes to win elections in an open democratic society. This question is not addressed directly because this book is focused on the policy and legislative struggles that take place in Washington, based on the composition of Congress, but it can be addressed briefly here.

In the case of the Republicans, an understanding of their success begins with their ability to appeal to many members of the electorate on the basis of shared non-economic concerns, such as race, religion, and ethnicity, which are just as "basic" and "real" as social class in terms of shaping social identities and voting behavior, as seen in the fact that the "religious cleavage" is almost twice as large as the "class cleavage" (Nieuwbeerta, Brooks, and Manza 2006). Further, they find resonance with many Americans on the basis of a common sympathy with the deep strain of antigovernment sentiment in the American belief system. Republican success also includes their efforts at voter suppression through a wide range of stratagems (Davidson, Dunlap, Kenny, and Wise 2004; Piven, Minnite, and Groarke 2009). Finally, as a tertiary factor that is sometimes overstated, Republicans did enjoy a large advantage in campaign spending from the 1930s through the 1980s.

In the case of the Southern Democrats, the starting point for understanding their electoral success can be found in the exclusion of African Americans and many low-income whites from the polling booths from the 1890s until the mid-1960s. They also took advantage of appeals to white voters through shared racial resentments and an especially strong form of antigovernment ideology. This Southern version of antigovernment ideology is extreme due to the fact that the South's white population was subjugated twice in the space of one hundred years by the federal government, first in the Civil War and then through both legal and military measures in the 1960s. Issues related to religion, guns, and sexuality were added to Southern whites' list of grievances by the 1970s, all framed in terms of impositions of one sort or another by the federal government, which is resisted on everything except the federal spending that the Southern delegation in Congress provides to the South in far greater amounts than the federal taxes collected in that region.

As the brief overview in the previous two paragraphs suggests, it is possible to demonstrate employer dominance of the electoral process *in the districts and states that provided the votes for the conservative coalition.* However, as already explained, this book focuses on policy and legislative struggles, not on how elected officials arrived in Washington. It makes reference to elections only when there were significant changes in the composition of Congress that made a difference in legislative outcomes. Further, the general public comes into the picture only in those instances in which corporate-financed opinion-shaping committees, liberal-labor organizations, or disruptive social movements attempted to influence congressional decisions by mobilizing average citizens to pressure Congress and by publicizing poll results allegedly reflecting the will of average citizens.

POWER INDICATORS

To provide suggestive statistical evidence of the changes that occurred after 1938, I make use of three social indicators that are in good part reflections of the power struggles I analyze. *Income inequality* is discussed in terms of the Gini coefficient, a standard measure of inequality that can range in theory between zero, which would indicate perfect equality, and 1.0, which would indicate that one person has all the income or wealth. In reality, this statistic usually ranges between 0.200 and 0.700 for distributions of income in most modern nations. In this book, I make use of the Gini coefficient for the incomes of urban male workers, the most useful subset of employees for my purposes because they were more likely in the postwar era to be well paid and/ or unionized. Its value can be seen by the large declines and increases in it over a sixty-seven-year period: it was 0.418 in 1937, 0.317 at its low point in 1953, 0.401 in 1985, and 0.475 in 2004, a journey that reflects much of the analysis presented in this book (Kopczuk, Saez, and Song 2010).

Second, I often report the *effective tax rate* on the top 1 percent of income earners, which is the percentage of their total incomes this small group actually pays in federal income taxes after deductions and loopholes are taken into account. This rate is useful because it can change quite dramatically depending on the outcome of battles over taxes. To provide an idea of how widely this rate fluctuated over most decades between 1930 and 2010, it was 6.6 percent in 1930, 21.6 percent in 1940, 58.6 percent at its high point in 1944, 26.3 percent in 1967, and 22.1 percent in 1986 (Brownlee 2000, pp. 51, 60, 61). Third, I discuss *union density,* which is best defined for my purposes as the percentage of salary and wage workers who are members of unions, as determined by monthly surveys and telephone interviews. However, I use the percent of nonagricultural workers in unions, which yields very similar results, for years before 1948, when there is no information on union rates for wage and salary workers, and sometimes thereafter for continuity. As with the Gini coefficient and the effective tax rate, there is wide variation over time, from 7.5 percent in 1930 to 26.9 percent in 1940, to 35.4 percent at its peak in 1945, followed by a gradual decline to 26.3 percent in 1962 and 22.3 percent in 1980, and then a descent to 11.8 percent in 2011 (Bureau of Labor Statistics 2012; Mayer 2004, p. 22, table A1).

The changes in these indicators are useful because they broadly reflect the outcomes of the policy conflicts that I discuss, with the Gini coefficient declining when union density and the effective tax rate on the top 1 percent are increasing. Conversely, the Gini coefficient generally increases when the effective tax rate and union density are declining. These three statistics therefore can be considered "power indicators" as well as social indicators. However, they are affected to some extent by factors other than the results of power struggles, which is why I used the phrase "broadly reflect the outcomes of the policy conflicts that I discuss" at the start of this paragraph. The effective tax rate, for example, is also influenced by fluctuations in the business cycle and very dramatic upheavals, such as economic depressions and wars. It is also influenced by the "bracket creep" that results from sustained inflationary periods, which pushes a higher percentage of the top 1 percent into the very highest of the tax brackets that existed until the Reagan era. But any "noise" in the three power indicators is not a serious problem and is not unique to power indicators. All the indicators used in the social sciences have measurement problems, including those used in economics, which often appear to be the most rigorous (Morgenstern 1963).

With those qualifications in mind, income inequality provides an indication of the degree to which the corporate rich are winning victories that lower their taxes or freeze the minimum wage and/or unemployment benefits, because those types of successes usually lead to increases in income inequality shortly thereafter. Based on these and similar policy conflicts, the trajectory of the Gini coefficient in the postwar era becomes a revealing reflection of postwar power struggles. In the case of union density, it provides an indication of the potential for developing a working-class political identity, which is heightened for several reasons when union densities are high, starting with the feeling of social solidarity that can come from belonging to a union. High union density also means greater exposure to discussions and literature concerning the economic benefits of union membership. Unions also provide information about the political candidates opposed to them, and they bring heightened attention to government decisions that might help or hinder unions. In the end, union density is a useful power indicator because it reveals the potential for class-based voting and for success in clashes with employers over wages, hours, working conditions, and the right of unions to exist.

In addition to serving as power indicators, the changes in income inequality, the effective tax rate on the top 1 percent, and union density are three of the changes over the long swing of the postwar era that are in need of an explanation, each with importance in its own right in terms of the quality of life for most people. The research in this book suggests that the changes in all three of these power indicators were the result of the corporate community's increasing dominance of government at the expense of the liberal-labor alliance, which was weakened by its inability to incorporate African Americans on an equal basis or make any headway in replacing segregationist Southern Democrats with more liberal legislators.

CONCLUDING CAVEATS

This book is not a complete history of everything that happened between the late 1930s and the early twenty-first century. It only deals tangentially with the key foreign policy and military decisions that had a major role in making it possible for the United States to become the dominant world power during this time period. Domestic economic and social issues, along with international trade policy, are more relevant to understanding resurgent inequality.

Nor does the book discuss cultural changes and social issues during this time period, many of which were life-changing in terms of their impact on gender relations and on young people of all races, ethnicities, and sexual identities. At the same time, cultural shifts had an equally profound but very different impact on conservatives, who tend to resist any changes in the established order, especially in relation to sexual and religious issues (Jost and Sedanius 2004; Lakoff 1996; Tomkins 1964). The many cultural and social changes also received an enormous amount of attention from reporters, writers, and pundits. But these issues enter into this account only to the degree that the corporate-conservative or liberal-labor alliance tried to use them as part of their pursuit of power.

This book is about power, who has it, and how they use it. It concludes that power is even more important than profits for the corporate leaders who involve themselves in the realm of national policy through a variety of trade associations, foundations, think tanks, and policy-discussion organizations. In fact, this concern with power explains why corporate moderates could not fully embrace Keynesian economics and why they eventually abandoned it.

NOTES

1. This pathbreaking work, which began in the early 1970s based on the graph-theoretic approach developed by Richard Alba (1973) and the network algorithms developed by Phillip Bonacich (1972), has been ignored by many social scientists. They overlook the role of a rigorously outlined and repeatedly replicated policy-planning network that generates many large-scale policy proposals as well as many of the experts and corporate officials who are appointed to government positions in both Republican and Democratic administrations. The way these groups supply corporate officials and experts for government positions is demonstrated once again in this book, but it was done in a more systematic fashion for the 1970s by Michael Useem (1980) and Harold Salzman and G. William Domhoff (1980). For original network studies of the corporate community for some of the years covered in this study, see Peter Mariolis (1975), Beth Mintz and Michael Schwartz (1981), Mark Mizruchi (1982), and John Sonquist and Thomas Koenig (1975). For studies of the close relations among mainstream think tanks and policy groups during this same time period, which show the ultraconservative groups to be on the margins, see Val Burris (1992). For a study of a 30 x 30 matrix containing think tanks, policy-discussion groups, and elite social clubs from across the country using an algorithm based on Boolean algebra, which showed the Business Council, the Committee for Economic Development, the Conference Board, and the Links Clubs in New York were the main members of a "bridge group," see Phillip Bonacich and G. William Domhoff (1981). For a study with a 1970 interlock matrix consisting of 201 corporations, the twelve private universities with the largest endowments, the eleven foundations with the largest amount of assets, seven civic and cultural groups, and six policy-discussion groups, using an algorithm developed by Mizruchi (1983), which found that IBM, the Conference Board, General Foods, Chemical Bank, the Committee for Economic Development, New York Life, Yale University, Morgan Guaranty Trust, Consolidated Edison, and the Rockefeller Foundation were the ten most-central organizations in the network, see Harold Salzman and G. William Domhoff (1983). For an interview-based study of several hundred elites in different institutional sectors in the early 1970s, which used the graph-theoretic approach to discover a core of 227 leaders from all institutional sectors, see Richard Alba and Gwen Moore (1978).

2. There is a small stratum of well-off professionals, such as architects, physicians, various types of noncorporate lawyers, and professors at elite private colleges and universities, that is situated between the two classes; only the physicians among them come into the picture in this book due to their opposition to national health insurance and Medicare.

Chapter Two

The Rise and Sudden Decline of the Liberal-Labor Alliance, 1934–1938

The widely praised reforms of the early New Deal, enacted before there was any semblance of a liberal-labor alliance, provided temporary respite to several million unemployed people through a variety of emergency relief, public works, and conservation programs. But they were kept small, constantly criticized, and shut down whenever any signs of recovery appeared. In contrast, much was done for the major economic interests that had been humbled by the stock market crash in 1929 and the Great Depression. The rescue began with the Banking Act of 1933, which was fashioned in good part by the bankers who served as top appointees in the Department of the Treasury during the Hoover administration. Roosevelt initially opposed and only later reluctantly agreed to one of the most crucial elements of the reform effort, government insurance of bank deposits, which he warned could be used by unsavory bankers as well as conscientious ones. Most big banks on Wall Street opposed deposit insurance for their own reasons (Freidel 1973, pp. 235–236, 441–443).

However, deposit insurance was heartily supported by the owners of small banks in states and congressional districts in the South and West that were represented by Democrats. They had the backing of Southern Democrats, including such highly visible figures as Vice President John Nance Garner (who also owned a small bank in Uvalde, Texas) and Jesse Jones, a Houston multimillionaire who headed Roosevelt's Reconstruction Finance Corporation, which underwrote the various legislative rescues with nearly $50 billion in loans to banks, railroads, and other corporate entities throughout the 1930s (that's $600 to $680 billion in 2012 dollars, a massive bailout by any standard) (Olson 1988).

The Emergency Banking Act also included a reform that forced the powerful Wall Street banking houses to choose between commercial banking and investment banking, which is known as "Glass-Steagall," after its original Senate and House sponsors. First suggested in 1929 by President Herbert Hoover, this change already had been put into practice in March 1933 by the world's largest bank at the time, Chase National Bank, but most Wall Street leaders opposed it. It was championed by those leaders in the Senate and House that had major roles on the banking and currency committees, which accumulated damning evidence that several Wall Street firms were stealing from their customers in various ways, such as using their deposits to make speculative gambles in the stock market and to provide loans to their own officers. The reform passed in the Senate without a single dissenting vote (Carosso 1970, chapter 16).

Financial institutions, and in particular insurance companies, were stuck with many potentially worthless mortgages, but the Home Owners' Loan Act of 1933 saved the day by making it possible for the government to purchase mortgages from people falling behind in their payments. The act gave mortgage lenders safe government bonds in exchange for their mortgages and provided the distressed homeowners with lower-cost loans, a rare bailout of both financiers and average people; 20 percent of all mortgages were soon owned by the government agency created by this act (Schlesinger 1958, p. 53; Smith 2007, pp. 325–326). Congress also supported a plan devised by the real estate industry to revive home construction and make long-term, low-interest loans more readily available through the passage of the National Housing Act of 1934 (Gotham 2000, 2002).

The early actions by Roosevelt and the new Congress also bailed out one of the Democratic Party's most powerful constituencies, the plantation masters of the South, who along with other agricultural interests were suffering declining crop prices due to their excessive production in the face of low demand. The plan that saved agribusiness, embodied in the Agricultural Adjustment Act, was developed within the corporate policy-planning network of that day. It handed government subsidies, financed by a tax on the processors of agricultural products, to plantation owners growing the three main Southern cash crops (cotton, tobacco, and rice), and to wheat and corn farmers throughout the country, in exchange for voluntary reductions in crop acreage. Corporate moderates saw these subsidy payments as the best way to reduce agricultural production and the pressure to dump surplus crops on the world market, which might lead to retaliation and thereby interfere with the expansion of industrial exports by large American corporations. The US Chamber of Commerce and large-scale agricultural interests championed the plan. It sailed through Congress in the spring of 1933 with the backing of Southern Democrats, who had been crucial to Roosevelt's nomination as the party's standard-bearer and controlled all the key committees in Congress through the seniority system (see Domhoff and Webber 2011, chapter 2, for the full story of the Agricultural Adjustment Act based on archival findings).

A National Industrial Recovery Act, written by representatives of the corporate community, soon followed. It was meant to arrest the downward spiral of prices and wages in the non-farm business sectors by allowing organized business owners in each sector of the economy to create codes of fair competition that would set minimum prices and maximum levels of productive output, along with minimum wages and maximum hours for their employees. In exchange, the corporate leaders were supposed to include representatives of workers and consumers in their deliberations, but this actually happened less than 10 percent of the time. In theory, these separate and self-policed code authorities would eliminate cutthroat competition, reemploy workers, and increase purchasing power, thereby restarting the economy, but the plan did not work and was spared an agonizing reappraisal when it was declared unconstitutional by the Supreme Court in May 1935 (Domhoff 1996, chapter 3; Himmelberg 1976/1993).

With finance, agriculture, industry, and real estate interests seemingly taken care of, the White House and Congress turned their attention to the many self-serving and often illegal activities carried out by the New York Stock Exchange, whose shenanigans led angry corporate leaders in many parts of the country to join Roosevelt in calling for tighter regulation of the stock market by an independent government agency. In conjunction with the banking legislation passed in 1933, the Securities Exchange Act of 1934 in effect prohibited financiers from cheating each other and saved unknowing middle-class investors from losing their money to gamblers and swindlers. It also protected the economy from a wide range of destructive practices that had undermined many corporations. As one scholarly expert on Wall Street explained, the new legislation "reduced opportunities for corporate theft and restricted the methods by which individuals, while inflicting pecuniary damage on each other, could derange the entire economy" (Parrish 1970, p. 232). The new regulatory agency established by the legislation was given a wide degree of discretion in setting standards, which made it more susceptible to control by the industry itself (Carosso 1970, pp. 363, 379).

Although the first two years of the New Deal primarily served the interests of the ownership class, a burst of union organizing, which was an accidental consequence of the National Industrial Recovery Act, and the arrival of even more Northern liberal Democrats into Congress after the 1934 elections, marked the beginnings of a liberal-labor alliance that seemed to have the potential to alter the existing power structure. With the Southern Democrats showing an apparent willingness to go along with any regulatory or spending legislation that did not interfere with race and labor relations in the South, the New Deal reached its high-water mark in 1935. An overwhelmingly Democratic Congress passed the National Labor Relations Act, the Social Security Act, and an omnibus "wealth tax," which raised marginal rates on income over $500,000 to 75 percent and created a new progressive corporate income tax that reached 15 percent for any profits over $40,000. In 1936, in a further effort to curb the concentration of corporate power, Congress passed a graduated tax on profits that were not distributed to shareholders.

Shortly thereafter, Roosevelt was reelected with 60.8 percent of the vote and the Democrats increased their overwhelming majority in the Senate by gaining six seats, leaving the Republicans with only sixteen members. Moreover, the Democrats and the progressive independents that usually allied with them won an additional fifteen seats in the House, giving them a 347–88 margin over the Republicans. At that point the liberal-labor alliance seemed poised for further victories, especially because it had contributed to the Democratic landslide in many key industrial states. In particular, three industrial unions in the newly emergent Committee of Industrial Organizations (CIO) provided campaign workers, signed up new voters, organized campaign speakers, and funded national radio broadcasts. They were especially instrumental in galvanizing low-income voters to vote Democratic in Pennsylvania, Ohio, Illinois, and Indiana. They also provided significant campaign funding to Democratic candidates for the first time in American political history, an unprecedented $800,000 (Webber 2000, pp. 111–114). (Later, CIO came to stand for the Congress of Industrial Organizations.)

Roosevelt and the liberal-labor alliance were poised to build on this string of successes in early 1937, with legislation closing loopholes that allowed the rich to evade taxes by such subterfuges as incorporating their yachts and deducting their expenses for horse farms as losses on a hobby. Roosevelt soon began to make plans for further tax reforms in 1938, including increases in the tax on undistributed profits, a progressive tax on capital gains, and a levy on tax-free federal, state, and municipal bonds (purchased in abundance by the wealthy). These projected tax increases "aroused fear and hostility among large corporations" because they "correctly viewed Roosevelt's tax program as a threat to their control over capital and their latitude for financial planning" (Brownlee 2004, p. 98). The ascendancy of the liberal-labor alliance seemed as if it might be at hand.

But the New Deal was in serious trouble by early 1937, success on tax reforms notwithstanding. Southern Democrats were deeply incensed by the sit-down strikes in the North that were leading to the rapid unionization of some of the largest corporations in the country. They were further inflamed by efforts by the CIO to unionize the South. The interracial nature of the CIO's efforts in both the North and South added to Southern white enmity. Simmering Southern hostility toward the New Deal exploded into outright opposition after Roosevelt attempted to liberalize the Supreme Court in early February through a proposal to add new appointees to supplement those justices who were over age seventy. Led by one of Roosevelt's closest allies, Senator James Byrnes of South Carolina, the Southern Democrats decided the time was right to capitalize on the widespread congressional animosity to Roosevelt's policies by blocking any initiative that might lead to an attack on racial segregation and provide an opening for a political coalition of black and white workers. "Throughout 1937," concludes historian William Leuchtenburg, "these two issues—Court packing and the sit-downs—were repeatedly linked" in order to claim that Roosevelt "was condoning an assault on property rights" (Leuchtenburg 1963, p. 243). Their resistance began with a series of amendments, resolutions, and delays on labor-related issues, starting with Byrnes's amendment to a coal-mining bill, which declared sit-down strikes to be illegal.

The amendment won thirty-six votes even though Roosevelt's supporters promised to take up the issue of sit-downs after the coal bill passed. Southern senators then settled for a nonbinding Senate resolution, sugar-coated with platitudes about the usefulness of collective bargaining, which condemned sit-downs as illegal and contrary to public policy (Patterson 1967/1981, pp. 136–137). Not yet satisfied, Byrnes soon organized an attempt to cut back on funds for government jobs and welfare payments by insisting that the emergency caused by the Great Depression had passed. Then the gatekeepers on the House Rules Committee, controlled by Southern Democrats and Republicans, voted in June to postpone consideration of Roosevelt's Fair Labor Standards Act, which was aimed in good part at curbing any advantages conferred on Southern businesses by low wages, long hours, and the widespread use of child labor. The conservative war against the New Deal had begun.

Roosevelt compounded his problems in early 1937 with his decision to reassure business of his support for private enterprise by balancing the budget, in part through ordering a very large cut in the work-relief efforts of the Works Progress Administration and the virtual shutdown of Public Works Administration construction (Huthmacher 1973, p. 153; Piven and Cloward 1971/1993, pp. 111–117). In conjunction with a separate decision by the Federal Reserve Board to shrink the money supply, the result was a sharp downturn in the economy. The rapid rise in unemployment undermined unionization efforts and shook voter confidence in the New Deal, which in turn emboldened conservative Democrats on Wall Street and in the South to join with Republicans in early 1938 to eviscerate the undistributed profits tax and eliminate the progressive corporate income tax. In addition, the final version of the Fair Labor Standards Act excluded four-fifths of the labor force (including most agricultural workers), trimmed the proposed minimum wage from forty-four cents to twenty-five cents, and set the maximum hours that could be worked per week at forty-four instead of forty. The legislation was still a triumph for the New Deal because it eliminated child labor and established the principles of minimum wages and maximum hours, but it also generated further hostility toward liberal-labor reforms among the planters and manufacturers in the South.

At the same time that the conservative coalition was flexing its muscles, the strength of the spending coalition was revealed in the congressional reaction to a new spending bill Roosevelt put forward in April 1938, just five days after the conservative coalition had rejected his proposals for further tax reform. Following the addition of amendments in both the House and the Senate to increase the amount of spending on farm subsidies, housing, and earmarked government projects in favored congressional districts, the bill rolled through both houses of Congress. For example, only eleven Democrats in the House opposed the bill; even twenty-three of the House Republicans, who were usually solidly united against any New Deal proposal, voted for the bill (Patterson 1967/1981, p. 238).

The bargain between Northern and Southern Democrats on spending was discussed frankly and openly on the floor of the House at the time by a machine Democrat from New York. He began by noting that parity prices for farmers were passed when he and the mayor of New York convinced New York Democrats to change their vote by adding an amendment to the Works Relief Act, a public spending bill that would primarily benefit cities. He then recited earlier instances in which the New York vote made a difference, such as a cotton bill of great concern to Southern Democrats. In the process, he continued, "at those times we had certain assurances of reciprocity," which is a far more precise term than the usual "horse-trading" or "logrolling" metaphors often used in talking about the exchange of political favors (Campbell 1962, p. 115). It reaches back to the deeper essence of the "gift exchanges" that are found in cultures throughout the world, which reveals that it is very difficult for people to ignore the moral requirement of reciprocity that burdens any gift with the potential for strong feelings of shame and guilt (Mauss 1924/1969).

The continuing nature of the spending coalition can be seen in the fact that between 1953 and 1960 Southern Democrats voted for agricultural subsidies 93 percent of the time, Democrats from the northeast 64 percent of the time, and Republicans only 18 percent of the time. And, revealing the reciprocity mentioned by the New York Democrat in 1938, between 1961 and 1968 Southern Democrats voted 69 percent of the time for public works, urban construction, and other projects supported by almost all Northern Democrats, but Republicans supported these projects only 17 percent of the time (see Sinclair 1982, pp. 21, 108, 145, for detailed original research on these and other voting patterns).

Reflecting the tenuous nature of citizen support for the liberal-labor alliance in terms of both turnout and voter preference, the Republicans loosened Democratic dominance of Congress in 1938 by gaining eighty-one seats in the House and eight in the Senate. As a result, Southern Democrats once again became a majority of the Democrats in the House, thereby adding to the power they already had within the party through seniority, control of key congressional committees, and a willingness to use the filibuster whenever they felt their core interests were threatened. At that point the majority of Southern Democrats in both houses joined with the resurgent Republicans to form a durable conservative voting coalition on issues having to do with support for unions, civil rights, taxes, and business regulation. The remaining tax on undistributed profits was repealed, and conservatives launched investigations into the allegedly pro-Communist sympathies of the CIO and the National Labor Relations Board. Attempts to amend the National Labor Relations Act were barely set aside after Roosevelt replaced the most liberal member of the labor board with a moderate and acquiesced to cuts in the board's funding. The labor board remained under constant siege by Southern Democrats and Republicans for the next forty-five years, making it increasingly less useful to union organizers (Gross 1981, 1995).

Not long after the initial battle over changing the labor board, executives and financiers from corporations and Wall Street began to arrive in Washington to manage the War Department as the government slowly recognized the threat of war in Europe and Asia and started to mobilize its military capability. The threat became more urgent after the Nazi invasion of Poland in September 1939, and the rapid escalation of Japanese attacks on China, French Indochina, and the Dutch East Indies. In the process, the newly appointed corporate officials worked closely with the conservatives in Congress to dismantle many New Deal programs and institutions. In 1941 Roosevelt appointed his erstwhile ally, James Byrnes, to the Supreme Court, a clear departure from his five previous appointments to the court.

Due to the economic impact of the new recession, the continuing conflicts over union organizing in the South, and the wars with Germany and Japan, the liberal-labor alliance lost whatever chance it had to solidify a major challenge to the corporation and plantation capitalists who ruled America at the time. As a result, it lost almost every major legislative battle it fought over the next forty-five years and failed to realize any of the larger hopes it had entertained for the postwar era. It had to settle for minor extensions of the Social Security Act in relation to old-age benefits, unemployment insurance, and disability benefits, which usually required support from one or another group within the conservative coalition to pass muster in Congress.

And yet, despite this stark reality, many social scientists and historians portray the years between 1945 and the 1970s as the era of a liberal ascendency that brought prosperity and abundance to an increasing number of Americans through the forward-looking efforts of Democratic presidents and the influence of the liberal-labor alliance. There was indeed greater prosperity in the decades after the war, and more income equality as well, but they were not the result of a liberal-labor ascendancy.

Chapter Three

Leadership for Corporate Moderates, 1939–1945

Corporate moderates created their new leadership group, the Committee for Economic Development, in the summer of 1942 based on two interrelated concerns. First, they believed that the revived standing they were enjoying because of their prominent role in the rapid conversion to a wartime economy would not last if the economy sank into the doldrums that still lingered as late as 1940. As the president of Procter & Gamble put it in a meeting with other corporate leaders in 1941, "The challenge that business will face when this war is over cannot be met by a laissez-faire philosophy or by uncontrolled forces of supply and demand" (Collins 1981, pp. 81–82).

In other words, corporate moderates thought they had to accept at least some government involvement in the economy to ensure that another depression did not occur. They further concluded they had to plan for the postwar era. But they also understood that the ultraconservatives among them, as embodied in the National Association of Manufacturers and the US Chamber of Commerce, still wanted to severely limit the government's role. Corporate moderates believed that the ultraconservative approach was certain to depress the economy even further in the event of an economic decline. They also knew that ultraconservatives could lobby very strongly for their own views due to their close ties with the conservative coalition in Congress.

Second, the corporate moderates were concerned because government planners and private groups supported by the liberal-labor alliance were carrying out most of the publicly visible planning for the postwar economy. They knew through their own experience, as well as through media accounts and discussions with their economic and political advisors, that liberals and labor had coalesced into a loosely knit policy and electoral coalition within the Democratic Party through success in helping to pass the National Labor Relations Act, and through working together for liberal candidates in the 1934 and 1936 elections. They also knew that by the early 1940s most members of the liberal-labor alliance, which until then had many different tendencies within it, had found a common path through the idea that government could provide the basis

for creating a new economic program that created a wide range of government spending and social insurance programs (Brinkley 1995). Liberals and union leaders, and
perhaps especially the very liberal leaders within the United Auto Workers, were also
beginning to realize that Keynesian economics "served as a convenient rationalization
for what they were already doing," taxing those who could afford to pay and spending
the revenues on programs that helped people in need (Leuchtenburg 1963, p. 246).

The corporate moderates' fears in relation to their conflict with the liberal-labor
alliance over wages, taxes, and union organizing were most directly expressed in early
1941 at meetings of the Business Advisory Council, at the time a quasi-governmental,
quasi-private policy-discussion group made up of a cross section of American corporate
leaders. The BAC, as it was usually called, was created in 1933 by Roosevelt's secretary
of commerce, a longtime corporate lobbyist with a South Carolina plantation pedigree
and many years of service to the Democratic Party. Although the BAC was a government advisory group, the corporate community itself selected its members, with the
presidents of General Electric and Standard Oil of New Jersey (renamed Exxon in
1972) leading the way. Through consultations with the foremost policy groups and
trade associations of that era, the corporate leaders made a deliberate attempt to enlist
business statesmen. At the outset, forty-one members held dozens of seats on corporate boards, linking together eighteen of the sixty largest banks, railroads, utilities,
and manufacturing corporations according to my tabulations, but there were several
members from medium-sized businesses outside the main corporate strongholds as well
(McQuaid 1976, 1982).

During the 1930s the BAC prepared reports for the president and consulted
directly with him from time to time. Although its advice was often ignored in the first
five years of its existence, especially on key provisions of the National Labor Relations
Act and the initiatives to raise taxes on the wealthy and their corporations, the BAC's
members and reports played an important role in the formulation, passage, and institu-
tionalization of the Social Security Act (see Domhoff and Webber 2011, chapters 4 and
5, for new archival findings on the origins and implementation of the Social Security
Act). Due to the solidification of the conservative coalition after the 1938 elections
and the gradual conversion of the economy to military production in 1940 and 1941,
Roosevelt relied increasingly on the BAC for advice in bringing corporate leaders into
top government positions (Holl 2005; McQuaid 1982).

CORPORATE DOMINANCE DURING WORLD WAR II

Corporate involvement in the conversion to a wartime economy through leaders suggested by the BAC gradually led to corporate dominance of military production once
the war began, despite ongoing attempts by members of the liberal-labor alliance,
usually called "the New Dealers" at the time, to develop a decision-making role for
themselves. This reliance on the corporate community was generally thought to be
necessary due to its ability to carry out large-scale production faster and better than
could new government-managed plants or a new network of previously uncoordinated

small businesses. In particular, a handful of large steel, aluminum, auto, and airplane manufacturers appeared to have a monopoly on the machinery, resources, and skills that were needed for making tanks and airplanes.

Moreover, high-ranking military officers preferred to work with the corporate leaders they had come to know through the Army Industrial College established by the War Department in 1924, which centered on preparing career military officers to take part in future industrial mobilizations. The school was created at the urging of the corporate leaders who directed the War Production Board during World War I, and corporate executives were among its primary lecturers. They included financier Bernard Baruch, one of the sixty richest people in the country at the time, who had been in charge of the War Industries Board in World War I. In fact, Baruch's management of industrial production during World War I, along with his generous campaign donations to Democrats and continuing involvement in military preparation in the two decades between the wars, made him a respected figure on military production issues among corporate, political, and military leaders before and during World War II. Roosevelt therefore believed he had to reach an accommodation with the financiers and large corporations he often criticized in his first eight years in office if the military was to have the necessary weaponry in a reasonable period of time (Blum 1976; Catton 1948, pp. 29–30; Schwarz 1981, p. 335).

The military departments that controlled war contracts and procurement were managed by corporate executives, some recently commissioned as military officers, some not (Millett 1954, p. 290). Many of those not taken into the military hierarchy were "dollar-a-year men," meaning that they were paid their full corporate salaries by their home corporations so they would not have to suffer a pay cut to join the government. In effect, it was a corporate subsidy of government, and it may have served as a reminder to these executives that they were still part of the corporate community. Once the procurement division set the contracts, the supervision and delivery of the war materiel was turned over to the ordnance division, which was also honeycombed with businessmen (Campbell 1946, pp. 3–4). As for who received the contracts, the answer is the largest companies in the corporate community. The top 1.3 percent of industrials, which accounted for 38.4 percent of civilian industrial output at the outset of the war, produced about 70 percent of all war materiel. The top ten corporations received 30 percent of the contracts, and two-thirds of the contracts went to the top one hundred corporations (Hooks 1991, p. 149).

At the same time that corporate executives and their conservative political allies took increasing control over the wartime economy, New Dealers were frozen out or pushed to the fringes. However, members of the liberal-labor alliance were able to raise objections from several remaining outposts, including a planning committee at the War Production Board, a chair of the Smaller War Plants Commission within the War Production Board, and a CIO official and an AFL official who were among the several vice chairs at the War Production Board. None of these positions had great influence, but those occupying them did have an official status, and they did have access to liberals in Congress and to the mass media. Then, too, there were one or two committees in the House and Senate controlled by centrist or liberal Democrats, and they often were charged with investigating the complaints and claims by the New Dealers. Although New Dealers had very little influence on wartime defense production, they were later able to use their minor positions to put forth their own views on the reconversion to a peacetime economy (see Waddell 2001 for the full story of the corporate ascendancy during World War II).

THE NATIONAL RESOURCES PLANNING BOARD

The corporate leaders within the Business Advisory Council focused most of their concerns about losing out during the transition to a peacetime economy on a small government agency, the National Resources Planning Board (NRPB). Originally housed in the Department of the Interior, the NRPB became one of the growing number of agencies within the White House in 1939 as a minor part of a legislative package meant to strengthen the president's control of the executive branch, in spite of strong objections by conservatives in Congress. The reconstituted NRPB was overseen by a three-person advisory group, led by Roosevelt's retired uncle, Frederic Delano, a former railroad president, Chicago civic leader, and advocate for city and planning.

By then seventy-six years old and long retired, Delano was joined first and foremost by Charles Merriam, a political scientist at the University of Chicago, who had been active in Republican reform politics since the Progressive Era and helped to start the Social Sciences Research Council in the mid-1920s, among many policy-related activities in which he was involved. The third member, George Yantis, a lawyer for lumber and pulp companies in the state of Washington, as well as the Speaker of the House in the state's legislature, had an interest in regional planning and served as a key political contact for Roosevelt in the Northwest. However, he had only a minimal involvement in the activities of the NRPB (see Reagan 1999, chapter 8, for the origins of the NRPB and the careers of Delano, Merriam, and Yantis).

Delano, Merriam, and Yantis were in turn advised by a two-person committee created to provide the NRPB with the business point of view: Henry S. Dennison, president of Dennison Manufacturing Company, which he inherited from his father; and Beardsley Ruml, the treasurer of Macy's Department Stores in New York. By 1939 Dennison had enjoyed a long career as an innovator in the corporate community. He favored progressive management techniques, supported unemployment insurance and old-age pensions, and was an early member of the BAC. A heart attack in late 1941 at age sixty-four greatly reduced his involvement in subsequent events. Ruml, in contrast, was just coming into his own and soon would be a major leader in the early CED.

The son of a physician, Ruml earned a PhD in psychology from the University of Chicago in 1917 and worked in the army's testing program during World War I. He went to work after the war for a new consulting firm that tried to create worker-employer harmony through the application of psychology to personnel management. He began an executive career in 1921 as an assistant to the president of the Carnegie Corporation (one of the earliest policy-oriented foundations) and then served as the director of the Laura Spelman Rockefeller Memorial Fund from 1922 to 1928, granting an unprecedented amount—$41 million—to the social sciences between 1923 and 1928, which is the equivalent of $551.7 million in 2012 dollars (Fosdick 1952, p. 199). When that fund was merged into the Rockefeller Foundation in 1929 as its social sciences division, Ruml became the director of the smaller Spelman Fund for two years, providing grants to urban policy-planning groups, and then took a position as the dean of social sciences at the University of Chicago for three years. It was at this point that he became the treasurer at Macy's from 1934 to 1945 and then chair of its board of directors. He was a director of the National Bureau of Economic Research and became a founding trustee of the Committee for Economic Development (Reagan 1999, chapter 6).

As an advisory group with a small budget that only met with the president from time to time, the NRPB in fact had little or no influence in the government, but it was staffed by a handful of liberal economists, political scientists, and planners who could draw upon their many counterparts at the local level and in universities. The NRPB was therefore able to publish a long string of pamphlets and reports that built on various Keynesian ideas to propose a full-employment economy, a series of social insurance programs, and greater government involvement in the economy. The NRPB's ability to gain media attention and energize the liberal-labor alliance, which still had a visible minority presence in Congress, was worrisome to the corporate leaders and the conservative coalition (Clawson 1981; Reagan 1999, chapter 8).

Moreover, Delano and Merriam gave Roosevelt an outline in January 1941 for a proposed Economic Bill of Rights for all Americans, such as the right to a remunerative job, a decent home, health care, and a good education, which received publicity at the time and was spelled out in more detail in periodic reports. The board's most comprehensive statement, *Security, Work, and Relief Policies,* which was already in draft form by late 1941, was finally sent to Congress in late 1943, with an outline for a liberal benefits program that paralleled similar programs in European social democracies. Roosevelt then called for the new Economic Bill of Rights in his State of the Union speech in January 1944.

Three months after Roosevelt's speech, however, the conservative coalition expressed its displeasure with the idea of an economic bill of rights by defunding, and thereby disbanding, the planning board. In the process Congress also stipulated that the NRPB's functions could not be undertaken by any other government agency, thereby making it difficult if not impossible for the federal government to engage in planning to the extent envisioned by liberal and leftist Keynesians (Bailey 1950, pp. 26–27). For the time being at least, congressional committees controlled by Southern Democrats would be the government's planning agencies.

THE ORIGINS OF THE COMMITTEE
FOR ECONOMIC DEVELOPMENT

Anticipating the likely liberal-labor campaign for a new liberal welfare state, the Business Advisory Council appointed a Committee on Economic Policy to look into the issue of domestic postwar planning at about the same time that the NRPB members were meeting with Roosevelt in early 1941. The BAC chair and its new economic policy committee brought their concerns to their most direct contact in government, secretary of commerce, Jesse Jones, the conservative Texas lumberman, home builder, and bank director who had chaired the Reconstruction Finance Corporation for Roosevelt since 1933. Roosevelt added the secretary of commerce position to Jones's portfolio in 1940, which further enlarged his very extensive network of contacts in the corporate community (Jones 1951).

Jones already was well aware and equally concerned that organized business appeared to be falling behind the National Resources Planning Board and other outposts of the liberal-labor alliance in thinking ahead to the postwar era. He pledged to work with the BAC in developing a domestic postwar program that would concentrate on private investments instead of the list of large government investment projects that the liberal groups were compiling.

Strictly speaking, however, private business was more involved in postwar planning than the BAC and Jones asserted in public, or than is fully appreciated in most accounts of the postwar era. In fact, such planning began shortly after World War II broke out in Europe, when an already established private policy-discussion group, the Council on Foreign Relations (CFR), founded in 1919, created a War-Peace Studies project with the approval of the State Department and a large grant from the Rockefeller Foundation. It soon engaged the participation of several hundred business and financial leaders, academic experts, and former government officials in the work of several different study groups, which concerned themselves with a wide range of economic, political, and military issues. The Economic and Financial Group, whose business members came mostly from the New York area, was by far the most important of these committees in the long run because it worked out the proposals that became the framework for American foreign and economic policies after World War II. The stream of reports from each study group was sent to both the White House and the State Department. The work of the War-Peace Studies project was supposedly confidential, but its ideas were mirrored in many major publications, such as *Fortune,* which also began holding Fortune Roundtable discussions about the American future in 1939; these discussions were then summarized in the magazine itself (Shoup 1974).

By the summer of 1940, the Economic and Financial Group already had concluded that the full productivity of the American economy as currently constituted could only be sustained (without resorting to the considerable government intervention favored by the liberal-labor alliance) if corporations were able to invest, purchase raw materials, and sell products in an area that included Western Europe, South America, and the British Empire, an area that came to be defined as the "Grand Area." The Grand Area strategy also included Southeast Asia because of the need for nearby trading partners for Japan, which was meant to insure that there would be no clash between the American and Japanese economies in the future. The War-Peace Studies project also argued for the necessity of an International Monetary Fund (IMF) and an International Bank for Reconstruction and Development (better known as the World Bank), including an outline for how they should be organized (see Domhoff 1990, chapters 5 and 6, for a document-by-document account of how this planning unfolded and then became the basis for postwar American foreign and economic policy).

The planning by the War-Peace Studies project provided an internationally oriented economic framework within which it might be possible to overcome the liberal-labor alliance's desire for a more government-directed and nationally oriented economy that would provide greater income and security for wage workers and unemployed Americans. However, there was one problem: this planning was about international economics, large companies with overseas markets, and commercial and investment banks with interests in many countries. It did not have any direct focus on smaller companies or the thousands of regional and local economies that feared a return to high unemployment after defense production ended. With this gap in mind, Jones instructed the National Economics Division in the Department of Commerce to do a survey of corporations in the summer of 1941 to learn about their investment plans for the postwar era. To the department's apparent surprise, the survey revealed that only General Electric had done more than think about the matter. The result of this unexpected finding was, first, a departmental report in November 1941, *Markets After War*, and then a proposal, *A Program for Postwar Planning*, in January 1942. The planning proposal argued that the BAC and the Department of Commerce should work together to create a businessman's committee "to encourage postwar planning by individual firms" (Collins 1981, p. 82). This proposal became the starting point for the CED, an organization that soon made it possible for the corporate moderates to expand their visibility and influence in both the corporate community and Washington.

Both documents were prepared by a temporary departmental employee, economist Arthur Upgren, who within a year became the chief economist for the US Chamber of Commerce, followed by employment as a vice president of the Federal Reserve Bank of Minneapolis and as a professor of economics at the University of Minnesota. Whatever the reasons for choosing Upgren to prepare the Department of Commerce reports (a decision I was not able to trace), his role is significant and worth mentioning because he was also one of the four economic advisors to the Economic and Financial Group within the War-Peace Studies project. He therefore understood the general postwar economic framework envisioned by the Council on Foreign Relations within which any new BAC-sponsored planning group would be working.

A series of meetings between Jones and BAC leaders over a three-month period shaped the ground rules for proceeding. They included a decision to exclude participation by representatives from farm groups and churches, thereby increasing the likelihood of general agreement and forceful reports. There was an almost complete overlap between the BAC and the CED in the first two years. Fourteen of the twenty founding CED trustees in 1942 were present or former members of the BAC, and three of the remaining six were appointed to the BAC the next year.

As the plans for the CED matured, Jones sent Roosevelt a note in mid-June explaining what he was up to: "It is our plan to create a nationwide committee of business and industrial representatives to study the post-war economic situation from the standpoint of fitting business and industry into the conditions that will follow the war." However, Roosevelt did not like the idea, writing to his secretary of state, who was in close contact with the War-Peace Studies project members, that "I think there is a real danger in having Jesse Jones expand his thought as contained in this letter." When Roosevelt finally wrote back to Jones a month later, he tried to discourage his project by claiming that "on all domestic issues, these studies by each agency of the government should be coordinated through Mr. Frederic Delano [the chair of the NRPB]" because "there is a great danger of confusion if several committees of this kind are set up" (see Waddell 2001, pp. 136, 197n46, for this evidence of tension between Roosevelt and Jones over bringing business leaders into the planning process on domestic issues). Jones moved ahead anyhow, all the more determined to make sure that the new Committee for Economic Development would have no official connection with the government.

The CED's incorporation papers, filed in September 1942, were modeled after those of The Brookings Institution to make clear that the organization, though made up of business leaders, was strictly nonpartisan and not a lobbying group. Instead, it was said to be concerned with the general public interest, which would be ascertained through careful research and consultation with academic experts. It is in that sense that the members of the organization are best defined as corporate moderates. Or, as political scientist Clinton Rossiter described CED leaders in his 1950s book *Conservatism in America,* they were "liberal conservatives—liberal enough to be seen as "just another bunch of New Dealers" by ultraconservatives, and conservative enough to be characterized by liberals as "Wall Streeters with brains" (Rossiter 1955, pp. 182–183).

Because of their relative independence and their belief that there was a need for some government involvement in the economy, CED leaders were able to suggest policies that often were perceived as the midway or compromise point between the ultraconservatives in the corporate community and the leaders of the liberal-labor alliance. In doing so, they showed continuity with a moderate strain in the corporate community that had searched for compromises when challenged by populists, reformers, or labor leaders in the past. This moderate current within the corporate community went back at least to the turn of the twentieth century with the creation of the National Civic Federation. This first national-level policy-discussion group, modeled after a similar group concerned with Chicago, brought together corporate leaders, union officials, and academic experts in an attempt to find new solutions to what was then called "the labor question" (Green 1956; Weinstein 1968). In fact, historian Robert M. Collins (1981, p. 84), who has written the most detailed scholarly book on the CED from its founding to its successful involvement in the tax cut in 1964, believes that "the ideology of the new group was strikingly similar" to that of the National Civic Federation.

The chair of General Foods served as the chief fund-raiser the first year of the CED's existence, and the chair of Continental Can took the same role in the second year. Sidney Weinberg, the lead partner in the rising investment banking firm of Goldman Sachs, was the vice chair for finance both years, providing a direct link to Wall Street. Despite the size and importance of these three firms, the CED was careful to raise most of its funds in modest sums, ranging from $10 to $1,000, from businesses of all sizes, so that the organization would not be regarded as beholden to a few large corporations. It followed the advice of Alfred P. Sloan Jr., the president of General Motors from 1923 to 1937 and the chair of its board of directors in the 1940s. Sloan counseled the CED finance committee, "Personally, I think it is a mistake to get too large an amount, relatively, from too small a number of people. The reaction is bound to be that there are a few financing the thing for their own selfish purposes" (Schriftgiesser 1960, p. 28). As a result, the CED solicited 2,224 separate contributions to raise $1.7 million over the two-year period, which is $22.3 million in 2012 dollars (Committee for Economic Development 1944b, p. 17).

To ensure that the CED had a neutral image with the general public, the organizing committee decided that its efforts "would be jeopardized if the Chairman were a leader of such outstanding national prominence that his very name would attract an exaggerated public attention and perhaps lead to unwarranted expectations." It therefore recommended "a forward-looking energetic chairman, widely and favorably known to business, but unencumbered with undue national prominence" (Schriftgiesser 1960, p. 27). The trustees then selected Paul Hoffman, who was the president of Studebaker, the second-largest automobile company in the late 1930s, as well as a vice chair of the Business Advisory Council. Notably, and as most CED trustees knew, Hoffman had been advocating the formation of an independent research and discussion group for well over a year. He was joined in this endeavor by his close friend and CED vice chair, William Benton, a former advertising executive, who served as a University of Chicago vice president and helped manage, and then purchased, *Encyclopedia Britannica.* As Hoffman and Benton conceived of the research group, it would include academic experts as well as corporate leaders willing to devote some of their time to formulating public policy proposals.

The trustees were therefore prepared to accept Hoffman's suggestion that the CED should have a research-and-policy component. Ralph Flanders, the president of a relatively small business, Jones and Lamson Machine Company, a Vermont tool and die maker, who was also a director of the Federal Reserve Bank of Boston, was named the chair of the CED's Research and Policy Committee. He was known in the corporate community for his coauthorship of a forward-looking book on full employment that he wrote with three other progressive businessmen of the 1930s, including Dennison of the NRPB advisory committee; the book was drafted by the liberal economist John Kenneth Galbraith, who was just at that moment learning more about Keynesian theory (Dennison, Filene, Flanders, and Leeds 1938). Following his appointment as chair of the new Research and Policy Committee, Flanders also became a member of the Economic and Financial Group of the CFR's War-Peace Studies project, which shows that corporate leaders were well aware of the CFR planning efforts. His presence in both groups signified that there would be a direct link between the two corporate groups.

The CED leaders then worked very carefully to select the right balance of academic advisors. They wanted to include a range of views, but they did not end up with any visible liberals or ultraconservatives. "I don't think there has ever been a group so carefully checked and double-checked," Hoffman later commented (Schriftgiesser 1960, p. 61). They began with a respected Harvard expert on labor relations as the chair of a new Research Advisory Board: Sumner Slichter, who was the outgoing president of the American Economic Association when he agreed to advise CED. Trained at the

University of Chicago, as were a majority of the economists involved with the CED in its early years, he had been a Harvard professor since 1930. Slichter was somewhat sympathetic to the New Deal but had been skeptical of many of its economic policies and was not a supporter of Keynesian theory.

Although there were no strong liberals among its academic advisors, the CED did have a very visible liberal economist of that era on its staff, Gardiner Means, best known as the coauthor with A. A. Berle Jr. of the 1932 classic *The Modern Corporation and Private Property.* Means was suspect in corporate eyes for his work arguing that some large corporations had enough power in their specific markets to set their own—"administered"—prices. He also had been an employee of the National Resources Planning Board when its members and top employees met with CED leaders Hoffman, Flanders, Benton, Ruml, and Chester Davis, by then the president of the Federal Reserve Bank of St. Louis, for a discussion of mutual interests in the spring of 1943. Despite criticisms of the CED by some ultraconservative business executives for employing Means, he stayed with the organization until his retirement in 1958 (Schriftgiesser 1960, pp. 35–36). Moreover, a telegram he sent in 1945 to a CED trustee, the president of a large meatpacking company, suggested he was in fact in tune with what the trustees were trying to accomplish: "Am awfully tired of hearing business men define role of government in negative terms. Big fact is that government has to do more than in the 1920s. Up to business to say what more [is] so that it [the government] won't take on more than is necessary" (Waddell 2001, p. 137).

In addition to generating policy statements with the help of academic advisors, which were disseminated throughout the corporate community and government circles, the periodic gatherings of trustees for serious discussion of specific issues had two other very important functions. First, they were providing the trustees with a more sophisticated overview of the big issues and an understanding of the varying perspectives that contended within government policy arenas. In effect, the CED established a new training ground for those corporate executives who had the inclination and ability to see beyond the interests of their own specific companies. It thereby helped to create policies that would benefit the corporate economy, and in the process it prepared and legitimated its trustees for appointments to government positions. Second, the interactions between corporate officials and academic experts led many of the experts to have a greater understanding of the business viewpoint, which in turn sometimes led them to be interested in serving in policy-oriented positions in government. More generally, these two crucial functions are implicit in all of the corporate-financed policy-discussion groups, as demonstrated in studies documenting that government appointees from the corporate community very often are members of such organizations (Domhoff 2013, chapters 4 and 7; Salzman and Domhoff 1980; Useem 1980, 1984).

GRASSROOTS POSTWAR PLANNING BY THE CED

For all the effort that the CED leaders put into creating a respected Research and Policy Committee and a diverse Research Advisory Board, their more immediate concern was the mobilization of local businesses for their own postwar planning to help fend off public acceptance of the liberal-labor alliance's efforts. This task was undertaken by the CED's Field Division, which was set up only after the National Association of Manufacturers and US Chamber of Commerce agreed to its creation on the condition that it would be disbanded shortly after the war ended. This massive effort was carried out under the leadership of Marion Folsom, the treasurer of Eastman Kodak, who also was the chair of the BAC's Committee on Economy Policy.

Born and raised in southeastern Georgia, where his father was a merchant and a trustee of Southern Georgia College, Folsom was educated at the University of Georgia and the Harvard Business School, and then joined the treasury department at Eastman Kodak in 1915. After serving as a captain in World War I, he returned to Eastman Kodak and was soon promoted to assistant treasurer. During the 1920s he became involved in issues concerning unemployment and old-age insurance in upstate New York, providing the company's very conservative president with constant updates on new developments. In the process he became a well-known business figure, working with reformers in New York City interested in developing social insurance legislation. During the 1930s he served as a member of Roosevelt's Advisory Committee on Social Security, playing a substantive role in the formulation of the Social Security Act and in aiding its passage by providing a bridge to members of Congress from his native South. He became a member of the BAC in 1934, so he had considerable experience with government and policy issues by 1942 (Jacoby 1997).

In early 1944, a year after agreeing to direct the Field Division, Folsom also became the staff director of the House of Representatives' newly formed Special Committee on Postwar Economic Policy and Planning, chaired by a very powerful Southern Democrat from Mississippi named William Colmer. The committee looked at the whole scope of postwar planning and issued many reports. At one point the CED trustees hosted a dinner attended by sixteen of the eighteen members of Colmer's committee; Folsom later reported at a CED meeting that many of the CED reports on the details of the postwar transition "came out at the right time" to be of use in Congress (Whitham 2010, p. 20). Folsom's appointment as a congressional staff director is the first of many examples of specific linkages between the CED and government that involve either direct appointments or policy proposals.

By the end of 1944, nearly 3,000 local committees, all of them independent entities that simply drew upon information and guidance provided by the CED, were making plans for their cities' postwar future (Schriftgiesser 1960, chapter 3). As one highly visible outcome of this effort, the CED published a report, *American Industry Looks Ahead* (Committee for Economic Development 1945a), five days after Japan's surrender in August 1945, which stated with certainty that widespread fears about the possible return to high unemployment were unwarranted. Based on research by Slichter and others, along with estimates from local committees of what could be done in their cities, the report claimed there would be between fifty-one million and fifty-seven million jobs, several million more than what most other forecasters claimed. The high-end estimate turned out to be very accurate, although critics later claimed the CED had arrived at its accurate prediction through a flawed methodology (Schriftgiesser 1960, pp. 58–59).

Flawed methodology or not, the report gave more credibility to the CED in the short run and boosted the spirits of local businesses. And in fact, the conversion to peacetime production was carried out much faster than skeptics had feared. It is unlikely that private investments in local communities across the country could have substituted for what really mattered over the next few years—the surge in consumer spending, greater government domestic spending through a variety of programs, and, from 1950 to 1953, a large increase in defense spending due to the Korean War. Nevertheless, local business communities had regained their swagger, and many of their employees may have attributed the return of prosperity to these local efforts.

With the Field Division's primary mission completed by the summer of 1945, the CED closed it down at the insistence of ultraconservatives in the Chamber of Commerce, even though the committees had worked well in bringing together businesses, agricultural interests, and even union leaders on local policy issues. The shutdown was a good example of the ongoing differences between those C. Wright Mills (1948, pp. 23–27, 240–249) identified at the time, based on a systematic reading of the business press, as "sophisticated" conservatives, who try to stay ahead of trends and work out acceptable compromises, and "practical" conservatives, who take a short-run view and fight any proposals that might give any ground to rival power groups or the government.

MANAGING THE POSTWAR TRANSITION

In spite of the success of its Field Division and optimistic projections about the number of peacetime jobs that would be created, the CED took a cautious approach to the postwar transition, partly because it might be proven wrong about the economy, but even more because it knew that the liberal-labor alliance wanted to take advantage of the transition to institute some of its long-term plans. The CED leaned in the liberal-labor direction on several issues, such as longer and more generous unemployment benefits, plans for backup spending on government construction projects in case the expected level of consumer demand did not materialize, provisions for on-the-job training for new positions, and maintenance of price controls on selected products for a year or two after the end of the war. But it sided with ultraconservative business groups on the issues that mattered the most to the corporate community—how war contracts would be terminated (fast and generously), the liquidation of government-owned production facilities (sell the relatively few that were useful for peacetime production to private companies, with some preference for smaller businesses, and scrap the others), and the timing of the reconversion to a peacetime economy (wait for the war to be over before resuming any production of consumer goods).

In making its specific policy recommendations between 1943 and 1946, the CED drew upon the best expert advice it could find on each issue, including experts who were working for the government at the time. It also drew upon the information and expertise of trustees who were part of the war effort, starting with Ernest Kanzler, chair of the Universal Credit Corporation in Detroit, who was a high official at the War Production Board; and Weinberg of Goldman Sachs, the assistant to the chair at the War Production Board, who spent much of his time coordinating between the War Production Board and the corporate community. They also could rely on the knowledge and contacts of the CED's executive director, John Fennelly, a former investment banker with a major firm in Chicago, who had worked with Hoffman on the financing of Studebaker in the 1930s. During the early years of the war Fennelly served as an assistant to several key officials at the War Production Board, then took a position in the Washington offices of the CED between June 1943 and November 1944, which involved much back and forth with his former colleagues as well as work on CED policy statements (Fennelly 1965).

All of the CED policy statements were put into the hands of key decision makers in Washington, including members of congressional committees. Colmer's House committee on postwar planning and its less active Senate counterpart, chaired by Walter George of Georgia, provided the main focus, and there is reason to believe that the CED reports had an impact on their work. As Folsom told his fellow trustees in 1945, the list of reports issued by the Colmer Committee was almost identical with the list published by the CED (Whitham 2010). Overall, however, the congressional committees on postwar planning "never really accomplished much" by way of furthering any specific postwar plans (Reagan 1999, p. 239). Their most important function was to replace the disestablished National Resources Planning Board and ensure that no other New Deal outposts within the government continued any of its planning efforts, thereby blocking any significant government involvement in the reconversion to a peacetime economy.

When the war with Japan ended sooner than expected in mid-August 1945, the decontrol and reconversion processes were far faster than the CED advocated due to pressures from both the ultraconservatives and agricultural interests. The War Production Board's controls on raw materials were removed two weeks after Japan's surrender. Controls on wages, vehicle purchases, gasoline, and processed foods were gone a few weeks after that, leaving little possibility that the Office of Price Administration could control prices on the items remaining under its purview. In early September, President Harry Truman asked Congress to repeal the excess profits tax, a type of wartime tax first used in World War I to siphon off profits that were far higher than in peacetime due to lucrative military contracts. The repeal, which went into effect on January 1, 1946, convinced organized labor, already concerned about the loss of overtime pay, that it had to strike for large wage increases very quickly. Labor's decision turned out to be a fateful one that misread the mood of the general public and alienated many white-collar employees and inhabitants of small towns and rural areas that were not yet comfortable with the idea of unions. More generally the chaotic reconversion process left business, labor, and consumers angry with the Truman administration. Inflation and major strikes became the defining features of early postwar political conflict (see Bernstein 1965 and 1967a for accounts of the sudden transition and the subsequent impact of the way it was handled; see also Bernstein 1967b).

THE CED JOINS THE BATTLE OVER THE POSTWAR TAX STRUCTURE

As the arguments over reconversion and postwar planning were unfolding, the CED was doing its homework on tax issues in an effort to find a moderate way through the minefield of tax battles that had marked the previous eight years. They did so knowing that the president and the liberal-labor alliance already had tried to raise the issue of war revenues in 1940 and 1941 to revive their goal of instituting higher tax rates on wealthy individuals and extremely profitable corporations. Roosevelt made numerous statements to this effect in 1940 and 1941, and then claimed in 1942 that no one should make more than $25,000 a year during a difficult two-front war in which everyone should have to sacrifice, which is $350,000 in 2012 dollars (Brownlee 2004, p. 209). The result would have been marginal tax rates as high as 90 percent for a handful of individuals, along with high and progressive rates on corporations. These high corporate tax rates would include an excess profits tax with rates ranging from 20 to 60 percent, which would clearly fall upon the biggest and most profitable corporations, most of which were likely to be involved in providing supplies and war materiel to the military.

Rejecting Roosevelt's agenda, the conservatives who controlled the tax committees in both houses of Congress substituted an excess profits tax with a range of 25 to 50 percent in 1940 and 35 to 60 percent in 1941. Crucially, they also enlarged the tax base to include lower-income individuals and made the rates at the high end far less progressive for both individuals and corporations than Roosevelt suggested. But, at the same time, they resisted the ultraconservatives' push for a general sales tax, so they had taken a moderate course. At that point the New Dealers decided they were satisfied with the outcome. They realized that it might be wise to accept a mass-based income tax as the most politically defensible way "to ensure a permanent flow of revenue to federal programs of social justice" (Brownlee 2004, p. 112).

To keep tax payments flowing on a timely basis throughout the year, the New Dealers in the Department of the Treasury proposed a system of monthly withholding taxes on interest and dividends as well as incomes, an approach known as "collection at the source." It had been used in the Civil War and World War I, and most recently in collecting the Social Security payroll taxes legislated in 1935, as well as in Canada and Great Britain. The Treasury officials advocating this plan also understood that the use of a withholding tax would make it easier to increase or decrease tax revenues on a monthly basis in order to cool off or stimulate the economy. That is, they saw tax withholding as a useful tool for managing consumer demand. In contrast, conservatives inside and outside of government initially objected mightily to withholding, claiming the system was administratively impossible and would lead to financial strains for the many families that would have to pay taxes for both 1941 and 1942. Due to their protests and influence, the idea of withholding taxes on interest and dividends quickly disappeared. Then, CED trustee Ruml came up with a plan to smooth the transition to monthly income tax withholding by forgiving the previous year of income taxes entirely. Since only a few percent of employees owed income taxes for 1942, and therefore would receive a massive windfall, Roosevelt objected in a message to Congress that the plan was unconscionable (Blum 1967, p. 59).

Ruml ignored the president's criticisms and instead built on his legitimacy as a former philanthropy executive and the current chair of the Federal Reserve Bank of New York to orchestrate an extensive media campaign in favor of his proposal, paid for by Macy's. At the same time, Ruml extolled the virtues of the Treasury's plan for monthly income tax deductions and embraced it as if it had always been a part of his own plan. He testified several times before congressional committees and gave numerous speeches to business and service organizations, which quickly won large-scale public support for his ideas according to opinion polls. The argument over tax forgiveness then stalled passage of the Revenue Act of 1943 for several months, finally resulting in a compromise that in effect gave Ruml 75 percent of what he originally proposed (Bank, Stark, and Thorndike 2008, p. 103).

The liberal-labor alliance's defeat on tax forgiveness for the well-to-do was followed by congressional rejection of Roosevelt's renewed call later in 1943 for large tax increases on personal incomes to keep wartime deficits at a minimum. Although the conservative coalition increased the excess profits tax to as high as 95 percent on the most profitable corporations, with a 10 percent refund promised for after the war, it also added numerous new tax loopholes for various business sectors, including steel and mining. These changes led Roosevelt to veto the bill with the claim that it was not "for the needy but for the greedy" (Brownlee 2004, p. 114). He then became the first president to suffer a congressional override on a revenue bill.

Although the number of taxpayers skyrocketed from 3.9 million in 1939 to 42.6 million by 1944, the top 1 percent of household incomes nonetheless had to be taxed at a marginal rate of 50 percent to 90 percent on any earnings over $25,000 to help control inflation and keep the debt from rising to even more massive proportions. Consequently, the effective tax rate on the top 1 percent of income-earners climbed to 58.6 percent in 1944, four times what it had been in World War I and nearly three times what it had been in 1940. As a result, the top 1 percent ended up paying 32 percent of the personal income taxes that were collected during 1945. The latter figure provides an indication of just how essential taxes on the wealthy were for the war effort, as well as a window into how highly concentrated the income distribution was at that time (Brownlee 2000, pp. 60, 116).

The Committee for Economic Development entered the tax fray in 1944 by issuing a policy statement with two major goals that seemed difficult to reconcile: maintaining large government revenues while at the same time reducing the steep taxes that were being paid by high-income individuals and corporations. The trustees began by enlisting help from university and government experts on public finance, led by University of Wisconsin economist Harold Groves, who worked within a reformist tradition established a few decades earlier by another Wisconsin economist, John R. Commons. Based on his experience working for the National Civic Federation for three years at the turn of the century, Commons decided that lasting reforms had to have the support of the corporate moderates through an appeal to the profit motive. He came to this conclusion in part because the reform efforts he had worked for prior to his years with the National Civic Federation had all failed, but also because he and other reformers suffered many defeats between 1906 and the early 1920s as the leaders of a progressive-minded think tank, the American Association for Labor Legislation (Commons 1934).

After Groves's ideas were critiqued by other experts, his analysis and recommendations appeared as a book, *Production, Jobs, and Taxes* (1944), in which he argued that a reasonable and balanced tax plan is one that does not depress consumption or reduce the incentive to invest. To have a productive economy, he claimed, taxes on personal incomes and estates were the best ways to raise funds for the government. He eliminated corporate income taxes because he thought they suppress investment, a claim that was rejected for lack of evidence by liberal tax experts (Musgrave 1947). From Groves's perspective, any tax on corporate income should be considered as simply a method of collecting personal taxes on dividends at the source, which the recipients of dividends would then deduct from their income taxes. As a result, two-thirds of federal taxes would come from the personal income tax, with most of the remainder coming from taxes on tobacco and alcoholic drinks.

Relying heavily on Groves's recommendations after working through them in great detail, the result was the CED's first major policy statement, *A Postwar Federal Tax Plan for High Employment* (1944a). The CED's tax proposal, one of dozens offered at the time by business and labor groups, soon emerged as one of three comprehensive plans that were given serious attention. It also staked out enough original territory to earn plaudits in articles in the left-leaning *The Nation,* the liberal *New Republic,* and the most visible business magazine of the day, *Fortune,* as the best taxation plan put forward by a business group (Bank 2010, p. 198). It even mollified ultraconservatives to some degree by arguing for somewhat lower rates on high-income individuals and for the conventional business view that taxes on corporations should be eliminated. Just over 221,000 copies of the 1944 statement were distributed by August 1945, compared to a range of 27,000 to 137,000 for five statements concerning the details of the postwar transition (Committee for Economic Development 1945b, p. 13).

The CED report began with the argument that taxes had to be higher than they were before the war because of the many necessary burdens the federal government now shouldered—defense, international obligations, likely veterans' benefits, and paying off the debt. But taxes could nonetheless be lower than the high wartime levels and still bring in the large revenues that would be needed. To achieve fairness without creating a drag on productivity or consumption, the CED followed Groves's recommendation in asserting that the personal income tax was the best starting point from an economic and government point of view. It allowed for productivity growth and could bring in large revenues by including lower-income earners, thereby generating international confidence in the strength of the government. Viewed from the standpoint of individuals, the report claimed, income taxes are potentially transparent to everyone in terms of general payment levels, can be made more equitable through progressivity, and can allow for different personal circumstances through dependency deductions and income averaging over the space of several years (Committee for Economic Development 1944a; Schriftgiesser 1960, p. 82).

Following Groves once again, the report presented a further surprise to the corporate community by arguing for higher estate and gift taxes. It claimed that "death taxes," as it called such taxes, "are less likely to have a depressing effect on incentives to enterprise than the collection of equal amounts from businessmen during their lifetime" (Committee for Economic Development 1944a, p. 36). It further broke with business orthodoxy by opposing the use of general sales taxes at the federal level, and also wanted to limit specific taxes on certain products, called "excise" taxes in that bygone era, except in the case of alcohol, cigarettes, and maybe gasoline, especially if gasoline taxes were used to build highways.

To raise half of the $18 billion that the CED thought the federal government needed each year—a figure that did not include Social Security benefits or interest on the national debt—the basic income tax rate should be somewhere between 16 and 20 percent, with the CED's preference being for an 18 percent "normal" rate before progressivity and personal deductions were added into the calculations. It then presented a table in which it compared the effective tax rates for 1944 with what the rates would be under its preferred plan, which eliminated taxes on those making less than $2,000 a year and provided for effective tax rates that ranged from 9 percent at the bottom rung to 69.7 percent for those making over $5 million a year. These rates were 20 to 40 percent lower than the wartime rates, with the largest reductions for those making over $50,000, the equivalent of $653,000 in 2012 in terms of purchasing power. Basically, the success of the plan depended upon the retention of a tax base of just over forty million taxpayers.

Although the CED's plan broke with business orthodoxy by rejecting sales and excise taxes while opting for progressive income taxes, the names attached to the report were not those of young or liberal executives, or of representatives from small marginal companies. Perhaps the most prominent name of the era on the Research and Policy Committee was that of Thomas P. Lamont, the chair of the board of J. P. Morgan Bank, the famous bank that had provided leadership on Wall Street since the onset of the corporate era in the 1850s; Lamont himself had been an advisor to presidents and statesmen since World War I. The presidents of two Federal Reserve banks, the dean of the Harvard Business School, and the president of the US Chamber of Commerce also served on the Research and Policy Committee, and the list of trustees in general by this time included top officers at Boeing, Coca-Cola, Continental Insurance, General Motors, and Quaker Oats.

Nor was the statement lacking in orthodoxy when it came to corporate taxes. It first of all recommended an immediate elimination of the excess profits tax once the war ended. Based on Groves's recommendations once again, the CED agreed with ultraconservatives that taxes on corporations should be eliminated because it was both morally wrong and harmful to the economy to tax the same income twice, first when it is earned by corporations and then again when it goes to individuals as dividends from stocks and bonds. Abolish "double taxation" became the corporate community's slogan. However, there was irony and political amnesia in the CED's concerns about double taxation because corporate leaders had suggested it in 1936 as part of their successful battle against the corporate tax they disliked the most, the undistributed profits tax (Bank 2010, pp. 146–147, 179–180). There were also good reasons to doubt that claims of double taxation had any validity, starting with the fact that large owners knew beforehand they would have to pay a price for the many advantages conferred upon them by organizing as corporations rather than partnerships (Paul 1954, pp. 423–425).

For the CED, the way to end the alleged immorality and burdens of double taxation would be to tax corporations at the same normal 18 percent rate as individuals would pay, and then exempt individual stockholders from paying any taxes on the dividends they received. "To remove the inequity and the repressive effect of double taxation on stockholders' income," the report said, corporations should withhold taxes on "behalf of its stockholders," making the dividends they received "exempt from the standard tax" (Committee for Economic Development 1944a, p. 20). In effect, the CED was suggesting that the corporations withhold taxes on dividends in the same way they already did on employee incomes. The net result of this proposal from an individual point of view would be that stockholders, who have high incomes through dividends, would pay far lower tax rates than those who earn high incomes from a salary, such as executives and administrators, or from a professional practice, such as medicine or law.

Although the liberal-labor alliance agreed with the CED that progressive income taxes were better than sales taxes, its proposals called for much steeper progressive rates on both high incomes and dividends for individuals. It also wanted high progressive taxes on corporations, arguing from past experience that low taxes on corporations might encourage them to hold on to their earnings, thereby taking money out of circulation that was needed to stimulate the economy. These views were expressed through the Coordinating Committee for a Progressive Tax Program, led by representatives of the CIO. The leadership also included "fourteen other labor, consumer, professional and church organizations," which charged that the corporate plans would relieve the "99,000 wealthiest individuals and corporations" of the tax burden they should shoulder (Paul 1954, p. 418).

With the rival plans presented to it by business and the liberal-labor alliance in hand, the Ways and Means Committee offered its own proposal in 1945. It called for a reduction in corporate taxes in general for the benefit of several hundred thousand corporations. But the committee also wanted to postpone the repeal of the excess profits tax until 1947, because only about 20,000 corporations earned enough to pay the tax. Top corporate leaders reacted vehemently to this idea, indicating just how important abolishing the excess profits tax was to them in restoring both their power and their profits. After intensive lobbying, the tax legislation enacted at the close of World War II was close to the corporate standpoint in that the excess profits tax was indeed abolished, a major accomplishment that reduced the top tax rate from 95 percent to 38 percent. In addition, the emphasis on mass-based income taxes and a flat tax for corporations was in keeping with what the CED and ultraconservative members of the corporate community desired. Although there was talk about abolishing double taxation, corporate leaders did not push strongly on this issue because the excess profits tax was of far greater concern to them, second only to the undistributed profits tax on their list of least-preferred taxes (Bank 2010, pp. 201–202, 204–205).

However, the top marginal rate on individuals (85 percent, as compared to the 73 percent advocated by the CED) and the high flat tax on corporations (38 percent, as compared to the 18 percent advocated by the CED) were more than the CED trustees and other corporate leaders could accept. A united corporate community therefore entered into a long-term effort to reduce both of these taxes to levels that they felt were appropriate for them to pay given the importance of their risks, investments, and management skills in expanding the economy. At the same time, their general efforts in this regard were constrained by their need for a strong federal government and the resistance of the liberal-labor alliance, which was backed by the likelihood of a presidential veto as long as Truman or any other Democrat was president (Bank 2010, pp. 204–205). Corporate leaders therefore tended to concentrate on lobbying campaigns to reduce corporate taxes through creating as many different types of "tax expenditures" (a general term for tax breaks, loopholes, and tax incentives) as could be obtained for as many different sectors of business as possible (Howard 1997, pp. 3–4, 9). The process of creating these favors for businesses became a useful one for politicians in terms of obtaining corporation support and campaign funds, which made corporate success by means of this approach all the more likely. In effect, the new tax system drew corporate and political leaders into an even more necessary and lucrative form of gift exchange (Brownlee 2004, pp. 129–130).

The shifting nature of the argument over the types and levels of taxation—from undistributed profits taxes in the 1930s to excess profits taxes in the early 1940s to double taxation after 1945—obscured more basic issues. First, the argument ignored the fact that economic growth and corporate profitability may not be related primarily, or even secondarily, to tax issues. Second, as studies by the Department of the Treasury revealed at the time, there was in fact no good information available on the actual effects of taxation on the success of the economy (Bank 2010, pp. 206, 208; Paul 1954, pp. 429–431). More recent evidence suggests that lower tax rates on corporations, dividends, and capital gains have no impact on investment decisions (Burman 1999; Stewart 2011).

In effect, then, the corporate-conservative and liberal-labor alliances were arguing from preferences based on beliefs and values, shaped by concerns about power and ideology, even though both sides often brought highly selective economic evidence forth as the reason for their preferences. Put more generously and abstractly, the degree to which both sides were trying to legitimate their power and privilege, rather than economic self-interest, let alone the good of the economy in general, is unknown. It is within this context that the large and clear differences between the corporate-conservative and liberal-labor alliances on how the tax burden should be distributed make the effective tax rate for the top 1 percent of income earners a useful power indicator. All that said, however, it should not be overlooked that the corporate moderates and the liberal-labor alliance had reached a cross-class compromise that focused on income taxes with at least some degree of progressivity while at the same time minimizing the role of sales taxes and excise taxes.

THE CED GOES INTERNATIONAL

The CED originally did not intend to have a strong focus on the international economy, but in 1945 it issued two policy statements, based on two years of intensive discussions, that put it on the road to making international economic issues one of its major concerns.

In the process, it began to create the rules and institutions that were necessary for the phenomena that came to be known as "globalization." The first CED statement had a long-term impact in terms of increasing international trade, the second a short-term impact by providing a small compromise that aided in the creation of the International Monetary Fund and the World Bank. This work, which began with thorny issues related to tariffs and trade, was part of the organization's effort to complement the work by the CFR's War-Peace Studies project, whose business members, as noted earlier, tended to be from large New York–based corporations and financial institutions.

To provide the initial basis for discussions, CED leaders asked four prominent economists to write briefing papers. Three of the four were at the same time advisors to the Economic and Financial Group in the War-Peace Studies project, which provided linkages to the work that study group did between late 1939 and early 1943 and highlighted the role of economists as architects for the system that corporate leaders wanted to construct.

After numerous lengthy discussions within a subcommittee, which had to overcome many disagreements and hesitations, the CED published a general policy statement on international economics in 1945 under the title *International Trade, Foreign Investment, and Domestic Employment* (see Whitham 2010 for an analysis of the origins of this CED policy statement). At one key meeting, a draft of the report was discussed by a group that included three of the leading government experts on economic issues: a special advisor on economics to the secretary of war, a Department of State expert on international economics, and an assistant secretary to the treasury. The statement included an emphasis on the fact that the United States could not rely on foreign trade to generate high employment, which was contrary to what some CED trustees had believed at the outset. Instead, high employment would be a necessary basis for increasing international trade: "The greatest single contribution which the United States can make to high levels of trade and employment throughout the world is to develop and to maintain a high level of employment, production, and consumption within its own borders" (Committee for Economic Development 1945c, p. 5).

As one part of the meeting that included the three government advisors, the trustees discussed the problems involved in defining the separate roles of the International Monetary Fund and the World Bank in encouraging world trade, just when financial leaders from the allied nations were meeting to grapple with these issues without much success in Bretton Woods, New Hampshire. Several ideas put forth by the CED trustees seemed potentially useful to one of the government experts, who was the Department of the Treasury's key representative to the Bretton Woods conference. He therefore urged the CED to put out a separate statement that might help convince American ultraconservatives, who included many commercial bankers, to support the American proposals: "A report from this group would be most influential. I would like to make a plea that your forthcoming policy statement covers the immediate issues, on which your weight can be felt. The other things can be presented in another document" (Schriftgiesser 1960, p. 123).

After further discussions among themselves, the members of the Research and Policy Committee came up with a compromise that would deal with the American bankers' main concern: seemingly temporary currency loans from the IMF to countries with exchange problems could freeze IMF assets by in effect becoming short-term stabilization loans, thereby covering up an inability to pay government debts. The compromise simply made explicit that the World Bank could make such short-term loans to strapped nations as well as the long-term reconstruction and development loans that would be its primary focus. This was not quite the solution the Treasury representative had hoped for, but it was good enough to break the logjam that had developed. "This report is an important one and we don't want to make a mistake in how we handle it," he said in a memo to his boss, Secretary of Treasury Henry Morgenthau Jr. (Hurwitz 1990, p. 28; White 1945).

The Treasury Department then issued a press release saying that its top officials had read the report and thought its suggestions deserved very careful consideration. Within forty-eight hours of the official publication of *The Bretton Woods Proposals: A Statement on National Policy* (Committee for Economic Development 1945d), the stalemate ended. The CED received considerable acclaim in the media for its ability to fashion acceptable compromises. In fact, it was the first of several such compromises over the next several years as the committee gradually began to take the lead role within the corporate community on international trade issues.

With the compromise concerning the role of the International Monetary Fund accomplished, Congress wrapped up its trade-oriented legislative business for 1945 by extending the Reciprocal Trade Act, first passed in 1933, and the Lend Lease Act, which gave weaponry and needed goods to overseas allies in exchange for "considerations," such as opening the British empire to American investments and products. Congress also expanded the lending capabilities of the Export-Import Bank, which had been created in 1934 to help foreign countries finance the purchase of American-produced goods. In short, Congress set the stage for the postwar leadership role for the United States that leaders within the Council on Foreign Relations and Committee for Economic Development were advocating, usually against the opposition of the more nationalist ultraconservatives (McLellan and Woodhouse 1960).

THE GI BILL AND THE INVISIBLE WELFARE STATE

As part of its effort to limit unemployment and assure adequate consumer demand after the war, the CED and corporate moderates in general were strong supporters of a generous postwar benefits package for all veterans who had served at least ninety days, whether they had seen any combat or not. This package was brought together in the Serviceman's Readjustment Act of 1944, best known as the GI Bill. Today the act is sometimes thought of as a victory for the liberal-labor alliance, but that is only partly the case because the final provisions were the product of an ultraconservative veterans' organization and the conservative coalition. More exactly, the bill was in some ways a setback for the liberal-labor alliance's larger postwar plans to provide similar benefits for all citizens, even though its members ended up pleased with the generosity of the benefits provided to returning veterans.

Roosevelt's first message to Congress in relation to postwar benefits for veterans, sent in late October 1943, centered on educational benefits. Based on work by a committee of the disestablished NRPB, the message was followed one month later by further proposals on other topics. Critically, the president's plans were tied to a larger vision of national economic planning, money for education, and unemployment benefits for everyone. Two months later, however, Roosevelt's larger plans were preempted by a bill exclusively for veterans that was written in haste by a committee of a highly visible veterans' organization, the American Legion, best known for its support for teenage baseball leagues and its service to communities in times of disaster (Ross 1969, p. 94).

The American Legion was "conceived, organized, and financed" shortly after World War I by young civilian commissioned officers who had volunteered for service, all of them scions of the "American capitalist Establishment" (Campbell 2010, p. 14). Its leaders built on two elite organizations, the National Security League and the Military Training Camps, formed in 1915 in preparation for possible entry into World War I and to restore the physical vigor and assertiveness they thought were declining in the American character. The most central figure in forming the American Legion was Theodore Roosevelt Jr., the son of the famous president, and himself a stockbroker and adventurer, later to be an assistant secretary of the navy (1921–1923), governor of Puerto Rico (1929–1932), governor general of the Philippines (1932–1933), an executive at American Express, and a brigadier general during World War II. Several of the legion's other founders went on to equally distinguished careers and worked for the government in high posts during World War II.

From the outset, legion leaders lobbied for military training programs and the best possible benefits for veterans as part of their desire to nurture a more patriotic culture and stronger military. This effort led to a program for universal military training for reserve officers on college campuses and at camps during the summer months as part of the Defense Act of 1920, along with a Veterans Bureau established in the same year and then a veterans' hospital system over the next several years. Legion commanders also advocated financial aid for World War I veterans in the early 1920s, seeking money for them to buy farmland or a home, or as a one-time cash benefit up to $625 (about $8,400 in terms of purchasing power in 2012). After a Republican president vetoed their "bonus bill," in part due to opposition by the US Chamber of Commerce, legion leaders settled for life insurance policies in 1924 that would be payable to veterans in 1944 or to relatives at the time of a veteran's death. In 1930 they convinced Congress to provide free hospital care for post-service disabilities (Littlewood 2004, pp. 38–39).

Although the American Legion's GI bill included many provisions developed by the NRPB, Roosevelt was initially opposed to it because he saw it as "particularistic" legislation that did not fit with his desire to provide the same generous benefits to all Americans as part of the Economic Bill of Rights. He already had explained his position in regard to special benefits for war veterans in a speech to the American Legion convention in 1933, in which he said it seemed especially unfair to him that veterans should receive pensions for post-service disabilities when other Americans were not afforded the same support after debilitating injuries or illness. Indeed, at that point he used the temporary powers that were given to him by the Economy Act of 1933 to eliminate "just over 380,000 mostly non-service connected disability cases from the pension rolls" (Campbell 2004, p. 258). However, ten years later, with executives from large corporations directing the war effort, and with postwar planning in the hands of congressional committees chaired by congressmen from the Deep South, Roosevelt quietly acquiesced.

The American Legion's bill flew through the Senate in late March by a 50–0 vote under the sponsorship of Democratic Senator Bennett Clark of Missouri, who in 1919 was the first chair of the legion. However, it contained several liberalizing features that were urged by members of the liberal-labor alliance. It therefore faced strong opposition in the House from Southern Democrats, who feared that the educational opportunities and the year-long unemployment compensation provisions might help African Americans escape from segregation and low-wage seasonal work. This opposition was embodied in the chair of the House Veterans Affairs Committee, John Rankin of Mississippi, himself a member of the American Legion. Rankin claimed generous educational benefits would lead to too many overeducated and undertrained people, who would be subject to the influence of leftist professors in the process. He also openly expressed his concern that African Americans would not accept jobs as long as they received unemployment benefits. With the aid of other Southern Democrats and the conservative Republicans on his committee, his scaled-down version of the bill went to the House floor, where it passed by 388–0 despite a strong lobbying effort for the Senate version by liberals and legionnaires (Ross 1969, p. 116).

The final bill was made somewhat more liberal in the conference committee, but the conservative coalition put limits on the size of loan guarantees and eliminated direct loans to veterans. To maximize congressional and state-level control of federal executive agencies and minimize any interference in Southern race relations, the federal government's Office of Education was relegated to a secondary role in relation to veterans' education, the United States Employment Service's involvement in helping veterans find employment was marginal, and much of the actual work was put in the hands of state governments (Frydl 2009, chapter 2). With state-level control of most GI Bill programs firmly established, various benefits were improved over the next two years, making it a program that could have a positive influence on postwar America (Ross 1969, chapter 8).

As was briefly mentioned in the Introduction, the economic impact of this legislation throughout the postwar era was very large, especially if its later inclusion of veterans of the Korean and Vietnam wars, and the few remaining veterans from World War I, is taken into consideration. In addition to educational benefits for 7.8 million veterans of World War II, Korea, and Vietnam, it also included free medical care for all veterans of all wars, whatever the cause of the illness or injury; mortgage support for the purchase of homes, farms, or businesses; and life insurance. There was also preferential treatment for veterans seeking employment in the federal civil service; between 1953 and 1964, when the government stopped reporting the number of veterans in civil service jobs, veterans were about 60 percent of male federal employees. In total, over $20 billion was spent on all the programs combined between 1945 and 1955, a figure that includes about $14.5 billion for educational support. In the peak year, 1948, benefits for veterans accounted for 20.1 percent of the federal budget (see Campbell 2004, p. 260, and Ross 1969, p. 288, for this and other information on the impact of the GI Bill).

Sociologist Alec Campbell provides the most sweeping and informative view of the impact of veterans' benefits in making a strong case that they added up to "an invisible welfare state" in the postwar era. Not only were nearly half of adult males the veterans of one war or another by 1970, with a gradual decline to 41 percent by 1980, but government benefits accounted for 20.3 to 36.4 percent of all nondefense, nondebt-service outlays between 1946 and the early 1950s, with a gradual decline thereafter that reflects the increasing size of the elderly population receiving Social Security pensions, Medicare, disability payments, and welfare benefits. This invisible welfare state was not only important for the lives of millions of Americans but also provided government support for the economy throughout the postwar era, especially when the higher salaries earned by those educated through the GI Bill are added to the picture (Campbell 2004, pp. 251–254; Ross 1969, p. 289).

A WIDER PERSPECTIVE ON THE WAR YEARS

The corporate community and the conservative coalition shaped most of the major decisions during World War II on both military and civilian issues. Responding to the lingering economic depression from the 1930s and the rise of a liberal-labor alliance that had an alternative vision of American society, corporate moderates developed their own postwar plans through the Council on Foreign Relations and the Committee for Economic Development. This planning resulted in the International Monetary Fund, the World Bank, and legislation to increase international trade. The CFR and CED also offered plans for the postwar transition and supported generous benefits for veterans.

Roosevelt, with his emphasis on a progressive income tax, set the terms for the postwar tax structure, but the CED and the conservative coalition limited its progressivity to some extent, insisted that it include all but the lowest-income members of the social ladder, and shaped it as much as possible to fit corporate preferences. Still, all members of the corporate community, not just ultraconservatives, found the taxes on them and their corporations to be too onerous, setting the stage for an argument that has gone on ever since.

The conservative coalition's dominance of Congress is reflected in systematic studies of its successes and failures between 1939 and 1945. In the House, for example, it appeared eighty-one times in that seven-year period and won on seventy-two of them (Shelley 1983, p. 34). Even more telling, it never lost on the labor issues on which it most frequently coalesced (Katznelson, Geiger, and Kryder 1993). It also eliminated several other New Deal agencies in addition to the National Resources Planning Board, including two within the Department of Agriculture. The conservative coalition was clearly in charge legislatively (Waddell 2001).

As for the CED, its trustees decided to continue their work for at least three more years, even though some leaders within the National Association of Manufacturers and the US Chamber of Commerce wanted the entire organization to disband at the same time as it closed down its Field Division. The trimmed-down CED also retained its Public Information Division, whose primary task was to see that copies of CED reports were covered in the mass media and put into the hands of corporate executives, university professors, and government policy makers.

Although the liberal-labor alliance did not enjoy a single legislative success between 1939 and 1946, and suffered the dismantlement of several New Deal agencies, unions reached 14.3 million members in 1945 and a high point in union density of 35.4 percent for all nonagricultural workers that was never attained again (Mayer 2004, p. 22, table A1). In addition, union leaders worked with liberals on planning new legislation that would build on the plans of the defunct National Resources Planning Board. They did so on the basis of widely shared understandings that the liberal-labor alliance would make full use of Keynesian economics in order to provide a "rationale for their political position" (Brownlee 2004, p. 104). Furthermore, there had been a dramatic decline in income inequality in the years since 1938. With higher tax rates on those with high incomes, and with virtually everyone working at good wages or with overtime pay, the overall Gini coefficient for full-time nonrural male wage and salary workers fell from 0.430 in 1938 to 0.366 in 1945. Conversely, the effective tax rate on the top 1 percent of income earners had risen from 6.8 percent in 1932 to 21.6 in 1940 and 58.6 in 1945 (see Goldin and Margo 1992 and Krugman 2007, chapter 3, for overviews of the changes in income inequality).

As the postwar era began, the liberal-labor challengers felt fortified for a renewed effort due to the growth of unions and the apparent usefulness of the liberal and left versions of Keynesian economics for their purposes.

Chapter Four

The Postwar Years and the Truman Administration

CONFLICT OVER THE EMPLOYMENT ACT OF 1946

The first attempt by the liberal-labor alliance to exert more influence in the postwar era began amid the excitement created by the end of the war, high employment, large increases in the number of university students, and robust consumer spending. Adding tension to this heady brew, there was rapid inflation after the removal of price controls and widespread strikes by unions, which resented the hasty removal of the excess profits tax and price controls.

The Employment Act of 1946 seems like a minor matter today because it ended up delivering far less than it originally promised. But in its original form, the "full employment bill," as it was first called, built on the work of a wide range of liberal-labor planning and research groups. Most critically, the bill stated that "the federal government would underwrite the total national investment necessary to ensure full employment" (Bailey 1950, p. 23). It shared many ideas in common with the National Resources Planning Board's 1943 report to Congress, *Security, Work, and Relief Policies*. In effect, and as most of those who paid attention to politics at that time knew, it was the first move by the liberal-labor alliance to gain greater power during the postwar era.

In practical terms, the language in the first draft of the Employment Act meant the government could make loans available to private industry and local and state governments. Such loans would be offered if it were determined through economic projections that there would be a shortfall in the amount of investment needed to bring about full employment. Called a National Production and Employment Budget, this package of economic projections was basically a calculation of how large the economy had to be in order to ensure full employment. Even more radically, the proposal stated that "if such loans were not applied for or utilized in sufficient quantity to bring about full employment, Congress would then appropriate for public works and other federal projects the amount of money needed to accomplish this end" (Bailey 1950, p. 24). Put more directly, the liberal-labor alliance wanted government to take over the investment function from capitalists when necessary. The potential for private profits would no longer dictate whether or not investments were made.

Virtually all members of the corporate community found the draft legislation completely unacceptable when it first appeared. The ultraconservatives felt confident that they had the votes to block the legislation due to the size of the conservative coalition in the House, as already demonstrated by its many successes in eliminating New Deal agencies and programs after 1941. Taking no chances, they nonetheless organized a large lobbying effort under the direction of a vice president at General Motors, who also served as a director of the National Association of Manufacturers (Collins 1981, p. 104). The legislative process and the final shape of the act are especially interesting because the CED trustees stayed apart from the successful corporate lobbying effort; then they played a low-key role in turning the defeated proposal into legislation that was useful to corporate moderates in furthering their own vision of how the government should be involved in the economy. This vision included the plans for the expansion of international trade discussed in the previous chapter.

The full employment bill went through seven further revisions (based on comments on the original proposal) before being introduced into the Senate in late January 1945. The revised version put as much emphasis upon creating consumer demand through compensatory government spending as the original version did on the idea of government investment, which can be described as a shift from a "left" Keynesianism, with an emphasis on planning, reforms, and regulation as well as spending, to a "liberal" Keynesianism, with an exclusive emphasis on the use of taxing and spending tools to stimulate the economy (Friedberg 2000, pp. 88–91). This change in emphasis was a disappointment to some of the bill's most liberal supporters outside of government because it no longer included the guarantee of the right to a job and the authorization of spending to fulfill that guarantee. However, there was still a sentence that said, "There are hereby authorized to be appropriated such sums as may be necessary to eliminate any deficiency in the National Budget" (Bailey 1950, p. 48).

By that point the CED was preparing for its compromise approach after authorizing Flanders and his Research and Policy Committee to craft policy recommendations. Perhaps the most important member of the Research and Policy Committee in terms of this specific issue was Eric Johnston, the owner of several small businesses in Spokane, Washington, and a founding CED trustee. His success as president of the Spokane Chamber of Commerce led to his election as the president of the US Chamber of Commerce by those who hoped he would be able to bend the national chamber in a more centrist direction. By the time the Senate was ready for hearings in July, Flanders, Ruml, and Hoffman were prepared to testify on the bill. They urged that the word *full* be dropped from its title because full employment was impossible to attain and suggested the substitution of the word *high*. They also suggested a compromise that would replace the government agency designed to create the National Production and

Employment Budget with a government-appointed commission of private citizens to make recommendations to the president on economic policy from time to time. The commissioners would draw on a staff for expertise and consult with advisory committees appointed by various established interest groups in the private sector. In effect, instead of giving the president a staff that could prepare an economic forecast and help plan for action under his direction, the CED was calling for a quasi-independent mini-CED within the federal government that would not be completely beholden to the president. However, in agreement with the original legislation, the CED spokesmen said there should be a joint congressional committee that would review proposals by the commission.

As CED employee Karl Schriftgiesser wrote in an informative history of the first eighteen years of the CED, Flanders, Ruml, and Hoffman were not lobbying Congress in making their case. Instead, they were invited by congressional leaders to testify as independent representatives of a nonprofit, non-lobbying group, thereby preserving their nonpartisan stance (Schriftgiesser 1960, p. 91). Based on this kind of arrangement, CED trustees ended up testifying ninety-nine times before congressional committees between 1945 and 1966. During this time CED employees also testified to congressional committees (Schriftgiesser 1967, p. 20n1).

It is also noteworthy that Johnston did not testify for or against the bill. Nor did he allow any other leaders or employees in the US Chamber of Commerce to testify because he was not prepared to oppose the bill without providing an alternative, a decision that increased tensions with ultraconservatives inside the organization. Reflecting this tension, many top executives in state-level or local chambers expressed their strong opposition before congressional committees, thereby publicly revealing the divisions within the loosely knit federation of chamber organizations.

After a dozen revisions following the public hearings, the employment bill passed the Senate by a vote of 71–10 in late September 1945. There was no real opposition because the corporate community, plantation owners and other large-scale commercial farmers, and leaders of the conservative coalition decided to make their stand in the House, where they were in a much stronger position. Furthermore, the authorization of spending had been removed, to the disappointment of some members of the original drafting committee, "who felt that the bill was being hopelessly emasculated" (Bailey 1950, p. 59). However, the bill was very satisfactory from the view of its liberal sponsors, even though there was no obligation for the government to make investments, because the possibility of such spending was retained through a successful amendment.

At this point the National Association of Manufacturers, local and state chambers of commerce, and the American Farm Bureau Federation vocally supported the conservative coalition's attempt to stop the bill in the obscure House Committee on Expenditures in the Executive Departments, to which it had been purposely assigned by the conservatives on the Rules Committee. Once the bill was blocked, however, the corporate moderates in the US Chamber of Commerce (in which they temporarily had a strong position because of Johnston's role as president) and the CED broke ranks with the ultraconservatives. They argued once again that there should be a commission to provide the president with economic advice and a joint committee of Congress to receive the report. This time Flanders was able to circulate advanced copies of the report entitled *Toward More Production, More Jobs, and More Freedom* (Committee for Economic Development 1945e), which was about to be released.

Flanders's new testimony to Congress, along with behind-the-scenes drafts of a compromise bill provided by the staff of the US Chamber of Commerce, attracted the favorable attention of a Southern Democrat from Mississippi. A former member of a local chamber of commerce, he was in a position to dictate the terms of the House bill because he was the swing vote on a five-person subcommittee appointed to redraft the legislation. He removed the main planning mechanism, namely, the National Economic Production Budget, as well as any suggestion that the government would have to spend money based on economic forecasts. But he did include a Council of Economic Advisors (CEA) to prepare a President's Economic Report, along with the new joint committee of Congress advocated by the CED and other corporate moderates. Robert Collins (1981, pp. 105–106 and 245n81) provides the details on how the last stages of this process operated, concluding, "The congruence of the Chamber draft with the House substitute and with the final legislation is remarkable."

Although conservatives had control of Congress, the liberals in the Senate were able to influence the bill's final shape when it arrived in the conference committee appointed to iron out differences between the Senate and House versions. In particular, they insisted that the three-person Council of Economic Advisors suggested by the national chamber be retained (Bailey 1950, pp. 226–227). More generally, the liberals ensured that the bill made the White House responsible in principle for the overall functioning of the economy, even though events soon showed that Congress does not usually follow the suggestions in CEA economic reports.

Due to the relatively minor nature of the accommodations to liberal demands, it would seem that the US Chamber of Commerce might be on its way to working with the CED to steer a moderate course for the corporate community. However, Johnston's farewell speech at the end of his three-year tenure as president in May 1946, which called for the continuation of the new policies, was met with a muted reaction. Johnston had alienated many chamber directors by his generally moderate stances on several issues and by directing his staff to create the compromise proposals that were incorporated into the Employment Act by the House committee. In the words of one local chamber executive who attended that annual meeting, the US Chamber had "gone Conservative" again (Collins 1981, p. 122). It headed back to an ultraconservative stance, only slightly less unbending than that of the National Association of Manufacturers, until the arrival of the Eisenhower administration in 1953, when it sometimes took more moderate positions on some issues. After his final speech, Johnston became the president of the Motion Picture Association of America, the trade association for the movie industry, but he stayed on as a CED trustee and remained on the Research and Policy Committee for many years.

CED leaders, in comparison, expressed satisfaction with the general outcome because of their belief that a more active government was needed to ensure the level of employment that would keep the liberal-labor alliance at bay. In addition, they also had come to realize that the United States needed to show Great Britain and other allies that it would not allow the US economy to sink into another Great Depression if it was going to convince them to open up their economies to American trade and investments. This international dimension is often overlooked in understanding the corporate moderates' acceptance of the Employment Act in its final form. But as Flanders wrote in the foreword to the report on *International Trade, Foreign Investment, and Domestic Employment,* "We cannot plan for nor expect to achieve a high level of productive postwar employment within the United States without paying close attention to the expanded influence of our international economic position" (Committee for Economic Development 1945c, p. 3). Although the Employment Act was not the creation of the CED and the Council on Foreign Relations, as finally formulated it was completely compatible with, and even helped to create, the new world economy they wanted to build. From their standpoint, it served as a down payment on the promise to ensure that a nascent international economic order would not be pulled into a worldwide depression by a sudden decline in the US economy.

The final bill also had implications concerning the nature of the postwar relationship between the corporate community and the federal government because it included a specific mandate for the Council of Economic Advisors and the Joint Committee on the Economic Report to utilize the work of "private research agencies" (Bailey 1950, pp. 231–232). Thus, the CED, The Brookings Institution, the National Bureau of Economic Research, and similar private organizations assumed a more formal standing. With the National Resources Planning Board long removed from the scene, and with no other government agency allowed to take over its functions, the Employment Act helped to ensure that what little planning there was to be in postwar America would take place outside the government, within organizations closely related to the corporate community in terms of their financing and high-level governance. The Employment Act thereby blurred the line between the federal government and the private sector, which helped to reinforce corporate dominance.

The corporate community's success in making use of the CEA as a direct link between the policy-planning network and government is demonstrated most directly by the fact that twenty-four of the forty-one people appointed to it between 1945 and 1983 served as consultants for either the CED or the Commission on Money and Credit (a special one-time policy commission sponsored by the CED in the late 1950s), sometimes before their service on the council, sometimes after. Many of the appointees also had consulted for other think tanks or policy-discussion groups, although almost half of them were young economists whose primary contacts were within the academic community. Most striking of all, eleven of the thirteen chairs of the CEA in that time period previously had been employed by or consulted for the CED or a major think tank. Six had been advisors to the CED, six had an affiliation with the National Bureau of Economic Research, four were associated with The Brookings Institution, and three had an affiliation with the American Enterprise Institute, an ultraconservative policy organization founded by the US Chamber of Commerce in the 1940s and revitalized in the 1970s. There were very few career differences between the seven Republican and six Democratic appointees to the chair position, except in the case of two liberal chairs appointed by Democratic presidents (see Domhoff 1987 for a more detailed accounting of the careers of CEA appointees before and after their service).

The defeat suffered by the liberal-labor alliance at the hands of the corporate community on the scope of the Employment Act put an end to strong liberal economic initiatives for many years to come. The coalition did not try anything nearly as bold concerning economic policy until the 1970s, when its plans for creating a national planning agency, along with ideas for generating new jobs through government, were thwarted in the midst of the corporate moderates' right turn. In fact, the liberal-labor defeat in 1978 on a toned-down version of the original full employment bill signaled the end of whatever legislative power unions and liberals had wielded in the forty-three-year period that began in 1935 with the passage of the National Labor Relations Act.

THE CED AND THE MARSHALL PLAN

The CED followed its involvement in the establishment of the International Monetary Fund in 1945 and the passage of the Employment Act in 1946 with the biggest success in its entire history, the selling of a $12.7 billion, four-year program of financial aid to sixteen European countries to an isolationist Republican Congress and the ultraconservatives in the corporate community in 1947. Known as the Marshall Plan because it was formally introduced by Secretary of State George Marshall, a leading World War II general, the aid it offered was the equivalent of $130.6 billion in 2012 dollars. The CED also had a hand in marketing the Marshall Plan to a large portion of the general public, which didn't like the idea that the United States was supposedly giving taxpayer money to foreigners without any strings attached any more than ultraconservatives did.

Hoffman was again one of the key leaders, not only because of his prominent role in the CED but because he had a good working relationship with the Republican leader on foreign policy, Senator Arthur Vandenberg of Michigan. Once Truman accepted Vandenberg's suggestion to appoint a blue-ribbon presidential commission to study Marshall's call for massive aid to economically crippled European countries, several of which had strong Communist parties, five of his nine corporate appointees, including Hoffman, were trustees of the CED, and several of the others were members of the CFR. Three of the six academic representatives were members of the CED's Research Advisory Board. More generally, the ideas for the Marshall Plan came out of postwar discussions in the policy-planning network (Eakins 1969; Hogan 1987).

Hoffman and other CED leaders wrote the compromise that dealt with the major sticking point for ultraconservatives: giving money to seemingly "socialist" economic systems, which were in fact capitalist welfare states whose governments were controlled by social democrats. In order to accomplish the two main corporate goals in backing the plan—guarding against Soviet-backed Communist takeovers and creating new customers for American corporations—the corporate moderates convinced the ultraconservative members on the panel that the statement should say that each country would be free to choose its own economic system. Since this point continued to raise concerns among ultraconservatives, the CED soon thereafter published its own statement in support of the Marshall Plan, *An American Program of European Economic Cooperation.* It stated that the trustees firmly believed the American free enterprise system was the best way to create a productive economy, but that they also thought it was fair and just that "each country must be left free to decide on its own methods of organizing production" (Committee for Economic Development 1947a, p. 15; Schriftgiesser 1967, pp. 118–119).

In addition, the CED report (Committee for Economic Development 1947a, p. 22) suggested that the program should be carried out by a new agency directed by people chosen from "the large number of able men who served our country during the war and gained fruitful experience with questions similar to those presented by the program of cooperation." In effect, the report provided the basis through which the Republicans in the Senate could justify their insistence that the program be taken out of the State Department and headed by a corporate executive in charge of a new independent government agency.

The work of Truman's blue-ribbon commission and the CED was complemented by a private citizens' committee established from behind the scenes by CFR leaders (see Wala 1994 for a highly revealing case study of this massive opinion-shaping effort). This committee pointed out to wary citizens that the grants would not only revive European economies, and thereby make Communism less attractive, but would also help the US economy as well because most of the money had to be used to buy American machinery and consumer goods. In effect, the Marshall Plan money—and later, programs that gave aid to other countries to buy military equipment or rebuild their economies—can be seen as a form of domestic economic pump priming by the American government because the money never left the country (Eakins 1969, pp. 166–167). All of these aid programs had the consequence of generating the government spending called for by the liberal-labor alliance in the early 1940s without creating any further direct government involvement in the domestic economy.

Once the Marshall Plan legislation finally passed in April 1948, Truman appointed Hoffman as head of the European Economic Cooperation Administration at the insistence of Senator Vandenberg. Hoffman in turn included several CED trustees among the numerous corporate executives who staffed his agency in the United States and in the European countries receiving aid. But criticism of the program returned with the election of a larger number of ultraconservative Republicans to Congress in 1950. It was ended in 1951, two years earlier than originally planned, partly because it was already successful, but also because the conservative coalition was complaining that government spending had grown too large with the military buildup for the Korean War that began in late June 1950.

RESHAPING THE NATIONAL LABOR RELATIONS ACT

The CED played little or no role in the most significant corporate victory on a domestic policy during the Truman era, the 1947 revision of the National Labor Relations Act, but it did quietly support many of its key provisions. Officially named the

Labor-Management Act of 1947, but best known as the Taft-Hartley Act, this new labor legislation severely hampered organized labor's ability to establish new unions in nonunionized economic sectors, perhaps especially in the least unionized parts of the country.

The corporate community's victory was all the more significant because the original National Labor Relations Act was enacted in 1935 despite its vigorous opposition. That defeat was especially frustrating for the corporate moderates on the Business Advisory Council, starting with its chair, Gerard Swope, president of General Electric, and Walter Teagle, the president of Standard Oil of New Jersey, who was the chair of the BAC's industrial relations committee. To their regret, they had originally suggested a meeting with union leaders in 1933 to deal with the unexpected upsurge in union organizing generated by the passage of the National Industrial Recovery Act, and then proposed the creation of a National Labor Board that would consist of six business executives, six union leaders, and a representative of the government, Senator Robert F. Wagner of New York (McQuaid 1979, 1982).

The arrangement had several similarities with the National War Labor Board that had worked to the corporate community's satisfaction during World War I, just fifteen years earlier. In particular, the National War Labor Board operated on the basis of "proportional representation," which stated that a union could only represent those workers who voted for it, not all the employees in the company. This meant that the established craft unions, joined together as the American Federation of Labor (AFL), could look out for their own members while ignoring the far greater numbers of unskilled industrial workers. In suggesting a labor board in 1933, the business leaders were assuming that the craft-union leaders once again would accept the same sort of cross-class bargain. Moreover, during the 1920s, Swope, Teagle, and several other corporate moderates had created employee representation plans to meet and confer with employees in individual factories within the larger corporation. Thanks in part to the apparent success of these employee representation plans, Swope, Teagle, and other corporate moderates thought they had little to fear from unions.

With both Swope and Teagle as members, the National Labor Board had several successes in its first few weeks in ending strikes using a five-step procedure drafted by Swope: (1) the strike would end immediately; (2) the employers would reinstate strikers without discrimination; (3) the board would supervise a secret election by workers to determine whether or not they wished to have a union as their representative; (4) the employer would agree to bargain collectively with the representatives of those workers who voted to be represented by a union; and (5) all differences not resolved by negotiation would be submitted to an arbitration board or the National Labor Board itself. However, several large industrial companies managed by ultraconservatives soon defied the board's authority, leading Wagner to instruct the reform-oriented corporate lawyers and Ivy League law professors temporarily staffing the board to draft a tougher version of the original provisions. Ominously for the corporate community, it included a clause stating that a majority vote for a union would be sufficient for it to have the right to represent all of the workers in a given "bargaining unit," which could consist of part of a company, an entire company, or several companies in an industry, depending on the circumstances.

The corporate moderates unanimously rejected majority rule because they wanted to continue to deal separately with craft and industrial unions and retain their employee representation plans as well. But several AFL union leaders were no longer willing to accept proportional representation due to changes in their own circumstances, which led them to side with Wagner and generate an unbridgeable gulf. In particular, John L. Lewis, the president of the United Mine Workers, was determined to organize the steel workers because the steel companies would not allow him to organize the coal miners in the many mines owned by steel companies, which left his union completely vulnerable to the employers (Dubofsky and van Tine 1977). Sidney Hillman, the president of the Amalgamated Clothing Workers, faced a similar problem; he needed to organize textile workers to protect his clothing workers union (Fraser 1991).

The corporate moderates might have conceded the point on majority rule if the issue only concerned coal miners and garment workers, but the growing sense of unity between craft and industrial workers in other industries, especially in auto, rubber, and other heavy industries, raised the specter of large industrial unions throughout the economy. In the end, no corporate leaders, whether moderates or ultraconservatives, wanted the government to have the power to help create a fully organized working class (see Domhoff and Webber 2011, chapter 3, for an analysis based on new archival materials).

The nascent liberal-labor alliance then showed its understanding of power in Congress by agreeing to exclude domestic and agricultural workers from the purview of the act, which meant that Southern Democrats could feel free to vote for the act because the plantation owners' primary labor force would not be covered by it. The exclusion of agricultural workers also made it easier for Progressive Republicans in the Midwest and West to support the act, thereby further dividing the nationwide employer coalition (Farhang and Katznelson 2005). Even then, Roosevelt might have tried to weaken the proposed law or put it aside if he had not already entered into a political alliance with Lewis, who voted for Hoover in 1932, and Hillman, a supporter of the Socialist Party in the past. Moreover, he did not finally give his public support to the bill until the liberal-labor alliance demonstrated that it could produce a voting majority in the Senate that included his close political allies from the earliest days of his presidential candidacy, the Southern Democrats (Domhoff and Webber 2011, pp. 138–140).

Southern concerns with racial exclusion were paralleled by successful efforts by leaders of the AFL to eliminate a clause in the legislation that would have outlawed discrimination by unions (Frymer 2008, pp. 24, 29). Moreover, the traditional craft-union leaders, the bulwarks of the AFL, were wary of some provisions of the law that they thought might favor the drive for the industrial unions advocated by Lewis and Hillman, but those provisions nonetheless remained in the legislation. As the craft leaders feared, Lewis and Hillman broke with them several months after the law passed due to their refusal to support an all-out effort to create permanent industrial unions at a time when the largely unskilled workers employed by large corporations were clamoring for union representation. Putting the split between craft and industrial unions to one side for the moment, the new legislation contained risks for unions in general because in accepting it they "gave up many of their traditional organizing weapons in return for certain statutory guarantees of protections to be enforced by the NLRB" (Gross 1995, p. 144).

To complicate matters even further, and as noted briefly in this book's Introduction, the Southern Democrats began to criticize the law in early 1937 because of the CIO's use of sit-down strikes and its efforts to create integrated unions in the South. By 1938 Southern leaders in the House of Representatives had combined forces with the National Association of Manufacturers, thereby bringing Northern and Southern employers into an alliance to weaken the act. Then an unexpected partner, the AFL, joined the employer coalition because its officers were convinced that the National Labor Relations Board (NLRB) was aiding its upstart rival, just as they had predicted it might three years earlier. For the AFL, the NLRB decision that "could not be forgiven" occurred in June 1938, when it ruled that the entire West Coast would be the bargaining unit for longshoremen and warehousemen, thereby eliminating small AFL affiliates in four ports. AFL officials were further upset by a ruling concerning a company in Alabama, leading to plant-wide elections in which the five hundred "white, highly skilled mechanics" would be outnumbered by the one thousand African American laborers (Gross 1981, pp. 56, 59, 85).

The result was a widening of the divide between the craft and industrial unions, creating a major problem for the liberal-labor alliance that never fully healed over the next several decades—a split that was complicated by differences among blue-collar workers in race, ethnic origins, religion, and skill levels. After charging that Communists dominated both the labor board's staff and the CIO, the AFL leaders sent their lawyers to private meetings with NAM lawyers beginning in July 1938 to work out amendments to the National Labor Relations Act that might serve their common interests. The Southern Democrat/NAM/AFL coalition then wrote a bill in 1939 that became the major basis for the 1947 legislation, a fact the AFL later tried to deny or ignore (Gross 1981, pp. 3, 67ff).

Roosevelt and the liberals in Congress were able to fend off the proposed legislative changes in 1939–1940 because of the impending war effort. The industrial mobilization in turn revived organizing efforts that had slowed considerably due to strong resistance by large industrial corporations after a remarkable growth in union membership from just over three million in 1935 to almost nine million in 1940. The renewed upsurge then led to the establishment of a National War Labor Board on the basis of the World War I formula of having representatives from labor, business, and the general public rule on strikes and grievances until the war ended. Although the corporate executives on the war labor board resisted rulings that would aid unions, the public and labor representatives gradually came to agree to accept a "maintenance of membership" provision through which newly employed workers would automatically be part of unions in exchange for a no-strike pledge by union leaders, thereby providing a huge boost to union membership that never would have happened outside the war context (Gross 1981, chapter 13).

Southern Democrats continued to search for ways to hamper union organizing and found the opening they were looking for when Lewis, who had refused to sign the no-strike pledge, ordered the mine workers to strike for a $2-a-day wage increase in early June 1943. In response, Congress passed the War Labor Disputes Act, which gave the president the power to take over industries essential to prosecuting the war that were threatened by strikes; it also prohibited unions from using membership dues for campaign donations to political candidates. Roosevelt vetoed the bill, but Congress easily overturned it. A year later, Roosevelt used the act when ten thousand transit workers went on strike to protest a ruling by the Fair Employment Practices Commission that the city's transit authority had to employ African Americans as trolley and rapid transit operators, one of many indications during the war years that racial divisions would remain a major problem for unions in the postwar era.

Once the war ended, the conservative coalition seized the opportunity provided by the immediate upsurge of postwar strikes to pass a series of crippling amendments to the National Labor Relations Act in July 1946, most of them based on the anti-labor legislation already drafted in 1939. Only a veto by Truman, upheld by liberals and moderates in the House, saved the union movement from an immediate postwar defeat. A few months later, the Republicans won control of both the Senate and House, at a time when 65 percent of those polled in a nationwide survey thought "well" of the US Chamber of Commerce, but only 50 and 26 percent thought the same about the AFL and CIO, respectively (Collins 1981, pp. 92–93).

Building on the anti-union amendments fashioned by the Southern Democrats, NAM, and the AFL in 1939, the Taft-Hartley Act put its greatest emphasis on adding new rights for management in relation to labor, which in effect gave it more latitude to pressure workers. It also added a list of unfair labor practices that hampered union organizing by outlawing tactics that were used in the 1930s to win union recognition, such as mass picketing, secondary boycotts, and jurisdictional strikes, the latter of which involve disputes over work assignments handed out by employers. Drawing on the precedent in the War Labor Disputes Act, another statute gave the president the power to represent the general public's interest through the declaration of an emergency, which would delay a strike with a sixty-day cooling-off period. Still another statute limited the power of labor-board appointees by giving their top staff member, the general counsel, more discretion as to what cases to investigate and bring before the board. The law included a direct attack on the several CIO unions that were led by members of the Communist Party by making it necessary for union leaders to sign an affidavit stating they were not Communists (Gross 1981, chapter 13; 1995, chapter 1). It also decreed that employer contributions to a union health fund were illegal, which effectively abolished a union-controlled benefits fund that the United Mine Workers had won for its members in a 1946 strike. Unions therefore had to share responsibility with management and put the money into a trust (Brown 1999, p. 158).

In addition, the act legitimated laws already passed in five states that allowed employees to decline to pay dues to an established union if they so desired. (These laws are called "right-to-work laws" because employers insist that their support for the right to resist joining a union is based upon a principled defense of the rights of individual workers.) Although eighteen more states passed such laws by the end of 1963, they were repealed in Delaware, Indiana, Louisiana, and New Hampshire, which meant that there were nineteen right-to-work states in 1965, all of them in the South, Great Plains, and Rocky Mountain regions (see Dixon 2007 and 2010 for sociological studies of right-to-work laws). Although there was no strong evidence that right-to-work laws impede unionization in studies carried out through the late 1980s, more recent research suggests a modest decrease in unionization rates, but not in wages, during the first forty years after Taft-Hartley (Moore 1998). Whatever the facts may be, the important point is that both the corporate community and the liberal-labor alliance thought that these laws mattered greatly. The result was decades of legislative conflict over Section 14b, the clause that allows states to have right-to-work laws (Gall 1988).

The CED's statement on collective bargaining, which had no impact on the legislative process, and is therefore useful only as an indication of how corporate moderates viewed unions, supported most of the key provisions of the act. It suggested more freedom for employers to tell their side of the story to their employees, limits on the power of appointed board members by giving more decision-making latitude to the board's general counsel, and a ban on both secondary boycotts and jurisdictional strikes. It agreed with other business groups that foremen and other supervisors should be defined as management and excluded from union bargaining units. It also argued for strengthening a current government mediation agency, Conciliatory Services, and turning it into an independent Federation Mediation Service; this widely shared business recommendation was included in the final legislation as the Federal Mediation and Conciliation Service (Schriftgiesser 1967, pp. 161–162).

Several provisions of the Taft-Hartley Act played a significant role in the gradual decline of the union movement since its passage. However, it is difficult to pinpoint any one act or ruling as "the" turning point in undermining the union movement because unions already had lost their most potent pre-war organizing tactic, the sit-down strike, which was opposed from the outset by the National Labor Relations Board and then declared unconstitutional by the Supreme Court in 1939. Moreover, the Taft-Hartley Act was followed in the 1950s by numerous anti-union rulings by the NLRB and further legislative changes and court decisions that hampered union organizing. One of the most damaging decisions by the Supreme Court was issued in 1951, which declared that it was illegal for a union to close down an entire construction site over an argument with a single contractor or subcontractor, an issue that is usually discussed using the phrase "common-situs picketing," which will reappear in several later chapters (Gross 1995, pp. 83–84, 341).

When union leaders signed on with liberals in supporting the National Labor Relations Act in 1935, they were well aware of the risk they were taking by giving up traditional organizing tactics in exchange for promises of government protection through the NLRB and the courts. They took that risk in part because they were having little or no success except for a few business sectors in which employers could not afford to bring in replacement workers for one or more of several reasons, including high skill levels (e.g., printing), geographic isolation (e.g., coal mining), and time sensitivity (e.g., railroads) (Kimeldorf 2013). Furthermore, the usefulness of the original act for union organizers was not automatic. Its value depended on the protection and possible extension of the several specific statutory guarantees that were included in it. But the Taft-Hartley Act and many later decisions by both Congress and the NLRB narrowed or withdrew those guarantees in what turned into a class struggle at the legislative and regulatory levels.

However, the Taft-Hartley Act did result in one unanticipated consequence for the corporate community. It reinforced union leaders' resolve to bargain for health and pension benefits, despite strong opposition by most corporate leaders, as the only way to overcome the challenges to the long-term viability of unions created by the new law. The possibility for such negotiations was created by two separate government decisions during World War II. The Internal Revenue Service ruled that corporations could count health and pension benefits as expenses for tax purposes, and the National War Labor Board ruled that wage controls did not apply to increases in fringe benefits. After a postwar drive to unionize the South failed badly, thereby making it impossible to unseat or gain compromises from Southern Democrats, several labor leaders realized that any improvements in worker security would have to come through collective bargaining for social benefits, not government programs.

But it was the Taft-Hartley Act's challenge to the very existence of unions that changed the terms of the power equation. As political scientist Michael K. Brown concludes, "unions found that collectively bargained social rights provided an escape hatch from the threat to their security posed by Taft-Hartley. Fringe benefits obtained on union terms provided the 'virtual equivalent' of a closed shop." When the National Labor Relations Board backed wartime government rulings in 1948 by deciding that bargaining other health and welfare funds was legal, and then received support for that decision from the courts, it "opened the door to bargaining over social rights and left legislative derailment as the only way to shut down unionized welfare capitalism." After a Truman-appointed strike settlement board ruled in 1949 that the steel industry had to accept the United Steelworkers' demand for pensions and social insurance "in the absence of adequate Government programs," the die was cast, to the outrage of steel executives and other industrialists (see Brown 1999, pp. 154, 159, for the information and quotes in this paragraph).

IMPROVING CORPORATE MODERATE PLANS FOR SOCIAL SECURITY

Unlikely as it may sound, the same corporate moderates who failed to defeat the new labor law in 1935, led once again by Swope of GE and Teagle of Standard Oil, were the key figures in the formulation of the Social Security Act that passed in the same year. Indeed, the major features of the old-age insurance program were based on corporate experience over the previous twenty years. They included three principles considered essential by the corporate moderates: benefits levels must be tied to salary levels to preserve values established in the labor market, there could be no government contributions from general tax revenues, and there had to be both employer and employee contributions to the system in order to limit the tax payments by corporations. In addition, corporate contributions to the system were not to be taxed. These assertions about the role of the corporate moderates are documented elsewhere (Domhoff and Webber 2011, chapter 4).

The three essential features of old-age pensions, along with several parts of the unemployment insurance program, were written into the Roosevelt administration's draft plans in good part by employees of Industrial Relations Counselors, Inc., an advisory firm on labor relations founded and financed by John D. Rockefeller Jr., which primarily served companies in which he had an ownership stake. After the advisory firm's main ideas survived a difficult legislative gauntlet, the pension plan, passed in July 1935, was generally satisfactory to the corporate moderates. As in the case of the National Labor Relations Act, Southern Democrats insisted on the exclusion of agricultural and domestic workers as their price for support.

The creation of unemployment insurance proved to be a much more complicated and intense struggle because an unlikely alliance of Southern Democrats and the reformers in the John R. Commons/University of Wisconsin tradition rejected the corporate moderates' vision of nationwide unemployment insurance administered by the federal government. Anything close to nationwide standards was threatening to the Southern plantation owners' low-wage view of the world, and it did not fit with the emphasis on state-level programs by the Wisconsin reformers as the safest way to secure employer support. Moreover, organized labor and liberal social reformers rejected the corporate moderates' call for payments into the unemployment fund by workers as well as employers. The result was state-level unemployment insurance that had lower benefits and was easier to stigmatize because workers did not make contributions. Even worse, perhaps, the legislation gave states the discretion to set their own minimum payment levels and the number of months of coverage. As a result, and in contrast to what eventually happened with old-age social insurance, it proved to be impossible to stabilize a long-term unemployment insurance program with increasing benefits and greater control by a federal administrative bureaucracy (see Domhoff and Webber 2011, chapter 4, for a very detailed analysis of the complex and many-sided battle over unemployment insurance).

In 1937 Congress appointed the Advisory Council on Social Security to suggest ways to improve the provisions for what was then called old-age social insurance and is now usually called "Social Security benefits," the term I will use in keeping with the contemporary meaning of that term. It included several businessmen, starting with Swope and Folsom, but also a prominent insurance company executive from Philadelphia, Albert Linton. Six union representatives were appointed, three from the AFL and three from the CIO, but they seldom attended meetings and had very little impact. There were seven professors, mostly economists, along with the general secretary of the National Consumers' League and a recent president of the Association of Schools of Social Work (Berkowitz 1987, pp. 62–66). The council ended up making recommendations that shaped Social Security benefits even more to the liking of the corporate moderates, while at the same time drawing support from liberals and social workers.

The council was chaired by J. Douglas Brown, an industrial relations expert, who worked closely with Industrial Relations Counselors, Inc. from his position as an industrial relations professor at Princeton. He played a central role in drafting the old-age insurance provisions of the original act, and then chaired a special committee of the Social Science Research Council that studied ways to improve the act (Domhoff and Webber 2011, pp. 211–214). Drawing much of its staff and several policy recommendations from the Social Science Research Council, the council first of all recommended a large reduction in a reserve fund insisted upon at the last minute by Roosevelt so that money would not be needed from general tax revenues several decades hence to sustain the program. Corporate leaders wanted this change because some of them feared that the reserve fund might be used to raise benefits, help pay for public housing projects, or perhaps even to buy private enterprises. The advisory council also urged higher pension payments, higher benefits for married couples, the extension of benefits to widows at age sixty-five, the extension of benefits to the dependent children of deceased recipients, and the payment of benefits beginning in 1940 rather than waiting until 1942, as originally planned. In addition, it recommended the extension of coverage to the self-employed, agricultural workers, and domestic workers (Berkowitz 1987, p. 72).

Labor leaders, liberals, social workers, and organizations representing the elderly favored the recommendations because of their concern that low-income people might not otherwise have enough money to live on, and Keynesian economists liked the changes because they might stimulate the economy. Insurance companies liked the new amendments because they left plenty of room for their profitable private plans for employees with higher incomes, especially for the corporate executive plans that were their biggest customer target. Other corporate leaders were satisfied that taxes and benefit levels were modest.

Congress accepted most of these recommendations, but no new occupational categories were added, which reflected the continuing desire of the Southern Democrats and ultraconservatives to exclude low-wage workers, especially agricultural workers. Very significantly in terms of future arguments over the solidity of Social Security reserves, the reduced fund was made into a trust fund with a strong unanimous statement from the advisory council, endorsed by Congress, which was meant "to put to rest claims that the Treasury bonds in which the Social Security funds were invested were somehow not real and in some way represented a misuse of funds" (Altman 2005, p. 132). The ultraconservatives had made such claims from the moment the Social Security Act passed, but the transformation of the reserves into a trust fund based on a thousand years of Anglo-Saxon and American custom, precedents, and laws did not deter them from continuing their efforts to undermine public confidence in a government program they heartily despised as contrary to their deeply held values about the need for individual autonomy and the limited role of government in caring for citizens.

Building on the model of the 1937 advisory council, a new seventeen-person advisory council was assembled in 1947, after a long period in which the conservative coalition had frozen benefits in order to stop the expansionary plans developed by the Wisconsin reformers that staffed the Social Security Administration. As a result of the conservative coalition's concerted efforts, means-tested old-age assistance became more important in terms of both number of recipients and the size of the benefits, putting guaranteed pensions in a precarious position by the late 1940s (Brown 1999, pp. 112–113). At this juncture, however, all moderates and many ultraconservatives in the corporate community were in general agreement that expansionary changes could be made in old-age insurance, thanks to the conservative way in which the system was administered and to educational efforts by CED trustee Folsom of Eastman Kodak, who chaired the social insurance committees of both the NAM and the US Chamber of Commerce (Manza 1995).

The chair of US Steel headed the new advisory council, but he rarely attended meetings and left most decisions to the associate chair, Sumner Slichter, the Harvard economist and CED advisor, who by that point was a consultant for several major corporations. Slichter in turn worked closely with the chair of the 1937 council, J. Douglas Brown, the industrial relations expert from Princeton. The new council also included two business holdovers from the 1939 committee, Folsom and Albert Linton, the insurance company executive. Along with a policy analyst from the AFL and another from the CIO, Slichter, Brown, Folsom, and Linton were part of a six-person steering committee (Altman 2005, pp. 152–153).

At Brown's suggestion, the steering committee hired a former Social Security administrator, Robert M. Ball, whom Brown had come to know after Ball took a position at a new University-Government Center on Social Security, which provided training sessions for professors and federal employees about the Social Security program. Ball, whose previous work as a Social Security employee had given him the opportunity to develop an understanding of the business viewpoint, proved to be both knowledgeable and pragmatic, which made it possible for him to introduce new ideas and fashion compromises, a role he was to play for the next thirty-six years in relation to new developments in the Social Security system (Berkowitz 2003, pp. 55–73).

The representatives of organized labor, by this point eager and forceful participants in the process, wanted to raise the level of income that could be taxed for Social Security purposes to $4,800, with most corporate leaders insisting on a much lower level, $3,000; the advisory council compromised at $4,200 (Altman 2005, pp. 155, 165). Benefits were increased by 77 percent, but most of this increase simply overcame the 74 percent rise in prices since the first payments were made, and the increase was only two-thirds as large as the rise in wages since 1939. The advisory council also recommended the inclusion of self-employed, agricultural, and domestic workers, but most agricultural workers in the South would still be excluded because they worked part-time or seasonally (Quadagno 1988, p. 148). A majority of the advisory council also advocated the addition of disability insurance, but Folsom and Linton were opposed, as were the US Chamber of Commerce and the American Medical Association.

Congress once again accepted most of the recommendations, but it pared down the number of occupations to be included. Disability insurance was supported in the Senate but lost to the conservative coalition in the House. In general, Social Security became somewhat more inclusive, but not more generous. More important from the liberal-labor perspective, the changes seemed to guarantee that old-age pensions, not means-tested old-age assistance, would be the way in which most of the elderly would receive benefits in the future.

THE CED SOLIDIFIES ITS FISCAL AND MONETARY POLICIES

As the corporate community prepared to fight Communism in Western Europe and organized labor at home, while at the same time accepting the main thrust of the Social Security Act, the CED announced its position on fiscal policy in 1947 with a statement on taxing and budget policy. That statement was followed in 1948 by a detailed policy proposal on the way in which fiscal and monetary policy should be used in combination to stabilize a growing economy at a high level of employment. Taken together, the two statements constituted the CED position on economic policy for the next twenty years. The reports had a major impact on government policy by the 1960s, making it possible for the CED to navigate between both the liberal-labor alliance and the ultraconservatives.

Taxes and the Budget: A Program for Prosperity in a Free Economy (Committee for Economic Development 1947b) created a halfway position between the ultraconservatives, who wanted balanced budgets, and the liberal Keynesians, who wanted to manage future economic downturns through tax cuts and increases in government spending. In addition, the liberal Keynesians wanted to head off periods of inflation by raising taxes on the well-to-do and cutting government expenditures, which would decrease buying power and at the same time provide enough of a government surplus to pay down the federal debt. CED trustees opposed both of these liberal-labor policy preferences without at the same time embracing economic orthodoxy about balancing the budget each year.

Although the CED trustees believed that the ultraconservatives' economic plans would slow the economy, and thereby risk falling profits, depression, and worker unrest, they did not adopt the liberals' approach because of its emphasis on manipulating the tax rate and using government spending policy to heat up or cool down the economy. They feared that the inexact art of forecasting recessions, as called for in the National Production Budget included in the original full employment bill, might lead liberal experts to recommend policies that would justify increasing government expenditures year after year. In the interest of limiting such expenditures as much as possible, the CED suggested its own formula for a "stabilizing budget policy," which called for setting tax rates at a level that would balance the budget over a period of several years while providing for a high level of employment.

The concept behind this policy was first proposed by Keynesians in the Department of the Treasury in the late 1930s, then picked up and promoted by Beardsley Ruml. Using his own terminology, Ruml set out to convince the corporate community that the budget should be balanced, but over a period of several years, which is why he called it the "stabilizing budget policy." This goal would be accomplished by allowing tax receipts to be lower in times of economic recession, thereby leading to automatic deficit spending by the federal government. This temporary deficit spending, including higher outlays for unemployment benefits, would then lead to higher tax collections once the economy recovered, thereby making it possible to pay down the government debt and to soak up excess purchasing power.

There was no suggestion that the government should make investments in the economy, hire unemployed workers, or increase spending, which remained anathema to most of the corporate moderates and would have been impossible to sell to their ultraconservative brethren—and most members of the conservative coalition—in any case. Using intentionally dry phrasing, the CED first explained the idea as follows at the end of its statement on postwar taxes in August 1944: "The Committee deems it wise that the tax structure and the budget should be so drawn as to make possible substantial reduction of the federal debt at a high level of employment. As much debt should then be retired as is consistent with maintaining high levels of employment and production" (Committee for Economic Development 1944a, p. 24).

The trustees prefaced this vague statement by saying they were not concerned about the size of the debt as long as the country had the resolve to pay it off in order to protect government integrity. However, eagle-eyed reporters were not fooled. *Time* said that "it looks as if CED were prepared to accept deficit financing when national income falls below $140 billion," and *Life* spelled out the CED philosophy even more clearly: "They aim to balance the budget only when the economy is balanced first" (Schriftgiesser 1960, p. 84). *Fortune's* comment was even more blunt about the CED's phraseology: "Doubletalk aside, the CED advocates deficit financing when there is unemployment" (Collins 1981, p. 131). Ruml later explained the success of his new formulation as follows: "Business people will almost without exception agree with two principles. The first is that we ought to have a balanced budget. The second is that the country ought to have high employment. Put those two together and you get the 'stabilizing budget,' a balanced budget at high employment" (Neal 1981, p. 36). High employment was defined as 96 percent of the workforce, that is, a 4 percent rate of unemployment, which was seen as acceptable because it was said to consist primarily of people who were changing jobs (now called "frictional unemployment") or temporarily lacking the skills to find a job in a changing economy (now called "structural unemployment").

A year later the CED provided a seventy-five-page synthesis of its full program in *Monetary and Fiscal Policy for Greater Economic Stability* (1948). The report began by more openly challenging the sanctity of balanced budgets while at the time criticizing the efforts at forecasting and demand management by the strong contingent of liberal Keynesians still active in and around the federal government. It went on to put greater stress on the use of monetary policy (i.e., changes in the size and rate of growth in the money supply) by the Federal Reserve Board to stimulate the economy when necessary or reduce demand if inflation increased. The statement argued that monetary policy is a better alternative than the liberal Keynesian effort to use increased government spending to maintain high employment for two main reasons. First, the Federal Reserve Board and its Open Market Committee can move more quickly than Congress. Second, monetary policy can have a more immediate impact by simply buying or selling government securities on the open market, increasing or decreasing the banks' reserve requirements, changing the rate at which banks can borrow from each other overnight (called the "federal funds rate"), or changing the rate at which banks can obtain short-term loans from a Federal Reserve bank ("the discount rate"). Moreover, the CED's emphasis on monetary policy over fiscal policy fit with the straightforward policy prescription for dealing with slumps put forward by monetary economist Milton Friedman of the University of Chicago, who claimed that the Federal Reserve Board could produce rapid recoveries from recessions "simply by purchasing enough bonds for cash to flood the economy with liquidity" (DeLong 2012).

In addition, but not directly stated, CED trustees had more faith in the Federal Reserve System ("the Fed"), which is powerfully influenced by the corporate community, than in the administration or Congress (Fuccillo 1969, p. 318). Moreover, the CED enjoyed a close relationship with the Fed, and several trustees were directors of one of the twelve regional banks. In addition, Ruml, Flanders, and Chester Davis had served as the presidents of the Federal Reserve banks in New York, Boston, and St. Louis in the years shortly before the report was issued. Thomas McCabe, the president of Scott Paper Company and an original CED trustee, was appointed as the chair of the Federal Reserve Board in early 1948, while the report was being written. Moreover, Fed economists often served as CED advisors (Collins 1981, p. 150).

Perhaps best of all from the CED point of view, a mix of fiscal and monetary policies "requires no expansion of the traditional functions and powers of government," as plainly stated at a later point by the president of Northwest Bancorporation in Minneapolis, who chaired the subcommittee (Thomson 1954). However, despite the CED's private concerns about the expansion of government power, its major public claim was that fiscal and monetary policies are complementary, not antagonistic, with no mention of their worries about the government becoming too powerful (Stein 1969).

Although this new approach seemed very satisfactory and sensible to corporate moderates, there was a major stumbling block to its implementation. During World War II the Federal Reserve Board agreed to use interest rates to support the price of government bonds at their initial (par) value. This approach helped to keep the debt as small as possible, but at the same time it limited the Fed's ability to exercise its power to shape the economy by raising or lowering interest rates at will in the face of economic changes. The concentration on maintaining the value of government bonds continued after the war, but the CED openly challenged it in its 1948 report on monetary and fiscal policy. Soon after the report appeared, McCabe gave it a strong public endorsement.

Within a few years, the 1948 CED statement and its aftermath led to a widely shared implicit agreement that a combination of fiscal and monetary policies—in effect, a commercial or conservative Keynesianism—would be used to keep the economy growing. Basically, the CED and other corporate moderates argued that the government should be involved in fiscal and monetary policy ("macroeconomics"), but that it should keep its hands off the details of the market system ("microeconomics"), according to a historical account by Herbert Stein (1969), who wrote shortly after his retirement from twenty-three years as an economist for the CED. However, the ultraconservatives constantly grumbled about or resisted this solution to problems of slump and boom, and the liberal-labor alliance continued to challenge it in the name of higher social spending and more government involvement in the economy through regulation and/or planning.

In retrospect, a commercial Keynesianism that emphasized the use of monetary policy turned out to be enormously useful for a power struggle with the liberal-labor alliance. On the one hand, it could induce recessions by raising interest rates, which in effect made unemployment for workers, not higher taxes for the corporate rich, the way in which inflation would be controlled. On the other hand, its method for stimulating the economy, tax cuts, meant that the size of the federal government could be kept as small as possible.

RECESSION, THE COMMUNIST THREAT, AND THE KOREAN WAR

Unemployment varied between 3.5 and 3.9 percent in the six months before the 1948 presidential elections, which was good news for Truman. But in spite of the efforts by the CED and other policy experts to craft conservative policies to avoid recessions, depressions, and inflation, unemployment gradually rose over the next eleven months to a high of 7.9 percent in October 1949. The liberal-labor alliance called for antirecession measures as union membership declined during the downturn, but Truman, the corporate community, and the conservative coalition were unwilling to initiate stimulus spending because of their overriding concern with deficits and the possibility of inflation. Most of all, the fear that the government would grow and limit free enterprise continued to loom very large for them (Friedberg 2000, pp. 96–97). However, McCabe and the Federal Reserve began to buy government securities in June 1949, and they lowered the reserve requirements for banks, which had some influence in reviving the economy by increasing the money supply. The Treasury Department quietly accepted the change because it made debt financing less expensive for the government.

But as the recession lingered into October, members of the liberal-labor alliance called for the resignation of the chair of the CEA, Edwin G. Nourse, a former agricultural economist at The Brookings Institution, who had long-standing associations with the Chamber of Commerce, the National Association of Manufacturers, the Conference Board, and the American Management Association (Hess 1972, pp. 16–19). A man of caution when it came to government spending, Nourse remained concerned about the potential for inflation. He urged business leaders to take the lead in stopping the economic slide by making investments and keeping workers on the job, but they of course did not respond because it would be unprofitable for their corporations. He also claimed that deficit spending could be as dangerous as military risks. This surprising assertion alienated members of the bipartisan foreign policy network, whose members were increasingly concerned about the ongoing conflict with the Soviet Union over Communist Party actions in several countries in Western Europe that were experiencing severe economic difficulties.

As foreign policy leaders became ever more convinced that Soviet intentions were antithetical to American interests, Secretary of State Dean Acheson and his advisors in the State Department and the Council on Foreign Relations began thinking in terms of a substantial military buildup in Western Europe. Nevertheless, Truman asked the Defense Department to cut its spending by $2 billion in July 1949. The most conservative members of the Truman administration, along with leaders in Congress, agreed that the Soviet Union was a menace but insisted that the need to control deficits should constrain any increases in military spending (Friedberg 2000; Schriftgiesser 1960, p. 167).

At this point Acheson and his aides received support from an unanticipated source, Leon Keyserling, a very liberal member of the CEA. Keyserling, who had a Harvard law degree and two years of graduate work in economics at Columbia, was urging a strong stimulus program through increases in nonmilitary domestic spending. Already speaking publicly for a major demand stimulus, Keyserling assured the foreign policy experts who consulted him that a dramatic increase in defense spending would not harm the economy, and might even help it. As one of Acheson's assistants later wrote, "Keyserling and I discussed these matters frequently; though he wanted to spend the money on other programs, he was convinced that the country could afford $40 billion for defense if necessary" (Nitze 1980, p. 169). When the Soviets successfully tested an atomic bomb in August 1949, and the anticipated Communist victory occurred in China a month later, the momentum shifted in favor of those who favored major rearmament. Nourse resigned as chair of the CEA in November, and Keyserling became the acting chair.

In the light of the Soviet and Chinese Communist successes, Truman ordered a major reevaluation of the country's foreign and military policies, with foreign policy advisors asking Keyserling and other economists in the Truman administration for their advice. The resulting national security policy statement, "United States Objectives and Programs for National Security," which came to be known as National Security Memorandum No. 68 (NSC-68), recommended a 300 percent increase in military spending over the next few years to rearm Western Europe and station 100,000 American troops there as well. To allay ultraconservative fears of possible negative impacts on the economy, the report embodied Keyserling's earlier arguments.

Despite the urgent tone of NSC-68, it still seemed unlikely that the military spending proposal would go anywhere because Truman and most Republicans in Congress opposed it. They also felt confirmed in the rightness of their economic path because the economy had begun a slow recovery in November 1949, with the unemployment rate falling to 5.4 percent over an eight-month period, perhaps aided by the ultraconservative tax cut of 1948, along with new domestic spending triggered by the Marshall Plan and the Fed's actions to ease credit. Then the sudden and unexpected North Korean invasion of South Korea in June 1950 changed the economic and military equations as American troops were sent into action to repel the attack.

Under the circumstances, the corporate moderates were immediate supporters of both increased taxes and far greater defense spending. But they also formed the Business Committee on Emergency Corporate Taxation, headed by Ruml and including the top officers of over one hundred major corporations, to fight unsuccessfully against the restoration of the excess profits tax favored by Truman and the Democrats. Instead, they preferred corporate tax increases, as expressed in a CED statement calling for "a temporary 'defense profits' tax consisting of a flat rate of 15 percent on corporate profits on top of a somewhat reduced normal corporate tax rate of 38 percent." Nevertheless, Congress imposed an excess profits tax of 30 percent on top of a progressive regular rate on corporations that rose from 45 percent to 47 percent. As part of the bargaining, the corporations were able to gain assent for a 70 percent ceiling for the combined corporation and excess profits taxes, far lower than the taxes they paid during World War II (see Bank 2010, pp. 213–215, for the tax information and quotation in this paragraph).

Tax arguments aside, corporate executives returned to the government to lead the war mobilization. One of the CED's most publicly visible trustees, Charles E. Wilson of General Electric, who was also a member of the Business Advisory Council, became head of the Office of Defense Mobilization, a position similar to one he held during World War II, when he was executive vice chair of the War Production Board. In turn, CIO leaders within the liberal-labor alliance viewed defense mobilization as an opportunity to increase their role in economic governance. They called for new forms of cooperation between unions, corporations, and the federal government, and asked for decision-making positions on the War Production Board, but corporations resisted and Wilson ignored their suggestions.

Even with a war being fought by American troops in South Korea, it was not a foregone conclusion that ultraconservative Republicans and their backers, who tended to be focused on Asia and Latin America, would support spending for troops and rearmament in Western Europe, as called for in NSC-68. In anticipation of this problem, the corporate moderates created a new lobbying and opinion-shaping organization, the Committee on the Present Danger, in December 1950, five months after the new war began. The fifty-four-member group included Paul Hoffman, four other CED trustees, and an economist on the CED's Research Advisory Board, as well as numerous leaders and members in the CFR. In a campaign reminiscent of the effort to sell the Marshall Plan three years earlier, along with even more direct lobbying of Congress, the Committee on the Present Danger pulled out all the stops in an effort to convince the general public and Congress of the importance of taking NSC-68 seriously. Within a year, Congress agreed to troops in Western Europe and funding for European rearmament (Friedberg 2000; Sanders 1983).

The increase in defense spending, along with military assistance to European countries, which used most of the money to buy American weaponry, replaced the $3.7 and $4.1 billion spent on the Marshall Plan in 1949–1950 and 1950–1951 in providing an unexpected major economic stimulus to the American economy. It accelerated a recovery that was already under way and brought unemployment down from 5.4 percent in June 1950 to below 4.0 percent for most of 1951 and 1952. It then fell below 3.0 percent until the last three months of 1953, with low points of 2.5 percent in May and June of that year, a postwar record that the economy would never again come close to attaining.

However, in spite of Keyserling's arguments about the slack in the economy in 1950, the Fed still insisted that war spending was likely to bring about inflation. It therefore took the opportunity to raise the discount rate in August 1950, to the displeasure of Keyserling and the Department of the Treasury. A public argument followed, with the Treasury Department finally accepting an "accord" in March 1951. Whether the Fed's decision was an economic or strategic one, it had the consequence of restoring the Fed's pre-war independence. It set the stage for the use of high interest rates and the inevitable rise in unemployment that would follow in order to tame inflation in the future (Hetzel and Leach 2001; Schriftgiesser 1967, pp. 45–46).

A LIBERAL-LABOR VICTORY ON HOUSING?

In mid-July 1949, just as the battle over defense spending was heating up, a long-standing argument between the liberal-labor alliance and urban real estate interests seemed to have ended with the passage of the Housing Act. At first glance it appeared that the liberal-labor alliance won a major victory with the enactment of this legislation because it authorized the construction of 810,000 units of public housing over the ensuing ten years, increased the Federal Housing Authority's ability to provide mortgage insurance, and permitted the Federal Housing Authority to finance rural homeowners. But the act ended up as a subsidy for the real estate interests that long had hoped to transform low-income downtown neighborhoods into cleared land for the expansion of commercial, educational, and cultural areas. As a result, central business districts, universities, hospitals, museums, and theaters were expanded and enhanced at taxpayers' expense.

The story of the Housing Act therefore provides an opportunity to bring urban real estate interests into the power equation, and to show how they received a powerful assist on their most critical issue from CED trustee Ralph Flanders in his role as a senator from Vermont, an assist that allowed them to capture all the increase in land values for themselves. The story of the Housing Act is also prototypical of what actually happened with many later pieces of legislation that are often catalogued as victories for the liberal-labor alliance.

Large-scale urban real estate owners and developers, as indicated in Chapter 1, are a distinctive segment of the ownership class. They make profits through efforts to increase land values by intensifying the use of land, whether for downtown expansion, new shopping malls, high-rise apartment complexes, upscale suburbs, or Las Vegas gambling casinos (Logan and Molotch 1987/2007). They join together in local growth coalitions to make plans and maintain group discipline. Nationally, they are organized into a powerful federal lobby through the National Association of Real Estate Boards, the National Association of Building Owners and Managers, the Mortgage Bankers Association of America, and the US Building and Loan League. Historically, the intensification of land use was most often accomplished by attracting railroad centers, stockyards, ports, factories, office buildings, and corporate headquarters to a fledgling city, but government buildings, universities, cultural centers, and, increasingly, stadiums, entertainment complexes, and tourism also bring in valuable paying customers for the hotels, stores, and restaurants that enhance land values the most.

For the most part, local growth coalitions and the corporate community are in full agreement on policy issues, but tensions can develop between them because corporations can move to new locations if a growth coalition is not able to keep its city free of unions, high taxes, and business regulation. Such departures often leave declining land values and devastated growth coalitions in their wake. There also have been serious conflicts over air and water pollution caused by corporations, with railroad executives and manufacturers casting aside the concerns of real estate owners. But dirty air and water became a major issue in the 1960s nonetheless, in good part because of efforts by local growth coalitions in Pittsburgh, Los Angeles, and other cities, which worried about a possible decline in land values due to peoples' fear of developing health problems if they kept their residences or businesses in a smoggy city (Gonzalez 2005).

With the rise of the automobile and suburbanization in the 1920s, downtown land values faced a threat that accelerated with the depression in the 1930s and the increased urban migration of African Americans from the rural South in the 1940s and 1950s. The real estate interests first responded with the Housing Act in 1934, which provided support for the housing industry, and by the next year they were developing plans for the federal government to subsidize the purchase of land for redevelopment in low-income neighborhoods (pejoratively labeled "slums") near downtown areas (Gotham 2000, 2002). Although it might seem that it would be easy for wealthy private developers to purchase this land for the department stores, office buildings, and luxury apartment towers they wanted to construct, in fact slumlords were reluctant to sell because of the good profits they made, and besides, the costs of demolishing the existing buildings were high. "As a result," as one expert on the origins and legacy of the Housing Act of 1949 explains, "few private developers undertook the redevelopment of slum tracts" (von Hoffman 2000, p. 304).

To deal with these daunting problems, in 1941 the National Association of Real Estate Boards put forth a plan developed by its research arm, the Urban Land Institute, which called for metropolitan land commissions that could use the power of eminent domain to clear slums. In addition, city governments would receive loans from the federal government to pay for the "write-down" on the land that was purchased. More bluntly, the difference between what the real estate interests had to pay the slumlords and the price they could afford (and still make a profit on their new buildings) would be paid with government loans backed by taxpayer dollars. However, developers quickly realized that loans would not be good enough; it would take subsidies from the federal government to make clearance and redevelopment financially feasible.

As the growth coalitions polished their plans for urban redevelopment in the postwar era, they faced problems from the liberal-labor alliance as well as ultraconservatives, who opposed federal spending in cities. In 1934 liberal housing advocates, who favored increased attention to public housing, had opposed their legislative proposals, as did civil rights activists, consumer activists, and organized labor. The AFL had called the growth coalitions' proposal the "anti-housing bill." However, the liberal-labor alliance was unable to have any impact on this New Deal measure, demonstrating the close relationship between growth coalitions and urban Democratic machines and the conservative coalition more generally (Gotham 2000, p. 303).

In 1937 liberals put forward their own legislation for subsidized rental housing sponsored by unions and other nonprofit organizations. They also called for public housing on vacant land on the edge of cities, thereby threatening downtown land values.

To counter this challenge, the growth coalitions joined with Southern Democrats and machine Democrats in securing several crippling amendments. One such amendment limited public housing to low-income people, thereby stigmatizing the whole venture at the outset. Another stipulated that federal aid had to be given to local public housing authorities, which meant that growth coalitions might be able to block the program at the local level if they could not shape it to their liking at the national level. Finally, funds were limited to the point that only 130,000 units were completed by 1941, when the conservative coalition was able to end financial support for the program. Most of the new units had to be packed into small areas because there was so little money for land purchases, which of course made it more likely that the new housing tracts would turn into unattractive places to live.

By the early 1940s the liberal-labor alliance also had its own solution to the problem of purchasing land from slumlords, one that had the added benefit of underwriting city finances. They agreed with the growth coalitions that the federal government should subsidize the lion's share of the land purchases, but in return the cities would pay one-third of the costs and have the right to lease the cleared land to developers, thereby providing cities with a major income stream that would decrease dependence on property and sales taxes.

Congressional hearings on bills prepared by the Urban Land Institute and the liberal-labor alliance were held before Colmer's Special Subcommittee on Post-War Economic Policy and Planning in 1944–1945, thereby setting the stage for later legislation. In 1946 strategists in the liberal-labor alliance suddenly offered to support the urban redevelopment bill sought by the growth coalitions if cities would own the land and if public housing were built for those who were displaced. They also insisted that residential areas cleared of low-income housing had to be returned to "predominantly residential uses," with "predominantly" eventually defined as over 50 percent (von Hoffman 2000). Not surprisingly from a power perspective, the growth coalitions opposed the liberal-labor provisos because they gave city governments too much potential power and independence. The result was a stalemate until 1949.

In an attempt to make housing legislation more acceptable to the growth coalitions, Senator Flanders put forth three compromises that were included in the Housing Act of 1949. The first mandated that federal money be given to the local community in one lump sum, which made it more difficult for federal agencies to monitor a local program in any detail. The second stated that a unit of slum housing had to be torn down for each unit of public housing that was built, which would clear land for developers and at the same time keep the housing supply tight. The third compromise, and by far the most important from the growth coalitions' point of view, allowed city-cleared land to be sold as well as leased to private developers, which meant that growth coalitions could capture all the profits if they controlled the city government, as they almost invariably did at the time.

Even with these concessions, however, the growth coalitions tried to block the final bill because it still contained a strong emphasis on housing in redevelopment areas and the provision for new public housing. Once the bill was enacted over their objections, which is why the bill seemed at first to be an unalloyed liberal-labor victory, the growth coalitions were able to limit funding for it through their strong influence with the Appropriations Committee in the House. They also suggested to local real estate leaders that they lobby for passage of state legislation that would allow them to set up local redevelopment agencies that could compete with local housing authorities for federal grants.

In good part due to these roadblocks, but also because of the rise in defense spending discussed in the previous section, neither redevelopment plans nor government housing construction went anywhere until the Republican takeover of the White House and Congress in 1953, which made it possible for the real estate interests to amend the law to their liking. Their recommendations were sent to Congress through a presidential commission dominated by bankers, savings and loan officials, and real estate and development leaders. The key change created an exception to the rule that residential areas had to be restored to predominantly residential usages. The new provision allowed another 10 percent of federal grant monies for a given project to be used for nonresidential uses, pushing the non-housing percentage up to 60 percent. The commission also proposed that the program should encompass slum prevention as well as slum clearance by including neighborhoods that might become slums if they were not redeveloped. In practice, this provision became a license to create self-fulfilling prophecies by city neglect of essential services and repairs while real estate interests criticized and denigrated these neighborhoods in the media.

The combination of these two new Republican provisions freed local growth coalitions to move ahead with their plans, especially in the large cities in which growth coalitions fortified by corporations with local headquarters had been planning for very large changes since the end of World War II. The US Chamber of Commerce reversed its previous disapproval of housing legislation and backed the new amendments. Once the legislation passed, requests for money burgeoned and numerous programs got under way. Tellingly, no local grant requests were refused in the first two years (Sanders 1987). Then the gradual enlargement of the exception rule made the program even more attractive to developers. The non-housing percent was increased to 70 percent in 1959, to 80 percent in 1961, and to 85 percent in 1967. By then the costs of buildings constructed by universities and other nonprofit organizations counted as part of a city's one-third contribution, which made redevelopment all the easier for growth coalitions and drew them closer to universities and their administrators (Rossi and Dentler 1961). In the process, the program provided local economies with a Keynesian stimulus program courtesy of the federal treasury, which is an example of why construction unions are usually very strong supporters of local growth coalitions.

In short, the real estate lobby won a complete victory over the liberal-labor alliance even though it took several years to do so. Urban "redevelopment" became urban "renewal," a very different program than what liberals had envisioned. Far more housing was torn down than was built. Of the 810,000 public housing units that were mandated by the Housing Act of 1949, only 332,000 were completed by 1961. As will be discussed in later chapters, the same powerful urban lobby also won victories in later years as well, sometimes in spite of opposition from the US Chamber of Commerce.

THE BIG PICTURE ON THE TRUMAN ERA

As the Truman administration wound down in late 1952, the Committee for Economic Development and the Business Advisory Council had clearly established themselves as the spokespersons and leaders for the corporate moderates. Building on the fact that the corporate community reestablished its legitimacy through its contribution to the war effort, corporate moderates were able to modify the Employment Act of 1946 and to provide significant support for the creation of the Marshall Plan. They also were the most powerful supporters of the expansions and improvements in the Social Security system passed in 1950, just as they were in 1939.

As for the corporate community as a whole, it not only won a major victory over organized labor with the passage of the Taft-Hartley Act but, in conjunction with the conservative coalition, also was able to block almost all of the legislation it opposed. The Truman administration, with strong backing from the liberal-labor alliance, had proposed federal aid for education, an increase in the minimum wage, national-level standards for unemployment benefits, and improvements in Social Security, but the only successes were on Social Security (supported by the corporate community), public housing (very little of which was built), and increases in the minimum wage (in exchange for agreeing to the elimination of some occupational categories from the program) (Roof 2011, chapter 2). More generally, the conservative coalition formed 140 times in the House between 1946 and 1952 and lost only thirteen votes, a 90 percent success rate. It formed 177 times in the Senate and lost only fifteen times, with a perfect record in three years in which it formed twenty or more times, for a 92 percent success rate overall (Shelley 1983, pp. 34, 38). Most of these victories once again concerned labor issues, which by then were of even greater concern to the Southern Democrats than in the past because of increased attempts at unionization in the South, including ongoing attempts at biracial organizing (Katznelson, Geiger, and Kryder 1993).

The list of successes for the conservative coalition also included the defeat of a national health insurance bill in 1950, a legislative battle that will be mentioned in Chapter 6 as part of the background to the passage of Medicare in 1965. Even the one seeming success for the liberal-labor alliance, the Housing Act of 1949, ended up as a victory for real estate and development interests. It perhaps goes without saying by this point, but it should be noted that the public housing built in the South was completely segregated (Brown 1999, p. 127).

With the economy generally strong except for the 1949–1950 recession, income inequality continued to decline, from a Gini of 0.369 in 1946 to 0.317 in 1953, its all-time low before or since, just at the time when the unemployment rate was below 3.0 percent for the first nine months of the year (Kopczuk, Saez, and Song 2010). Consistent with declining income inequality, the tight labor markets caused by war production after 1950 led to the growth of the union movement, especially for the CIO unions. As a result, union density for nonagricultural workers reversed a postwar drop from 35.4 percent in 1945 to 30.4 percent in 1950 by rebounding to 33.8 percent in 1953 and 34.8 in 1954, levels never attained again (Mayer 2004, p. 22, table A1).

The effective tax rate on the top 1 percent of households went down in the first years after the war, from 42.1 percent in 1945 to 32.2 percent in 1952, in part due to a cut in the top marginal rate from 94 percent to 82 percent, which passed in 1948 over a Truman veto. However, the rollback on progressive tax rates was slowed because of the necessity of paying for the Korean War. The corporate community also muted its complaints about "double taxation" of corporate profits, which became little more than a talking point. Lower tax rates in general and faster depreciation allowances on new investments were more important to it, especially because the excess profits tax was certain to be eliminated after the war ended (Bank 2010, pp. 192, 213).

Specific numbers aside, the CED's conservative version of Keynesian economics had gained a legitimacy that would be useful to the corporate community in future battles over tax rates. It provided a strong rationale for both moderate and conservative elected officials to claim that tax cuts, which they often wanted to enact for their own political reasons, are the best possible economic stimulus when the economy declines. At the same time, the liberal Keynesian rationale for tax increases in times of robust economic growth could be ignored by both corporate executives and elected officials by drawing on long-standing fears of government incompetence, favoritism, and excess. When the liberal-labor alliance pressured for tax hikes to dampen inflation, there were delays that made any increases too little and too late to matter. Delays and continuing inflation then opened the way for corporate executives to argue that high interest rates were the best way to tame inflation because they registered their impact simply, quickly, and directly through the reduction of consumer demand. This policy choice contributed to inequality by raising unemployment and cutting incomes at the lower end.

Generally speaking, then, the CED's overall perspective and specific policy suggestions seemed to be proving very beneficial for the corporate community, and the trustees had voted to make the organization a permanent one. However, the ultraconservatives remained unconvinced by CED successes. They continued to advocate a strong antigovernment, balanced-budget, high-tariff, and isolationist viewpoint through pamphlets, books, and radio shows (Fones-Wolf 1994). CED trustees believed these messages to be so counterproductive that they launched their own economic education campaign with funding from the Ford Foundation, headed at the time by CED founding trustee Paul Hoffman. In 1952 these efforts at economic education were turned over to a newly created nonprofit organization, the Joint Council for Economic Education. Renamed the Council for Economic Education in the 1980s, it now centers its attention on attempting to influence how elementary and high school students are introduced to economic ideas, primarily through working with teacher education programs and providing curriculum guides and materials for classroom use (Domhoff 2010, pp. 132–135).

The continuing disagreements between corporate moderates and ultraconservatives at the time are revealed in an exhaustive study of business ideology carried out by means of a content analysis of all available publications, media advertisements, and radio commercials generated by corporations and their associations between July 1, 1948, and June 30, 1949. Its authors concluded that a predominant "classical creed" was embodied within the US Chamber of Commerce and NAM, but they also found a "managerial" variant, which in their view reflected the role and interests of the largest corporations. In addition, they noted a postwar extension of the managerial view, as exemplified by the efforts of the Committee for Economic Development. This extension stated that the "system does not function perfectly," making it necessary to employ some Keynesian ideas and use government to introduce the necessary corrections (Sutton, Harris, Kaysen, and Tobin 1956, pp. 215–216).

As the size of the CED gradually increased from several dozen trustees to over one hundred, the Research and Policy Committee also grew from twenty to forty. This growth made it necessary to establish a smaller Program Committee with about a dozen members, drawn from the Research and Policy Committee, for setting an agenda and coordinating work by various subcommittees. At about the same time, an Executive Committee with from five to seven members came to provide the leadership of the organization. Trustees moved in and out of these two committees on a regular basis, and a wider range of trustees took part in subcommittee deliberations, annual meetings, and fundraising campaigns, but from then on the core of the organization at any given time consisted of forty to fifty executives and six or seven staff members.

Chapter Five

Corporate Moderate Frustrations

The Eisenhower Years

Members of the CED and the Business Advisory Council had their greatest direct involvement in the government during Dwight D. Eisenhower's two-term presidency, starting with their large role in helping the widely admired war hero become a respected civilian as the president of Columbia University from 1948 to 1950. They also helped him create the American Assembly in 1950, a discussion forum that brought together people from various organizations, profit and nonprofit, to talk about a different policy issue every six to twelve months. Both of these leadership positions burnished Eisenhower's credentials as a statesman concerned with major policy issues (Griffith 1982, p. 98; Jacobs 2004). He even became a CED trustee for a brief time in 1948, which made him suspect to many ultraconservatives, though he had little or no active involvement in the organization.

CED members were among the key supporters of Eisenhower's campaign. For example, the chair of the CED at the time, Walter Williams, the chair of Continental, Inc., a mortgage banking, insurance, and real estate company in Seattle, and a former president of the American Mortgage Bankers Association, chaired Citizens for Eisenhower, and Paul Hoffman was the chair of its Advisory Council. Another CED trustee, Howard Petersen, the chair of Fidelity-Philadelphia Trust Company, who figures prominently in this and succeeding chapters, was chair of the campaign's finance committee. Lucius Clay, a former army general, who had known Eisenhower for twenty years and by then was chair of the board at Continental Can Company, used his role in the Business Advisory Council as a basis for organizing a series of meetings between other corporate chieftains and Eisenhower (McQuaid 1982, p. 171).

After the elections, several CED trustees joined the administration, starting with the two men who served successively as his secretary of the treasury, Ohio mining executive George Humphrey (1953–1956), and Texas corporate lawyer Robert

Anderson (1957–1960). Williams moved from chair of Citizens for Eisenhower to undersecretary of commerce, and founding trustee Marion Folsom was appointed the undersecretary of the treasury (1953–1954) and then secretary of health, education, and welfare (1955–1958). The chair of the CED trustees early in the Eisenhower administration, the president of Hart Schaffner and Marx, was tapped as a special assistant in the White House. Two years later his replacement as CED chair, the chair of Crown Zellerbach, was appointed ambassador to Italy, where he had earlier served as a Marshall Plan administrator. A CED trustee was the director of the Federal Deposit Insurance Corporation, and another was director of the Office of Defense Mobilization. Reflecting on these and other Eisenhower appointees early in the administration, which included top officers at General Motors and J. P. Stevens, the second-largest textile manufacturing firm, *Business Week* wrote that they "represent the views of a particular type of forward-looking businessman, a sort of progressive conservatism" (Schriftgiesser 1960, p. 162).

Eisenhower's CEA chair, Arthur F. Burns, was a Columbia University economist and the director of research at the National Bureau of Economic Research. A moderate conservative who prided himself at the time on being a registered Democrat, Burns was joined on the council by Neil Jacoby, an original member of the CED's Research Advisory Board, and Walter W. Stewart, a retired Wall Street investment banker, who had chaired the board of directors of the Rockefeller Foundation from 1943 to 1950 and then became a fellow of the Institute of Advanced Studies at Princeton.

Six days before Eisenhower left New York for his inauguration, a group of eight CED trustees, including the presidents of Federated Department Stores, General Electric, Libby-Owens-Ford Plate Glass, and Northwest Bank Corporation, held a well-publicized meeting with him in which they gave him a nine-page statement with suggestions on how he should proceed. It first reiterated the principle that the country could afford whatever national security programs were needed, although it added they could be carried out more efficiently than in the past. It then asked for a liberalization of trade policy through lower tariffs, streamlined customs procedures, the elimination of shipping restrictions, and the provision of more government loans to countries that wanted to increase trade with the United States. It next warned that anti-inflation measures should be at the ready because the big burst in defense spending for the Korean War had brought the unemployment rate to such a low level that inflation might flare up. At the same time, the statement also suggested that the administration should have a list of projects it could undertake if unemployment grew rapidly after the war ended (Schriftgiesser 1960, pp. 164–165).

Most of all, the CED trustees wanted to see tax reforms and reductions, starting with cuts for high-income earners, as soon as it was clear that they were feasible. However, it added that those tax reductions should not be immediate, as the Republican platform had promised, because of the potential for inflation at that moment. This call for delay angered the National Association of Manufacturers, the US Chamber of Commerce, and leading Republicans in Congress, which wanted tax cuts in order to limit government spending (Schriftgiesser 1960, pp. 166–167). Even in the 1950s— that is, well before Reagan Republicans frankly stated that they wanted to reduce taxes in order to "starve government" and "defund the left"—it was clearly understood that tax cuts would be the best way to make government programs too expensive to sustain.

Based on the CED trustees' support for Eisenhower and their direct access to him, it might be assumed that the corporate moderates' policy viewpoints would enjoy even more success during his presidency than they had during the Truman administration. But such was not to be the case. In fact, the CED proposals were usually delayed or watered down by ultraconservatives and the conservative coalition. Ironically, the Eisenhower administration ended up primarily as eight years of stasis for the CED leaders. The best that can be said for the corporate moderates during these eight years is that they could take part of the credit for the fact that no liberal-labor initiatives with any immediate impact, except for disability benefits for those over age fifty, were enacted.

BLOCKED ON TARIFFS, SOME SUCCESS ON FOREIGN AID

The CED's problems began with the issue on which it had come to have its strongest and most direct role, tariff reduction, an increasingly larger part of its work because its trustees had decided that internationalizing the economy was important. Efforts by corporate moderates played an important role because 1953 marked the first year since the passage of the highly protectionist Smoot-Hawley Tariff Act in 1929 in which the traditionally high-tariff Republicans controlled the presidency and both houses of Congress. Because many ultraconservative Republicans continued in the protectionist tradition, the moderate and mostly internationalist Republicans who ran the CED could no longer rely on traditional free-trade Democrats in Congress, especially from the South, to support their program. Now they had to ensure that the Republicans would move in a free-trade direction, not revert to protectionism.

The fact that many CED trustees came from the Republican Midwest (e.g., the chair of General Mills in Minneapolis; the chair of Burroughs in Detroit; and the president of National Cash Register in Dayton, Ohio) provided a good entry point. In anticipation of an Eisenhower administration, the CED had been working on a new policy statement on foreign economic policy meant to reinforce the directions that had been undertaken through the Marshall Plan. The report appeared as *Britain's Economic Problem and Its Meaning for America* (Committee for Economic Development 1953). As the title implies, the report focused on the need to strengthen the British economy by making it possible for the United Kingdom to sell more products in the United States. A strong British Empire was seen, just as it had been by postwar planners in the early 1940s, as important to the United States for both economic and geopolitical reasons. That is, a strong British economy would make it possible for more American exports to go into the British Empire, but it also would ensure that Britain would remain a strong political ally. However, the report is also of more general significance because it called for lower tariffs and the removal of other trade restrictions for all American allies, not just Great Britain.

Despite the CED's Republican credentials and the economic expansion that might follow if its plans were adopted, legislation for liberalizing trade restrictions went nowhere in the new Congress. To the dismay of internationalists in the corporate community, the Eisenhower administration had to settle for a one-year extension of the Trade Agreements Act and a special investigatory commission, which was supposed to come up with trade recommendations for the next legislative session. The seventeen-member commission included three Republicans and two Democrats from each house, along with five businessmen, one economist, and one labor leader.

Paralleling the government commission, the CED formed its own subcommittee on the issue. It included top officers from many major companies, including General Electric, Standard Oil of New Jersey, Bankers Trust, and the H. J. Heinz Company. Most interesting of all in terms of the CED's eventual success on tariff reduction during the Kennedy administration, the committee was chaired by Petersen, the Philadelphia banker who served as the national finance chairman for the 1952 Eisenhower presidential campaign and became a special advisor for trade for President John F. Kennedy in 1961. Petersen's first job was as a lawyer with a Wall Street law firm in the 1930s. During World War II he served as an assistant to the secretary of war and from 1945 to 1947 as an assistant secretary of war, which gave him a part in helping to revive the German economy. After the war he joined Fidelity-Philadelphia Trust Company and became active in the CED.

As head of the CED subcommittee, Petersen spent a considerable amount of time talking with leading spokespersons for protectionist industries. One of the few protectionists in the CED, William C. Foster, a longtime manufacturing company executive, had served as undersecretary of commerce (1946–1948) and as an administrator of the Marshall Plan (1950–1951). He was also the president of the Manufacturing Chemists Association, a staunchly protectionist business association. In other words, the subcommittee was a textbook example of the role the CED tried to play within the corporate community: Petersen was an internationalist on trade policies who was learning to deal with the concerns of the protectionists in the business world (Schriftgiesser 1960, p. 182).

Petersen and other CED trustees working on trade policy also became acquainted with the research director for the government commission, Alfred C. Neal, an economist and vice president for the Federal Reserve Bank of Boston. Neal had a PhD from the University of California, Berkeley, and had taught at Brown University before Flanders, the president of the Federal Reserve Bank of Boston at the time, asked him to join the bank as the head of its research department. He later became a senior vice president in charge of administration. Shortly after the government trade commission completed its work, the CED hired Neal as its first paid president, a position he held for the next twenty years (Schriftgiesser 1960, p. 211).

The report by Petersen's subcommittee, entitled *United States Tariff Policy* (Committee for Economic Development 1954), made the case for expanding both imports and exports; it used standard economic doctrine to claim that specialization by countries tends to raise the standard of living in all countries through more efficient use of resources. It also argued that the United States needed to encourage more imports if other countries were to have the money to buy American exports, a point to be kept in mind when ultraconservatives began to complain several years later that foreign companies were "invading" American markets. Finally, in a noneconomic argument, the report insisted that low tariffs are necessary to help American allies, especially Great Britain, which relied far more on trade than did the United States. That is, geopolitical concerns entered into the argument once again. Despite efforts at compromise, two corporation presidents on the Research and Policy Committee refused to sign the report, and two or three companies withdrew financial support from the CED on the basis of it (Schriftgiesser 1960, p. 182).

Despite generally supportive reports by the government commission and the CED, the Eisenhower administration lost ground on the tariff issue in the 1955 legislative session. The largely protectionist Congress only gave it permission to lower tariffs by 15 percent over the next three years and tied the administration's hands slightly through a number of protectionist amendments (Pastor 1980, p. 103). These setbacks were somewhat unexpected in that Democrats had taken control of both the House and Senate after the 1954 elections, which meant the key committees were chaired by seemingly low-tariff Southern Democrats, not Republican protectionists. In the past their strong efforts had been essential in holding any losses to the protectionists to a minimum.

But something else had changed between 1953 and 1955 besides the return to Democratic control of Congress. The textile industry, by then largely relocated to the South, began to demand tariff protection for the first time. After dominating the American market in the years during which American allies were still rebuilding from the war, the textile manufacturers were feeling a slight pinch from foreign imports. However, the new competition came as no surprise to the CED trustees. A few years earlier they had urged several foreign countries, especially Japan, to rebuild their economies by starting with labor-intensive industries such as textiles, and had anticipated that they would be selling in the American market in exchange for American corporate access to their markets (Hunter 1959, chapter 10). Although less than 10 percent of the American market had been captured by lower-cost imports, the gradual increase made the Southern textile owners fearful about the future. Working through their long-standing trade association, the American Textile Manufacturers Institute, industry leaders put on a vigorous campaign throughout the South, holding dozens of meetings with other business executives and encouraging them to contact their congressional representatives. They ran ads, sponsored letter-writing campaigns, enlisted the support of textile workers, and lobbied in Washington.

An ultraconservative named Roger Milliken, head of his family's privately held textile company, Deering Milliken, served as their de facto leader. He had moved his company headquarters from New York to South Carolina in 1954 to be closer to the many plants he had relocated there, but he immediately found himself in clashes with labor organizers. In 1956 he threatened to close a plant in Darlington, South Carolina, if workers voted for unionization, which they then did by a narrow margin. The immediate shutdown that followed was the beginning of a resistance to the rulings of the National Labor Relations Board that went on for thirty years before Milliken finally prevailed (Gross 1995, pp. 193, 362n5).

The efforts by the textile owners apparently had an impact on Southern Democrats, especially those from Georgia and Alabama, who quickly changed from philosophic free traders to cautious protectionists (Bauer, de Sola Pool, and Dexter 1963, pp. 60,

359–360). This meant that the ultraconservative nationalist industrialists of the North and the Southern-based textile industry were lined up against the internationalists on trade issues. Given the power of the conservative coalition in Congress, there was no contest when it decided to take on the internationalists on tariff issues.

Not surprisingly, then, the legislative struggle for renewal of the Trade Agreements Act in 1958 did not lead to a victory for the corporate moderates or the Eisenhower administration. Though renewal was granted for four years, the ultra-conservatives convinced Congress to constrain the executive branch even further by granting Congress the right (by a two-thirds concurrent vote) to "force the President to implement a recommendation of the Tariff Commission." Congress also rewrote a national security escape clause "so that virtually any domestic industry could obtain protection from foreign competition if it were determined that such competition were weakening the internal economy and thereby impairing national security" (Pastor 1980, pp. 103–104).

In spite of these setbacks, the CED continued its efforts by publishing two more reports calling for liberalized trade policies. A subcommittee chaired by Thomas Cabot of the Cabot Corporation in Boston sounded warnings about possible exclusion from the new European Common Market in 1959 if the government did not change its tariff policies. Then an emerging balance of payments problem became the theme of *National Objectives and the Balance of Payments Problem* (Committee for Economic Development 1960b). This report was produced by a subcommittee chaired by economist Emilio G. Collado, who had worked as a member of Neal's research staff for the government commission to examine tariff policy. He was soon thereafter hired as the treasurer of Standard Oil of New Jersey, followed by his appointment as a CED trustee (Schriftgiesser 1967, pp. 123–124).

Although the CED did not achieve the success it had hoped for on tariff issues, it did make some progress in obtaining more federal aid for underdeveloped countries. Its arguments came to be framed in the context of competition with the Soviet Union for influence in the Third World, while adding that such aid was necessary "regardless of what the Russians do," not only to "protect our vital, immediate interests" but "to help the underdeveloped countries build the kinds of societies with which the West can live in cooperation and peace in the long run." An April 1957 report, *Economic Development Assistance,* warned that the Soviets had recently widened their relations with underdeveloped countries, thereby opening up "a new broad path of assault on the Free World by international communism." The CED also made a successful case for the establishment of a development loan fund (see Schriftgiesser 1960, pp. 184–186, 217, for characterizations of the reports mentioned in this paragraph).

A few months after the development assistance policy statement, a founding trustee, Donald K. David, serving as the CED's chair, expressed heightened corporate concern about the Soviet Union at a celebration of the organization's fifteenth anniversary. He did so by drawing attention to its recent unexpected launching of a small space satellite, a major accomplishment at the time. Behind the booster rockets and the satellite, said David, who was a director of the Ford Motor Company and General Electric and the vice chair of the Ford Foundation, "there is a social system of human institutions that, in this case, has made the correct decisions about what was important to achieve and has motivated and organized efforts to do it" (Schriftgiesser 1960, p. 217).

Vice President Richard Nixon, scientific experts, and a CED trustee who was a former deputy secretary of defense were present to speak on the issue as well (Committee for Economic Development 1957). Nine months after the Soviet satellite was launched, corporate moderates became backers of the National Defense Education Act, passed in September 1958, which supported national defense by funding educational institutions at all levels over a four-year period. This step was the first of several that gradually led the CED trustees to become strong advocates of federal aid to education, as reflected in later policy recommendations. It was a direction that brought the CED into further conflict with the US Chamber of Commerce, which rejected the idea of any federal aid to education on the grounds that education was a state and local matter.

Claiming that the challenge from the Soviet Union would require increased emphasis on foreign aid and further support for scientific and technological education, the CED issued a report on *The Problem of National Security* in 1958. It argued that the United States faced "a continuing situation of constant danger with which we apparently must live for many years" (Schriftgiesser 1960, p. 187). To reassure ultraconservatives and the general public that the country could increase defense spending while at the same time maintaining a strong economy, it twice echoed a statement CEA chair Leon Keyserling had given corporate moderates and foreign policy analysts nine years earlier: the United States "can afford what we have to afford," with the words underlined the second time (Committee for Economic Development 1958c, pp. 27, 52).

LIMITED SUCCESS ON TAX-AND-SPEND POLICIES

The CED put forth many suggestions on how to improve tax policy during the Eisenhower years, which of course meant adopting the CED viewpoint, but as in the case of tariff policy, it did not have any major impact. The ultraconservatives first of all ignored the CED plea to wait on any tax cuts by eliminating excess profits taxes immediately, although reductions in income taxes did not take effect until January 1954.

As the economy began to weaken in late 1953, with unemployment creeping up to 4.5 percent by December, the CED published *Defense against Recession* in March 1954, suggesting that the time had arrived for further reductions in income taxes. The Eisenhower administration decided to take a wait-and-see attitude even while reaffirming that it would use tax cuts and increased government expenditures if necessary. Instead, it relied primarily on monetary policy and the rise in unemployment and welfare benefits as a source of spending. In addition it accelerated the pace for government spending on defense and interstate highways. Still, the administration did make some use of fiscal policy in that it allowed the previously approved reduction in income taxes, which had not been meant by the ultraconservatives to serve as a stimulus, to take effect as scheduled, and then approved a reduction in excise taxes (Collins 1981, pp. 156–157). Although the administration's overall response was less than assertive, it did reject ultraconservative concerns with budget deficits and liberal-labor calls for increased government spending. Meanwhile, unemployment increased to 6.1 percent by September, then fluctuated between 4 and 5 percent over the next two years.

Reductions in defense spending and higher interest rates moved unemployment upward once again in the first half of 1958, from 5.8 percent in January to 7.5 percent in July. By spring of that year the CED's Program Committee was arguing for a one-year tax cut of 20 percent for individuals if there was not a distinct improvement within two months, but that deadline came and went (Committee for Economic Development 1958a). Without any strong pressure or support from corporate moderates in general, and in the face of opposition by the ultraconservatives, Eisenhower decided to wait on tax cuts. Instead, he again used other forms of fiscal stimulus by authorizing an acceleration in highway aid and convincing Congress to pass a program to stimulate housing construction—via support for mortgages—through the Emergency Housing Act of 1958. The idea of using government funds to support home mortgages as an economic stimulus was not a new one. It began in the early 1930s and had been deployed in a small way by Eisenhower in 1954, and would be used again in the 1960s and 1970s (Carliner 1998, pp. 308–309). After the launching of the Soviet satellite, there were also increases in spending for defense, education, and research.

For the most part, though, Eisenhower decided to rely on lower interest rates to trigger an economic recovery, which stimulated an upswing in housing construction and increased purchases of cars and other durable goods. Still, unemployment remained between 5 and 6 percent throughout 1959 and most of 1960. It reached 6.1 percent for the November presidential elections, to Nixon's lasting frustration, and it was 6.6 percent when John F. Kennedy was inaugurated, which is about 2.5 times what it had been during the Korean War. Mild stimulus policies were not working, and the CED's tax-cut remedy had not been tried.

THE PUZZLE OF RISING INFLATION

Inflation, always a major concern within the corporate community, was not a problem during the first three years of Eisenhower's presidency. With the Federal Reserve Board ever vigilant on the issue, Eisenhower abolished the extensive wage-price controls put in place on an emergency basis at the onset of the Korean War within three weeks of taking office. However, the fact that prices and wages did not fall as unemployment gradually climbed in the mid-1950s generated concern that something was not quite right according to the conventional understandings of economics. Then, when inflation increased to about 5 percent in 1957 and 1958, mainstream economists and corporate leaders alike expressed both surprise and consternation: inflation within a recession was not something they had anticipated (Schriftgiesser 1960, p. 199).

From the White House's point of view, no amount of inflation should be tolerated. It might lead to runaway inflation and a devaluation of the dollar, thereby creating problems with the balance of payments in international trade. Moreover, Republicans claimed the current inflation was of a new type, "cost-push," caused by increases in the costs of factors of production, such as raw materials and higher wages due to union demands. No longer was inflation simply a matter of "demand-pull," too much money seeking to buy too few available goods. All talk of raw materials aside, the determination of wages through collective bargaining was considered to be the main culprit.

As inflation continued into 1958, the White House announced the creation of a Cabinet Committee on Price Stability for Economic Growth, chaired by Nixon, and including several cabinet members and the chair of the CEA. Allen Wallis, the dean of the business school at the University of Chicago, and a member of the CED's Research Advisory Board, was appointed executive vice chair to carry out the detail work for the committee. The committee issued several reports with the help of economists in the private sector, including Herbert Stein of the CED, and sent Wallis on a nationwide speaking tour in an attempt to alert a wide range of civic associations to the grave dangers of inflation.

The liberal-labor alliance opposed the White House's approach from the start. Its leaders and economists said that administered prices, whether set by overt collusion among corporations or through price signals sent by the actions of the dominant corporation in an industry, were the main cause of inflation, which should be remedied by more vigorous antitrust activity by the government. Moreover, according to its spokespersons, the low level of inflation was not a serious problem. Instead, rising unemployment was the primary issue at this juncture because it left many families destitute while slowing the overall growth of an economy that needed to produce more in order to provide for everyone. As usual, then, the rival coalitions had developed very different analyses of the problem, with most Republicans agreeing with the corporate community that union power and cost-push inflation were a major concern, and most non-Southern Democrats agreeing with the liberal-labor alliance that the emphasis should be on administered prices and policies to reduce unemployment.

The arguments about inflation between the White House and the liberal-labor alliance were paralleled by similar debates within the CED, which established a subcommittee on inflation in the fall of 1955. Contrary to the claim by the liberal-labor alliance that price-fixing by corporations was the main problem in controlling inflation, the CED felt that the market already was protected from oligopolistic corporations by the antitrust laws. The CED claimed, however, that there was no comparable protection for the general public interest from powerful unions.

Slichter, still one of the CED's top economic advisors, counseled its trustees that gradual inflation in the range of 2 to 4 percent was not a problem, but they did not accept his analysis (Schriftgiesser 1967, p. 77). Instead, subcommittee members largely echoed the position taken by the White House and its main point man on inflation, Wallis. Like Eisenhower, they considered inflation to be a cause for alarm, "an evil which must not be tolerated ... a cruel tax on people who live on fixed incomes," leading in 1958 to very conservative policy recommendations in *Defense against Inflation* (Committee for Economic Development 1958b, p. 11). While frankly stating that a good understanding of inflation did not exist, the report primarily blamed unions for both inflation and rising wages.

According to the CED analysis, wage demands by unions were the main problem because they tended to outrun increases in the "rate of productivity," a concept defined by a relatively simple index, the rate of increase in total output per worker per hour. Although increases in the rate of productivity depend primarily on the introduction of new machinery and improved work organization, corporate leaders used the index to imply that their employees were the problem, either through lack of effort or union rules that stifled organizational and technological innovations. Making the corporate claim even more questionable, the index is distorted by the movement of workers from occupations in which productivity gains were low at the time, such as farming, to manufacturing jobs in which productivity often increases rapidly due to the introduction of new technologies. Moreover, the productivity index can decline if workers move from manufacturing to service jobs that are labor-intensive, as began to happen in the 1960s and 1970s. In addition, issues that have nothing to do with technology, work organization, or worker effort, such as inflation and changes in currency valuation, also can distort the index (Berkowitz 2006, pp. 66–67). As early as 1957, the Joint Economic Committee of Congress registered criticisms of the index, but its various shortcomings were lost from sight as it became the basis for major political battles over the next two decades (Gordon 1975, p. 119).

Problems with the measurement of productivity gains aside, the CED policy statement recommended that the package of wages and benefits for employees "should rise as fast as—but not faster than—the rise of output per man-hour for the economy as a whole." However, the wage-benefit package should not absorb the whole productivity gain because the rate of profits should grow, too. The CED then offered a suggestion that was resisted by some trustees and advisors, who feared it seemed to confer legitimacy on voluntary wage-price guidelines set by the government, even though the subcommittee stated that it strongly rejected government controls on wages and prices during peacetime: "We must rely on the forces of competition and on the *voluntary exercise of restraint* in price and wage policies by business and labor to prevent this [inflation] from happening" (Committee for Economic Development 1958b, p. 15, my italics). However, voluntary restraint did not fit with the laws of competition, as CED advisor Jacoby, until 1955 a member of the CEA, pointed out in the context of a long letter to the CEA chair: "The hortatory approach to the problem of containing inflation is not merely ineffective; it is also contradictory in the sense that it asks people to behave noncompetitively" (Gordon 1975, p. 116). Thus, as in-house critics of the CED formula for wage-price guidelines had feared, it generated tensions within the CED for the next seventeen years, until the possibility of such guidelines was finally laid to rest.

As also feared by the in-house critics, the CED's formula opened the door to wage-price guidelines, however voluntary, that would be determined by economic experts employed by the federal government, and within a few years the Kennedy administration took advantage of the opportunity. The issue was usually debated using the vague concept of an "incomes policy," which can be broadly defined as any approach to influencing the economy (and especially controlling inflation) that does not rely exclusively on the traditional market system and the minimal governmental laws needed to support it. By the late 1950s, one form or another of an incomes policy had been tried in a few Western European countries, usually involving multiparty negotiations that brought together employers, organized labor, and government officials to determine prices, wages, and taxes.

Although union demands were seen as the immediate problem, the CED inflation report said that the federal government bore the formal responsibility for inflation because it did not take the actions that were necessary to combat it. The subcommittee then advocated higher interest rates through actions by the Federal Reserve Board and an amendment to the Employment Act of 1946, which would state that the maintenance of a low level of inflation was as important as stimulating high employment (Schriftgiesser 1960, p. 203). Next, in a clear indication that most CED trustees did not think that the Taft-Hartley Act went far enough in limiting the power of organized labor, the report concluded, "There is an urgent need for objective consideration of the proper extent, character and uses of union power in our society. Existing laws should be reviewed to see whether they give or leave a degree of power to labor organizations that is not in the public interest" (Committee for Economic Development 1958b, pp. 15–16). That is, it would be up to the government to tame organized labor.

FURTHER SETBACKS FOR ORGANIZED LABOR

Building on the Taft-Hartley Act of 1947, the corporate community made further progress during the Eisenhower years in limiting the regulatory and legal support for unions. It did so first and foremost through the deployment of corporate-oriented practitioners of labor law, often with experience as aides for Republicans on congressional labor committees, or former staff members for the National Labor Relations Board.

Fully aware of the tenuous relations over the previous seventeen years between the craft-based AFL and several of the industrial unions in the CIO, Eisenhower tried at the outset of his administration to fashion labor legislation that would bring the AFL unions—some of which had supported his campaign—into the Republican fold. He began by offering them concessions on picketing and strike activities at construction sites. Much of the negotiating between Eisenhower and George Meany, the president of the AFL, occurred through Eisenhower's secretary of labor, a plumber who was highly recommended for his cabinet position by Meany. But the complex set of concessions, the details of which need not concern us here, was completely unacceptable to the ultraconservatives. They were represented in the administration on this issue by the secretary of commerce, who organized other cabinet members against it and made well-timed leaks to the mass media (Gross 1995, pp. 78–85). The secretary of labor resigned eighteen months after his appointment, and the AFL was left with no choice but to ally with the CIO as much as possible. Indeed, the rebuff by the Republicans, along with the continuing corporate attacks on all unions, were among the factors that led to the merger of the two rival union confederations into the AFL-CIO in 1955 (Roof 2011, p. 88).

While Eisenhower was trying to win over the AFL, he was also making conservative appointments to the NLRB, which soon began to issue rulings that strongly favored corporations. First, the new board majority rapidly expanded the rights of employers to resist unions through speeches and pamphlets that bordered on threats of job loss, which went beyond what the Taft-Hartley Act had mandated. It further restricted union organizers' ability to use some of their most potent economic weapons, such as boycotts of companies and picketing of delivery sites. In addition, Eisenhower appointees to the board exempted even more medium-sized and strictly local firms from its purview than was called for in the Taft-Hartley Act, and made it easier for employers to fire union activists (Gross 1995, pp. 102–103).

The board majority replaced longtime staff members in regional offices with conservatives, and by December 1954 it had reversed most of the precedents developed by Democratic boards between 1937 and 1952. At the same time the new NLRB majority ignored the practices of the increasing number of firms that aided corporations in defeating unionization drives and in developing ways to bring about the decertification of already established unions. Their methods included the use of psychological tests to screen out potential employees with leadership abilities and of seemingly neutral discussion groups to identify employees who might be sympathetic to unions (Smith 2003, chapter 4).

Buoyed by their success within the NLRB, the ultraconservatives turned their attention to corrupt leadership and criminal behavior in several unions through hearings in the Senate, chaired by the senior Democratic senator from Arkansas, John Stennis. Although the main fireworks came a few years later, the hearings began in 1955 and provided material for headlines and television clips from testimony, wiretaps, and subpoenaed documents, with the International Brotherhood of Teamsters, the International Longshoremen's Association, and the United Mine Workers as the major targets.

The legislation that emerged from these hearings, the Labor-Management Reporting and Disclosure Act of 1959, had a complex and circuitous history, starting with rival bills created by the labor committees in the House and Senate in 1958. However, the final act was based for the most part on a version written by corporate lawyers serving on the US Chamber of Commerce's Labor Relations Committee (Gross 1995, p. 140). The chamber's draft was introduced on the floor of the House through a rarely used parliamentary procedure by a Democrat from Georgia, Phil Landrum, and a Republican from Michigan, Robert Griffin, leading the bill to be called the Landrum-Griffin Act in most accounts.

The Landrum-Griffin Act was aimed first and foremost at boss control and racketeering in the labor movement, requiring unions to hold secret elections that could be reviewed for fairness by the Department of Labor. It gave more rights and protections to union members, required unions to file financial reports with the government, and in other ways limited the power that leaders had over their members. However, the chamber's lawyers also took the opportunity to hamper union organizing by making it illegal for a unionized business to agree to demands by union organizers that it cease doing business with nonunion companies that unions were trying to organize. It also strengthened the laws against secondary boycotts through the closing of small loopholes. Laws that restricted picketing were made even more constraining by prohibiting roving pickets from being present when the delivery trucks of anti-union companies arrived at their destinations (Gross 1995, p. 139).

Unions were clearly on the defensive in the face of the revelations during the congressional hearings, but leaders within the AFL-CIO were confident they could limit the damage. Their confidence was heightened because they had contributed campaign workers and money to the Democratic Party's success in the 1958 midterm elections, which gave the party margins of 64–36 in the Senate and 283–153 in the House (McAdams 1964, p. 4). They further believed they might be able to remove some of the more onerous provisions of the Taft-Hartley Act as a trade-off for accepting the new restrictions on the unions' management of their financial resources. In making their calculations, however, organized labor ignored the fact that the conservative coalition still had the potential for 59 votes in the Senate (24 Southern Democrats, 35 Republicans) and 245 in the House (92 Southern Democrats, 153 Republicans).

The chair of the Senate Labor Committee, John F. Kennedy of Massachusetts, who already had his eye on the 1960 presidential race, tried to convince his union allies that changes in the Taft-Hartley Act should not be included in the new legislation, but the labor leaders rejected his arguments. With Kennedy's acquiescence, the Senate passed the union's version of the bill in April 1959 (Gross 1995, p. 141). But the Senate version was not able to survive in the House, in which the conservative coalition had the support of 95 Democrats, including all 92 Southern Democrats, and 136 of 153 Republicans. The result was a surprising victory for the Landrum-Griffin version of the act.

Before joining with Republicans in voting for the revised legislation, however, the Southern Democrats insisted upon the elimination of several clauses they feared might provide openings for civil rights efforts in the South. In addition, the Republicans promised to continue to join the Southern Democrats in blocking civil rights legislation in the future, casting aside any pretense that it was any longer the "Party of Lincoln" when it came to civil rights. All the while, the NAM and US Chamber of Commerce reminded Southern Democrats that passage of the act was essential to keep unions out of their region and thereby maintain its attractiveness to industry (McAdams 1964, p. 212).

The final version of the act that emerged from the compromises within the conference committee was not as restrictive for unions as the House bill fashioned by Landrum and Griffin had been. But the outcome was primarily a defeat for unions nonetheless because it strengthened the regulation of internal union affairs by government officials far more than AFL-CIO leaders desired and added the restraints on secondary boycotts and roving pickets discussed earlier in this section. However, the impact of these defeats was obscured by the fact that the new legislation had no immediate negative effects for the large established unions that practiced some semblance of internal democracy. Instead, its impact was more serious for the long run because it made organizing new unions much more difficult, especially in smaller industries, and particularly in the South.

Moreover, there were small favors for construction unions on picketing issues in the final bill, suggesting that some Republicans still hoped to win support from them. In addition, the bill also required anti-union consulting firms to "file an 'Agreements and Activities Report' within thirty days after agreeing to persuade their client's employees to reject unionization" (Smith 2003, p. 102). This provision quickly led to the decline of this new form of union busting. The most important of these firms, Labor Relations Associates, which figured prominently in the Senate hearings, was a thinly disguised arm of Sears, Roebuck. Founded by the director of the company's employee relations department in 1939, with the ostensible goal of providing advice to any company that needed its services, it primarily funneled Sears, Roebuck money to the Teamsters in exchange for the Teamsters' help in decertifying unions. Fully exposed during the Senate hearings, it went out of business in 1962 (Smith 2003, pp. 98–102).

SMALL GAINS FOR LABOR ON SOCIAL SECURITY

The liberal-labor alliance fared better on Social Security issues during the Eisenhower years than it did on union issues. Organized labor again took a very active interest, particularly in the face of renewed efforts by the ultraconservatives to constrain any further growth in the program. Basically, the ultraconservatives wanted to limit benefits to a single flat sum for anyone over age sixty-five, whatever a person's work record or previous income levels. Tensions over the issue declined somewhat after Eisenhower rejected the ultraconservative proposal. He thereby sided with the corporate moderates, who favored the strengthening of Social Security through raising the cap on the amount of a person's income subject to the Social Security tax and slight increases in benefit levels. Moderates also wanted to enlarge the Social Security pool by expanding coverage to include public employees, self-employed professionals, farm owners, farm workers, and domestic workers, and to make pensions slightly higher for some beneficiaries by only counting years in which the person could work enough months to contribute to the pension fund (Altman 2005, pp. 180–181). The ultraconservatives and the American Medical Association (AMA) opposed all of these changes, but the bill passed in August 1954 after self-employed professionals were removed due to AMA lobbying.

The biggest advance for the liberal-labor alliance on a social-insurance issue during the Eisenhower years came in 1955, when the Social Security Act was amended to include disability benefits for anyone over age fifty who was permanently disabled. With concerted congressional lobbying by organized labor for the first time on a Social Security matter, a strong disability amendment passed the House in spite of the fact that the Eisenhower administration and the AMA opposed it. The bill was delayed by the conservative coalition in the Senate Finance Committee, but then, after the committee deadlocked six to six on a recommendation, it went to the floor for a vote by the full Senate. At this point liberal and labor lobbyists made two key concessions that opened the way for partial success. They supported an amendment that would give states control of the program, which met the key demand by Southern Democrats, and they agreed to exclude employees under age fifty, which neutralized opposition from insurance companies. In exchange, a majority of Southern Democrats in the Senate voted for the compromise and the insurance industry did not lobby against the bill (Quadagno 2005, pp. 53–55). In 1958 Congress extended the disability program to include benefits for the families of disabled workers, and in 1960 it was extended to include employees under age fifty.

THE EISENHOWER ERA: RETROSPECT AND PROSPECT

The corporate moderates had their moments and registered some small gains during the Eisenhower years, but the ultraconservatives in the corporate community and the conservative coalition in Congress had the largest impact on most policy decisions. The few successes for the liberal-labor alliance involved the several changes in the Social Security Act, along with a federal supplement to unemployment compensation passed in 1958, all of which were very large steps in terms of the lives of low-income people.

In addition, the liberal-labor alliance could take part of the credit for the civil rights legislation introduced by the Eisenhower administration in 1956 and passed in 1957, which created a Civil Rights Division within the Department of Justice and a bipartisan Civil Rights Commission empowered to investigate and make recommendations concerning violations of civil and voting rights. The first report from the Civil Rights Commission led to the Civil Rights Act of 1960, which strengthened voting provisions to some extent but had little immediate impact (Sinclair 1982, p. 86). In fact, civil rights activists interpreted the 1960 act as a defeat because the conservative coalition would not accept the Civil Rights Commission's recommendations to mandate federal voting registrars and give the attorney general the power to seek injunctions to protect voting rights. They knew well that Senate Majority Leader Lyndon Johnson of Texas had taken the strongest provisions out of the act in order to maintain a degree of consensus between Northern and Southern Democrats, a compromise that angered the leaders of the United Automobile Workers (UAW) (Boyle 1995, chapter 5).

The liberal-labor alliance also could take some satisfaction from the fact that it led the effort to block Republican legislation to amend the Employment Act to include the CED's recommendation that it should include concern for inflation among its objectives (Schriftgiesser 1967, pp. 81–82). In addition, liberal members of the House were heartened by the fact that they had been able to create their own caucus, the Democratic Study Group, to do research and follow floor votes more closely in an attempt to make them more effective legislators. Shortly thereafter, eighty members signed the caucus's liberal manifesto (Roof 2011, pp. 78, 136–137).

At a glance, the labor movement appeared to be more politically robust at the end of the 1950s due to a merger of the AFL and CIO in 1956. The visibility and strike successes of several big unions that had major contracts with the corporate giants in steel, auto, rubber, and other major industries contributed to this impression, as did the activism and calls for greater government spending by the UAW. Organized labor also had an impact within the Democratic Party because of the financial and human resources it could provide to Democratic candidates (Roof 2011, p. 89). However, less than a majority of union members were registered to vote, and not all of them voted Democratic (Boyle 1995, chapter 5). Further, the number of workers in unions had stagnated at about 17 million between 1954 and 1960, and the percent of non-agricultural workers in unions had declined from its near-high point of 34.8 in 1954 to 30.9 percent in 1960 (Mayer 2004, p. 22, table A1). Most of all, the union movement suffered significant defeats at the hands of the National Labor Relations Board and through the passage of the Landrum-Griffin Act.

Unions were in fact in a defensive and declining position in the overall power structure, even if their top leaders did not grasp—or admit to—that reality. Instead, they concentrated on the fact that they had defeated right-to-work initiatives in five of six states in 1958 (the loss was in Kansas) and contributed to the large gains made by the Democrats in both the House and the Senate in that same election. The national-level leadership of several unions also gave strong support to civil rights legislation, with the hope that African American voters would help to liberalize the Democratic Party in the South and thereby break the Southern Democrats' stranglehold on Congress.

But the liberal-labor alliance faced serious potential problems in the electoral arena because of the unwillingness of white workers to support the integration of African Americans into craft unions, especially in the construction industry (Frymer 2008, pp. 54–65). In 1959 the National Association for the Advancement of Colored People (NAACP) passed a resolution warning labor leaders that it might ask the National Labor Relations Board to decertify the many unions that were discriminating against black workers at the local level in both the North and the South. When black trade unionists brought several resolutions concerning discrimination to the floor of the annual AFL-CIO convention in that same year, the only support for the defeated measures came from the UAW (Quadagno 1994, p. 62; Roof 2011, p. 120).

Far overshadowing the successes of the liberal-labor alliance, the conservative coalition, working with a large operational majority during the first six years of the Eisenhower administration, won on most of its issues. More generally, it had won an impressive 92.4 percent of the votes on which it formed between 1939 and 1956 (Brady and Bullock 1980, p. 557). Due to the large influx of non-Southern Democrats into Congress after the 1958 elections, however, the operational size of the coalition fell to slightly less than a majority in both the House and Senate for the first time in the postwar era. It nonetheless won 57 percent of the time in the House on thirty votes and 67 percent in the Senate on eighty-six votes, including on the crucial Landrum-Griffin Act (Shelley 1983, pp. 34, 38). Its major losses were on the two civil rights bills, which seemed minor at the time but in hindsight can be understood as small steps that gave further leverage to the civil rights movement.

As for the US Chamber of Commerce, it had little to complain about during the Eisenhower years. It had supported state ownership of coastal lands, which freed the oil companies from regulation of their offshore drilling by the federal government, along with bills that helped the nuclear energy industry and one that reduced farm price supports, and of course it was all for the Landrum-Griffin Act. But it lost three times in its opposition to improvements in Social Security. It opposed a modest raise in the minimum wage, federal funds to build housing, and any federal assistance for higher education, all of which passed. This pattern of what it did and did not support continued for the next twenty-four years with generally the same outcomes.

The Eisenhower years showed once again that changes in the level of military spending had a significant impact on the economy. The spending on tanks, battleships, and airplanes was a reaction to what were perceived as deadly threats to the Grand Area that defined the American sphere of economic and political influence, as best shown by its leveling off or decline when the danger seemed to have passed for the time being

(Goertzel 1985). But such spending did provide a major economic stimulus after the Korean War began, and from then on it put a high floor under government spending even when it was not increasing. "In fat years and lean," as Bernard Nossiter, a veteran *Washington Post* economics reporter, put it in his retrospective account of the American economy from 1950 to 1990, "high levels of military outlays (ranging from 5 percent to 3 percent of the economy since 1950) have put a floor under effective demand, a break on every slide." Taking the Eisenhower administration as a case in point, $11 billion in defense cutbacks between July 1953 and July 1954 contributed to the rise in unemployment from 2.6 percent to 5.8 percent, and a reduction of $1 billion in mid-1957 contributed to a sharp but brief recession (Nossiter 1990, pp. 76–78, 204, 210–211). Later research on defense spending on the Korean War and other wars suggests that Nossiter was on the right track; every dollar in government outlays generates a $1.50 in nongovernment spending (Krugman 2012a, p. 236). More generally, with programs for veterans, the elderly, the disabled, and the unemployed also in place by the end of the Eisenhower era, the government had come to resemble an insurance company that controlled a large military establishment (Krugman 2011a).

As a result of higher unemployment rates and the continuing movement of unionized industries to the low-wage, anti-union South, the Gini coefficient for male urban workers crept up from its all-time lowest point of 0.317 in 1953 to 0.326 in 1960. In contrast, the effective tax rate on the top 1 percent of households was down to a little less than 25 percent by the late 1950s, half what it had been at the end of World War II. When these two figures are combined with the drop in union density, it seems clear that the liberal-labor alliance lost ground during the Eisenhower years in general as well as on many specific pieces of legislation.

As the Eisenhower era ended, the ongoing importance of the differences between the corporate moderates and the ultraconservatives was reaffirmed through a 1959 survey of corporate executives' perspectives on domestic and foreign policy issues. The researchers received complete responses from 152 of 302 business leaders. They held positions in one or more of six business groups between 1952 and 1959, including the National Association of Manufacturers, the US Chamber of Commerce, and the Committee for Economic Development, along with three minor groups, the ultraconservative American Enterprise Association, the equally conservative Tax Foundation, and the liberal National Planning Association, which are not relevant to this book because they were smaller or soon faded from view.

The largest number of respondents, fifty-nine in all, held what the two researchers called "fundamentalist" views on both types of issues. Thirty-three were fundamentalist on domestic issues and progressive on foreign policy issues, and thirty-four held "progressive" views on both types of issues. Of the forty NAM respondents who could be clearly classified, 75 percent were fundamentalists, 12.5 percent were progressive only on foreign policy issues, and 12.5 percent were progressives on both types of issues. Conversely, fifteen of twenty-four CED respondents were progressives on both types of issues (62.5 percent), 29.1 percent were progressives solely on foreign policy issues, and only two (8.3 percent) were fundamentalists (Woodhouse and McLellan 1966). Based on these findings, there is little or nothing that needed to be updated in

C. Wright Mills's (1948) earlier characterizations of "practical," "old-guard" conservatives and "sophisticated" conservatives, or in the large-scale study in the late 1940s that
documented the distinction between a classical and managerial creed (Sutton, Harris,
Kaysen, and Tobin 1956).

With the differences between corporate moderates and ultraconservatives in mind,
it is now time to see if the corporate dominance during the twenty-one years between
1939 and 1960 continued into the Kennedy and Johnson administrations, which by
the 1980s were viewed as the heyday of American liberalism.

Chapter Six

Corporate Moderate Successes in the Kennedy Years

Although the corporate moderates had few notable successes during the Eisenhower administration, it turned out that the CED's many reports from that era prepared the way for victories on trade and tax issues during the Kennedy administration. President Kennedy and his cabinet not only shared much in common with the corporate moderates on economic and trade issues but also needed some business support if they were going to make any inroads into the conservative coalition. Dashing liberal-labor hopes going into the 1960 elections, Republicans made major gains in the House, giving the conservative coalition a solid working majority. As a result, Kennedy, who had served in Congress from 1946 to 1960, always had the conservative coalition in the front of his mind as he tried to figure out the right timing for spending and civil rights bills in relation to other legislative projects (Schlesinger 1965, pp. 628–629, 657).

Moreover, the liberal-labor alliance seemed to be receding in importance outside Congress by 1961 because "union membership was declining, attempts to organize the unorganized were generally unsuccessful, and the AFL-CIO was torn by an internal jurisdictional battle between craft unions in the building trades and industrial unions in the mass production industries" (Gross 1995, p. 146). As noted in the previous chapter, it also faced growing tensions with the NAACP and the civil rights movement due to the resistance of craft union leaders and many members of the rank-and-file in both craft and industrial unions to any form of integration, North or South.

In keeping with Kennedy's concern to build strong links to the corporate community, several of his cabinet appointees were corporate leaders or members of the policy-planning network. For example, Dean Rusk, the president of the Rockefeller Foundation and a member of the Council on Foreign Relations, was appointed secretary of state; Robert McNamara, president of the Ford Motor Company, became secretary of defense; and C. Douglas Dillon (head of the investment banking firm of Dillon, Read, a member of the Council on Foreign Relations, and the undersecretary of state in the Eisenhower administration) became secretary of the treasury.

The secretary of commerce, Luther Hodges, onetime head of a textile mill and the former governor of North Carolina, also fit this mainstream pattern. But he unexpectedly had issues with the leaders of the Business Advisory Council, which complicated Kennedy's relationship with the corporate community. In February 1961, Hodges asked BAC leaders to reconsider the continuance of the CEO of General Electric as their chair in light of the fact that the company recently had pleaded guilty to taking part in a massive price-fixing and bid-rigging scheme that involved twenty-nine companies in the electrical equipment industry. Shortly thereafter, at least partly in response to congressional and journalistic criticisms of the BAC's secrecy and exclusive relationship with government, Hodges also asked its leaders to include more small-business representatives and to allow reporters to cover its meetings. Rather than totally accept Hodges's suggestions, the BAC made a unilateral withdrawal from its quasi-government role five months later and changed its name to the Business Council, announcing it was available to consult with any department or agency of the executive branch.

Although the several corporate appointees in the Kennedy administration provided direct lines of access, and the White House made immediate overtures to the reconfigured Business Council, corporate moderates knew that Kennedy was not in agreement with them on all issues. For example, he appointed the general counsel for the United Steel Workers, Arthur Goldberg, as his secretary of labor, and appointed moderates and liberals to head the Securities and Exchange Commission, the Federal Trade Commission, and the Federal Communications Commission. Most of all, Kennedy's first two appointees to the National Labor Relations Board were liberals, creating a new Democratic majority that made several controversial decisions. These decisions triggered strong opposition in the corporate community and the formation of a new corporate committee to do battle with organized labor. In addition, the president's executive order permitting the organizing of public-employee unions, issued in January 1962, heightened corporate wariness and led to a series of reports from organizations in the policy-planning network.

Kennedy's appointees to the Council of Economic Advisors also had a strong liberal cast, although not so strong that they were unacceptable from the CED's point of view. The chair, Walter Heller, a Keynesian economist from the University of Minnesota, and before that a CED staff member in 1946–1947, helped draft the CED's 1947 statement on tax policy. Ten years after his employment with the CED, Heller wrote a critique of its stabilizing budget policy in which he said that it could be improved upon "by increasing its reliance on discretionary relative to automatic fiscal controls." First, however, his critique noted that "having toiled rewardingly in the CED vineyards as a consultant and technical advisor on budgetary policy, and having been among the worshippers at the shrine of fiscal automaticity, I should perhaps note that this reappraisal has not been entirely unagonizing" (Heller 1957, pp. 634, 651). That is, Heller became a somewhat more liberal Keynesian in the intervening years, although he still agreed with the CED position that tax cuts were preferable to the increases in government spending still advocated by left-leaning Keynesians as a better way to stimulate the economy.

The two other CEA appointees were Kermit Gordon, a professor at Williams College and an economic advisor to the CED, and James Tobin, an innovative liberal Keynesian economist at Yale (he was awarded the Nobel Prize in Economics in 1981). Moreover, Kennedy appointed Paul Samuelson of MIT, by far the most visible and respected Keynesian economist in the United States, and the winner of the Nobel Prize in Economics in 1970, as one of his consultants. Samuelson was serving on the CED's Research Advisory Board at the time, which suggests that the corporate moderates were more willing to listen to liberal Keynesian ideas by the 1960s.

In addition to its ties to the Kennedy administration through its former employees and consultants working for the CEA, there were other early indications of direct CED connections, as recounted in a confidential memo that CED chair Donald K. David sent to all trustees at the time of the CED's annual meeting. He began by claiming, in relation to a report by Samuelson to the president on recession policy, "it just happened that this distinguished CED consultant was not only fully aware of CED's position regarding anti-recession policy, but almost completely embraced it as his own" (David 1961, p. 1). David also thought that a "Republican CED trustee from West Virginia, Dave Francis, Mayor of Huntington, who has been working to get CED ideas put to work in fighting chronic unemployment," had influenced the Kennedy administration's plans for spending on area development programs (David 1961, p. 2). (In addition to being mayor of Huntington, Francis was the president of Princess Coal, a major coal mining company.)

David expressed pleasure that the secretary of labor had "announced the establishment of an Office of Automation and Manpower, the duties of which sounded like a listing of the proposals of the CED policy statement on distressed areas which will be released a week from next Monday." The secretary of labor not only talked about "retraining programs, allowance payments, vesting of pensions, and the care needed in relocating plants, but also urged both management and labor to do something to 'create labor mobility.'" David went on to say that "our expert in this field tells us that for a public official to endorse 'labor mobility' is most extraordinary, if not unprecedented" (David 1961, p. 2).

In addition, David noted that an expert who consulted for the CED on housing issues had been appointed as an assistant in charge of planning for the Housing Administration and that two of the members of the task force that created the plans for Kennedy's Alliance for Progress, which passed with great fanfare and a large budget in 1961, were consultants to the CED on its report on *Cooperation for Progress in Latin America* (Committee for Economic Development 1961a). In concluding, however, he also reminded his colleagues it was no time to boast about these successes. He ended his three-page double-spaced report by saying, "This is a record of which we can be proud. On most of it we must remain silent" (David 1961, p. 3).

It is very likely that the CED chair, speaking to a trustees' meeting, exaggerated the influence of the committee on the substance of the various policies he mentioned, especially in the case of Samuelson, whose stature made him a force in his own right and hardly very concerned with the CED. However, David's remarks show at the least that the CED approved of these policies and that it had direct connections to the Kennedy administration through shared advisors.

THE TRADE EXPANSION ACT

The CED and corporate moderates in general had their first and most clear-cut success during the Kennedy administration with the passage of the Trade Expansion Act of 1962, which went significantly beyond previous trade legislation in allowing the executive branch to negotiate lower tariffs. The potential for success for the corporate moderates on this issue was most clearly signaled by the appointment of banker and CED trustee Howard Petersen, a major fundraiser for Eisenhower in 1952, as the president's special trade advisor. He was put in charge of drafting new trade legislation with the help of a staff of ten (Pastor 1980, p. 106; Preeg 1970, pp. 44–45). Just as he had done in his work with the CED, Petersen also served as a negotiator with the protectionist industries: "The campaign by the administration on the chemical industry was carried as far as a private meeting between Petersen and industry leaders in February at a session of the Manufacturing Chemists Association in New York" (Bauer, de Sola Pool, and Dexter 1963, p. 351). In the case of the even more politically crucial textile industry, a White House aide who worked for Petersen, lawyer Myer Feldman, a Democrat and a longtime aide to Kennedy since his Senate days, carried out the final negotiations.

The CED tried to aid in the process by publishing a new report in 1962 on trade policy, *A New Trade Policy for the United States,* just as the legislative process began. It argued that a more expansionary trade policy would stimulate the economy and help deal with unemployment, unused productive capacity, and the balance of payments problem. It warned that the United States could be shut out of the European Common Market if it did not open its own markets and that Third World countries might "turn to the Soviet bloc" if "they cannot find markets in the Free World" (Committee for Economic Development 1962a, pp. 5–6). It provided eleven specific recommendations in regard to the nature of the policy negotiations with foreign countries, along with a discussion of the size and distribution of tariff reductions by the United States.

After the Kennedy administration agreed to impose import quotas on foreign textiles and increase subsidies for Southern cotton growers, the industry agreed to the overall bill. And once the textile industry accepted the deal, the protectionists in Congress ended their opposition. As one study of the bill concludes, "It was the indirect effect of the administration's approach to and conversion of the textile lobby and to numerous other businessmen that indirectly affected Congress" (Bauer, de Sola Pool, and Dexter 1963, pp. 78, 362, 422). The bill as agreed to by the White House and Congress also included a provision for "adjustment assistance," which made it possible for the government to give financial compensation to those industries and workers that were directly harmed by import competition, even though the CED and the ultraconservatives in Congress did not favor that provision. Instead, it was a concession that Kennedy insisted upon to win support from organized labor. That concession to labor aside—and it was rarely used after the legislation passed because of continued resistance by the conservative coalition—the bill was a complete victory for the corporate moderates.

Once the bill was signed, a CED trustee from a multimillionaire San Francisco shipping family, William M. Roth, was named the president's special representative for trade. At the same time, the CED organized a major study that searched for a common North American–European trade policy in relation to Japan and Southeast Asia. It did so with the help of a four-year grant for $750,000 from the Ford Foundation and through the involvement of its "sister committees" of corporate leaders in Japan and several European countries. Petersen, who had resigned his White House position and returned full-time to his position at Fidelity-Philadelphia Trust Company, headed the new Subcommittee on East-West Trade. The subcommittee included the presidents or chairs of American Electric Power, Bank of America, Crown Zellerbach, Gillette, MGM, Pitney-Bowes, Sperry and Hutchinson, and Standard Oil of California, and the editor-in-chief of Cowles Magazines and Broadcasting. The advisors to the committee included an economist from the University of California, Berkeley, and the director of the European Institute at Columbia University (Committee for Economic Development 1965a).

The European Committee for Economic and Social Progress, consisting of corporate executives from France, Germany, and Italy, and the Japanese Committee for Economic Development, contributed input to the CED subcommittee's deliberations through position papers and the attendance of some of their own expert employees at subcommittee meetings. They also wrote supporting or dissenting comments that were published as part of the final report. The CED's counterparts in Europe and Japan were part of the infrastructure that was in the process of creating a more fully globalized economy. The CED's 1965 annual report noted, "There was a very large area of agreement on trade and credit policy toward the East by these groups of businessmen and scholars in the five leading industrial countries, policy toward Red China being the biggest exception." It then added that "the agreement between these five groups probably exceeded that achieved by their governments," which may be a commentary on the growing solidarity within an enlarged international corporate community, and also on the problems it faced in dealing with separate governments (Committee for Economic Development 1966c, p. 6).

Roth and his many assistants, guided in part by suggestions in the CED report and those in many other reports as well, then led the lengthy negotiations that culminated in a pact among fifty nations, finalized in 1967, that decreased tariffs on industrial products by one-third (Schriftgiesser 1967, p. 136). These negotiations were a very crucial step in the internationalization of the economy that corporate moderates had been advocating for over twenty years.

THE KENNEDY TAX CUT

The second big issue for the corporate moderates during the early 1960s was the need for major tax cuts to stimulate an economy that had gradually become more sluggish over the full course of the Eisenhower administration. Kennedy initially responded with several small pump-priming measures that were passed during the administration's first six months, including an increase in the minimum wage and the extension of unemployment benefits beyond their normal period. He called for an Area Redevelopment Act aimed at providing jobs through economic development programs in New England, Michigan, West Virginia, and Kentucky, which were suffering from the loss of old industries or the modernization of coal mining. A new housing bill was meant to provide a stimulus for urban economies. A year later, Congress passed the Manpower Development and Training Act, the first federal job training program, which was aimed at retraining workers who were losing their jobs to automation and technological change.

In addition, Kennedy used an executive order in early February to initiate a pilot food stamps program for low-income families. It was similar to one that had been used briefly in the late 1930s and then legislated on a trial basis in 1959, although the Eisenhower administration chose not to use it. The program was of special concern to Southern Democrats and other agricultural interests as a potential way to deal with agricultural surpluses. Although not foreseen at the time, it was destined to become a major piece of the federal government's safety net by 1975. Based on Kennedy's campaign claim that the Eisenhower administration had allowed the Soviet Union to move ahead of the United States in missile production, there was also a modest increase in defense spending. In terms of the overall economy, though, the combined increases in domestic and defense spending provided very little stimulation; an unemployment rate that had reached 7.1 percent in May 1961 fell to only 5.7 percent by the end of Kennedy's thirty-four months in office.

In effect, a CED campaign to sell Kennedy on its formula for a strong economy began with the release of a brief report, *Growth and Taxes: Steps for 1961,* a few weeks after he was inaugurated. It first recommended tax reductions for people in the higher brackets because high taxes were a burden on "effort, talent, enterprise, and investment" (Committee for Economic Development 1961c, p. 3). The report also advocated major changes in the way depreciation allowances were determined in order to give businesses more leeway about how much to deduct from their taxes to replace aging plants and equipment.

With a clear eye on creating more domestic jobs, the Kennedy administration countered with a legislative proposal that would provide a tax credit for new investments in plants and equipment for production within the United States. In return, it wanted to tax undistributed corporate profits that were kept in Europe and to discourage offshore tax havens, among several reforms. Recalling their battles with Roosevelt over the undistributed profits tax during the New Deal, no business groups liked this proposal. Although the conservative coalition rejected the undistributed profits tax, the investment tax credit passed a year later. At the same time, the changes in depreciation allowances advocated by the CED were made through actions that could be taken directly by the secretary of the treasury, who simply updated already approved depreciation schedules. In the end, then, business received two quick tax breaks, not just the one for which it lobbied.

Kennedy, who understood Keynesian economics and the case for a tax cut, remained hesitant because he did not want to be labeled as a big spender. But as economic conditions deteriorated over the next few months, including a very large one-day decline in the stock market in late May 1962, the idea of a tax cut seemed to take on more urgency. When Kennedy made a purposely vague announcement in June that he would propose tax reductions of one sort or another in the relatively near future, with the nature and size of the cuts still to be decided, the jockeying over how the tax breaks would be distributed began in earnest. However, the issue was complicated by Kennedy's desire to bring about tax reform at the same time, which was out of the question as far as all business groups were concerned, including the CED. Moreover, there were difficult problems facing the tax cutters because large reductions could be given to higher earners with relatively little loss of revenue, but even small reductions for the large majority, who now paid a large share of the total income taxes, would shrink the tax take considerably. Although tax reductions for the wealthy were the strong preference of the corporate moderates, it would not be politically easy for Democrats to pass big tax breaks for the rich and the corporations without including something for middle-income Democratic voters.

In December 1962, Kennedy presented his more specific plan for reducing taxes to a meeting of the conservative Economic Club in New York City. He attempted to short-circuit the objections he feared he would face by assuring the assembled executives and financiers that he also would avoid any "rush into a program of excessive government expenditures" (Schriftgiesser 1967, p. 108). Due to his mistaken belief that the primary concern of his audience was balancing the budget, he was surprised and pleased to receive far more applause and approval than he anticipated. As Stein, still the CED chief economist at the time, later pointed out in subtle and politically savvy detail, the corporate community was more than ready for tax cuts that boosted the economy and perhaps made future cuts in government expenditures more likely. Once again, that is, well before the idea became explicit in the Reagan years, virtually all corporate executives clearly believed that tax cuts would "limit and forestall the growth of expenditures," even if the tax cuts did not turn out to stimulate the economy as much as corporate moderates anticipated (Stein 1969, p. 433).

To show its support for Kennedy's proposal, which it was able to anticipate as far as its general outlines, thanks in part to informal communications between CED and CEA economists, the CED released a statement on *Reducing Tax Rates for Production and Growth* (Committee for Economic Development 1962b) on the morning of his scheduled speech. The headline on page one in the *Washington Post* announced that an "$11 Billion Cut in Taxes Urged by CED; Experts See Slash Aiding US Growth; Economic Group Would Postpone Reform Legislation" (Schriftgiesser 1967, p. 106). Kennedy read the report soon after his return to Washington; a few days later Heller told Stein that Kennedy was impressed with it (Collins 1981, p. 186). As if to confirm that point, Kennedy arranged for copies of the report to be given to each member of Congress.

The chair of the subcommittee that wrote the report, Frazar Wilde, chair and president of Connecticut General Life, was very familiar with all the issues because of his involvement in the discussions of taxing and finance within the CED over the past four years. The new report called for an $11 billion tax cut over the next two years, which would be accomplished by reducing the top marginal income tax rate from 90 percent to 65 percent between 1963 and 1965, along with a reduction in the corporate tax rate and a reduction in the capital gains tax.

In addition to advocating tax reductions of about the same size as those proposed by Kennedy, the CED report warned against trying to combine rate reduction with revenue-raising reforms because it would delay enactment of the tax legislation. It favored a two-step reduction in corporate taxes, from 52 to 47 percent, and then from 47 to 42 percent, if federal spending was held at its 1963 budget levels. However, it also recognized that cuts for middle-level individuals were politically necessary: "The hearts of the CED members belonged to reduction of the corporate profit tax and of the upper-bracket individual income taxes, coupled with restraint of federal spending. But they knew that for political reasons, and perhaps also for good economic reasons, the package would also have to include reduction of income taxes across the board and increased deficits, and they were willing to accept that" (Stein 1969, p. 419).

The CED's new statement provided Kennedy's tax-cut proposal with further legitimacy and political cover to his right. However, Kennedy's proposal dismayed members of the liberal-labor alliance. Its economists, led by spokesperson John K. Galbraith, believed that there was a far greater need for increased public spending, and they had been telling Kennedy that for many months. Although serving as Kennedy's ambassador to India, Galbraith criticized Kennedy's Economic Club speech as "the most Republican speech since McKinley" (Stein 1969, p. 421). Thus, Robert Collins seems on target when he concludes that Kennedy hardly sold his tax cut to a reluctant corporate community, as folklore often has it: "The popular view of John F. Kennedy pulling a benighted business community, kicking and screaming, into the modern age of political economy is clearly mistaken. Above all, the outcome indicates the pervasive influence which the postwar corporatist version of Keynesianism had on subsequent economic policy in the United States" (Collins 1981, pp. 199–200).

While members of Congress maneuvered and postured, corporate moderates, led by Wilde and Henry Ford II, the head of his family's Ford Motor Company, created the Business Committee for Tax Reduction to lobby Congress and work through the media to influence public opinion. Four of the six organizers were CED trustees, and twenty-three of the fifty executives invited to the formal organizational meeting were CED trustees. Wilde and CED economic advisor Theodore Yntema, who became a vice president for finance at Ford Motor in 1946, were among those who testified in favor of the bill before the Ways and Means Committee. According to Collins, the Business Committee for Tax Reduction was "the action agency for the CED constituency during the tax battle." It grew to a membership of 2,800 and its budget made it the third-largest Washington lobby in 1963 (Collins 1981, p. 192), This effort is noteworthy in and of its own right, but it is also another of the many examples of the fact that the corporate executives who became the heart of the Business Roundtable in the 1970s were already well organized for political action in the 1960s.

Reflecting the continuing disagreements within the corporate community, the US Chamber of Commerce called for even larger tax cuts, but not primarily to stimulate consumer spending. Sticking with pre-Keynesian economics, at least in its rhetoric, the chamber claimed that a tax cut was needed simply to encourage investment. The NAM did not take a stand either way on the bill but made clear that it was for tax cuts on the traditional grounds of encouraging investment and limiting the size of government, which supports Stein's point that many corporate leaders supported tax reductions simply because they hoped such cuts would help to shrink the government.

When all was said and done, the proposals for tax reform were completely abandoned in favor of simply passing a $10.2 billion tax cut over a two-year period. The top income tax bracket was dropped from 90 to 65 percent, which was in line with the CED recommendation. Corporate taxes were lowered from 52 to 46 percent, the capital gains tax was reduced, and depreciation allowances for the purchase of business equipment were increased. The legislation ended up as primarily a tax cut for the corporations and individuals in high-tax brackets. It set major precedents for future tax cuts that contributed to the increase in income inequality.

Moreover, the corporate community and the conservative coalition insisted on expenditure restraint in exchange for supporting the bill, a fact that leaders in the CED and Business Council frequently pointed out to the new president, Lyndon Johnson, and his appointees during the subsequent four years. Their insistence on spending restraints placed serious limits on the early responses to the civil rights movement and the rising turmoil in inner cities, leaving Johnson in a situation in which his programs came along too late with too little in terms of what was needed (Brown 1999). Due to the battle to remove the emphasis on reform, the tax cut did not pass until March 1964, which proved to be timely in terms of boosting Johnson's upcoming presidential campaign.

TENSIONS AND SETBACKS ON WAGE-PRICE GUIDELINES

Fully aware of the likelihood that the large-scale tax cuts it thought would be necessary to revive the economy might lead to inflation, the Kennedy administration had plans to introduce voluntary wage-price guidelines into the policy mix soon after it took office. It also worried that a wage-price spiral might jeopardize the international competitiveness of American corporations: "We cannot afford unsound wage and price movements which push up costs, weaken our international competitive position, restrict job opportunities, and jeopardize the health of our domestic economy," Kennedy wrote in a special message to Congress two weeks after the inauguration (Barber 1975, p. 141).

In talking about wage-price guidelines, the administration was broaching the sensitive subject of an incomes policy, through which employers, organized labor, and government officials might reach some understandings concerning prices and wages. The idea was not at all to the liking of either the corporate community or organized labor, albeit for separate reasons. As a first step, Kennedy had appointed an Advisory Committee on Labor-Management Policy, consisting of top business leaders and major union presidents, which was charged with the responsibility of recommending measures to meet the goal of wage-price stability. In addition to sending a strong message to the corporate community and organized labor on the dangers of inflation, it was hoped that American allies would understand the advisory committee "as evidence that the Kennedy Administration was in earnest about wage and price discipline to ease the balance-of-payments problem" (Barber 1975, pp. 142, 153). However, the committee could not achieve consensus, and the corporate members strongly rejected any semblance of government guidelines or hearings in relation to price increases.

As the labor-management advisory committee floundered, the administration carried out discrete efforts behind the scenes (largely through members of the CEA and its staff) to limit the size of any wage increase resulting from the 1962 contract negotiations between the United Steel Workers and the steel industry. As part of this effort, Secretary of Labor Goldberg put his credibility on the line with organized labor by urging the steelworkers to keep their wage demands within the bounds set by productivity gains. Kennedy then talked personally with the president of the steel workers, leading to his reluctant acceptance of the Kennedy-Goldberg pleas to maintain political solidarity with the pro-labor president. The White House also thought it had reached an understanding with US Steel, the industry's price leader, that it would not raise prices. In fact, Kennedy and Goldberg had met with the president of the steel workers and Roger Blough, the chair of US Steel, as a way to finalize an agreement that had involved lengthy negotiations (Barber 1975, pp. 167–168). The settlement therefore occurred within a context that was consistent with the CED's 1957 report on inflation. In fact, the position the administration advanced was parallel ("almost word for word") to the CED's official recommendation back in 1958, but the policy was nonetheless unpopular in the corporate community, even among many corporate moderates in the CED (Schriftgiesser 1967, p. 89).

Two weeks after the settlement was announced, Blough asked for a White House appointment on only a few hours' notice and told Kennedy that US Steel had decided to raise its prices by $6 a ton. Kennedy was taken by surprise, but he knew he was not the first president to have problems with the steel industry. Truman faced three similar confrontations between 1946 and 1952, ordering the combatants to the White House to resume negotiations in 1946 and temporarily taking over the industry in 1952, only to have the Supreme Court rule that his action was illegal. The Eisenhower administration was drawn into an intermediary role in a steel strike in 1956 but kept its involvement secret, and it had to set the terms for the settlement of a 116-day steel strike in 1959, which specifically prohibited an increase in steel prices (Gordon 1975, pp. 128–129). A study prepared by two economists for the Joint Economic Committee in 1959 concluded that increases in steel prices "had contributed greatly" to inflation in the late 1950s (Barber 1975, p. 155).

With the prestige of the presidency and the concept of wage-price guidelines at stake, as well as his own image in the eyes of the union movement, Kennedy immediately took several highly publicized actions to force Blough to rescind the price increase. In doing so, he was taking on not only the steel industry but one of the most powerful members of the corporate community as well, because Blough was also the chair of the Business Council and a trustee of the CED. After beginning his career in the early 1930s at a Wall Street law firm representing the J. P. Morgan financial complex, which put together US Steel in 1901 in one of the biggest mergers of that era, Blough became the president of the company in 1955. He had an increasingly large role in most of the key events over the subsequent twenty years, including the steps that led to the formation of the Business Roundtable in 1972.

Kennedy's strong reactions to what he saw as a double-cross by Blough included threats of antitrust actions, other types of government investigations, and the transfer of government steel purchases to companies that did not raise their prices. At the same time, his aides used their contacts to convince Joseph Block, the president of Inland Steel, and also a CED trustee, to hold the line on prices. The battle was over in seventy-two hours when US Steel announced that it would rescind its price increases. For Blough and other corporate leaders, it was a worrisome reminder of the potential power of the government to dictate to the corporate community, at least in the short run (Schlesinger 1965, pp. 636–639).

Although the administration soon claimed that the outcome of its first serious attempt at institutionalizing restraint by both corporations and unions was on balance a successful one, even though there were subsequent piecemeal price hikes by most steel companies, it was hesitant thereafter to become actively involved in contract negotiations. In the aftermath, one of Kennedy's CEA appointees did a careful study of the experience of several European governments with wage-price policies and concluded that they did not do any better in holding down wages and prices, even though they had more power over these issues than did the American government (Barber 1975, p. 175).

Moreover, the episode reinforced organized labor's wariness of guidelines as more likely to restrain wages than prices, partly because wages are more easily monitored than prices but also because of the corporate community's general clout. In addition, agreeing to wage-price guidelines would imply that organized labor tacitly accepted the current distribution of income between wages and profits as being fair, but that seemed morally wrong to many union activists, liberals, and leftists, especially at a time when profits were soaring (Dark 2001, pp. 64–66).

KENNEDY, THE CORPORATE COMMUNITY, AND CIVIL RIGHTS

Although trade legislation, tax cuts, and wage-price guidelines were the essential items on the corporate moderates' agenda in the early 1960s, they were not the most visible and defining features of Kennedy's presidency. Instead, the headlines, and much of his time and energy, were given over to major Cold War crises, such as the failed invasion of Cuba in April 1961 and the Cuban Missile Crisis in the fall of 1962. Even more, these were the years of the sudden emergence of the civil rights movement to national prominence through nonviolent disruptions of normal routines, which began with sit-ins at lunch counters in Greensboro, North Carolina, in late January 1960, just as the presidential primary campaigns were getting under way. The sit-ins were followed by freedom rides into segregated bus stations in the Deep South in the spring of 1961, the integration of the University of Mississippi with the aid of federal marshals and troops in 1962, and the escalation of tensions in Birmingham, Alabama, in the spring of 1963, which led to a church bombing and the deaths of four preteen and adolescent girls in mid-September.

Kennedy took his first legal action against segregation two months after his inauguration when he issued an executive order that banned discrimination in hiring decisions on the basis of race, religion, or national origins by federal agencies or by companies that had federal contracts. In addition, it called for "affirmative action" in future hiring. Significantly, the order applied to unions that controlled apprenticeship programs as well as to the companies themselves. Named the President's Committee on Equal Employment Opportunity (PCEEO), it had a larger staff and budget than a voluntary and largely ineffective contract compliance committee established during the Eisenhower administration. It also had the power to ask for company employment statistics, to publicize the names of companies that discriminated, and to suspend government contracts (Delton 2009, p. 177; Golland 2011, chapter 2).

Kennedy appointed his reluctant vice president, Lyndon Johnson, as the committee's chair. Although hesitant to tackle the issue, Johnson took complete control of the committee once it became clear that he could not avoid what he saw as a politically risky assignment. The committee included many Kennedy loyalists, but Johnson hired one of his 1960 presidential supporters from the African American community, Hobart Taylor Jr., a graduate of the University of Michigan Law School, as the committee's special counsel. Taylor, whose father was a multimillionaire taxi company owner in Houston, was an ideal choice for Johnson. Not only was Taylor's father a longtime political ally and financial supporter of Johnson's, but Taylor himself was close to the leadership of the Democratic Party in Michigan through his employment in that state after law school.

Although usually opposed to government regulations on principle, corporate leaders did not respond negatively to Kennedy's order. In fact, some of them had a long history of publicly supporting fair employment, including CED trustees Fred Lazarus of Federated Department Stores and Fred Borch of General Electric, and some companies had gained experience in dealing with discrimination issues through their interactions with state-level Fair Employment Commissions. Lazarus, a vice chair at the CED and a leader in antidiscrimination causes in the Jewish community, had served on Eisenhower's version of the committee. A Republican, he was reappointed to serve on the advisory committee to Kennedy's PCEEO, on which he was joined by another CED trustee, Donald C. Cook, the president of American Electric Power, as well as several highly visible figures in a range of civic and cultural organizations.

Specific corporate leaders aside, the idea of fair and open employment fit with the corporate community's emphasis on the individual freedom of each worker. In addition, the industrial relations departments that corporations created after World War I (at least in fair measure to fend off unions) were well enough staffed to take on the responsibility for issues of integration and compliance, albeit with some additional training. Moreover, a fully integrated workforce did not conflict with an anti-union bias. As historian Jennifer Delton (2009, p. 279) points out in her detailed history of corporate compliance with civil rights laws, "Racial integration did not require that businesses give up their fundamentally conservative goals."

Shortly after the PCEEO was in operation, its director told the US Air Force that a new billion-dollar contract for Lockheed to manufacture massive cargo planes in its plant just outside of Atlanta would not be certified because the company was not in compliance with the new rules. At the same time, the NAACP Legal Defense Fund filed a lawsuit against Lockheed to test the strength of the new executive order. The California-based company agreed to what in the heat of the moment was called a "plan for progress." After negotiations involving the highest levels of Lockheed and several other companies, the companies pledged to change their hiring and promotion practices (Feild 1967, pp. 27–28). Several other defense companies soon signed on to similar plans, although there is reason to doubt their effectiveness in the first years (Golland 2011, chapter 2).

The National Association of Manufacturers, which first put itself on record in support of equal employment for African Americans and women at its annual meeting in 1940, gradually realized the possibilities for industry that the plans for progress contained. However, to ensure that companies would not be subject to any arbitrary government sanctions, its legal department sent a twenty-six-page statement to the PCEEO in June in an effort to clarify the details of the executive order and "to find solutions which will not endanger or deter in any manner the national defense effort"; to begin with, its lawyers asked for definitions of "discrimination" and "affirmative action" and a set of objective guidelines for determining if and when discrimination occurred (Delton 2009, p. 182). It wanted the government to establish procedures for appeals at official hearings on complaints brought against companies. It reminded the committee that the terms of government contracts were the province of the legislative branch, which implied that the issue might end up in the hands of the conservative coalition if the corporate community and the White House could not reach agreement on the issues NAM raised. The statement repeatedly mentioned that the cancellation of contracts might jeopardize national security. A year later, NAM hired a vice president from General Dynamics as its new president, who immediately expanded the association's efforts to end discrimination in employment.

Liberals in the Kennedy administration did not appreciate the pressure from NAM, but they set about to tighten up their procedures and guidelines. At the same time, Johnson appointed an Atlanta-based corporate lawyer to involve more companies in plans for progress within a context of voluntary compliance. However, the director of the PCEEO, an experienced fair-employment compliance officer from Michigan, doubted the efficacy of voluntary compliance and therefore advocated strong regulations and regular detailed compliance reports. At the same time, African American leaders in the NAACP and the Urban League publicly stated that the plans for progress were unlikely to be adequate.

The tensions within the PCEEO over the degree of regulation and enforcement became public when the Southern Regional Council, a small liberal outpost in Atlanta, issued a report claiming that most of the companies it had studied were not in compliance. It also noted that the three largest companies in its study, Lockheed, Goodyear, and Western Electric, were living up to their promises. But the positive side of the report did not make it into newspaper headlines. Johnson, annoyed by the negative publicity his committee was receiving, eased out the Atlanta lawyer in September 1962. At the same time he made his friend Taylor the executive vice chair, which eliminated the need for the liberal executive director, who was considered a pro-Kennedy appointee by Johnson.

From Johnson's point of view, Taylor proved to be an excellent liaison to corporate leaders, who continued to embrace the idea of compliance through signing plans for progress. In June 1963 they organized and financed a new quasi-independent advisory council, consisting of nineteen executives from defense companies, calling it Plans for Progress. However, they insisted that it remain a part of the PCEEO, which kept them in formal contact with Johnson and Kennedy on employment issues. In effect, Plans for Progress was a more specialized example of the original Business Advisory Council created by the corporate community in 1933. By that point an initially wary NAM supported Plans for Progress, touting it as a way to "maintain the credibility of voluntarism and to increase businesses' leadership role in equal employment opportunity" (Delton 2009, p. 182). The association also saw Plans for Progress as protection against criticisms and possible boycotts. As part of this new effort, NAM hosted workshops for corporate executives, and in late 1963 it helped organize an informational session about Plans for Progress that brought sixty-four company representatives to the White House. It then held a follow-up meeting with those companies.

With few exceptions, the union movement reacted very negatively to the executive order, which banned discrimination by their apprenticeship programs as well as discrimination by employers. Most—but not all—industrial unions signed a voluntary pledge to end discrimination, which they called Union Programs for Fair Practices to distinguish it from Plans for Progress. However, most of the craft unions refused to sign such a pledge, and even after they eventually did so, they continued to exclude African Americans from apprenticeship programs, or refused to take them into their unions if they gained accreditation through government programs. They saw the PCEEO as the beginning of an attack on what they had slowly achieved, a job niche that paid well and that could be passed on to their children or the children of their friends and neighbors. In sociologist Jill Quadagno's (1994, p. 65) telling phrase, they felt they had "property rights" in their jobs that were more basic than the right to equal access. More abstractly, the construction unions resisted on the basis of the gradualist version of liberalism that had been articulated by the liberal-labor alliance in the postwar era, which made it difficult to counter their arguments against any form of affirmative action (Sugrue 2001).

The general union resistance to integration soon led to protests and temporary shutdowns instigated by African Americans at construction sites in the North, especially in Philadelphia, where months of serious confrontation developed just as events in Birmingham were unfolding in April 1963. Although some of these demonstrations were called in support of the nonviolent protesters in Birmingham, the Northern activists were reacting to two years of adamant resistance to their efforts at local job integration by white craft workers, and they showed little respect for a nonviolent approach. When Kennedy sent his secretary of labor and members of his White House staff to survey the situation in several different cities, their reports revealed an increasing potential for violence. This alarming conclusion led Kennedy to make a major civil rights speech on June 11. Eleven days later, he issued a second executive order related to civil rights, this one explicitly banning discrimination on all construction sites that involved a federal contract. The day after the executive order was announced, Walter Reuther, the liberal and assertive president of the United Auto Workers, joined Martin Luther King Jr. in leading a "Walk for Freedom" in Detroit. But few of the 125,000 to 200,000 marchers were white (Sugrue 2008, p. 298). Shortly thereafter, the importance of the new executive order, and any possible confrontations over it, were overshadowed by Kennedy's announcement that his administration had begun the process of drafting new civil rights legislation that would deal with all forms of discrimination.

Despite new assurances by several top union leaders of a willingness to change their policies, the most that the construction unions would do was to support training programs, which provided Kennedy with a line of least resistance (Quadagno 1994, pp. 64–74). He shifted the emphasis of the Manpower Development and Training Act to African Americans in large urban areas and was receptive to new pilot programs designed to prepare African Americans to be workers through remedial education and job-training programs. In the process of what was in good part a stalling operation in the hope that craft unions would slowly integrate, the Kennedy administration in effect shifted the onus for the exclusion of African Americans from whites' determination to protect their jobs to the alleged educational and psychological deficiencies of black applicants.

Although the Manpower Development and Training Act was by then reasonably well established on the basis of support by congressional Democrats, the new pilot programs emerged from already existing foundation-funded pilot projects, which had their origins in the late 1950s. These private programs had been created in response to the rising urban tensions generated by a combination of the continuing migration of African Americans to major Northern cities, the fierce resistance to neighborhood integration by most Northern whites, and not least, the pressures that urban renewal projects put on black neighborhoods.

THE FORD FOUNDATION, THE CED, AND THE INNER CITY

In the face of white resistance to both union and neighborhood integration, the Kennedy administration, in the persons of Attorney General Robert F. Kennedy and his staff, was receptive to overtures from administrators at the Ford Foundation concerning their new pilot programs for dealing with the rising urban tensions. From a present-day perspective, at a time when there are large numbers of massive foundations with assets in the billions, it is difficult to comprehend the size, impact, and stature of the Ford Foundation. In 1968, despite a number of immense grants of unprecedented proportions over the previous fifteen years, it had four times more assets ($3.7 billion) than the second-ranked Rockefeller Foundation and ten times more than another prominent policy-oriented foundation, the Carnegie Corporation, and it held two-thirds of the total assets possessed by the thirty-three largest foundations (Nielsen 1972, p. 22). Employing by far the largest staff of experts on a wide range of topics, the Ford Foundation was truly the nine-hundred-pound gorilla of the foundation world. However, the Ford Foundation did not work alone. Usually starting with three or four other large New York foundations, it strived to create a network of funders for each policy issue of interest to its trustees, and to gradually shift as much of the financial support as possible to the other foundations once a program was established, thereby freeing its budget to support new initiatives. It also established contact with, or created, university-based research institutes and consortiums on a wide range of issues, including population control, the conservation of resources, international relations, and urban affairs.

As part of its network focus, the Ford Foundation's trustees developed close working relations with the CED. This process began when founding CED chair Paul Hoffman served as its president from 1950 to 1953, but it came to full fruition when CED trustee Donald K. David, a close advisor to the Ford family, became the vice chair of its board in 1953. With his extensive corporate contacts through serving as the dean of the Harvard Business School from 1942 through 1955, along with his involvement in the CED, David was fully trusted by Henry Ford II and the other trustees. At the same time, the board included two other CED trustees, James F. Brownlee, a Wall Street investment banker and the chair of the board of Minute Maid Corporation, and Roy E. Larsen, the president of Time, Inc., who sat on the boards of numerous corporations and policy groups while overseeing the publication of *Time, Life, Fortune,* and several other magazines. Another CED trustee, J. Irwin Miller, the president of Cummins Engine, joined the foundation's board in 1961.

Policy-oriented grants were given out through three main programs—one for international affairs, one for education and research, and one for public affairs. From the outset, the public affairs program concentrated on the inner city, a term I use to denote both black and white neighborhoods. Significantly, many of these neighborhoods were in the way of downtown expansion, or else near elite universities (e.g., Yale, Columbia, and the University of Chicago), which felt threatened by black migrants and were in need of land for their own expansion. The foundation began its public affairs efforts with a start-up grant of $250,000 ($2.1 million in 2012 dollars) in early 1955 to the American Council to Improve Our Neighborhoods (ACTION), a new nonprofit advocacy organization in which Larsen of Time, Inc. and the CED played a large role.

ACTION was established in November 1954 in response to President Eisenhower's Commission on Urban Renewal and Housing, which claimed that the implementation of the urban renewal program recently legislated by Congress would be aided by "the formation outside of government of a broadly representative national organization to help promote and lead this dynamic program for renewal of the towns and cities in America" (President's Advisory Committee 1953, p. 2). ACTION's board of trustees included bankers, corporate executives, and real estate developers as well as urban planners and housing experts from major cities across the country. Its ambitious program included three main aspects: (1) a research division that would amass all available information on how to carry out a sound program, (2) a technical assistance program to provide expert advisors to both private and governmental groups interested in this issue, and (3) a national advertising campaign to generate public concern with neighborhood decline. Time, Inc. made a movie to extol urban renewal's virtues, and the Advertising Council ran a national ad campaign for it through newspapers, magazines, and television. Its articles in major magazines led to a concentration on New Haven, Connecticut, the home of Yale University, as the ideal example of what urban renewal could accomplish (Domhoff 1978, pp. 41–44).

About the same time as the grant to ACTION was awarded, the foundation hired Paul Ylvisaker, a political scientist teaching at Swarthmore, to head its Public Affairs Program. Ylvisaker, with a PhD from Harvard, had an interest in cities and expertise in rural migrations, along with practical experience in urban politics as the executive secretary to the reform mayor in Philadelphia, where a major urban renewal program was under way. As Ylvisaker explained in an oral history after he left the foundation, he began his new job by meeting with the "power structures" in fourteen cities, along with the mayors and the superintendents of schools: "We were always working in that setting of powerful men," he explained, "keeping their ties intact and judging things from that point of view" (Ylvisaker 1973, pp. 15, 20).

Ylvisaker also had conversations with the foundation's trustees, who told him that the foundation could not address the issue of race directly, despite the obvious racial dimensions of the urban tensions with which he would be dealing. This prohibition was later corroborated in a historical study of the foundation's urban program during its early years (O'Connor 1996, pp. 591–592). Ylvisaker's oral history clearly reveals that he and other members of the foundation's staff were constantly checking with both foundation trustees and city leaders. As he remarked in relation to creating a community foundation in Cleveland, Ohio, which became the main funder of that city's urban programs and the prototype for the Ford Foundation's efforts to create community foundations throughout the country, he thought it made sense to check with key leaders there because he knew that Donald K. David, his superior at the foundation, would be talking with them, too (Ylvisaker 1973, pp. 46–47). Ylvisaker also met with experts on cities and minority populations, and hired some of them as consultants. While these consultations were going on, the foundation started giving large grants to universities for research on metropolitan areas and urban problems, including a center on urban and regional problems cosponsored by MIT and Harvard. The reports from these projects became a key source of information for Ylvisaker and gave him "a network of able associates around the country" (Tittle 1992, p. 106).

Thanks to this large network and his own training, Ylvisaker knew that most neighborhood improvement and community development associations in large cities were attempting to maintain white neighborhoods that could retain and attract middle-class whites. In addition, the terminology used by the social scientists that studied neighborhoods reinforced the view that African Americans were seen as a threat. For example, a 1957 book on African Americans in Chicago by two prominent sociologists spoke of "penetration," "invasion," "consolidation," and "piling-up" as the four stages in the racial change of a neighborhood from white to black. "Piling-up" referred to the point at which "the number of blacks exceeds the original number of whites" due to the desperate need for housing on the part of African Americans and the willingness of slumlords to overcrowd their rental properties in a search for higher profits (see Molotch 1972, pp. 4–6, for an account of how some mainstream social scientists viewed black migration).

Ylvisaker and the staff members for the programs the foundation sponsored also knew from their close contacts with leaders and activists in black communities that the level of militancy was rapidly increasing. They came to believe that black leaders had to play meaningful roles in any new programs, which made the situation both an opportunity for reforms and a threat of further disruption. The consultants and staff experts disagreed among themselves on just how to bring about desired changes and on how much black participation should be encouraged, which led to serious intellectual and personal disputes. However, all of them sought reform and incorporation, not pacification or resubjugation, that is, a forward-looking and accommodative strategy. As a result, they were heartily criticized and opposed by both machine Democrats and ultraconservatives, who wanted to maintain the status quo as much as possible (Knapp and Polk 1971, p. 11).

In 1959, the Ford Foundation announced a "Great Cities School Improvement" program to aid inner-city schools in ten large industrial cities, headed by Benjamin Willis, an African American who was superintendent of the Chicago city school system (O'Connor 1999, p. 175). However, Ylvisaker and his staff soon realized that a school program was not going to be enough, so they added a comprehensive program to aid "Gray Areas," which were defined as "slums or rapidly changing neighborhoods abandoned by the middle class and inhabited by low-income families, racial minorities, and recent migrants from rural areas or other cities" (Ford Foundation 1961, p. 55). According to Ylvisaker, the project was a way to deal with the opposition to urban renewal projects that were supported by foundation trustees (Ylvisaker 1973, pp. 23–25).

Basically, the foundation's overall goal was to bring about a "comprehensive involvement of other community resources—social, health and welfare agencies; urban renewal and housing bodies; the courts and the police; and religious organizations" (Ford Foundation 1961, p. 24; see also Halpern 1995 for a detailed account of these programs). As part of this vision, the foundation spent $26.5 million between 1961 and 1965 to support community action agencies in Boston; New Haven; Philadelphia; Washington, DC; and Oakland, California. There were also preschool programs, a youth development program, and a program to introduce police officers to the background assumptions and long-term goals of the project.

Ylvisaker began working with the Kennedy administration in 1961 after his immediate superior, a foundation vice president, met with one of Robert Kennedy's aides in Washington to explain the Gray Areas program and a similar pilot program for dealing with gang conflicts. Soon thereafter, the foundation, the White House, the National Institute of Mental Health, and New York City jointly funded a pilot program to tackle problems of juvenile delinquency and crime by involving teen gang members in more constructive activities (O'Connor 1996, pp. 599, 612). This and other government collaborations with the Ford Foundation were meant to remain small and be tested in a step-by-step fashion before they became any larger.

The CED efforts paralleled those of the Ford Foundation and often built on the foundation's initiatives. In 1957 the CED created an Area Development Committee to focus on urban-metropolitan issues, headed by the chair of Lever Brothers, with Ylvisaker serving as one of its advisors in its early years. The Area Development Committee's first policy statement, *Guiding Metropolitan Growth* (Committee for Economic Development 1960a), drew on reports by members of the foundation's network of experts. Raymond Vernon of Harvard, the leader of the Ford-financed New York Metropolitan Regional Study, wrote a CED supplemental booklet, *The Changing Economic Function of the Central City* (Vernon 1959). It "raised fundamental questions about the progressive downgrading of urban values" (Schriftgiesser 1967, p. 172). Political scientist Robert Wood of MIT, a participant in the Joint Center for Urban Studies at Harvard and MIT, and also a member of the New York metropolitan study, contributed a similar report, *Metropolis against Itself* (Wood 1959), which suggested that some urban functions might be better served by metropolitan governments. The 1960 CED statement, fashioned on the basis of these and other advisory reports from experts, supported urban renewal, advocated metropolitan-wide planning and economic development, and criticized local governments for not meeting their full responsibilities. It thereby provided the framework for an urban agenda that the CED adapted to changing circumstances over the next twenty years, often in close conjunction with new initiatives sponsored by the Ford Foundation (Schriftgiesser 1967, chapter 19).

The CED also drew on the Ford Foundation network and other social scientists for policy statements related to education and the revival of depressed areas. *Paying for Better Schools* (Committee for Economic Development 1959) supported federal expenditures for consolidated schools in low-income and rural areas in states in which per-capita income was less than 80 percent of the national median, a formula that would bring aid to Maine and most Southern states. The sums involved were modest, and there would be no strings attached to them, but a very divisive issue that had been debated since the 1940s lurked in the background: the use of federal funds to support segregated schools in the South. Fourteen of the fifty-two CED trustees on either the subcommittee or the Research and Policy Committee opposed publication of the new policy statement because they believed that school funding should remain a state and local responsibility.

Working through its Area Development Committee, the CED next reached beyond schools to support federal aid for local low-income economies through a report on *Distressed Areas in a Growing Economy* (Committee for Economic Development 1961b). The report expressed approval for various economic programs that had been discussed during the Eisenhower administration and then proposed by Kennedy in his first year in office, which led to the Area Redevelopment Act of 1962 with strong support from most congressional Democrats. The CED's statement first reaffirmed its support for schools in states with low per-capita incomes. It then suggested that such support be extended to include federal vocational aid and unemployment insurance for workers who were being retrained through federally supported programs, such as the one embodied in Kennedy's 1962 Manpower Development and Training Act. It also urged the federal government to build government facilities in distressed areas and to provide more rapid depreciation allowances to corporations that build plants in them. Finally, it seconded a Ford Foundation proposal that a highly visible federal executive should have responsibility for coordinating the various programs for distressed areas (Schriftgiesser 1967, pp. 174–177). The statement did not lead to the two acts that passed in 1962, but it did express support for the substance of this type of legislation.

THE GENERAL SIGNIFICANCE OF THE KENNEDY YEARS

In combination with the Trade Expansion Act passed in 1962, the passage of the tax cut in 1964 marked the fulfillment of the CED's basic goals when it formulated its agenda in the 1940s. At the same time, CED trustees and other corporate moderates showed their willingness to consider new issues by lending their support to the administration's efforts to cope with the civil rights movement in the South and inner-city tensions in the urban North. They also published statements supporting federal aid to schools in low-income states and backed federal programs for retraining workers and aiding depressed areas. Along with the support many of their individual corporations gave to Plans for Progress, these policy statements signaled their acceptance of the civil rights and social welfare legislation later passed during the Johnson years. Even the NAM was supportive of government programs to integrate the workforce, which made the passage of the Civil Rights Act in 1964 much more possible by taking some of the pressures off the conservative Republicans in Congress that might have opposed it otherwise.

As for the US Chamber of Commerce, its successes were few and far between. It opposed all of the education, urban, and farm support programs that passed between 1961 and 1963. In all, the chamber took a stand on fourteen pieces of legislation during the Kennedy years, losing on all but four of them. These defeats became a major reason why journalists and social scientists came to believe that business as a whole was now sharing power in a pluralist fashion with elected officials and a variety of interest groups. The conservative coalition also suffered several defeats in the same years, thanks in part to the modest nature of the programs Kennedy proposed and support for them from corporate moderates. The conservative coalition formed 150 times in the Senate, but it seldom realized its full potential, winning on only 53 percent of the occasions. It formed less frequently in the House, 54 times, but won more often, with a 63 percent success rate (Shelley 1983, pp. 34, 38). However, it maintained its preeminence on issues related to unions during the Kennedy years, as will be shown in Chapter 8.

Income inequality, the effective tax rate, and union density did not change much during Kennedy's three years in office. The Gini coefficient was 0.329 in 1961 and 0.325 in both 1962 and 1963. Union density was down only a percentage point or two, to 28.5 percent. The effective tax rate fell to 23.6 percent in 1963, a figure that would not be surpassed until the end of the first Reagan administration.

The end of the Kennedy administration also marks the end point for Robert Collins's in-depth archival research on the CED, so his summary of the impact of the committee during its first twenty-two years provides a useful foundation for my analysis of its role—and the role of corporate moderates in general—from the mid-1960s to the end of the first Reagan administration. In his view, the CED "dramatically" moved the "spectrum of business opinion" from an insistence on a balanced budget each year to the acceptance of several useful Keynesian insights: "To be sure, the shift was as uneven as it was gradual; but the 1964 tax cut proved conclusively that the doctrine of the annually balanced budget, the linchpin of pre-Keynesian orthodoxy, no longer held together the disparate forces of organized business." Put more specifically, "The CED's variant of Keynesianism promised economic stability with minimal enlargement of the civilian public sector, stressed automaticity, and depended on manipulation of government revenues, rather than increased spending, in an emergency" (Collins 1981, pp. 194, 198).

For all the roadblocks and delays caused by the ultraconservatives on economic issues, the policy debates within the political arena for the following decade concerned which version of Keynesianism would prevail. Would there be reliance on tax cuts to revive the economy and on restrictive monetary policies to cool it off, as the CED urged? Or would there be greater expenditures by government in the face of downturns, and even the expanded use of government projects to increase employment, as the liberal-labor alliance advocated, along with higher taxes on upper-income groups and lower government expenditures if inflation threatened?

Future debates aside, between the years 1942 and 1964 the corporate moderates' approach to economic, tax, and domestic policy issues had won out every time over the liberal-labor position, although the corporate moderates were sometimes beaten by the ultraconservatives. The only victories in which the liberal-labor alliance took part were on mild stimulus measures that helped lower-income people, including unemployment insurance, expansion of Social Security benefits, training programs for low-income workers, and food stamps. Corporate moderates accepted all of these measures, and a significant number of Southern Democrats supported several of them in exchange for state-level control of the programs and a disproportionate share of the rewards for Southern states.

Although corporate moderates supported a wide range of government-based benefit, education, and training programs in the early 1960s—providing a dramatic contrast with the positions taken by the US Chamber of Commerce—they nonetheless joined ultraconservatives in opposing several decisions made by the Democratic majority on the National Labor Relations Board. They also disagreed with Kennedy's executive order in 1962 permitting representation for public employees. These decisions and the ensuing conflicts are discussed at greater length in Chapter 8. But first it is necessary to see how events during the Johnson administration heightened corporate conflict with the liberal-labor alliance as well as increased the tensions between organized labor and the civil rights movement.

Chapter Seven

Corporate Moderation and More Success

THE JOHNSON YEARS

Coordination between the corporate community and the White House increased in 1964 and 1965 in the face of the civil rights challenge and the escalation of the Vietnam War. Johnson also conferred often with the two most powerful leaders in the union movement, George Meany, still president of the AFL-CIO, and Walter Reuther, still head of the United Auto Workers and the de facto leader of the most liberal segment of the union movement. Johnson also enjoyed the benefit of a solidly growing economy in 1964 and a booming economy in 1965. Unemployment declined from 5.5 percent at the end of 1963 to 5.0 percent at the end of 1964 and 4.0 percent at the end of 1965, a level that approached the low rates during the Korean War. These years are the main basis for the belief that Keynesian-based policies could lead to prosperity for all Americans.

However, the increases in government revenues that resulted from the robust economic growth did not tempt Johnson to abandon the limits on government expenditures championed by the corporate community, even in the face of growing unrest and disruption by African Americans in both the South and North, and despite urgent pleas for more spending by the liberal-labor alliance. Instead, he intended to abide by his reassurances to the corporate community that he would keep the budget under $100 billion.

QUIET CORPORATE SUPPORT FOR CIVIL RIGHTS

As might be expected from the defense contractors' generally positive reaction to Kennedy's executive order on discrimination in hiring, most moderates and even some ultraconservatives within the corporate community were quiet supporters of the Civil

123

Rights Act of 1964. Although NAM's staff lawyers expressed concerns about the law, and some trustees were against it, the organization did not openly oppose its passage (Delton 2009, pp. 205–206). In the case of Title VII in the act, which is the clause that concerned corporate leaders the most because it dealt with discrimination in employment based on race, religion, or gender, they were well prepared for implementing it due to their involvement in Plans for Progress and a series of seminars that had been sponsored by NAM.

Moreover, it was drafted to anticipate possible corporate objections. As Jennifer Delton (2009, pp. 35–36) explains, "Thus, Title VII specifically stated that accidental or inadvertent discrimination (of the sort that resulted from seniority, testing, and educational level) did not violate the law; that nothing in the law required an employer to maintain a racial balance in his workforce; that, in fact, any deliberate attempt to maintain a racial balance would violate the law; and that nothing in the law required employers to abandon bona fide qualification tests, even if, because of cultural or educational differences, members of some groups did not perform well on the tests."

In addition, the enforcement provisions were weaker than those advocated by liberals and the civil rights leaders. The Department of Justice could not file lawsuits against employers that practiced discrimination, which meant that aggrieved individuals would have to sue their employers over discrimination issues, a much more difficult and costly task until the rise of class-action lawsuits by the civil rights, feminist, and environment movements in the late 1960s (Yeazell 1987, pp. 240–244). The Equal Employment Opportunity Commission (EEOC), the agency charged with monitoring compliance, was given only a small budget and staff and needed a year before it could investigate the huge backlog of complaints that it received. However, it became effective and important within a few years, in part as an avenue to litigation against racially exclusionary unions by civil rights lawyers (Frymer 2008; Kelly and Dobbin 2001; Pedriana and Stryker 2004).

Once the legislation passed, the corporate community strongly supported it through Plans for Progress and another nationwide series of seminars sponsored by NAM "to help business owners and managers adjust to what it called 'the new era in industrial relations'" (Delton 2009, p. 183). Hobart Taylor Jr., by then an associate counsel to Johnson in the White House, continued to work directly with Plans for Progress, which gave the corporate community a link to the White House on employment discrimination issues. Johnson appointed Taylor to a three-year term as a director of the Export-Import Bank in late 1965, but he continued to be a liaison to Plans for Progress. By that point "308 companies with 8.6 million employees were enrolled" in Plans for Progress. Delton (2009, p. 188) sees a parallel with the CED in the role that Plans for Progress played in formulating the policies through which affirmative action was carried out: "Just as the CED formulated economic and trade policies, so too did Plans for Progress formulate affirmative action policies."

While the corporate community was helping to draw up guidelines and bring about compliance to the new law, unions were once again resisting, especially craft unions (Quadagno 1994, chapter 3). In a study of seventy-five cases brought before the EEOC between 1965 and 1968, only 24 percent resulted in satisfactory agreements.

African Americans were excluded from union membership in some cases, from hiring halls in others, and from apprenticeship programs in still others. Discriminatory seniority clauses and other methods were also employed, leading to "administrative futility" for the EEOC Act (Wolkinson 1973, p. 99, and chapters 2 and 5). At this point the civil rights movement turned to the courts, with dire budgetary consequences for many unions (Frymer 2008, chapter 4).

RESPONSES TO DISRUPTION AND POVERTY

To deal with rising discontent, Johnson also announced a new "War on Poverty" in his State of the Union address in January 1964. Drawing on the pilot programs developed by the Ford Foundation and the Kennedy administration, but launching them untested and on a scale that made their originators very uneasy, the new initiatives would include job programs, educational programs, and a variety of social service programs for people of all ages in low-income areas. Although a task force was created to discuss the details of the programs, Johnson made the basic budgetary allocations and designed the program with the help of the members of the CEA. He then selected a Kennedy in-law with an action orientation, Sargent Shriver, to head the Office of Economic Opportunity (OEO). Shriver previously managed the Kennedy-owned Merchandising Mart in Chicago, a huge warehouse for vendors, before turning his attention to politics and government during the Kennedy presidential campaign, so he was not an unknown in the corporate community.

Half of the $1 billion allotted for the War on Poverty was given to the Department of Labor for a work-training program to provide part-time work for young adults who were beginning or continuing their education. An additional $300 million was allotted to programs administered by the OEO, starting with a Job Corps, which provided educational and work experience to low-income youth from ages sixteen to twenty-four in vocational training camps and residential centers. Shriver, in a speech to the Business Council, asked its members to raise $30 million in tax-free funds for the matching grants cities had to spend to be part of the program. In the process he told the corporate leaders that the various programs would be subcontracted to private companies as much as possible (McQuaid 1982, p. 228).

The OEO incorporated the five community action agencies started by Ford's Gray Areas project into a new Community Action Program, along with twelve of the sixteen juvenile delinquency projects jointly sponsored by the Ford Foundation and the White House. The agency sought to assist communities in a wide variety of ways, including health education for children, summer work and recreational programs for youth, and health exams for all members of the community. It also helped low-income people obtain services and welfare support from local government agencies mandated by law. A Ford-funded program providing free legal services for the poor in New Haven, Connecticut, became the basis for the Legal Services program within OEO, which created over 250 local legal services agencies in cities and rural areas around the country to help both aggrieved individuals and the community action agencies in dealing with local governments.

The most popular of the new War on Poverty programs, Head Start, which offered preschool education and day care for low-income children, had varied origins, including the preschool programs that were part of the Gray Areas projects. VISTA (Volunteers in Service to America), which sent adult volunteers into a variety of settings, including low-income communities, also was part of the OEO. All of these foundation-sponsored programs also went through shaping and reshaping in a complex governmental policy process. But as a longtime Ford Foundation official later wrote, "Great Society efforts in education, manpower, legal services, housing, health services, and community action were clearly borrowed from these earlier [Ford Foundation] pilot programs" (Magat 1979, p. 121).

To make sure there were no surprises in store for corporate leaders when he intro-duced the War on Poverty and his other initiatives for 1964, Johnson hosted a dinner at the White House for the Business Council a few weeks before his State of the Union address. The secretaries of state, defense, the treasury, and commerce were on hand, along with members of the Council of Economic Advisors. As revealed by Johnson's secret taping system, he made a brief address in which he called for the Kennedy tax cut, an increase in private investment, and restraint on wage increases, but also argued for the War on Poverty he was about to announce (Grossman 2007, p. 24). He also used the occasion to repeat that he was "going to cut future federal spending far below the levels projected by the Kennedy administration" (McQuaid 1982, p. 226). Shortly thereafter, Business Council member and CED trustee John T. Connor, the president of Merck and Company, became the secretary of commerce.

Johnson also asked union leaders to support the War on Poverty, but to win their consent he first had to agree that no jobs provided through the Job Corps would compete with union workers or pay below the minimum wage. The UAW and its allies in the union movement were highly supportive of the general program, and one of Reuther's key lieutenants was put in charge of the Community Action Program. From the UAW's point of view, the program had the potential to help bring about a progressive coalition that encompassed the liberal sectors of the union movement, African Americans, low-income communities, churches, and student groups (Boyle 1995, pp. 188–191).

Although the food stamp program was not an official part of the War on Pov-erty, it played a low-key supporting role after it was made permanent by Congress in 1964, with an initial appropriation of $75 million to help 350,000 people. All Democrats supported the act, with most Republicans in opposition, although South-ern Democrats preferred a program for distributing surplus commodities and only supported food stamps in exchange for an increase in price supports for cotton and wheat. To ensure their control of the program, the Southern Democrats insisted that it remain in the Department of Agriculture, which gave them legislative jurisdiction over it through the congressional agricultural committees controlled by the conserva-tive coalition.

While the amount of money allocated to the War on Poverty programs might seem impressive at a first look, the program was underfunded from the start. In addi-tion, Johnson was taking some of the funds for it from other government programs, generating tensions among agencies and with the constituencies (mostly white) that benefited from those programs. Anticipating resentment to this approach, union and civil rights leaders urged Johnson to ask Congress for new budgetary allocations. However, Johnson dismissed their suggestions. Even a relatively small increase in social spending would take the overall budget beyond the $100 billion ceiling he had arbitrarily imposed for political reasons. The meagerness of the appropriations aside, several of the programs generated tensions within the Democratic Party from the outset because they were crafted at least in part to bypass, shake up, or lobby existing government agencies. This design reflected the poverty warriors' continuing concern that local and state governments were too beholden to traditional constituencies to be responsive to the insurgent African American community (Marris and Rein 1982; O'Connor 1996). Sure enough, many of the one thousand local programs established in the first eighteen months angered local growth coalitions by filing lawsuits and organizing public criticism, pickets, and boycotts against any government units that resisted them (Fisher 1994, pp. 123–131; Halpern 1995, chapter 3).

Within a year of the OEO's founding, it had been reined in by congressional legislation, which replaced the original idea of "maximum feasible participation" by low-income people in program governance with a requirement that one-third of the overseers of War on Poverty programs would be elected officials, one-third community volunteers at traditional agencies, and one-third representatives of the poor. In addition, most of the government funding was redirected to relatively uncontroversial programs. However, a few of the more confrontational programs survived in several cities, including Legal Services, and in the process incorporated local black activists into their operations, which helped some of them to develop administrative and political careers (Quadagno 1994, pp. 56–57).

NEW INITIATIVES AFTER JOHNSON'S LANDSLIDE VICTORY

Thanks to the strong economy and his apparent moderation on the Vietnam War, Johnson enjoyed great popularity going into the 1964 presidential elections. Moreover, his ultraconservative opponent, Senator Barry Goldwater of Arizona, had voted against the Civil Rights Act as an infringement on states' rights, thought that it might be a good idea to privatize Social Security, and talked about using nuclear weapons in Vietnam, all of which were beyond what most centrists and many moderate Republicans were willing to contemplate. Although some evidence suggested that middle-level white voters responded positively to the Goldwater campaign's racially tinged messages about busing, crime, school integration, and moral decay, they also feared Goldwater's anti-union views and his plans for Social Security (Phillips-Fein 2009, pp. 142–144).

The result was a landslide victory for Johnson, with 61.1 percent of the popular vote, along with major Democratic gains in Congress, giving the Democrats over 2–1 majorities in both the House (295–140) and the Senate (68–32). The election thereby changed the domestic legislative equation by shrinking the potential size of the conservative coalition to around 55 percent in both the Senate and the House (Shelley 1983, pp. 140, 141). However, in a sign of the major electoral realignment that was in the offing, Goldwater won five traditionally Democratic Southern states and Republicans captured seven House seats in the lower South for the first time since Reconstruction—five in Alabama and one each in Georgia and Texas.

Although flush with success, and with a likely strong revenue base for new spending programs, Johnson renewed his pledge to minimize government spending when he spoke to the annual CED meeting in Washington in late November. He reassured the assembled trustees that he understood the need for a "continuing drive for economy and efficiency" and vowed that the budget would "grow no more rapidly—and I would hope grow less rapidly—than our economy grows." But he also assured them that there would be no "reckless cutbacks" on federal education, vocational training, or retraining programs, all of which he knew were supported by the CED by that point (Schriftgiesser 1967, p. 112).

Within the constraints created by his solicitude toward the corporate community's desire to limit government spending, Johnson put forth many ambitious goals in his State of the Union address in early 1965. Most important in terms of power issues, he called for legislation to eliminate every obstacle to the right to vote, an education program to provide funds for every level from preschool to graduate work, health insurance for the elderly, a new initiative to "increase the beauty of America and end the poisoning of our rivers and the air that we breathe," a program to support the humanities and the arts, and "a national effort to make the American city a better and a more stimulating place to live" (Johnson 1965).

Most of the new programs envisioned by Johnson were formulated by a series of task forces in the second half of 1964 and early 1965, all of which worked under his close scrutiny. They drew together experts from the policy planning network, corporate executives, foundation administrators, civil rights leaders, and union officials to deal with issues concerning transportation, housing, education, the arts, and the environment. The landmark Voting Rights Act, which was drafted at record speed by constitutional and civil rights lawyers in the Department of Justice after violent clashes in Selma, Alabama, in February and March 1965, was the only exception (Graham 1990, pp. 163–170). As part of their deliberations, the task forces often drew from policy proposals that had been developed by the Ford, Rockefeller, or Carnegie foundations, or by nonprofit organizations they funded.

For example, the education task force was chaired by John Gardner, the president of the Carnegie Corporation, which had supported programs in education for several decades (Lagemann 1989; Weischadle 1980). This task force's recommendations for more federal support for education through a variety of avenues and formulas also had the support of a CED policy statement put together by a subcommittee chaired by Folsom; it expressed approval for increased federal spending on all aspects of education as a way to raise low incomes (Committee for Economic Development 1965b). By all accounts, the education task force had a big impact in bringing federal aid to education (e.g., Bernstein 1996, chapter 7; Graham 1984).

MORE CONFLICT OVER HOUSING AND URBAN RENEWAL

Although several of the task-force proposals were adopted by Congress in one form or another, the task force on metropolitan and urban problems, headed by Robert Wood of MIT, the former CED and Ford Foundation consultant, met with resistance because of the threats it posed to housing segregation. It included Ylvisaker of the Ford Foundation and Vernon of Harvard, both of whom served on the CED's Area Development Advisory Committee; the chief economist for the National Association of Mutual Savings Banks (which had a major interest in home loans); a planner who consulted for ACTION; and three experts on urban affairs from the University of California, Berkeley (Bernstein 1996, pp. 460–461).

The housing report began by endorsing the establishment of a Department of Housing and Urban Development (HUD), which would bring the Housing and Home Finance Agency, the Federal Home Bank Loan Board, and agencies for highway construction and waste treatment plants under one administrative structure. Earlier attempts to accomplish this goal had been rejected by the conservative coalition, partly out of a desire to protect the urban renewal programs carried out by the Housing and Home Finance Agency from any renewed emphasis on housing or urban services for low-income people. The task force's report suggested a new market-oriented government program of rent supplements, which would help the working poor blend into middle-income neighborhoods by paying a large portion of rental costs for families that could contribute one-fourth of their incomes toward rent. The report also argued that rent supplements would stimulate private housing construction and decrease the need for government-owned public housing.

Although the program seemed designed to appeal to market-friendly conservatives who disdained government controls, the conservative coalition eliminated the possibility of any black-white integration through rent supplements by giving local governments "the right to approve rent supplements before they were put into effect" and by limiting them to low-income families. These changes embodied a long-standing Southern Democratic strategy: "Keep direct benefits to individuals under local control" (Quadagno 1994, p. 93). Consistent with pressures from the growth coalitions, the Housing and Urban Development Act of 1965 expanded funding for existing programs, including matching grants for the construction of water and sewer facilities, and expanded mortgage programs for veterans and middle-income families.

MEDICARE AND MEDICAID: THE IRONY
OF A LIBERAL-LABOR SUCCESS

The passage of legislation establishing Medicare and Medicaid in July 1965 was in many ways a major triumph for the liberal-labor alliance over the American Medical Association and the ultraconservatives in the corporate community. However, the reasons for this success, and its considerable limitations, reveal a great deal about the American power structure.

Although the economics and politics of the Medicare battle are detailed and complicated, the essence of the matter from a power perspective is that hospitals and many physicians could not easily, or at least without embarrassing negative publicity, refuse treatment to the rising number of elderly and low-income patients who were unable to pay for the lifesaving treatments that were becoming increasingly available. However, they were not willing to treat the indigent for free, and there were limits to how much hospitals could shift their costs to well-off patients and insurance companies. In the end, the financial needs of hospitals, and to some degree physicians, trumped their antigovernment ideology. But the change occurred primarily because the liberal-labor alliance forced the issue, and then made enough concessions to gain their cooperation, along with the final Republican votes in congressional committees that were needed to pass the legislation.

The idea for government health insurance in the United States went back to the efforts of the American Association for Labor Legislation, the early think tank that tried to fashion reforms—in the tradition of John R. Commons—that were acceptable to the corporate community. However, the AMA always soundly defeated the American Association for Labor Legislation once it tried to move beyond workmen's compensation and industrial health and safety regulations (Moss 1996). During the Great Depression, Roosevelt permitted his cabinet-level Committee on Social Security to develop detailed plans for national health insurance, but he quickly abandoned those plans in the face of strong resistance from the AMA and its many supporters in Congress. Democrats revived the issue periodically, but there were no government payments for any kind of health care until the Southern Democrats agreed in 1946 to subsidies for the construction of hospitals. This legislation, which was the result of a lobbying campaign by the American Hospital Association (AHA) that began in 1939, passed on the condition that the new hospitals would not be integrated (Poen 1979, p. 87).

By the late 1940s, many nonprofit and public hospitals, which predominated in that era, signaled that they could not continue to care for indigent patients without government help. Similarly, leaders of Blue Cross, the insurance company sponsored by hospitals and physicians, told government officials that they could not offer affordable medical insurance to working-age adults as long as they had to sell insurance to the elderly as well. They were especially handicapped in competing with traditional for-profit insurance companies, which developed formulas ("experience ratings") that tended to eliminate elderly patients and concentrate on healthy young adults. Looming in the background, Blue Cross also worked with trade unions that had health plans, which laid the groundwork for a possible insurance industry–labor union alliance (Poen 1979, p. 137; Quadagno 2005, p. 24).

The American Medical Association and the US Chamber of Commerce blocked a liberal-labor plan for government health insurance for everyone in 1950 but allowed Congress to pass legislation through which the government could pay "medical vendors" that treated welfare recipients of any age, a term that could be interpreted to include payments to doctors at hospitals. At the same time, the liberal-labor alliance began to look again at an idea first proposed in the late 1930s and early 1940s: the creation of a hospital insurance plan that would be restricted to the Social Security

Administration's elderly beneficiaries. However, the idea of limiting a new proposal to the elderly, with the thought that success might open the way for including younger adults at a later date, was rejected at the top levels of the Social Security Administration because of its commitment to health insurance for all. Moreover, organized labor's interest in government health insurance had declined somewhat because of its increasing ability to achieve health care for its members and retired members through union contracts. In making this choice, union leaders fully understood that their stance left nonunionized workers high and dry, but they also knew they could not win universal health insurance without first diluting the strength of the conservative coalition at the voting booth.

Due to this mix of factors, government health insurance for the elderly did not become a priority for the AFL-CIO until 1957, shortly after Congress enacted a health care program for the dependents of military personnel and expanded the payments to medical vendors that provided services to welfare patients. Something else changed at that time as well. The automobile companies had insisted in the last round of collective bargaining that the UAW should no longer "demand negotiations for those in retirement" (Quadagno 2005, p. 57). Even without the warning from the automobile executives, union officials were painfully aware that more benefits for retirees meant lower wage increases for their current workers, a very difficult trade-off. Union leaders also knew it was a propitious moment for a new campaign because hospitals were coming under even more financial pressure; in fact, the American Hospital Association had let it be known that it was rethinking its opposition to government support for taking care of low-income patients of all ages (Altman 2005, p. 186).

As part of its campaign for hospital insurance, the AFL-CIO provided the major financial support for a new senior citizen's council, which proved to be very effective in organizing Social Security recipients as a pressure group (Marmor 2000, p. 18). The campaign also had the support of professional associations for social workers and nurses. In addition, union health insurance experts and legislative strategists worked closely with two experienced hands that knew the system best. Robert M. Ball, back at the Social Security Administration after his brief time out of government, provided advice from the inside. Wilbur Cohen, who worked for the Social Security Administration from 1935 until 1956, when he was pushed out by the Eisenhower administration, took time off from his position as a professor of social work at the University of Michigan and helped with strategy and lobbying (Berkowitz 2003, chapters 2 and 3).

The new approach adopted by the liberal-labor alliance was not immediately successful. Hospital insurance for the elderly was rejected by the conservative coalition, which was backed by substantial lobbying by the AMA, the newly formed Health Insurance Association of America, the Pharmaceutical Manufacturers Association, the US Chamber of Commerce, and the American Farm Bureau Federation. But the AMA and the private insurance companies, whether nonprofit or for-profit, also felt compelled to come up with alternative plans, most of which relied on federal subsidies to state governments or private insurance programs. At this point the AMA even asked its members to consider lowering their fees to elderly patients as a way to fend off government health insurance.

Liberal-labor hopes for health insurance were frustrated by the Democrats' loss of several dozen House seats in the 1960 elections. Their proposals therefore died in the Ways and Means Committee during the Kennedy years. The decisions to kill the proposals were made by the committee's chair, Wilbur Mills, a Democrat from Arkansas, who knew that support for hospital insurance for the elderly was about even within his committee and still short of a majority in the overall House. He did not want to force his colleagues "to clarify their public record with anything so concrete as a yes or no vote when there was little to be gained by it" (Marmor 2000, pp. 40–41). At the same time, the Austin-Boston alliance, still managed by two of its leaders from the late 1930s, agreed to the Kennedy administration's request to enlarge the Ways and Means Committee. They also agreed that no one would be appointed to the committee who might keep Medicare from going to the House floor if and when there were enough votes.

By 1962–1963, most Medicare opponents knew that they were fighting a losing battle. Rearguard legislation passed in 1960 to give federal matching grants to states to support hospital care for low-income patients was helping a mere 1 percent of these patients; only thirty-two states were willing to pay the state's share, and most of the meager federal subsidies were going to five large industrial states. The AHA came to the conclusion that its member hospitals needed some form of major federal support as costs increased and the number of elderly Americans, most of whom were unable to pay for hospital care, grew from 12 to 17.5 million between 1950 and 1962. Furthermore, the commercial insurance companies were doubtful that their new attempts to insure the elderly could be profitable. They began to think in terms of selling supplemental insurance to fill any gaps in a government plan (Quadagno 2005, p. 72). However, neither the AHA nor the Health Insurance Association of America dropped its official opposition to Medicare, and both continued to resist the liberal-labor plan as much as possible, while at the same time trying to shape it to their liking.

Due to the Democrats' strategy of delay and gradual change, and the realization by their opponents that private insurance was not sufficient, the Democratic landslide in 1964 meant that some form of health insurance for the elderly would be passed in the next congressional session. The Democrats came forward with their proposal for hospital insurance, which the Republicans countered through a bill adapted from a plan written by experts at Aetna, the giant private insurer. The Republican plan called for supplementary private insurance, in part subsidized by the government, which would pay for physicians' services as well as hospitalization. At the same time, the AMA tried to stave off the Democrats' proposal by updating past Republican plans for federal subsidies for the purchase of private hospital care. Renamed Eldercare, the AMA plan also included provisions for payment for physicians' services. The Ways and Means Committee then decided to include all three proposals in a single package: Medicare A, which provides hospital and nursing home insurance; Medicare B, which pays the doctors' bills; and Medicaid, an expansion of the AMA's Eldercare proposal to include hospital and physician payments for low-income patients of any age.

Despite this major compromise, many Republicans and the AMA still resisted, as did the US Chamber of Commerce, of course, with the opponents fearing any governmental expansion and the loss of professional autonomy for physicians. Northern and Southern Democrats, at this point mostly united, were therefore forced to include private insurance companies as intermediaries for Part B, giving the insurers an opening into a market in which they previously had only minor involvement. In the process, insurance companies also won the right to administer Part A, hospital insurance, as well. As for the AMA, it continued to resist on its own. It was successful in its insistence that physicians who worked in hospital settings, such as radiologists and anesthesiologists, must be able to maintain their independence by submitting their bills directly to the insurance companies, rather than through the hospitals, as both the hospitals and Medicare advocates desired (Marmor 2000, p. 54).

As this quick history demonstrates, Medicare and Medicaid never would have been created without the unflagging efforts of the liberal-labor alliance, which received most of its funding on this issue from the AFL-CIO. Ironically, the alliance ended up fashioning a compromise that saved the private insurance system. As the AFL-CIO's chief strategist on government medical insurance later explained, the liberal-labor alliance had no other choice than to save the private insurance system in order to obtain government insurance for the elderly. "What we were really doing," he explained, "was making voluntary insurance viable for almost all of the working population in the country" by having government pay for the elderly patients who made private insurance unprofitable. "Now without Medicare," he continued, "had this burden existed as a threat or had they attempted to meet it, their system would have broken down, which in either case would inevitably have brought on national health insurance" (Quadagno 2005, p. 75). In other words, the ultraconservatives in the corporate community, along with the AHA, the AMA, and the Republicans, forced a compromise that greatly benefited the medical-industrial complex and at the same time eliminated any strong public backing for national health insurance.

Moreover, the union officials that had done so much to bring about Medicare were not consulted on key details of the final legislation. The result was an agreement between the White House and the leaders of the conservative coalition that gave insurance companies a large administrative role. As labor experts presciently feared, this bargain opened the way for rampant inflation, especially because any attempts at price controls were also eliminated out of fear that physicians might boycott the program. According to two of the union experts who helped formulate the AFL-CIO's policies and strategies related to health and medicine, the labor movement actually had very little direct access to the White House on this issue. They thought the consultations the administration held with labor leaders were mostly meant to keep "the labor boys happy without anything of real substance happening as a result." Labor had "fought like the dickens against letting the insurance companies into this program" out of cost concerns, so "it was disappointing to be working on this for years and years in every detail, and then within a matter of an hour have the entire picture changed totally and be presented with this and not really have had a part in it" (see Quadagno 2005, pp. 74–75, for the information and quotations in this paragraph).

Due to the rejection of various policy suggestions put forth by the labor experts and the liberals in Congress, the costs of the program were soon twice what the administration originally estimated: "both hospital and physician charges more than doubled their past average rate of yearly increase" in 1966, the program's first year in operation (Marmor 2000, p. 51). In the process, the health insurance companies became a powerful lobby in and of themselves as they greatly increased their profits. The salaries of top-level hospital administrators grew rapidly, and more for-profit hospitals were able to enter the market and earn huge profits, often after buying up, or buying out and closing, a large number of nonprofit and public hospitals. More generally, medicine became an organized business sector that had strong incentives to overcharge patients and the government due to the fact that taxpayer subsidies were underwriting a big part of the bill. The new system thereby put a relentless inflationary pressure on medical costs. Over the first five years, hospital costs increased 14 percent and physician fees 6.8 percent, far more than most other costs were rising at the time (Marmor 2000, p. 98). Within a few years, health spending as a percentage of the gross domestic product was at least twice as high as in other industrialized democracies such as Canada, France, and Germany, even though millions of people still had no insurance coverage of any kind because they did not work for a large corporation or a government agency but were not poor enough to qualify for Medicaid (Krugman 2007, chapter 11).

In 1968 in a vain attempt to remedy the defects in the government's health insurance program, Reuther kicked off a new drive for national health insurance for everyone, eventually enlisting the entire liberal-labor alliance and gaining the backing of the most famous of the liberal senators, Edward F. Kennedy of Massachusetts. Reuther even thought that some corporate leaders might be supportive now that they faced stronger foreign competition and were looking for ways to lower their wage-and-benefit costs. However, the corporate moderates developed their own plans to foster greater coverage of employees through private health care plans.

A CED report issued in 1973, at a moment when it seemed possible that a more complete health insurance plan for working-age adults might be enacted, presented a full and refined statement of the corporate moderates' position. It began with a mandate that all large-scale employers had to offer health insurance plans to their employees, which would be supported by contributions from both employers and employees. Smaller employers would receive some degree of help in their payments by being part of private insurance pools, thereby making any government funding of employee health insurance unnecessary. The CED wanted this care to be delivered as much as possible through a massive increase in the use of health maintenance organizations (HMOs). Medicare would continue to cover the elderly and disabled, and there would be federally subsidized community trusts for any self-employed people who lacked health insurance, and for those who were part-time employees or unemployed (Committee for Economic Development 1973).

Despite the arguments back and forth after 1968, no new health insurance programs were enacted during the remainder of the twentieth century. The liberal-labor alliance did not have the strength to prevail in Congress, and the ultraconservatives and the conservative coalition did not like several features of the corporate moderates' plan. The effort to go beyond Medicare never made it out of a congressional committee in either chamber. There would be no legislation of any consequence regarding health insurance for the remainder of the twentieth century (Quadagno 2005, chapter 5).

When President Barack Obama's Patient Protection and Affordable Care Act passed in 2010, it was very similar to the CED proposal in 1973 in that Medicare would continue for those over age sixty-five, companies had to offer health insurance to their employees (those with one or more full-time employees in the CED plan, those with over fifty employees in the Obama plan), and individuals without coverage would be required to purchase health coverage (through community trusts in the CED plan, through state-level insurance plans in the Obama plan). Both plans provided government subsidies for insurance purchases by low-income people that were not eligible for Medicaid. The main difference is that the Obama proposal had to exempt millions of small businesses from offering insurance plans and give a bigger role to private insurance companies, by then vastly larger than they had been just twenty years earlier, or else it never would have passed (Potter 2010; Quadagno 2011).

MODEL CITIES, URBAN RENEWAL, AND FURTHER URBAN DECLINE

About the same time that Johnson signed the Voting Rights Act and the new Medicare legislation, he also convened a new task force on urban problems. The task force was again chaired by former CED consultant Robert Wood of MIT, but this time it included two corporate executives: Ben Heineman, the president of Chicago and Northwestern Railroad, who was active on CED's Area Development Committee; and Edgar Kaiser, a corporate moderate who headed the company he founded, Kaiser Industries. Reuther was the labor representative, in part because he had presented Johnson with a proposal for large-scale neighborhood rebuilding in a few demonstration cities. With the hope that Detroit would be one of the first demonstration cities, Reuther's proposal expanded on a plan appended to the previous housing task force's report by Detroit's mayor. Whitney Young, the president of the National Urban League, was included on the task force as a visible and respected member of the African American community. The experts on the committee were economist Kermit Gordon, a former administration official and by then the president of The Brookings Institution; Charles Haar, a Harvard law professor with an expertise in land-use law; and William Rafsky, the urban renewal administrator for Philadelphia. Senator Abraham Ribicoff of Connecticut, recently the secretary of health, education, and welfare, was the final member.

Members of the task force were aware of Johnson's preferences and also of the white resistance that any new program was likely to face. They also knew that President Kennedy had temporized on his campaign promise to eliminate discrimination in housing, waiting until after the 1962 midterm elections to issue a narrow executive order that prohibited federally funded housing projects from selecting tenants by race. Diluting the impact of Kennedy's executive order even further, it was interpreted by government housing authorities to apply only to newly constructed housing, which in any case continued to be segregated because new housing could only be built in black neighborhoods due to local pressures (Quadagno 1994, p. 92).

Members of the new task force were also well aware of the problems generated by both urban renewal and the community action agencies, and they were determined to avoid them. Urban renewal had been too much about bricks and mortar, they concluded, so they included social programs that in many ways were similar to those in the original Gray Areas program. As for the community action agencies, they were perceived as having been too confrontational with existing government departments and agencies, so the final decision on any local HUD programs was given to mayors. The program they proposed began with six large demonstration projects. The projects would have enough resources to show Congress and other cities what might be possible to achieve with a unified effort.

Despite these attempts to avoid past problems, leaders within growth coalitions and big-city mayors reacted negatively to the new program, and so did ultraconservatives and machine Democrats. As might be expected, elected officials worried that the new "Model Cities" program, as it came to be called, might drain money away from urban renewal. Conservatives on the Ways and Means Committee moved to limit the program to $12 million in planning grants, which resulted in a quickly assembled lobbying group, the Urban Alliance, consisting of leaders in the growth coalition, construction unions, and civil rights groups. It urged that the committee move the bill to the floor of the House as originally proposed, but with an extra $600 million for urban renewal to ensure the continuance of that program (Haar 1975, pp. 70, 95–97, 224). For political reasons, Congress expanded the program to include sixty-six cities of varying sizes, making it possible for every state to have a chance for at least one HUD demonstration project. The requirement that new housing had to be integrated was removed.

Once the revised program was in place in late 1966, it faced even more problems with growth coalitions, city officials, and neighborhood residents than it had with Congress. Most white Americans were simply unwilling to integrate their neighborhoods, as already shown by their rejection of fair housing initiatives in many cities and states in the previous three years, including a vote in California in 1964 by nearly a 2–1 majority. For white Americans, property rights trumped open access to housing (Quadagno 1994, p. 98). In addition, the liberal HUD leaders were hampered in their efforts by the fact that several agencies within the new department were very sympathetic to growth coalitions and had helped to keep African Americans out of white neighborhoods since the New Deal (Quadagno 1994, chapter 4).

With African Americans urging HUD to enforce executive orders and laws prohibiting discrimination in housing, the continuing local efforts to move ahead with urban renewal projects intensified the problems that many cities were experiencing. This was seen first and most tragically in Newark, New Jersey, in early 1967, after the city council voted to use any Model Cities funds it received—even though HUD decisions on grants were yet to be made—for a new medical and dental center on inner-city land, which meant tearing down 150 acres of ghetto housing. It was a clear expression of the concern with land values that are primary for growth coalitions, but in this case the result was strong criticism from the black activists who had taken control of the city's community action agencies, despite the new federal guidelines on how power in such agencies should be shared. As the protests mounted, an OEO evaluation team sent from Washington to assess the situation reported that there was a danger of violence (Quadagno 1994, pp. 49–50).

Not long thereafter, in July 1967, riots broke out after a black cab driver was arrested for improperly passing a police car and taken into a police station in handcuffs. Following reports that the cab driver had been beaten, and perhaps died, a crowd gathered and began throwing rocks at the station. (The cab driver was taken out the back door to a hospital, treated for the injuries he received at the hands of the police, and released.) As the unrest continued in the next few days, police shot and killed a black protester, which led to six days of rioting, twenty-five more deaths, almost 1,500 arrests, and $26 million in property damage.

FURTHER PRIVATE INITIATIVES IN THE INNER CITY

The cutbacks in community action programs and the shortcomings of the Model Cities program did not mean the complete abandonment of efforts to ameliorate conditions in the inner city. Instead, the corporate community and affiliated foundations developed a range of nonprofit organizations that focused on self-help and private enterprises. This revised approach was crafted under the leadership of a new Ford Foundation president, McGeorge Bundy, the son of a corporate lawyer in Boston, a former dean of the Harvard faculty, a leader in the Council on Foreign Relations, and a major architect of the Vietnam War as the national security advisor for both Kennedy and Johnson from 1961 to 1965. Bundy began by replacing Ylvisaker as the head of Ford's urban programs with a former Connecticut AFL-CIO official, Mitchell Sviridoff, who had left his union position to manage the Ford Foundation's Gray Area's project in New Haven and then became the human resources commissioner in New York City.

Bundy and Sviridoff decided to concentrate on building affordable low-income housing and providing financial support for new small businesses, which meant less emphasis on the social and educational services that were central to the original Ford program and the War on Poverty. The new program was built around a greater emphasis on nonprofit community development corporations (CDCs), which could raise funds from both private and public sources, including new corporate and community foundations controlled by corporate executives through both funding and leadership. As one former Ford Foundation official later explained, the original program was an "adjunct to government that concentrated on social service programs," whereas the new CDCs were "a proxy for local government, concentrating much more on economic development and on residential and commercial building and renewal, a distinction of considerable significance" (Magat 1979, p. 123). Theoretically speaking, the revised plan was an attempt to create an organizational structure relatively independent of local government and federal funding.

The new program also provided grants for technical assistance to already existing nonprofit organizations, such as urban churches. The CDCs could use foundation grants to stimulate matching government funds for housing and small commercial developments, with the Ford Foundation allocating $2.25 million ($15.4 million in 2012 dollars) for this effort in its first year. To encourage this initiative, New York's two senators, Democrat Robert F. Kennedy and Republican Jacob Javits, sponsored legislation that made it possible for the OEO to join the Ford Foundation in funding several CDCs in black and Latino neighborhoods in New York. The program was further solidified in 1969 with a Ford-inspired change in the tax code that made it possible for foundations to give money to nonprofit organizations attempting to make a profit on some of their projects (Liou and Stroh 1998). By 1972 the foundation reported that it had spent $75 million on its CDC-centered program, supplemented by $100 million from other sources, and it had plans to spend another $75 million in the next few years (Ford Foundation 1972, p. 3).

To encourage the CDCs and other new nonprofits in various cities to work together and "continue innovation and experiments not possible under federal support," which meant that ultraconservatives and the conservative coalition would not tolerate such efforts, the Ford Foundation gave $250,000 to the National Association for Community Development and $375,000 to the UAW's brief-lived Citizens' Crusade against Poverty (Ford Foundation 1966, p. 27). A Center for Community Development, a clearinghouse for ideas and employment opportunities, was financed as well, which signaled that alternative nonprofit structures for providing services to the inner cities were in place by the late 1960s.

FAILURE ON WAGE-PRICE GUIDELINES, DELAY ON TAX INCREASES

Johnson and the corporate moderates headed into 1965 with a firm resolve to keep taxes low and stay within the budget. But that year turned out to be the beginning of a rapid increase in social-services spending at a rate of 8 percent a year, and by 1966 increased war spending and rising medical costs were overheating the economy as well. The result was prosperity, rising corporate profits, tight labor markets, and inflation, the last of which created dilemmas for both the White House and the corporate community concerning (1) government involvement in wage-price issues, (2) the need for higher taxes, and (3) the power of unions.

For Johnson, wage-price guidelines were essentially out of the question by mid-1966, just at the time that inflation really took off, because of his failed efforts to make them work in the first two years of his presidency. Two weeks after Johnson assumed office in November 1963, the labor leader he worked so hard to cultivate, Walter Reuther, told members of the CEA that the UAW intended to demand large wage increases in the light of record profits at General Motors and other automobile companies during the previous year. Since the industry was making great gains in productivity as well as profits, Reuther in effect challenged the administration to "enforce the price guideposts in the automobile industry," which would mean wage increases without price increases (Cochrane 1975, pp. 199–200). Not only were automobile company profits high, but also Reuther worried that he would look weak to the rank-and-file by accepting only moderate wage gains while the Teamsters and the construction unions were winning large increases. When the CEA checked with its main contact at General Motors, executive vice president George Russell, a CED trustee, about holding firm on prices, it learned that GM would insist on a price increase if it had to raise wages by a significant amount.

In response to the likelihood that other union and corporate leaders were thinking much like Reuther and Russell, Johnson approved plans for a more elaborate system of gathering information and influencing contract negotiations in 1964 than Kennedy had been willing to consider. However, the AFL-CIO made its opposition to these efforts clear in May 1964 with a long statement saying that guidelines were unnecessary because "inflation is not today's threat. Today's threat is idle men, idle plants, and idle machines." This public announcement bothered Heller, still chair of the CEA at that point, who wrote to Johnson that this opposition was "pretty serious business so soon after you have told them you regard the guideposts as 'sensible and fair' and 'in the public interest'" (see Dark 2001, p. 65, for the statements by the AFL-CIO and Heller). Secretary of Commerce Connor, the former member of the Business Council, did not make any effort to enforce the guidelines (McQuaid 1982, p. 239).

Still, the steel workers did limit themselves to a 3.2 percent increase during contract discussions in 1965, only to see the steel companies ignore the implicit bargain once again by making small price increases on different products over a period of several months. Shortly thereafter, the wage-price guidelines were a dead letter as far as labor, corporations, and Johnson were concerned. Gardner Ackley, Johnson's CEA chair, summarized the government's dilemma, based on his experience going back to the Office of Price Administration during World War II, when he remarked that "somewhere, sometime, we have to find a way to convince the unions they cannot continually push wage costs up and to convince business that profit margins cannot continually rise" (Cochrane 1975, p. 262).

Wage-price guidelines aside, by late 1966 tax increases seemed to be the proper remedy for dealing with inflation in a situation in which government spending could not be cut. Tax increases for high-income earners and profitable corporations appeared to be especially needed. Johnson completely understood this basic point, but political considerations once again made him hesitate. Asking for a tax increase would be to admit that the Vietnam War was expensive and going badly. It would also incur the wrath of the large number of Americans with strong antitax sentiments, and perhaps put the large contingent of new Democratic members of Congress at risk in 1966 in their traditionally Republican districts and states. Equally problematic, the conservative coalition made it clear that the price for such an increase was cutbacks in social spending. But the reductions in social spending sought by ultraconservatives risked more conflict among black activists, organized labor, and city officials.

Instead of calling for wartime wage-price controls and a tax increase, as Democratic presidents did during World War II and the Korean War, Johnson initially asked the corporate community to show voluntary restraint in investing overseas, which might help tame inflation by reducing the growing balance of payments problem. Although the Business Council would not support a temporary suspension of the investment tax credit, Johnson was nonetheless able to convince Congress to take this small step. Then the CED rejected this legislative action in the context of a policy statement on *The Dollar and the World Monetary System* (Committee for Economic Development 1966d).

Instead, the CED called for cuts in both domestic spending and overseas development assistance (Schriftgiesser 1967, p. 129). That is, in late 1966 corporate moderates were still more concerned with defending the dollar through budget cuts than they were with the growing tensions in the inner cities and the South.

The CED also wanted to reduce the corporate tax burden by adopting a value-added tax, which would provide more revenue for the government and "a better balance in federal taxes on business," to quote the title of its new tax proposal (Committee for Economic Development 1966a). In the process, the corporate income tax would be dropped from 48 to 38 percent, the rate that prevailed before the Korean War, because high corporate taxes were said to deter necessary corporate investment. With Johnson delaying a request for a general tax increase throughout 1966, an inflation rate that had been a mere 1.3 percent from 1961 to 1965 increased to 2.9 percent in 1966 and to 3 percent in 1967 (Collins 2000, p. 75).

While 3 percent inflation may seem minor by later standards, it was upsetting to the corporate community and heralded as a sign of worse things to come by Republicans, who realized they had a good chance of bouncing back in the 1966 elections. And in fact, white centrist and moderate voters did cut deeply into the Democratic congressional majorities in those elections, perhaps partly in reaction to an unpopular war and rising inflation, but most of all in reaction to their increasing frustration with the demands of the civil rights movement. The Republicans gained forty-seven seats in the House, including two more in the lower South, restoring the strength of the conservative coalition. They also added three new seats in the Senate, including one in Illinois that had been held for eighteen years by a liberal Democratic incumbent, Paul Douglas, who received less than half of the UAW vote, a strong indication of just how disaffected white workers were becoming. But the impact of racial divisions was seen most dramatically in California, where UAW members who had voted two-thirds for Johnson in 1964 gave half their votes to the successful Republican challenger for governor, Ronald Reagan (Boyle 1995, p. 222).

Still, it was not until the fall of 1967, after rioting and destruction in Newark, Detroit, and dozens of other cities, that the White House and corporate community began to think about raising taxes and committing a significant amount of resources to dealing with African American poverty and other grievances. As might be expected from the close ties Johnson had established with the corporate moderates, he began his lobbying efforts for a tax increase by asking leaders in the Business Council for their support. They agreed to help, but only on the condition that he cut $6 billion from domestic spending as well. The CED provided a quick summary report arguing in favor of a tax increase, and then leaders in both the CED and Business Council lobbied Congress heavily on the issue (McQuaid 1982). But the tax increase that finally passed was too small and too late to matter: the inflation rate rose to 4.3 percent in 1968.

In addition to more government spending on a range of social welfare programs, Johnson made a major effort at restoring order through a corporate jobs program that would replace the unsuccessful government job training programs (Brown 1999, pp. 287–290). The new initiative developed quickly after he invited leading executives to the White House in late 1967 and asked for their help. The result extended the cooperation that led to the Plans for Progress organization to the creation of a new National Alliance of Businessmen, with many of the same companies involved. This time the business leaders agreed to hire and train long-term unemployed youth for entry-level jobs in the private sector. The new initiative was coordinated with the National Urban Coalition, headed by John Gardner, the former Carnegie Corporation president and secretary of health, education, and welfare. He was joined on the board of directors by a cross-section of the corporate community, labor leaders, civil rights leaders, and local public officials in advocating more dialogue and greater government attention to urban problems.

Managed by executives who were on loan from corporations, the National Alliance of Businessmen and its publicists estimated that it hired approximately 430,000 people over the next two years and provided summer employment for another 300,000. The program was formally subsidized by the federal government, but only one-fourth of the corporate participants applied for payments because of the government's documentation and auditing procedures. Once again, as with Plans for Progress, the corporate community saw its effort as a voluntary one, "a chance to show what the private sector could do" (Delton 2009, p. 229).

As with the government's previous jobs programs, many unions resisted the efforts of the National Alliance of Businessmen, which generated problems for the unionized corporations that participated in the program. As a result, nonunion companies were more supportive, especially those in defense and high-tech industries, which depended on government contracts and needed to show government officials that they were making strong outreach efforts to the African American community. Aside from conflicts with unions, the program faced criticism from liberals and African Americans for its all-white leadership. Adding to the program's woes, many corporate personnel managers claimed that they had great difficulties finding new workers who would show up regularly and benefit from the training program. As a result of these varied problems, the primary long-term benefit of the program was that it caused corporations to seek out and promote well-educated black executives who had been relegated to minor positions in the past, or could only find work in government agencies (Collins 1997).

THE CED MOVES OFF CENTER

The CED took a step in a more liberal direction shortly after Johnson's request for a tax increase and the formation of the National Alliance of Businessmen. It did so first of all through the publication in 1968 of a new set of policy recommendations in *The National Economy and the Vietnam War*. Kennedy's former secretary of the treasury, C. Douglas Dillon, recently elected to the CED board of trustees, joined with eight other members of the subcommittee in unanimously recommending a temporary tax increase, restraint in the growth of the money supply, and a reduction in the projected rate of increase in government expenditures. In terms of spending restraints, the subcommittee called for cuts in agricultural subsidies, highway construction, improvements for rivers and dams, and the space program. Notably, the policy statement abandoned the CED's previous efforts to reduce social spending. After stating that expenditures for new programs related to health, manpower training, welfare, education, housing, and community development had risen from $5.9 billion in 1960 to $7.5 billion in 1964, and an estimated $20.1 billion for 1969, the report pointed out that this was still only one-seventh of total federal spending (Committee for Economic Development 1968c, pp. 37–38). In making its recommendations, the subcommittee had the advice of two Democratic and two Republican economists. The Business Council changed to a somewhat similar perspective about the same time (McQuaid 1982, pp. 248–254).

Furthermore, the CED report said that most of the money that would become available when the war ended should be used to deal with problems of poverty and racial tension, rather than reducing taxes: "We, and we believe the country generally, are impressed by the need to do more than we have been doing to reduce extremes of poverty, improve the conditions of urban life, improve education, and to give positive support to equal opportunity to all without racial discrimination" (Committee for Economic Development 1968c, p. 45). Although the report was overly optimistic about how quickly the war would end, it proved to be the first of several CED reports that in effect expressed approval for the Democrats' ongoing efforts to strengthen the federal government's social insurance capabilities.

In the same year, the CED also signaled openness on other issues, such as reforms in campaign finance, which was considered surprising for a corporate group at the time. It did so by supporting better disclosure laws concerning major donors, tax credits of up to $50 to encourage small donors, and partial public funding of candidates (Committee for Economic Development 1968a). It also published a new set of recommendations advocating increased federal support for education (Committee for Economic Development 1968b). Taken together, the three 1968 CED reports were distributed to nearly 442,000 people (Committee for Economic Development 1969a, p. 12).

But the efforts to create more jobs and educational opportunities for African Americans by the National Alliance of Businessmen and the CED, along with the increased spending in urban hot spots, seemed to be doing little good in terms of quelling unrest as the 1968 elections drew near. Since the summer of 1964, and in the aftermath of the assassination of Martin Luther King Jr. in April 1968, there had been 329 major disturbances in 257 cities, resulting in 220 deaths, 8,371 injuries, and 52,629 arrests (Downes 1970).

THE CORPORATE COMMUNITY AND THE VIETNAM WAR

Although spending to deal with domestic upheaval increased between 1965 and 1968, far more of the government's effort and money were concentrated on the Vietnam War, which was not the province of leaders in the CED and the Business Council. Instead, the management of the war effort was the domain of the financiers, corporate lawyers, corporate executives, and policy experts who involved themselves in foreign affairs through the Council on Foreign Relations. By the late 1960s the stature of the CFR was even higher than it had been during World War II and its aftermath, with virtually every appointed official and outside advisor involved in prosecuting the Vietnam War drawn from its study groups, which had reasserted the need for Southeast Asia as part of the Grand Area first outlined by the Economic and Financial Group of the War-Peace Studies project in its 1940 report (Shoup 1977).

However, the distance between the CFR and the CED should not be overstated. Fifteen percent of the 206 CED trustees in 1968 were also members of the 1,400-member CFR. At the same time, nine of the twenty-five largest defense contractors had at least one top officer who was a trustee of the CED. In addition, six of those nine major defense companies were also among the twenty-five largest industrial companies in the country—General Motors (No. 1), Standard Oil of New Jersey (No. 2), Ford Motors (No. 3), General Electric (No. 4), AT&T (No. 12), and Westinghouse Electric (No. 17) (Kaufman 1970, p. 57). In short, defense companies were fully integrated into the larger corporate community through ownership patterns, overlapping directorships, and shared memberships in policy-discussion organizations (Johnson 1976).

In addition to the CFR members that held official positions in the Johnson administration, its leaders organized a forty-eight-person committee, the Committee for an Effective and Durable Peace in Asia, to support the war effort. Its ad in the *New York Times* and thirteen other newspapers across the country in early September 1965 expressed its agreement with Johnson's war goals in a ten-point statement of principles, stressing that he "acted rightly and in the national interest" in sending American troops into Vietnam. A Wall Street lawyer, Arthur H. Dean, the country's chief negotiator at the talks that ended the fighting in Korea and one of the drafters of the Nuclear Test Ban Treaty in 1963, chaired the committee. Although most of the forty-eight members were bankers, corporate lawyers, and college presidents, there were seven CED trustees, including the chair or president of Campbell Soup, Crown Zellerbach, and Hewlett-Packard. By 1967, however, there were growing doubts among CFR members about continuing to escalate the war, leading to a new study group on "A Re-examination of American Foreign Policy."

In late March 1968, a month after a punishing surprise attack by the Viet Cong on South Vietnam's capital city, including an assault on the American embassy, Johnson called together his senior advisory group on Vietnam for consultation in the face of divided opinion among his government advisors, most of whom favored de-escalation. Known formally as the President's Consultants on Foreign Policy, and informally as the "wise men," it was constituted in September 1964. Since its purpose was in part to bolster Johnson's presidential campaign, the formation of this new bipartisan advisory group had been duly reported in the *New York Times*. Most of the sixteen original members were members of the CFR as well as leaders on Wall Street or former top State Department appointees in the Truman, Eisenhower, and Kennedy administrations. The wise men supported Johnson's decisions to escalate the war, including the dispatch of combat troops, in July 1965, and reassured him again in early November 1967 that he was on the right path, although by the second meeting several of them had private doubts (Gibbons 1989, pp. 347–350; 1995, pp. 874–878; Isaacson and Thomas 1986, chapter 23).

At the March 1968 meeting, however, the great majority of those present thought that de-escalation, negotiation, and eventual withdrawal were the only sensible steps. Cyrus Vance, a Wall Street lawyer, the deputy secretary of defense in the Kennedy administration, and a CFR director, explained the group's thinking to a former State Department official who was writing a book on the dramatic change in Vietnam policy. "We were weighing not only what was happening in Vietnam," said Vance, "but the social and political effects in the United States, the impact on the US economy, the attitudes of other nations; the divisiveness in the country was growing with such acuteness that it was threatening to tear the United States apart" (Hoopes 1969, pp. 215–216).

The group also realized that there were real tensions between China and the Soviet Union, as well as between China and Vietnam, which made any coordinated effort against Western capitalism in the Third World less likely. Within this changed geopolitical context, and already well aware of the unlikelihood of victory, the wise men thought it was time to try to deal with the increasing disruption on the home front.

A WIDER CANVAS ON THE JOHNSON YEARS

In many ways the CED and Business Council were even more influential during the Johnson years than they had been in the past. The president worked very hard for their approval and constrained the budget for social spending to retain their support. Corporate moderates were slow to accept the need for higher taxes and to urge strong financial support to address the grievances of the black community, but Johnson asked them for help in lobbying for tax increases, then put them in charge of a new program for providing jobs for African Americans after rioting escalated in 1967. Although the tax hike Congress approved in 1968 did not work as well as planned, the successful effort to pass it is yet another instance of how organized the corporate moderates were in the 1960s. Four years earlier they had mobilized to support a tax cut. Now they were able to mobilize to support a tax increase in very different political and economic circumstances.

Due to the landslide election of 1964, the 1965–1966 Congress was the high point of the postwar era for liberal-labor legislation, which included the Voting Rights Act, Medicare, and increased support for education and urban areas. The liberal-labor alliance secured increases in the minimum wage over a three-year period that were greater than the inflation rate, bringing it to its highest level before or since in terms of purchasing power. Social Security benefits were raised in 1965 for the first time since 1958, although the 7 percent increase was not enough to catch up with inflation; in 1967 there was another increase of 13 percent, bringing benefits a little closer to what they had been in the 1950s (Altman 2005, p. 206).

The diminished conservative coalition won less than half of the relatively few challenges that it mounted in 1965–1966, 45.8 percent of 131 votes in the Senate and only 28.4 percent of 88 in the House (Shelley 1983, pp. 34, 38). Still, due in good part to the committee chair positions held by Southern Democrats, it extracted many concessions on key liberal programs before they reached the floor of one legislative chamber or the other. In conjunction with the urban growth coalitions and the big-city Democratic mayors, it also helped to set limits on the liberal-labor initiatives that appeared to be very progressive at the outset, with the axing of the market-oriented rent supplement program as one prime example.

Conservatives and machine Democrats were also able to turn the Elementary and Secondary Education Act of 1965 to their own advantage by leaving allocation decisions to the local level. As a result, 94 percent of the school districts in the country received funds, which greatly diluted the intended impacts on urban schools. Some suburban school districts used their funds as the occasion to lower local school taxes or expand enrichment programs. The act ended up in good part as "a boondoggle that benefited suburban whites, not the urban poor" (Sugrue 2008, p. 470). Nor did the conservative coalition falter when it came to a critical union issue, the desire on the part of labor leaders to amend Section 14b of the Taft-Hartley Act so that it would no longer allow individual states to retain their open-shop legislation. The changes labor sought were passed twice in the House during the 1965–1966 Congress, but they were defeated by filibusters in the Senate (Bernstein 1996, pp. 307–312). Moreover, the conservative coalition returned to its winning ways after the Republican gains in the 1966 elections. During those two years it won 59 percent of the votes on which it formed in the House and 65 percent in the Senate. The conservatives were especially hard on Great Society programs, with the Model Cities program one major victim (Manley 1970; 1973, p. 239).

Economically speaking, the Johnson years were good ones for people with jobs or Social Security benefits, even with the inflation that worried them—and which was the major concern of corporate spokespersons. Although part of this prosperity can be attributed to the positive effects of the tax cuts in 1964, war spending added a further stimulus, keeping the unemployment rate between 3.4 and 3.9 percent from February 1966 through January 1970, even longer than the three-year run below that level during the Korean War. (The fact that an extra several hundred thousand men and women were in the armed services during this time also meant that fewer people were competing for more job openings.) Reflecting the high levels of employment and good contracts for unions, the Gini coefficient, which had gone up to 0.329 between 1954 and 1962, declined to 0.318 by 1968, almost reaching its 1953 low of 0.317. In comparison, and consistent with the decline in income inequality, the effective tax rates on the top 1 percent of income earners went up slightly, to 26.3 percent, most likely due to the income-tax surcharge and the inflation that pushed more of the top 1 percent into the very highest tax brackets. In the midst of the prosperity, unions also gained a little over two million members from 1964 to 1968, reaching 18.9 million, thanks to the growth of public-employee unions, which made up for a decline in private-sector members (Goldfield 1987, p. 15). Despite the overall increase in union members, though, union density nonetheless fell from 30.9 percent in 1960 to 28.3 percent in 1964 and 27.9 in 1968 (Mayer 2004, p. 22, table A1).

Although the corporate moderates were supportive of civil rights and federal monies for schools, and tolerant of most aspects of the War on Poverty, they were not moving closer to the Democrats. They worried that the fraying liberal-labor alliance still might be able to create larger government social programs than they thought were sensible, demand policies for dealing with inflation that they did not like, or legislate further government support for both private and public-employee unions. In fact, trouble was brewing just below the surface throughout the 1960s on the issue of greatest concern to all members of the corporate community—the power of unions.

Chapter Eight

New Sources of Conflict between Corporations and Unions

The corporate moderates pursued a generally forward-looking agenda in the 1960s and had several clear successes, especially in their various efforts to deal with both the civil rights movement and inner-city turmoil in an ameliorative way that would minimize the repressive actions favored by ultraconservatives. But they also had increasing tensions with the federal government over the key power issue for all members of the corporate community: the ability to control labor markets by limiting the power of unions. In a nutshell, the corporate moderates were not prepared to cede any power to organized labor or the federal government, which limited their cooperation with the non-Southern wing of the Democratic Party. A recounting of the series of events between 1961 and 1968 that generated increased conflict between the corporate community and the federal government over rights for unions provides the groundwork for understanding several major defeats for organized labor during the Nixon administration.

THE NATIONAL LABOR RELATIONS BOARD
CHANGES DIRECTION

Although most of President Kennedy's high-level appointments were moderate political figures or members of the corporate community, this was not true for the appointments to the NLRB. Taking advantage of the unexpected opportunity to make two appointments in his first month in office, Kennedy quietly liberalized the board. His first appointment, Frank McCulloch, came from a liberal family that in the early twentieth century had been strongly supportive of integration. McCulloch graduated from Williams College in 1926, earned a law degree from Harvard, and then worked for a law firm in Chicago for five years in the mid-1930s. Leaving his legal career behind, he took a position as the industrial relations secretary for the Council of Social Action, a church-based organization in Chicago. From 1949 until his appointment as chair of the NLRB, he worked as an aide and liaison to unions for the liberal Democratic senator from Illinois, Paul Douglas.

Kennedy's second appointment was a longtime NLRB employee, Gerald Brown, a regional director working out of San Francisco at the time of his appointment. Brown had a BA in history from West Texas State and an MA in economics from the University of Texas in Austin. McCulloch and Brown joined with a holdover Eisenhower appointee, John Fanning, a Democrat with a law degree from Catholic University, to give the board a liberal majority throughout the 1960s. Fanning's first job after he received his law degree was in the Department of Labor, followed by a high-level position in the Department of Defense in which he was in charge of industrial relations and had dealings with many craft unions working on the construction of military installations. He was appointed to the board in 1957 at the urging of Eisenhower's second secretary of labor, James P. Mitchell, a former Defense Department executive and industrial relations manager at Bloomingdale's (Gross 1995, pp. 147–152).

Kennedy's labor advisors and friendly Democrats in the House attempted to aid the NLRB in its work by formulating a reorganization plan. It allowed the board's regional offices to make final reviews on issues of fact, rather than allowing appeals to the board itself. Their aim was to decrease the large backlog of undecided cases, which grew from 410 in 1958 to 1,151 in 1961, due in good part to the increasing number of requests by corporations for board-level reviews. But the US Chamber of Commerce and the National Association of Manufacturers objected vigorously, claiming that any delegation of authority would deny the right of review by "presidentially appointed board members," which they preferred because they thought that board members "were more vulnerable to political and public pressure than trial examiners obscured from public view" (Gross 1995, pp. 157–159). The conservative coalition then blocked the reorganization plan by a 231–179 vote in the House in July 1961. This outcome served notice that the NLRB was under close scrutiny by ultraconservatives in the corporate community as well as by congressional conservatives.

The new Democratic majority on the labor board then moved quickly to regulate collective bargaining more fully than in the past in order to force resistant corporations to take the process seriously. It began by restricting what employers could say to their employees about joining a union, ruling out any claims that they would go out of business, relocate, or shut down for some period of time. It also ruled that unions had greater latitude in picketing businesses and in passing out information about a company's anti-union tactics than the Republican-dominated board had allowed. In addition, it made penalties for violations of labor laws somewhat stiffer, although it was hampered in this regard by the refusal of many courts to enforce such orders and by the conservative coalition's ability to block new labor legislation. The new board majority further aided unions by defining the size of bargaining units in ways that gave labor organizers an advantage. Most critical of all in the eyes of employers, the three Democrats on the board ruled that authorization cards signed by a majority of employees in a company, stating their willingness to join a new union, were sufficient to merit union recognition. This decision made it possible to bypass the usual procedure of holding a representation election using secret ballots.

These and other decisions elicited immediate protests from the corporate community, but the NLRB majority dismissed these outcries as the usual overstatements by ultraconservatives. They did so based on the false assumption, widely shared at the time in liberal and academic circles, that the biggest and most reasonable corporations had come to accept collective bargaining as a stabilizing influence, especially when they could raise prices after a contract settlement to levels that more than compensated for the higher wages and benefits they had to pay.

THE CED DECIDES TO LIVE DANGEROUSLY—AND IS BURNED

Just as the Democratic majority on the labor board was beginning to adopt policies that supported collective bargaining, the CED was taking its first look at the issue of union power since it recommended a review of federal labor laws in its 1957 report on inflation. However, it did so in an unusual way that ended up generating tensions within the organization itself. Instead of appointing a policy subcommittee to examine the issue, it sponsored an independent nine-member commission to write a report recommending ways to improve labor-management relations. The commission included well-known economists and industrial relations experts, most of them from Ivy League universities, the University of Chicago, and the University of California, Berkeley.

As staff director for the study, the CED chose George Shultz, an economist at the University of Chicago's School of Business, who later became a key figure in the Nixon and Reagan administrations. The son of the president of the New York Stock Exchange Institute, which provided training for new stockbrokers, Shultz went to boarding school at Loomis, received his BA at Princeton, rose to captain in the marines during World War II, and earned a PhD in industrial economics at MIT in 1949. After teaching at MIT for several years, he served as a senior staff economist for the Council of Economic Advisors in the mid-1950s, and then joined the business school at the University of Chicago.

The recommendations by the CED-sponsored commission, issued in 1961, disagreed with the new procedural rules put forth by the National Labor Relations Board. In general, the commission thought there should be less regulation of the collective bargaining process, arguing that there had been too much government intrusion into the process and too much wasteful litigation (Committee for Economic Development 1961d). The National Labor Relations Board's staff found this claim highly objectionable, as stated in a report that responded to the committee's claim: "We witness daily, in the cases we process, the efforts of respondents to avoid and evade their duty to bargain by a variety of devices and stratagems" (Gross 1995, p. 174). The staff report concluded that collective bargaining would become a rarity if the recommendations by the CED's commission became public policy.

While the general thrust of the independent report seemed to lean in directions that would be favored by the majority of CED trustees, it made several claims that drew angry comments throughout the corporate community, not simply from ultraconservatives. For example, it questioned the idea that unions were the primary cause of inflation, noting that administered prices and unexpected shortages of raw materials were also major factors. It also said that unions were on the whole useful, and then added what turned out to be an incendiary suggestion: Section 14(b) of the Taft-Hartley Act, which granted states the right to pass "right-to-work" provisions, should be repealed so that collective bargaining could harmonize labor relations throughout the country. It triggered a firestorm of public denunciation of the CED in business journals and angry letters from non-CED business executives. The critics worried that the repeal of Section 14(b) might unravel their strategy to decrease union strength in heavily unionized industrial states by giving companies the option to move to union-free environments (Schriftgiesser 1967, pp. 166–167).

The National Right-to-Work Committee, an ultraconservative lobbying and opinion-shaping organization with close ties to the NAM, orchestrated much of the negative publicity. However, several CED trustees were upset as well, with a few threatening to withdraw their corporations' financial support. Caught by surprise, CED leaders pointed out that the report was not an official CED document because it was not prepared, discussed, or voted on by the trustees, but to no avail. Alfred C. Neal, who by then had been the CED president for five years, later said, "The labor study was a terrible mistake" (Hurwitz 1989, p. 20). As the criticisms continued, the CED leadership decided to develop an official CED statement on labor unions. William Stolk, the chair of American Can Company, chaired the subcommittee, which included Blough of United States Steel, Francis of Princess Coal, and several other top executives from major firms. Blough's views on this topic were well known in the corporate community before his appointment to the subcommittee due to a series of three lectures he gave at Columbia University in the late 1950s. He had argued that it was time to "raise the question as to whether the original purpose so many sincere people had in fostering the cause of unions has somehow gotten out of hand. The glacier-like forces of a powerful labor movement, including unions representing workers in hundreds of competitive groups, adopt objectives that largely contradict the competitive principle itself." He concluded, "Wages and costs have spiraled so far out of line that enough profits cannot be accumulated to buy the needed new tools" (*Time* 1958).

Two years of subcommittee meetings resulted in an official CED policy statement that took positions very close to those of the NAM. Directly contradicting the independent report, it asserted that unions are a primary cause of inflation because they are often able to win settlements that go beyond productivity gains. In a comment reminiscent of those first made by employers in the 1920s, it said that right-to-work laws are essential to protect the freedom and rights of the individual. In addition, the CED supported lockouts by employers on the grounds that they are equivalent to strikes by workers (Committee for Economic Development 1964). There was no follow-up to the report, and it did not tarnish the CED's generally positive public image. But the AFL-CIO condemned the report, which reminded them that the corporate moderates were as hostile to unions as ultraconservatives, although less likely to advocate blatant anti-union tactics (Schriftgiesser 1967, pp. 166–167).

NEW CHALLENGES TO THE "RIGHT TO MANAGE"

While the CED's policy subcommittee was discussing its forthcoming report on unions during 1963 and 1964, the National Labor Relations Board was issuing new rulings that represented a distinctly higher level of threat to both moderates and ultraconservatives in the corporate community. Although the issues were barely worthy of media attention in the context of the rising civil rights movement, they provided new openings for organized labor to take part in management decisions, including such volatile issues as the removal of some in-plant functions to other companies ("outsourcing"), the closure of whole factories, and the movement of factories to new locations. In the eyes of all members of the corporate community, the labor board's decisions on these issues were a challenge to their "right to manage," a phrase that had been invoked since the 1940s to indicate that a sacrosanct line had been crossed.

The first round in this protracted conflict, which the corporate community did not win until 1971, involved a seemingly minor matter: the outsourcing of maintenance work previously carried out by employees in a plant owned by Fibreboard, the 364th-largest publicly held company in the country. By farming this work out to a low-wage company, Fibreboard lowered its labor costs and undercut the union at the same time. To make matters more complicated, the Republican majority on the NLRB originally decided the case in favor of the corporations in early 1961, before Kennedy made his appointments to the board. But the local union protested that the company's decision should have been subject to collective bargaining because it involved changes in the work process and the layoff of workers, and the AFL-CIO lodged a strong protest. Shortly thereafter, with the two Kennedy appointees on the board, the holdover general counsel to the board decided that the case needed a new hearing. One board member was unable to participate, and another volunteered not to participate so that the case could be reconsidered in a timely fashion, which resulted in a 2–1 decision in favor of the union.

Corporate leaders were not only upset by a highly unusual board action that put the right to manage at stake. They also worried that the decision would "hamper economic expansion by prohibiting the movement of capital to lower wage areas; prohibiting employers from obtaining the lowest cost of production; preventing the discontinuance of unprofitable lines or products; [and] inhibiting automation, mergers, and consolidations" (Gross 1995, p. 173). In addition, they thought it would hinder them in meeting the foreign economic competition they had encouraged through their advocacy of lower tariffs: "Employers were particularly interested in becoming more efficient through technological change, ending inflationary contract settlements with unions, and in other ways seeking to overcome the labor cost advantage enjoyed by foreign competitors" (Gross 1995, p. 190). Fibreboard, with the encouragement of the corporate community in general, made an immediate appeal to the courts.

Moreover, the Fibreboard decision was not an isolated case. The board also generated corporate hostility through a ruling on Roger Milliken's 1956 decision to close his Deering Milliken plant in Darlington, South Carolina, simply because its local workers had voted for a union. Although the NLRB began its investigation of the shutdown in

1956, a series of delays and legal challenges kept the case from reaching the board until the new Democratic majority, joined by one Republican holdover, voted 4–1 that it was an unfair labor practice to shut down a plant in order to eliminate a union. The board held the company liable for back pay and ordered it to offer jobs to its former employees in its other mills in the South.

The result was another court appeal. Adding further attention to the legal process, Senator Sam Ervin of North Carolina, a strong supporter of the textile industry, agreed to argue the case for the company when it reached the Supreme Court. A 1922 graduate of Harvard Law School, Ervin was one of 305 lawyers in Congress who represented business clients in the mid-1960s (Bonafede 1965, p. 1). Most maintained connections with their law firms back home, which frequently were paid handsome retainer fees by major corporations with headquarters in New York and other large cities (Pearson and Anderson 1968, pp. 112, 119). Although practicing law while in Congress was not controversial at the time, liberal-labor critics were able to raise questions and gain media attention about Ervin's involvement in the Deering Milliken case because the stakes were so high and he was a senior member of the Senate. He easily brushed aside their objections, and the media dropped the matter.

THE SUPREME COURT MAKES LABOR LAW

In a context in which neither Kennedy nor Johnson was willing to back unions with executive orders forbidding government contracts to companies that violated labor laws, and the conservative coalition and the liberal-labor alliance could not break their congressional standoff over possible legislative resolutions to the conflicts, the Supreme Court in effect made labor law in the 1960s. From the point of view of ultraconservatives and Southern Democrats, the "Warren Court," overseen by chief justice Earl Warren, was anathema, a hotbed of liberals and radicals who destroyed the country's foundations through its earthshaking 9–0 ruling in 1954 that school segregation was unconstitutional. Their anger was reinforced by the court's "one man, one vote" reapportionment rulings between 1962 and 1964, which outlawed the thinly populated rural House districts that greatly favored the conservative coalition. Ultraconservatives were further outraged by court decisions between 1962 and 1966 outlawing mandatory school prayer, extending the right to privacy into the bedroom, and giving new rights and protections to those arrested for alleged criminal acts.

However, for all the court's liberalism on the rights of individuals, its decisions on labor issues tilted in the direction of the corporate community and set the stage for a corporate counterattack on unions. The court first upheld the Fibreboard decision on extremely narrow grounds, in effect saying that the top leaders' "freedom to manage the business" had not been abridged because "no capital investment was involved" and the company "merely replaced existing employees with those of an independent contractor to do the same work under similar conditions of employment" (Gross 1995, p. 192). But even this narrow victory was a hollow one for the labor board. Justice Potter Stewart wrote a separate concurring decision, which was joined by two other justices, that provided a new rationale for limiting union power. It did so with the vague assertion that employers were not obligated to bargain over decisions that were "at the core of entrepreneurial control" or were "fundamental to the basic direction of the corporate enterprise" (Gross 1995, p. 193). Those two phrases became the basis for many future court decisions at all levels.

As disheartening as the Fibreboard decision was for the liberal-labor alliance, the decision concerning Deering Milliken's shutdown in Darlington was an even greater setback. It gave employers the right to go out of business for any reason whatsoever, "even if vindictiveness toward the union was the reason for the liquidation" (Gross 1995, p. 193). It then sent the case back to the labor board for further consideration. The court also overturned two NLRB rulings that were based on the idea that employer lockouts created too great an imbalance of power over unions. The court held that power imbalances were not the issue. Employers had the right to lock out workers whenever they wished to do so, including during contract negotiations.

CORPORATE MODERATES MOBILIZE TO CHANGE LABOR LAWS

Despite these apparent victories in the Supreme Court for the corporate community, the decisions did not go far enough to satisfy even the corporate moderates, who decided to join with ultraconservatives in an attempt to bring about changes in labor law through the legislative process. They did so through the "No-Name Committee," a small group of management lawyers and industrial relations vice presidents from a dozen major companies, two of which had two CED trustees (AT&T and B. F. Goodrich) and five of which had one (American Smelting and Refining, Ford, General Electric, US Steel, and Sears, Roebuck). Lawyers from Columbia Gas and Electric, General Dynamics, Humble Oil and Refining, Macy's, and Union Carbide filled out the group (Gross 1995).

The organizational chores for the new committee, which eventually changed its name to the Labor Law Reform Group (LLRG), fell to Douglas H. Soutar, a lawyer employed as an industrial relations manager by American Smelting and Refining. In the course of carrying out his role within the LLRG, Soutar also inadvertently secured himself a place in the history of labor-management struggles because he was a detailed note-taker and careful record-keeper, including for his innumerable telephone conversations. After his retirement, he donated his files to the Industrial and Labor Relations Library at Cornell, thereby making it possible for James A. Gross (1995, pp. 200–205, 234–237) to tell the full story of the origins of the corporate community's new offensive and the emergence of the Business Roundtable.

With the LLRG providing the general framework, the corporate moderates hired three seasoned promanagement labor lawyers to draft new labor legislation for eventual introduction into Congress. One served as a legislative counselor to General Motors, Chrysler, and General Electric, a second represented Chrysler and General Motors after working on both the Taft-Hartley and Landrum-Griffin acts, and the third was an influential management attorney in Washington. Two had served on the National Labor Relations Board at one time or another. Their work was then checked over by a "Blue Ribbon Committee," which consisted of management lawyers specializing in labor issues at one hundred large corporations. The drafting work was also coordinated with the Labor Policy Association—a meeting ground for hundreds of corporations with labor-law offices—through its president, who was a former lobbyist for several corporations (Gross 1995, pp. 202–203).

With the work of the three draftsmen under way, aided by financial support from the Chamber of Commerce and NAM, the LLRG laid plans for "phase two," a large public education project aimed at the country's "thought leaders." It would also include a widespread media campaign directed by a major public relations firm. There was a third phase as well, an attempt to gain the help of a Southern Democrat in the Senate, who would hold hearings on the National Labor Relations Act. Lawyers involved with the LLRG would use the hearings to criticize the act and lay the groundwork for the changes suggested by the drafting committee and the Blue Ribbon Committee (Gross 1995, pp. 205–207). However, it was early 1968 before phases two and three were put into action.

THE RISE OF PUBLIC-EMPLOYEE UNIONS

Although the origins of the American Federation of Teachers, the International Firefighters Association, and the National Federation of Federal Employers went back to World War I, few public-employee unions managed to gain a toehold in cities and states until the 1950s, usually by signing up white-collar workers in municipal government. A bill introduced into both the House and Senate in the late 1950s to give federal employees the right to organize offered new hope, but it did not cause a stir until it was introduced once again at the outset of the Kennedy years. Suddenly, the bill was seen as threatening not only to most members of the conservative coalition but to government executives as well. Several Kennedy aides, fearful that Congress "might enact a bill that gave workers too many rights and unions too much power," suggested that the president issue an executive order "intended to placate his labor allies while ensuring that the advent of collective bargaining in the federal service would alter labor relations as little as possible" (McCartin 2011, pp. 35–36). Organized labor, in contrast, greeted the proposed legislation with enthusiasm, hoping to organize workers at the federal level and then turn to state and municipal employees in the parts of the country in which union organizing had failed.

Lawyers for the Department of Defense wrote the first draft of the preemptive executive order based on the claim that unionized employees might impede defense production. Ninety-two work stoppages between 1956 and 1961 by skilled craftsmen at the National Aeronautic and Space Administration were the primary basis of their concern. After learning of this effort, Secretary of Labor Goldberg took control of the process by creating a task force that included representatives from several departments and agencies, including the Department of Defense, the Bureau of the Budget, and the Civil Services Commission, all three of which wanted the most narrow order possible in order to limit union powers.

The executive order finally issued in 1962 was indeed narrow in scope. It emphasized that federal employees need not join a union, ruled out strikes, included few of the procedures the AFL-CIO requested, and was soon made even more restrictive through interpretations by the Civil Service Commission. But union leaders praised it in public because it gave them the right to organize federal workers. As the labor organizers had anticipated, there was a rapid rise in membership for most public-employee unions, including at the state and local levels, with twenty-three states passing laws permitting public sector bargaining by 1970. For the most part, they were states in which liberal unions had used a variety of activist tactics and the Democrats had a legislative majority (Miller and Canak 1995a). The growth in public-employee unions was "the biggest breakthrough for labor since the New Deal" (McCartin 2011, p. 43).

The corporate community's reactions to this new organizing drive broke along the usual moderate/ultraconservative lines. The NAM and Chamber of Commerce insisted that public-employee unions should be restricted to the right to meet and confer, but with no right to collective bargaining. The corporate moderates proceeded more cautiously by using their positions as foundation trustees to suggest background studies. The Carnegie Corporation provided money in 1966 for a joint study by two associations of governmental executives, the National Government Center and the Council of State Governments, which were part of a large urban policy-planning network that had been in place since the 1930s with the help of financial support from Rockefeller philanthropies (Brownlow 1958; Roberts 1994).

Shortly thereafter, in 1967, the Ford Foundation provided The Brookings Institution with funds for a parallel study. Formally published in 1971 but widely circulated before that date, the Ford/Brookings report suggested that public officials stress the right not to join a union in talking with their employees, and offered specific ways to discourage unionization effort. In effect, sociologists Berkeley Miller and William Canak (1995b, pp. 28–29) conclude, the report suggested ways in which public officials could "avoid unionization by contracting out public services to private employees, leaving them entirely to free enterprise, or by skillfully resisting union organizing drives." The corporate moderates thus wanted to use contracting out in government agencies in the same way they were using outsourcing in their corporations to lower labor costs and weaken unions. By 1970 the Ford Foundation had given $445,000 to a consortium of urban policy-planning groups to establish a new Labor-Management Relations Service to train government administrators to deal with unions. The Ford Foundation also helped create the National Public Employers Association, a national-level labor relations association for public officials at all levels of government. Its Business Research Advisory Committee included representatives from Eastern Airlines, Ford Motor, General Electric, and Republic Steel (Miller and Canak 1995b, pp. 28–29).

TRYING TO INFLUENCE CONGRESS AND PUBLIC OPINION

By late 1967 the Labor Law Reform Group had a final draft of its proposed changes in the National Labor Relations Act. First and foremost, the draft put more emphasis on the right of employees to join or not join a union, and on the right of management to talk with employees about this decision. The plans to shape public opinion and influence Congress were also in place, but at the same time members of the LLRG "knew that there was no chance of changing the law unless Republicans triumphed in the 1968 presidential and congressional elections" (Gross 1995, p. 205). The public education phase of the campaign was carried out by Hill and Knowlton, the world's largest public relations firm, which handled publicity and lobbying for numerous industries, including tobacco (by denying that smoking was bad for health), pharmaceuticals (providing advice throughout Senate hearings concerning the marketing of untested drugs), and steel (during large strikes in 1952 and 1959). Its plan involved a nationwide effort that would be conducted without revealing its origins in the LLRG. As part of its effort, Hill and Knowlton said it would "meet privately with leading liberals" to learn how to overcome liberal objections; it also prepared editorials to send to hundreds of small newspapers and longer stories for nationwide magazines with which it had close connections (Gross 1995, pp. 207–208).

The LLRG's main legal counsel (i.e., main lobbyist) for the congressional phase of the campaign was a Washington lawyer who had worked on the Landrum-Griffin Act with other corporate lawyers, first as the general counsel to the House labor committee, then as a White House liaison to Congress. With Soutar playing an intermediary role, the LLRG then coordinated its efforts through Senator Ervin, fresh from his triumph at the Supreme Court on the Deering Milliken case, to orchestrate public hearings beginning in late March 1968. The setting would be a very unusual venue, a select subcommittee of the Senate Judiciary Committee appointed by Ervin, who would serve as chair. This strategy allowed the corporations and their supporters in the Senate to bypass the more liberal Senate Labor and Education Committee.

The subcommittee was created ostensibly to examine the freedom to join or not join a union from several independent perspectives, but 70 percent of the testimony came from corporate lawyers working with the LLRG, although none of them mentioned this fact. Many LLRG witnesses were especially critical of the Fibreboard decision, calling it "codetermination," which a labor lawyer from Olin-Mathieson attacked as "an alien doctrine, fundamentally contrary to the structure of US industry because it involved the worker in the management of the enterprise," a "socialist" idea imported from Europe. Their concern was to return to "traditional collective bargaining," which meant discussions limited to wages, hours, and working conditions. Problems arose, however, in early August when a liberal senator from Oregon, Wayne Morse, who was first elected as a Republican in 1945 and then became a Democrat in 1955, revealed the full story behind the hearings in the *Congressional Record*. Two days before the 1968 elections, the *Los Angeles Times* ran an in-depth exposé in which spokespersons for both the Chamber of Commerce and Hill and Knowlton acknowledged that a coordinated campaign had taken place (see Gross 1995, pp. 211–212, for the information and quotations in this paragraph).

In terms of impact, the hearings were completely obscured by anti-war demonstrations, the scramble for the Democratic presidential nomination after Johnson announced he would not run again, and the assassinations of Martin Luther King Jr. and Robert F. Kennedy. Although the Republicans gained five seats in the Senate in 1968, including the one held by Morse in Oregon, and five in the House as well, the labor committees in both houses still had too many non-Southern Democrats to make significant changes in labor laws possible. The overall campaign therefore ended in failure, but it once again revealed just how coordinated one hundred or more corporations were for lobbying Congress and connecting with opinion-shaping organizations. It also showed their determination to prevail one way or another on this issue, and prepared them to work closely with future presidents on labor issues.

A BROADER PERSPECTIVE ON HEIGHTENED CLASS CONFLICT

As has been demonstrated in earlier chapters, there were several ongoing disagreements between the moderates and ultraconservatives in the corporate community. Those disagreements widened in the 1960s because the corporate moderates supported a wide range of spending programs that were resisted by the ultraconservatives and the core of the conservative coalition. But as this and earlier chapters show, the corporate community was united in its opposition to unions. This is the defining issue when it comes to understanding class conflict in the United States, because defeating unions is the central power concern for the owners of all income-producing properties.

At the same time, there was nothing by way of settled case law to reassure the corporate community that its interests were secure, as demonstrated by the back-and-forth reversals of National Labor Relations Board decisions, first during the Eisenhower years and again in the Kennedy-Johnson years. If the board was a "mini-Supreme Court" for labor law, as it was meant to be, it was an extremely partisan one. Corporate moderates therefore remained staunch supporters of the Republicans because they did not want to risk liberal Democratic appointments to the NLRB or, even more critically, the Supreme Court. The few corporate owners and managers who remained Democrats after 1935 were either Southern conservatives or members of religious or ethnic minorities that were discriminated against by white Protestant business owners throughout the country (Domhoff 1990, chapter 9; Webber 2000).

Any hope or belief that class conflict had declined since the 1930s and 1940s was gone by the mid-1960s at the latest, as manufacturing companies faced stronger competition from abroad and a need to automate their production processes. Corporations were not willing to have their "right to manage" challenged under any circumstances, but they thought the issue was especially critical in the new competitive environment created by tariff reductions. From the point of view of liberal union leaders, though, it still seemed possible that the corporate leaders might accept the need for government insurance programs to socialize the growing costs of expensive corporate benefit programs. However, the corporate community did not want to risk government gaining any more legitimacy and power than it already had, and in any event the Southern Democrats would have fought such plans with great intensity to preserve the low-wage economy and racialized way of life in the South. The union leaders in the liberal bloc proved to be very wrong, perhaps because they thought the primary issue for corporate leaders was profits, not power.

As the turmoil generated by activists in the black community and the anti-war movement continued to escalate after 1965, it soon became apparent that the liberal trade unions could not organize a large voting coalition in support of the government programs they favored. Even in the case of the most progressive industrial union, the UAW, Reuther's hopes for an enlarged welfare state on the basis of a black-white workers' coalition in both the North and the South, with the segregationist Southern Democrats finally displaced, were "little more than ashes" by 1968. The UAW simply did not have the ability "to maintain a cross-class, biracial coalition committed to continued reform." Instead, it lost the support of its major allies and the confidence of many of its white members: "For very different reasons, African-Americans, white workers, liberals, and the New Left all came to see the UAW, as they saw the Johnson Administration, as a prop for the status quo," historian Kevin Boyle concludes in a concise summary of his study of the UAW between 1945 and 1968. Far from any notion that labor had sold out or betrayed its promise, its story was one "of struggles fought—and lost" (see Boyle 1998, pp. 230–231, for the information and quotations in this paragraph).

To make matters worse, long-standing tensions between Reuther and Meany were exacerbated by Meany's support for the Vietnam War and foot-dragging on integration, which led Meany to suspend the UAW from the AFL-CIO after it failed to pay its dues as part of a protest against Meany's policies. Reuther then formed a new Alliance for Labor Action that drew "the most unlikely of partners," the Teamsters, noted for corruption and political conservatism. The failure of the Alliance for Labor Action reflected the UAW's isolation from the rest of the labor movement at that point (Boyle 1995, pp. 246–247).

Although union membership in the private sector declined during the 1960s, that fact was cold comfort for the corporate community. It was far more concerned that the most powerful of the private-sector unions, such as those in construction, steel, and autos, could still use slowdowns, work stoppages, and strikes to win wage increases and better benefits in a context of tight labor markets and domestic turmoil, which would raise costs for the largest corporations. As a consequence, reducing union power became the primary concern for both moderates and ultraconservatives in the corporate community, whether the immediate issue was inflation, wage rates, profit margins, or foreign trade.

This renewed emphasis on defeating unions occurred just as Richard M. Nixon prepared to assume the presidency, thanks to a narrow victory over Hubert Humphrey in the popular vote (by a 43.4 to 42.7 percent margin), which led to a 301 to 191 victory in the Electoral College. Nixon's triumph was in part made possible by the defection of white Democrats to the third-party candidacy of Alabama's segregationist governor, George Wallace, who won five Southern states and 13.5 percent of the nationwide popular vote, thereby showing that his success in Democratic primaries in 1964 was no temporary aberration. His strong support in two highly populated Midwestern industrial states, Ohio (with 11.8 percent of the vote) and Illinois (with 8.5 percent), may have contributed to Nixon's narrow victory in them. All that said, Nixon's victory probably owed even more to the white Democrats who cast their votes for him instead of Humphrey. Whether they turned to Wallace or Nixon, the white vote for the Democratic ticket plunged by nineteen percentage points between 1964 and 1968 in many industrialized Northern cities. As a case in point, "half of the voters in UAW areas [i.e., city neighborhoods or suburban communities] had cast their ballots for conservative candidates, a profound change for a union whose members had been among the Democrats' most loyal supporters" (Boyle 1995, p. 256).

The Vietnam War was extremely divisive, and it left undying enmity between some groups and unending recriminations between many young adults of that era and war veterans from older generations. However, it is unlikely that very many defections to Nixon or Wallace by previous Democratic supporters can be attributed to support for the war or opposition to the anti-war movement. Instead, polls suggested that even though a majority of blue-collar and white-collar employees disliked the anti-war movement, they were opposed to the war as well (Hamilton 1975, chapter 5; Mueller 1973, 1984). It therefore seems more plausible that the defections were due to the backlash against government support for the civil rights movement's demand for integration. Within the UAW, for example, a majority of the members were adamant in their belief that the civil rights movement had gone too far too fast, and should go no further (Boyle 1995, chapter 10).

Labor leaders ignored the opinion polls and focused instead on how close Humphrey came to winning, thanks in part to the massive mobilization of union members to staff telephone banks, canvass neighborhoods, and bring supporters to the voting booths on election day. They thought that bread-and-butter issues would eventually overcome racial animosities. They also took heart from the growth of public-employee unions as a way to swell their ranks.

Chapter Nine

Corporate Policy Success and Economic Failure in the First Nixon Administration

Richard Nixon began his presidency with very little interest in economic policy, but it soon became his major concern. His original focus was on three goals: (1) ending the Vietnam War in a way satisfactory to American interests; (2) improving relations with China and the Soviet Union; and (3) pulling a majority of white workers, from both the North and the South, into the Republican Party as part of a long-term political realignment. At the outset, he also hoped to win over some African Americans through cautious support for affirmative action and the encouragement of more black-owned business enterprises, but by 1970 he had abandoned this effort in favor of an all-out use of coded racial appeals in building a new white people's party, including the white Cubans that had moved to the United States in the face of Fidel Castro's rise to power.

Not only was Nixon less interested in economic issues, he thought they were the least of his worries because unemployment was at a mere 3.4 percent in January 1969, and the inflation rate was down to 3.6 percent. Although he disliked corporate leaders as a group and spoke with disdain about Ivy Leaguers, he had confidence in the conservative Keynesianism advocated by the CED and the many Ivy League economists who consulted for it. In his only mention of economic issues in his inaugural address, he asserted, "We have learned at last to manage a modern economy to assure its continued growth" (Matusow 1998, p. 9). His plan was to keep unemployment around 4 percent while gradually lowering the inflation rate by another percentage point or two (Campagna 1994, p. 9).

Once Nixon decided on his general economic goals, he put little effort into picking his economic advisors, except for stipulating that there should be no Eastern bankers at the very top. Following the advice of Charls Walker, the executive vice president and chief lobbyist for the American Bankers Association, he chose the president of Continental Illinois Bank in Chicago, David M. Kennedy, as his secretary of the treasury. During the Johnson years Kennedy, a CED trustee, had chaired a presidential commission on the budget, which included four other CED trustees and advisors.

Kennedy picked Walker, the person who had recommended him for the treasury appointment, to be his deputy secretary of the treasury. Walker had been an economic advisor to the president of the Republic National Bank of Dallas before he became a bank lobbyist, and his appointment solidified the bankers' traditional control over the Treasury Department. In addition, Kennedy appointed a middle-level New York banker, Paul Volcker, as the undersecretary for international monetary affairs. Volcker, who had policy-oriented degrees from Princeton and Harvard, as well as two years of training at the London School of Economics, began his career as an economist for the Federal Reserve Bank of New York. He then became an economist for Chase Manhattan Bank for five years before joining the Kennedy administration in 1962 as director of financial analysis in the Treasury Department for a year, followed by two years as undersecretary for monetary affairs. He returned to Chase Manhattan as a vice president and director of planning in 1965, so he was a prototypical in-and-outer by the time he joined the Nixon administration in 1969, and went on to even bigger things in the Carter and Reagan administrations. Volcker worked closely with economist Murray Weidenbaum of Washington University of St. Louis, a former advisor to the CED, who was appointed an assistant secretary of the treasury.

As for the CEA, Nixon appointed a University of Michigan economist, Paul McCracken, as its chair. A centrist with a PhD from Harvard, McCracken had been a consultant to the CED since the 1950s and became a member of its Research Advisory Board in the 1960s. Herbert Stein, the longtime CED economist, who left the CED to become a fellow at The Brookings Institution in 1967, joined him on the CEA. McCracken and Stein had worked together in 1967 and 1968 as advisors to a CED subcommittee that reaffirmed the CED's traditional approach to fiscal and monetary policies, on which they were joined by four liberal economists who had been members of the CEA during the Kennedy and Johnson administrations (Committee for Economic Development 1969b). A Harvard economist and expert on consumer behavior, Hendrik Houthakker, became the third member of the CEA.

Two other individuals played a vital role in influencing Nixon's economic policies. The first, Arthur Burns, recently retired as president of the National Bureau of Economic Research, had been close to Nixon since Burns chaired Eisenhower's CEA, and Nixon planned to appoint him as the chair of the Federal Reserve Board when the position became open in early 1970. The second, George Shultz, the dean of the business school at the University of Chicago since 1962, was a frequent advisor to the CED throughout the 1960s, beginning with his involvement in the ill-fated independent labor report. Within the Nixon administration, he first provided advice from his position as secretary of labor (1969–1970), and then became directly involved in economic policy in 1971 as head of the recently created Office of Management and Budget. He took the lead role in economic policy as the secretary of the treasury from 1972 to 1974.

BATTLING INFLATION AND CONSTRUCTION UNIONS

Although Nixon's economic advisors were steeped in the CED tradition, they tended to put even more emphasis on monetary policy than did the original commercial Keynesians. They believed that interest rates were more important than tinkering with taxes, as CED reports from the late 1940s onward also insisted. In addition, several of them were influenced by the views of monetary economist Milton Friedman, a frequent informal advisor to Nixon at the White House, who argued that reducing the rate of growth in the money supply was the best way to control inflation. Although Keynesians rejected Friedman's single-minded focus on monetary policy, many of them were "shocked by just how similar" his monetary prescriptions were to the Keynesian view in a 1970 article he published (Krugman 2012a, p. 101). McCracken, a conservative Keynesian, described his views as "Friedmanesque" in a 1969 interview (Matusow 1998, p. 15).

In keeping with Nixon's desire to maintain as high a level of employment as possible in his effort to win over blue-collar voters, his advisors suggested a policy designed to gradually decrease the inflation rate, which had been an unacceptably high 4 percent in 1968. To accomplish this delicate balancing act, they suggested "moderate monetary restraint" as the main policy tool, which translated into a gradual increase in interest rates via the actions of the Federal Reserve Board. Drawing on the more traditional Keynesian side of the equation, they also wanted to reduce or eliminate the budget deficit, though they realized that this combination of policies was likely to reduce consumer demand, increase unemployment, and perhaps put the economy in a downward spiral. Publicly, the CEA said it expected unemployment to remain between 3 and 4 percent, but its private estimate for mid-1970 was 4.4 percent (it turned out to be 5 percent when the time came). Nixon ultimately accepted his advisors' recommendations, but he ordered the CEA to downplay the possibility of higher unemployment in public discussions (Matusow 1998, pp. 17–18).

However, the policy was never fully carried out. The Fed chair since 1951, originally appointed by President Truman, after a career as president of the New York Stock Exchange and the Export-Import Bank, raised interest rates faster and higher than the CEA expected. But inflation nonetheless rose at a fast pace in the early months of 1969 and throughout 1970, in good part because banks had found ways to bypass the higher interest rates and continue to satisfy the strong demand for loans by corporations by "borrowing heavily on the Eurodollar market, selling commercial paper through bank-affiliated holding companies, and selling assets under agreements to repurchase" (Marchi 1975, p. 306). In the process, interest rates reached their highest level since the Civil War, government spending was cut, and revenues grew due to the continuation of the surcharge on incomes and higher taxes on business. Although unemployment stayed around 3.5 percent throughout 1969, the eventual result was a recession and a new round of cost-push inflation. Unemployment grew to 6.1 percent by the end of 1970, but wages continued to climb as well (Matusow 1998, pp. 17–18).

Despite these varied government efforts, leaders within the corporate community complained that not enough was being done in a timely fashion. This was especially the view of executives who managed companies rushing to complete new factories, because wages and fringe benefits for construction workers had increased by 10 percent between June 1968 and June 1969. Wage increases in plant construction also contributed to a rise in housing prices due to the fact that workers who built residential housing insisted on the same wage and benefit scales established in industrial construction. Although the corporate chieftains publicly blamed the resulting wage increases on unions, they had contributed to the problem, and many of them understood that fact. In their search for higher profits and greater market share in a booming economy, they not only continued to borrow from banks in large amounts but also encouraged contractors to take on extra workers, and to pay overtime wages if necessary, to finish new projects on time. They thereby tightened labor markets over and beyond what a strong economy was already causing, which also made it possible for unionized industrial and construction workers to catch up with the inflationary spiral after three years in which they lost purchasing power. In some cases, workers were able to win settlements that improved their wages, temporarily pushing their gains above increases in the Consumer Price Index (Edsall 1984, p. 157).

The result was the creation in August 1969 of a new corporate organization to enforce self-restraint and provide aid to construction companies in battling unions. Called the Construction Users Anti-Inflation Roundtable, its members included many of the companies already in the Labor Law Reform Group, such as Alcoa, AT&T, General Electric, General Motors, Standard Oil of New Jersey, Union Carbide, and US Steel, most of which had at least one officer who was a CED trustee. In an article announcing the new organization, *Time* magazine took the opportunity to scold the corporate executives for their lack of restraint, noting that "some of those companies have been among the worst offenders in demanding quick completion of plants, whatever the cost and however much the jobs disrupt work on other projects" (*Time* 1969). General Motors, for example, caused shortages of construction workers in Ohio by insisting that construction firms work seventy-hour weeks to complete a plant that would allow it to compete with Ford Motor in the small-car market. By banding together and enforcing group discipline, the corporate giants hoped to ensure that they would no longer contribute to inflation by rushing factories to completion. As part of their effort to help construction companies resist demands by unions, they encouraged them to become "double-breasted," a euphemism for having a unit of the company that bid for nonunion contracts. Backed by the big industrial corporations, the Associated General Contractors of America developed a strike insurance fund to provide money to companies that resisted union demands for wage increases that exceeded the inflation rate.

The new group was informally called "Roger's Roundtable" because Roger Blough, by then retired as chair of US Steel, but still a member of the Business Council and a trustee of the CED, was its prime mover and founding chair. As Douglas Soutar, the convener of the Labor Law Reform Group, said many years later, he thought Blough was the key person "in everything," self-effacing and widely respected for his leadership throughout his long business career (Soutar 1996). But it was also the case that the steel industry was under especially strong pressure to hold down construction costs due to increasing international competition from foreign mills that were more productive than the American plants and had lower labor costs (Swenson 2002, pp. 308–310). In fact, Blough (1968/1972) had already called for import quotas because the steel industry was losing a big part of the American market and could no longer pass along rising production costs to its corporate customers.

In a dagger aimed straight at the heart of the construction unions, the Construction Users Anti-Inflation Roundtable asked the White House to suspend a 1931 law that put a floor under construction wages. Championed in that bygone era by Republicans James Davis, a senator from Pennsylvania, and Robert Bacon, a representative from New York, the law has been known ever since simply as "Davis-Bacon." Originally intended to keep contractors from making the lowest bids on a contract on the basis of extremely low wages for workers they would bring in from low-income regions of the country, Davis-Bacon required federal contractors to pay the local "prevailing wage" to construction workers. In practice, though, the prevailing wage soon came to be set by government officials through informal negotiations with construction unions, which meant that the wage usually did not decline and often increased.

Reacting to the wage increases in construction, Burns made similar suggestions to Nixon and his cabinet. In addition to suspending Davis-Bacon, the Construction Users Anti-Inflation Roundtable and Burns also wanted to expand training programs to increase the labor supply, reduce federal spending on construction, and forbid contracts that restricted hiring to private employment centers controlled by the trade unions. Shultz opposed suspending Davis-Bacon and bypassing union hiring halls, but with the help of one of his assistant secretaries, Jerome Rosow, the former vice president of labor relations at Standard Oil of New Jersey, he reshaped apprenticeship programs by taking the power to select new apprentices away from construction unions. Shultz thereby brought about some integration of the construction trades while also diminishing the unions. Based on predictions of an imminent labor shortage that never materialized, he also increased the size of apprenticeship programs. In tandem with the Construction Users Anti-Inflation Roundtable and the construction unions, he next established the Construction Industry Collective Bargaining Commission to mediate disputes and find new ways to moderate wage increases (Marchi 1975, pp. 310–311).

In the short run, though, inflation continued to rise. In late April 1970 Burns, by this time the chair of the Federal Reserve Board, gave a speech in which he said that demand-driven inflation was giving way to cost-push inflation caused by the wage-price spiral, which meant that "making monetary and fiscal policies still more restrictive not only would be ineffective but would invite recession" (Marchi 1975, p. 316). He advocated short-term controls, which led the secretary of housing and urban development, George Romney—a former president of American Motors and a former CED trustee as well—to call for a commission that would examine ways to control the spiral and save the housing industry from ruin. In October the Business Council sent the White House a "message of censure" because it had failed "to check excessive wage and price increases," and Shultz warned Nixon that to beat inflation he would have to use policies that might jeopardize any hope of Republican gains in the 1970 elections (Marchi 1975, p. 326).

THE CED TAKES A NEW STANCE ON INFLATION

As these events were unfolding in Washington, the CED moved beyond its traditional stance on dealing with inflation with the publication in November 1970 of *Further Weapons against Inflation*. The report endorsed the Construction Users Anti-Inflation Roundtable's approach to construction unions and advocated two new stopgaps after reaffirming support for the mix of monetary and fiscal policies the CED first recommended in 1947. One stopgap pointed in a conservative direction that was approved by virtually all trustees, with one or two liberal exceptions. The other suggested a more moderate path opposed by a sizable minority of executives at large corporations. The report sold 70,000 copies, a best seller by CED standards at the time, and "received more extensive and impressive news and editorial coverage than any CED statement in many years" (Committee for Economic Development 1971a, p. 10).

The project's staff director, Frank Schiff, had been hired the year before to replace Stein as the chief CED economist. Schiff received his PhD at Columbia in the early 1950s and taught economics there for a few years before taking a job with the Federal Reserve Bank of New York, where he came to know Volcker. His work in New York was followed by four years as the chief staff economist for the Council of Economic Advisors, from 1964 to 1968, and a year as deputy undersecretary of the treasury before joining the CED staff. Unlike Stein, he was not philosophically opposed to an incomes policy, which made it possible for him to be comfortable with whatever direction the trustees decided to take (Schiff 1990a, 1990b, 1994).

Although the report supported the continuing use of monetary and fiscal policies, it concluded that "demand compression," caused by the high interest rates and balanced budgets put in place by the Nixon administration, was not good enough in either the near term or the long run. Its failure, the report said, was revealed by the fact that settlements with unions in the first half of 1970 averaged 10.2 percent, compared to 8 percent in 1969, despite the considerable effort to limit the size of increases. Furthermore, lower interest rates and higher federal expenditures were needed to deal with "the urgent problems of our cities, education, poverty and welfare, health care, and the environment." The policy statement also flatly declared that tax increases would be necessary to pay for these essential programs if reductions could not be made in agricultural subsidies and in the defense and space exploration budgets (Committee for Economic Development 1970a, pp. 17–18).

The report concluded that the costs of fighting inflation through unemployment were "likely to be substantially greater than the American people would or should tolerate" (Committee for Economic Development 1970a, p. 11). It therefore advocated more extensive and generous unemployment benefits that would last longer. In other words, the budget cuts and high interest rates that are seen as purely economic issues by many policy makers are in fact implicitly premised on assumptions about the amount of suffering low-wage employees and the unemployed will accept without voting for liberal Democrats or venting their frustrations through potentially costly social disruption.

In addition to these moderate recommendations, there were several new conservative recommendations aimed at "increasing the efficiency of labor and product markets" as an important new way to decrease inflation. Under that rubric, "reexamination of existing labor legislation" stood "high on the agenda." The goal was to achieve "a better balance in the relative powers of unions and management" (Committee for Economic Development 1970a, p. 41). The report listed several ways to improve labor markets, beginning with programs to upgrade worker skills and to use newly emerging computer technologies to create a nationwide job market and increase labor mobility. Most of the recommendations, however, involved strategies to reduce union power. The CED also wanted the two states that allowed strikers to apply for unemployment benefits, New York and Rhode Island, to eliminate this possibility.

The statement provided specific recommendations in relation to the building trades unions, which paralleled those made by the Construction Users Anti-Inflation Roundtable. To help the localized and fragmented construction industry deal with the eighteen nationwide building trades unions, whose contracts usually expired at different times of the year, it advocated larger collective bargaining units and contracts that expired about the same time.

In a further effort to change the balance of power in the labor market for construction workers, the CED called for the elimination of restrictive work practices and voiced approval for the government apprentice programs established by the Department of Labor, applauding the fact that they would create a larger and more diverse pool of skilled construction workers. In addition, it suggested twice that "the possibility of having the [Davis-Bacon] Act suspended by the President should also be explored," first in the main body of the report and again in the summary (Committee for Economic Development 1970a, pp. 19, 50).

The statement endorsed more cooperation among the major companies that hired construction firms so they could regularize labor demand by coordinating their scheduling of projects, thereby loosening the labor market and perhaps reducing the need for overtime pay. It also provided a carefully worded endorsement of the Construction Users Anti-Inflation Roundtable that is notable for its indirect nature: "We regard as a particularly promising recent development the initiative being taken by a sizable number of the large national business firms on whose behalf much of the ongoing private commercial construction is undertaken (i.e., the major construction 'buyers' or 'users')" (Committee for Economic Development 1970a, p. 19).

As for measures unrelated to control of wages that might be of use, the report had a short list of improvements in product markets, such as better consumer information, the removal of minimum prices on some products, and the enforcement of antitrust laws. In terms of government's role, the report took aim at government purchasing programs, suggesting that the procurement of scarce products could be delayed. In that regard, it wanted the role of the Purchasing and Regulations Review Board in the Office of Management and Budget expanded so it could serve as a "public defender" of price stability (Committee for Economic Development 1970a, p. 46).

Beyond these structural recommendations, most of which tilted in a conservative, anti-union direction, the report also took an unexpected step in what was perceived as a more liberal direction. Abandoning the corporate community's seemingly unanimous distaste for wage-price guidelines, the report called for voluntary wage and price guidelines reminiscent of what had been tried in the Kennedy and Johnson administrations. For the time being at least, the CED's version would mean a three-person government Board on Prices and Incomes to analyze wage hikes and report their impact. It would suggest guidelines in advance of upcoming wage negotiations in critical sectors of the economy, and publicize its analysis of wage settlements. Adhering to the guidelines, however, would be voluntary. The statement did not make big claims for the likely success of this process, which was described at one point as a "possibly useful adjunct" (Committee for Economic Development 1970a, p. 22).

Twelve of the twenty-two subcommittee members agreed to the full set of recommendations without any reservations or dissents, including the chairs of Consolidated Can, General Foods, Trans World Airlines, and *Newsweek,* as did twenty-six of forty-eight members of the overall Research and Policy Committee. This slight majority felt that a wage-price board was needed because the administration's current policies were not likely to control the cost-push pressures exerted by those unions and businesses that had "a significant degree of discretion in setting wages and prices," which was a polite way of saying that both big labor and big business could override market signals (Committee for Economic Development 1970a, p. 52). However, six conservative trustees voted that the report should not be published, and over a dozen others wrote comments and reservations, which primarily concerned the wage-price guidelines or labor policies, although a few dissents addressed issues related to taxation or tariffs.

John Harper, the chair and president of the world's largest aluminum company, Alcoa, and a director of Mellon Bank, Goodyear Tire and Rubber, and Procter & Gamble as well as a trustee of Carnegie-Mellon University, made the most sustained critique of wage-price guidelines. In the mid-1960s he had experienced firsthand the power the government could wield on pricing issues when the White House threatened to sell a portion of the government's aluminum stockpile and to raise the ante in a price-fixing case involving the aluminum industry (Cochrane 1975, pp. 232–236).

Harper began his criticisms by praising the new inflation statement because it "contains many excellent suggestions to alleviate the inflation problem" but then wrote that he "reject[ed] completely the recommendations for voluntary wage-price controls and the establishment of new institutions to police such controls." He argued that "so-called incomes policy would automatically bring the government increasingly into private decision-making and if inflation still continued, the obvious next step would be mandatory controls," which would soon apply to profits as well as wages and prices. Reminding readers of arguments he had made to CED trustees at an annual meeting in Los Angeles in the spring of 1966, he repeated that he did not believe that a government board "could ever understand the complexities involved in determining the 'right' noninflationary price for many different industries and firms with literally hundreds of thousands of products of different quality, size, shape, and form," and even if it could, "the danger of paving the way for more government intervention in our economic system does not warrant taking the risk" (Committee for Economic Development 1970a, pp. 78–79). Five other trustees, including the presidents of Caterpillar Tractor, Merck and Company, and Corinthian Broadcasting, joined him in his comments.

Although Harper was the most vehement critic, the most frequent dissenter was Herman Weiss, the vice chair of the board at General Electric, who had only become a CED trustee in the months before he was appointed to the subcommittee. Trained in engineering at Case Institute of Technology in Cleveland, he worked his way to the top of GE over a thirty-seven-year career. Although he was critical of wage-price guidelines, most of his eight dissents strongly opposed other forms of government involvement in collective bargaining. Joined by Harper and three others, he also wanted to reduce income support for striking workers and their families well beyond the elimination of any possibility of collecting unemployment compensation in two states: "In addition to being ineligible for Unemployment Compensation, strikers should not be eligible to receive welfare payments, food stamps and surplus commodities, Community Chest and United Fund assistance." Corporations were being asked to finance strikes against themselves, he argued, and "the community as a whole is forced to finance the strike" (Committee for Economic Development 1970a, p. 76).

However, there were a few dissenting comments in a more liberal direction, many of which in effect replied to the conservative claims. Frazar Wilde, by then retired from Connecticut General Life, said there was a need for "a fully implemented incomes policy" (Committee for Economic Development 1970a, p. 73). There were also arguments for more job training programs, better unemployment benefits, and a national minimum wage to stabilize the economy. But liberal critiques were fewer and shorter than conservative criticisms.

The rejection of wage-price guidelines by the hard-line CED trustees, as well as any other form of government involvement in labor relations beyond the National Labor Relations Board and the Federal Mediation and Conciliation Service, marked the emergence of a serious difference of opinion within the organization. In effect, the dissenters wanted to rely on two confrontational options for dealing with inflation, which could be used separately or together. One would hold the line on wage increases, thereby forcing blue-collar and white-collar employees to absorb the costs of inflation through cuts in their real wages. This course was justifiable in their minds because they thought that workers had been making excessive wage demands. The other option would increase unemployment by using high interest rates set by the Federal Reserve Board to reduce consumer demand and business investments. The hardliners apparently did not share the other trustees' sense of urgency concerning a set of problems that mostly boiled down to poverty, high levels of unemployment, lack of health care, and poor educational opportunities for the low-income people who lived in large cities in all parts of the country. Nor did they seem worried that higher unemployment might lead to further social disruption.

MEANWHILE, BACK AT THE WHITE HOUSE

As the CED was putting together its 1970 report and urging it on the White House and Congress, Nixon was trying a variety of stratagems to win Republican control of Congress in 1970, but to no avail. After failing to make the electoral gains he hoped for, he decided to do everything he could to bring unemployment down from the 5.5 percent it had reached just before the 1970 elections to 4.5 percent for the presidential election two years hence. He therefore leaned on the Fed for easy money and talked in January 1971 about a "full employment budget" for the fiscal year that would begin on July 1, 1971 (Matusow 1998, p. 91). By this he meant the CED "high employment budget" championed by Stein, which would lead to deficits in the current circumstances. The CED's *Report of Activities* expressed its agreement with Nixon's new policy directions, and in the process gave itself credit for the idea of a high-employment budget (Committee for Economic Development 1971a, p. 11).

Even though Nixon now put greater stress on employment, he tried to maintain a gradualist policy for dealing with inflation to avoid alienating union leaders who supported his Vietnam policies. With the inflation rate averaging 18 percent for the first year of new government construction contracts, Nixon met in mid-January 1971 with members of the Construction Industry Collective Bargaining Commission, which he had appointed nearly two years earlier, and asked for a voluntary plan in thirty days that would curb inflation. But the business executives and labor leaders on the commission could not agree to a plan. Nixon then turned to the remedy favored by the Construction Users Anti-Inflation Roundtable and the CED, a suspension of the Davis-Bacon Act in February 1971, which led the CED (1971a, p. 9) to write in its annual report that its earlier recommendations "anticipated" Nixon's action. The suspension ended a month later with the trade unions agreeing to a new Construction Industry Stabilization Committee, "whose task it was to abate wage increases to something like the rate that had prevailed from 1961 to 1968" (Marchi 1975, p. 332). All settlements would have to be approved first by craft-level dispute boards and then by the new industry stabilization committee.

Although Nixon was not yet prepared to institute a wage-price freeze or make the transition to an incomes policy, partly because of strong divisions within his administration over taking those steps, the Business Council decided that it did not want to wait any longer for action. In a meeting at the White House with Nixon in May, J. Irwin Miller, the president of Cummins Engine and a former CED trustee, "espoused the immediate adoption of wage and price controls." Then the Business Council as a whole took "the unprecedented step of taking a straw vote on the issue, subsequently conveying to the president an expression of discontent at the administration's failure to secure smaller wage and price increases" (Marchi 1975, p. 340). Strikes in several different industries in the summer of 1971, which resulted in major wage hikes, including a 30 percent wage increase over a three-year period for the United Steel Workers, finally forced Nixon's hand (Matusow 1998, p. 110).

The new plan announced in early August instituted a ninety-day freeze on wages and prices, but not on dividends, interest, or profits. Even imminent pay raises negotiated earlier by unions on behalf of 1.3 million employees were frozen. Most interest groups and the general public, including the corporate community, responded to the freeze with strong approval, but unions reacted negatively because they thought it was aimed at them. As historian Allen Matusow (1998, p. 157) explained, "Everyone knew the real purposes of the freeze. It was to halt the excessive wage settlements driving up cost-push inflation."

In addition to the freeze, there was a proposal for reductions in taxes for both businesses and individuals to stimulate the economy and reduce unemployment. Since the tax cuts might feed inflation, the plan included tentative proposals for government spending cuts. However, Nixon assumed (correctly, as it turned out) that congressional Democrats would make even larger tax cuts and block spending cuts, which would provide a more vibrant economy for him to take credit for and good reasons to blame Democrats for any increase in inflation (Matusow 1998, pp. 151, 164).

On top of its direct challenge to organized labor, the Nixon administration "declared economic warfare against its astonished allies" in Europe and Japan (Matusow 1998, p. 162). It did so through two changes in international economic policy designed to stimulate the American economy and reduce unemployment, while at the same time helping American corporations sell more goods overseas. Capitalizing on the fact that the American dollar was also the international medium of exchange, the first change put an end to a postwar international monetary system built on the promise that foreign countries could convert American dollars to gold, which provided the stability (via monetary reserves for other countries) that was needed to rebuild the European economies devastated by World War II.

In the parlance of the day, the administration "closed the gold window," which in reality had been closed since the mid-1960s because there were by then more American dollars in Europe than there was gold in the bullion depository in Fort Knox, Kentucky. However, the fiction of gold being convertible to dollars was a useful one because it ensured American global dominance and postponed the day when the system of fixed exchange rates might have to be revised if inflation did not decline. The Treasury Department had therefore suggested in June 1969 that the fiction should be sustained as long as possible, even while claiming for appearances' sake that the department's preferred option was evolutionary reform: "Keep the gold window open for now, the report advised, but be prepared to close it if necessary" (Matusow 1998, p. 128).

The sudden closing of the gold window, which apparently caught most countries by surprise, left American trading partners with unpleasant choices for dealing with the fact that the inflated dollar (its high price was maintained by the fixed exchange rates) was exporting inflation to their countries. For example, they could continue to accept the flood of dollars let loose by the Fed's easy money policies—$10 billion in 1970, $30 billion in 1971—despite the negative consequences for their own economies. Or they could reevaluate their currencies upward, which would reduce any trade advantages their corporations had in relation to American companies. They might even restrict American capital inflow, but that would invite American retaliation. Their only reasonable choice was to allow the international market to determine the value of each currency, which is what eventually happened.

In closing the gold window, and thereby forcing a reconsideration of fixed exchange rates, Nixon was making the best of his options in terms of dealing with domestic economic problems and corporate concerns. In effect, the federal government's efforts to keep the dollar at a high value, along with inflation and high American wage rates, made American exports too expensive, rendering them less competitive in European and Japanese markets. At the same time, allowing imports to be less expensive made them more attractive to American buyers. In the process, both corporate profits and American jobs were being lost. To deal with these issues, Nixon could have pursued multilateral discussions of a new system of negotiated exchange rates, but that avenue had not been fruitful in the past. He also could have started negotiations for a system of "floating exchange rates," that is, rates set by currency markets, which might have proved to be a lengthy process.

Faced with serious inflationary and trade problems, the more attractive alternative for Nixon was simply to assert American power by refusing to convert dollars into gold, "thus reneging on dollar liabilities and expanding domestically without regard to international repercussions" (Dahlberg 1984, p. 586). Although Burns and leaders at the New York Federal Reserve Bank, which traditionally managed the country's international monetary affairs, expressed concerns that closing the gold window might trigger retaliation or more inflation, Nixon chose the option preferred by the Treasury Department if and when temporizing failed. He closed the gold window not only because he thought he had to do something to protect the dollar but "because he wanted to. It was his opening move in a historic offensive to correct the overvalued dollar and reorder the trading world to serve his political purposes" (Matusow 1998, p. 148).

Nixon's international power play also included a second thrust. He imposed a temporary 10 percent increase on those imports still subject to a tariff, thereby forcing other countries to negotiate new terms of trade with the US government or lose imports into the world's largest market. In exchange for removing this temporary tariff increase, the Nixon team wanted its trading partners to negotiate a new system of exchange rates and to lower certain of their tariffs that were hindrances to American corporations. It also wanted its economic and political allies to help pay for the expensive American military presence in their countries, which contributed to the trade imbalance. Moreover, just to make sure that American trading partners knew he meant business, the president announced a 10 percent reduction in foreign aid and provided new tax subsidies for American exports (Matusow 1998, p. 167).

The new international economic policies removed any conflict between the corporate community's domestic goals—low inflation and high employment—and an integrated world economy in which large corporations could prosper. Closing the gold window also dealt with several of the negative consequences of the American failure to control inflation between 1967 and 1971. It gave the Nixon administration the freedom to follow expansive domestic policies and continue to spend money abroad, while at the same time trying to control the wage-price spiral through the freeze. For all the confusion and consternation the package generated, it in fact furthered the interests of both the corporate community and the White House.

Shortly after the new economic policies were announced on August 15, Nixon appointed William Eberle, recently president of American Standard, a manufacturer of plumbing and heating equipment, as his special trade representative for negotiating needed changes in currency rates and tariffs. Not coincidentally, Eberle was the chair of a CED project on trade and currency issues that had arrived at many of the same conclusions as the Treasury Department and the White House based on over two years of discussions, so he was well prepared for his new position (Committee for Economic

Development 1971c). The government role took Eberle to dozens of meetings in capital cities across the world over the next three years. Another CED trustee, banker David M. Kennedy, Nixon's first secretary of the treasury, joined Eberle in these efforts as an ambassador-at-large, handling negotiations with Japan. By 1973, after many thousands of hours of negotiations and the failure of a new system of fixed exchange rates, the new international monetary system was based on floating exchange rates. The many advantages of this arrangement for trade among developed economies, such as automatic balance of payments adjustments, the absence of crises, and the freedom for each country to pursue different internal economic policies, outweighed the potential problems that could be caused by changes in the value of a currency, currency speculation, and the exacerbation of inflationary tendencies.

At the end of the ninety-day wage-price freeze, Nixon established separate pay and price boards, which were fashioned in part to satisfy organized labor. Their charge was to establish guidelines and limit the size of any increases that went beyond them. The pay board, with five labor representatives, five business representatives, and five public representatives, voted ten to five against retroactive pay increases for the 1.3 million employees whose raises had been frozen (Matusow 1998, p. 162). Its later decisions may have restrained wage increases somewhat, but several of its early settlements were very permissive. The price board, with seven public members, didn't even do that well, but inflation was declining for other reasons in any case. For Nixon and the corporate community, what mattered was the rapid growth in the economy after the failed effort at curbing inflation through demand restraint.

Although the issues involved in the wage-price freeze and closing the gold window were talked about in terms of cost-push inflation, balance of payments problems, trade barriers, and exchange rates, the underlying issues were clearly concerned with power. Would American unions continue to have the power to win wage increases under conditions of labor scarcity and inflation? Which countries might have to suffer inflation or unemployment, or both? Whose corporations would have the best opportunities to sell their products in other countries? For Nixon, the goal was to "keep the United States number one and help rally a new majority for '72" (Matusow 1998, p. 148). As for the corporate moderates, the pressures they exerted in favor of dramatic government actions showed they were willing to do battle with both the unions at home and their trading partners overseas, just as they had done with the unions and the Soviet Union from the 1940s through the 1960s.

THE CED REACTS TO NIXON'S ECONOMIC POLICIES

The CED reacted positively to Nixon's policy changes, as revealed by favorable comments in its annual reports and in new statements on trade policy and inflation. Its statement on *The United States and the European Community* (1971c), chaired by Eberle, expressed strong approval of the new economic policies. It also endorsed the strategic use of the temporary increases in tariffs on some imports to induce other countries to enter into negotiations, reiterating that the tariffs should be lowered or removed altogether only in return for changes in exchange rates and other concessions. It supported the continuance of wage and price controls for as long as they were needed. In effect, the report, which was finalized shortly after Eberle was appointed as the special trade representative, provided an outline and supporting information for his efforts.

A report on inflation issues from another subcommittee a year later, *High Employment without Inflation,* began with unequivocal support for Nixon's economic initiatives: "We believe that very forceful action had indeed become necessary to cope adequately with the twin problems of inflation and unemployment, and that the Administration's program of wage and price controls deserves the nation's broad support." Although the report mostly repeated previous recommendations and concentrated on creating the conditions that would make controls unnecessary, it added that wage and price controls would need to last until inflation was brought under control, which might take a considerable amount of time: "*If the stabilization objectives are to be fully achieved, demand and structural measures will have to be supplemented for the foreseeable future with wage-price (or incomes) policies involving some direct governmental concern with significant wage and price decisions*" (Committee for Economic Development 1972a, pp. 9, 17, italics in the original).

Although there were no votes against publication, the reservations expressed by hard-liners were if anything even harsher than those appended to the previous inflation report, so not all CED trustees were by any means happy with the government's interference in domestic markets. Harper of Alcoa and Weiss of GE, two of only four holdovers from the previous inflation subcommittee, were the most frequent and critical dissenters. Harper made sixteen comments, Weiss made fourteen; together, they accounted for thirty of forty-six memoranda of comment, reservation, or dissent by hard-line trustees. In addition, Harper, by then one of the main advocates for turning the Construction Users Anti-Inflation Roundtable into a more general organization, also joined four other trustees in ten dissents, including six dissents by Weiss, so he was part of twenty-six comments. Moreover, several trustees seconded his criticisms as well, so he was the most visible and central critic. As the chair and president of Alcoa, he was also the highest-ranking spokesperson for the new hard-line faction within the CED.

Weiss, with Harper joining him, repeated his 1970 assertion that the families of anyone on strike should not receive welfare payments, food stamps, surplus commodities, or help from the Community Fund or United Fund. This time he could refer to a recent study by researchers at the Wharton School, which claimed that strikes cost $365 billion a year in direct and indirect welfare support for strikers and thereby contributed to inflation by causing strikes to be longer and settlements more costly (Committee for Economic Development 1972a, p. 75; Thieblot and Cowin 1972).

But the most remarkable reservation concerning the report, which drew the approval of five other critics, including Harper, came from trustee Marvin Bower, who built up McKinsey and Co., a business consulting firm, over the previous several decades. According to Bower, the problem boiled down to a matter of national will and character, with the electorate shouldering a good deal of the blame. "The degree of the nation's 'will' (or resolve) is the determining factor," he began. "Unless the electorate and its leaders and legislators show a greater willingness than they are showing currently to pay for public services and benefits on a more current basis, and so avoid large and continuous budget deficits, then neither fiscal nor monetary policy nor any number of control phases will be successful in avoiding a high rate of (or even runaway) inflation." He then invoked history as evidence for the need for better self-discipline on the part of the American people: "History shows that control of inflation depends ultimately on the character of the people and their capacity for self-denial" (Committee for Economic Development 1972a, p. 65).

Although Harper was emerging as the policy leader for the hard-liners within the CED, Bower—with the help of his consulting firm—was in the process of becoming their ideological spokesperson and the person most willing to call for major changes in the organization's direction. Both men were among the five vice chairs of the CED at the time.

THE CED CONTINUES TO SUPPORT
GOVERNMENT SOCIAL BENEFITS

In contrast to the disagreements over how to deal with inflation, few CED trustees disapproved of several new reports that advocated enlarged government benefit programs. A 1970 statement, *Training and Jobs for the Urban Poor,* called for a special government program to train low-income inner-city residents for work in both the private and public sectors. It also recommended the establishment of nonprofit "Jobs Corporations" in metropolitan areas. A 1971 statement, *Education for the Urban Disadvantaged: From Pre-School to Employment,* expressed support for preschools and called for standards to hold schools accountable for the performance of their students. Two years later, *Financing Low-Income Housing* advocated housing allowances for low-income families, and *Building a National Health Care System* (discussed briefly at the end of the section on Medicare in Chapter 6) called for an all-inclusive system based on employer mandates, the continuance of Medicare, and a new program for low-income patients based on community trusts.

The corporate moderates' continuing support for ameliorative welfare and social policies also is reflected in the composition of its Research Advisory Board between 1968 and 1972. It included Wilbur Cohen, one of the architects of Medicare, by then the dean of the School of Social Welfare at the University of Michigan; and Daniel Patrick Moynihan, a sociologist employed as the director of the Harvard-MIT Joint Center for Urban Studies after several years as an assistant secretary of labor in the Kennedy and early Johnson administrations. Other visible policy experts from the 1960s on the advisory board were Mitchell Sviridoff, the former union official who joined the Ford Foundation as its vice president for urban affairs in 1966, and Paul Ylvisaker, the former Ford Foundation official who supported the pilot projects leading to the War on Poverty, and later a professor of public affairs and urban planning at Princeton.

However, by far the most revealing evidence for the CED's support for social initiatives, *Improving the Welfare System* (1970b), provided a plan for a national guaranteed minimum income with a floor of $2,400 ($14,232 in 2012 dollars) for a family of four. Appearing at a moment when the welfare rolls were climbing rapidly and the unemployment rate was low, it required recipients to work or enter a training program, with an exemption for mothers with children under the age of two. In addition to a guaranteed minimum income in exchange for work or training, the statement advocated a phased federal takeover of local and state welfare programs, and day-care programs for preschool children as young as age two. The Research and Policy Committee's vote to publish it was unanimous, and there were no conservative comments.

The report built on several years of work on this issue by corporate moderates and their advisors. The first influence was a series of meetings by business leaders who were called together in March 1967 by Governor Nelson Rockefeller of New York to answer the question, "If the problem of public welfare was given to you, what would you recommend as sound public policy in the next decade?" Led by Joseph Wilson, the chair of Xerox and a CED trustee, and with several other CED trustees on the steering committee, the group came to the conclusion that it could support either of two alternatives. One called for a "negative income tax," advocated by both Keynesian and monetary economists, in which individuals would receive year-end payments from the government if their incomes fell below a specified minimum. The other provided for "family allowances," in which government would provide monthly payments to families with low incomes to help raise their children. However, the Rockefeller group said that it "leans in the direction of a negative income tax" as long as the system contains "strong incentives to work" (Moynihan 1973, pp. 56–57). A presidential commission appointed by Johnson in 1967, with CED trustee Benjamin Heineman of Chicago and Northwestern Railways as chair, similarly advocated a negative income tax in a report that appeared in November 1969, but it did not include a work requirement.

The CED report appeared just after the House had supported Nixon's version of welfare reform and income maintenance. Called the Family Assistance Plan, it was developed by a staff of Democrats and Republican experts that included Moynihan of the Harvard-MIT center. It built on the idea of family allowances, not a negative income tax, which meant that it would not cover single individuals or couples without children. The plan called for a minimum annual income benefit of $2,400 through a combination of government payments and food stamps for families with children, so it is likely that the CED report had used the same figure to demonstrate solidarity with the Nixon recommendations. The new plan helped the working poor as much as, or more than, those on welfare, contained a workfare component for those on welfare, and was especially favorable for low-income African American families in the South. It was fashioned so that it would not cost more than $4 billion in the first year, which was considered the feasible economic and political limit by the Nixon administration (Committee for Economic Development 1970b).

The plan was not redistributive. One independent economic analyst who studied it in detail concluded that "these sums are so small as compared with total income that they would have an insignificant impact on the overall distribution of income," moving one percentage point of income from the nonpoor to the poor (Okner 1972, p. 352). Some liberal Democrats and virtually all welfare rights activists criticized the program because the income payments were lower than they had hoped for and would involve cuts for some welfare recipients in Northern cities. They also were critical of the work and training requirements, likening them to involuntary servitude.

While it might seem that support for such a program from the CED would be welcomed, Moynihan was not pleased by the arrival of its report because it called the Family Assistance Plan a mere "first step" and did not include a requirement that "women heads of households" had to work in order to receive the support payments. However, Wilson of Xerox did say at a press conference, "We want to see this legislation passed" (Moynihan 1973, p. 288).

The Family Assistance Plan endorsed by CED trustee Wilson had passed the House after careful scrutiny and considerable revision by the Ways and Means Committee, with Mills taking the lead for the Democrats. The ranking Republican on the committee, John Byrnes of Wisconsin, also worked very hard to improve and pass the bill. When Southern Democrats expressed concern on the House floor that a disproportionate number of the current welfare recipients were African Americans, Mills pointed out that most of the working poor, who would be greatly helped by this legislation, were white and lived in the South (Welsh 1973, p. 15). Mills and the House whip, Hale Boggs of Louisiana, convinced several fellow Southerners to support the revised plan, and Byrnes stressed its White House origins and its work requirement in order to sway any hesitant Republicans. Despite opposition from most Southern Democrats, the conservative coalition did not form and the bill passed by a strong 243 to 155.

With ultraconservatives inside and outside the government waging a spirited campaign to defeat the bill, members of the conservative coalition serving on the Senate's most powerful committee, the seventeen-member Finance Committee, blocked it in the summer of 1970. This majority consisted of seven Republicans from small states with few welfare recipients or African Americans (Arizona, Delaware, Idaho, Iowa, Nebraska, Utah, and Wyoming), and three Southern Democrats. These members had been placed on the committee to guard against attempts to raise taxes, reduce agricultural subsidies, or lower the depletion allowances granted to the domestic oil industry. Their rejection of the plan was spearheaded by one of the staunchest antiwelfare Republicans in the Senate, John J. Williams, the senior senator from Delaware, a rich state with very low welfare benefits. He made his opposition clear through statements he made and charts he presented at committee hearings. In the process, he argued that a guaranteed minimum income, in conjunction with food stamps and free medical care (which would be lost if too much money were earned), created disincentives to accept full-time jobs with low pay (Moynihan 1973, pp. 456–457). He was joined in his attack by the committee's chair, Democrat Russell Long of Louisiana. Long claimed to be for the legislation in principle but sabotaged it in numerous ways, including with misleading statements about it and procedural delays that kept it from coming to the Senate floor in a timely fashion as a rider on other bills (Welsh 1973, p. 17).

Although a representative of the National Association of Manufacturers testified that one of its own committees had found the plan's incentive structure workable, conservative senators insisted that they wanted more work incentives in the bill. As they well knew, their demands would raise the costs of the program well beyond what were considered reasonable limits. They also complained that the support for working adults was an expansion of welfare, which frustrated the proponents because they saw their program as a step toward shrinking the welfare rolls. On the liberal side of the table, an increase in work incentives raised the danger of forcing single mothers of preschool children to work outside the home. This upset liberal Democrats and was anathema to leftists and welfare recipients, who warned the Democrats against settling for small gains and created the National Welfare Rights Organization to bring pressure for higher welfare benefits.

After the White House made numerous revisions in the program in a vain attempt to satisfy members of the conservative coalition on the committee, the final vote of 10–6 against the plan included three negative votes from liberal Democrats. However, Moynihan (1973, p. 534) claims that it was too easy to blame liberals for killing the bill, which many commentators did at the time: "In the main," he said, the defeat was "a triumph of conservative strategy." Ultraconservatives on the committee made the program too costly through work incentives for any Republican to vote for it and too seemingly punitive for all but one of the four liberal Democrats to lend support.

Efforts were made to revive the plan in 1972, and a consensus between liberal Democrats and Nixon Republicans seemed to be close at one point. After once again passing the House, the new version lost in a 10–4 vote in the Senate Finance Committee, with liberals on one side and conservatives on the other. By that point there were no strong pressures to institute a new program. There had been no major urban riots since the summer of 1968, the upsurge in welfare recipients had leveled off, and there were fewer likely jobs for current welfare recipients with the unemployment rate at or near 6 percent in 1971 and between 5.6 and 5.8 percent during the first eight months of 1972. In the final analysis, however, it was the Southern Democrats' racial animus and their desire to maintain a low-wage workforce, in conjunction with the antigovernment mentality of hard-core Republicans, that blocked the program (Quadagno 1990; 1994, chapter 5).

Most important in the long run, the debate over the various policy options for helping low-income families legitimated year-end support payments from the federal government for the working poor, which came to be called the earned income tax credit (EITC), a far more positive name than "negative income tax." Corporate moderates saw the EITC as better than any of the alternatives for income maintenance because it does not distort low-wage labor markets in the way they believe minimum wages do. In fact, from the corporate point of view, the EITC is a wage subsidy to business that is paid for out of general taxes and can be understood as an offset for the taxes low-income workers pay into Social Security through the payroll tax (Quadagno 1994, p. 122). Moreover, members of the conservative coalition, who always oppose both welfare payments and the creation of government jobs, could champion it as an incentive to work and a bonus: "Southern Democrats, who have repeatedly blocked or reduced social welfare benefits for the poor (including Aid to Dependent Children and its successor, Aid for Families with Dependent Children) paved the way for the EITC" (Howard 1997, pp. 67, 74, 143–144). They also made the program more attractive to antigovernment ultraconservatives by excluding public-sector workers, which made it possible to keep wages low for state and local government employees in the South. In 2012 dollars, the program provided up to $5,830 for a family with two or more children.

The fate of the Family Assistance Plan aside, the fact that the hard-line CED trustees did not oppose educational and income maintenance proposals is revealing in terms of the nature of the conflict within the corporate moderates' camp. Improved government social benefits, especially at a time when the return of major disruptions by African Americans in the inner cities still seemed to be an outside possibility, were one thing. But government regulation of corporate practices, or strong wage-price guidelines that might turn into rules, were entirely different matters, because they had to do with power.

BIG CHANGES AT THE NATIONAL LABOR RELATIONS BOARD

While the arguments over inflation and the Family Assistance Plan were unfolding, the Labor Law Reform Group was working patiently with the White House to change the composition of the National Labor Relations Board in ways that would have long-term impacts on a whole range of management-union issues. LLRG members understood that the changes had to be gradual because of Nixon's desire to maintain labor leaders' support for the Vietnam War, control civil disturbances, and gain as much blue-collar electoral support as possible. They also realized that pro-labor Democrats controlled the labor committees in both Houses and could block anti-labor appointees. Despite these obstacles, the direction of the board was quietly changed in dramatic ways by late 1971.

With Douglas Soutar designated to work with the Nixon administration on all labor-related appointments, including to the NLRB, George Shultz rejected the LLRG's initial suggestion for a new chair of the labor board. Instead, he asked for a Republican who was not from either wing of the party. The result was the appointment of a corporate lawyer, Edward Miller, a partner in a large Chicago firm and a member of the Blue Ribbon Committee that helped guide the work of the LLRG. Miller said little about his views before or after his appointment, but he did indicate he believed that protecting the freedom of employees to join or not join a union was more important than the encouragement of collective bargaining. George Meany formally opposed Miller's appointment, but not so vigorously that Democrats on the Senate labor committee voted against him. Nor was there any opposition to Nixon's second appointment, Ralph Kennedy, a longtime staff member of the NLRB, who had become a regional director during the Eisenhower administration (Gross 1995, pp. 220–221).

Joining with a Republican holdover on the board, Miller and Kennedy diluted or reversed many of the decisions made by the board during the Kennedy-Johnson years. They began by ruling that the board was limited in the penalties it could impose on companies that violated the law, and then gradually allowed more anti-union statements by employers in the name of free speech. However, their most important decision came in 1971, when they ruled that there was no duty for corporations to bargain on decisions that involved "fundamental managerial issues," which effectively overruled the board's 1963 Fibreboard decision without explicitly doing so (Gross 1995, p. 226).

In a case involving General Motors' right to sell a truck dealership to an independent company that would be doing business in space it leased from General Motors, the majority ruled that General Motors had to bargain about the "effects" of the sale, but not about the sale itself, because the sale "was financial and entrepreneurial in nature" (Gross 1995, p. 193). The difference may seem small, but the Democratic majority had ruled in the Fibreboard case in 1962 that there was a duty to bargain about the decision itself, which meant before the decision was made. Although the Supreme Court supported the labor board's decision on narrow grounds in its 1964 opinion, the Republican majority now followed the comment in Justice Potter Stewart's concurring Fibreboard decision about management control over decisions that were "at the core of entrepreneurial control" or were "fundamental to the basic direction of the corporate enterprise" (Gross 1995, pp. 225–227). This change opened the way for outsourcing, plant removal, and plant closures, thereby facilitating the unimpeded movement of production to low-wage American states and Third World countries at the same time as communication and transportation costs continued to decline.

From that point on the battle between the corporate community and organized labor was fully joined at all levels. The new anti-union offensive also included the return of consulting firms that advised corporations on how to keep out or disestablish unions, which had been made possible by a Department of Labor ruling in 1963 that consultants had to report to it "only after communicating directly to their client's workers." The Labor Department's slight amendment to its earlier ruling made it possible for anti-union consulting firms and law firms to employ many old and new anti-union strategies, including the use of labor spies, by working only with management, thereby turning over direct contacts with employees to union-busting personnel on the companies' payroll. By the late 1970s there were dozens of such firms, with one of the largest, West Coast Industrial Relations Associates, claiming as many as 1,500 clients a year (see Smith 2003, pp. 102–104, for the information and quotation in this paragraph).

Anti-union consultants often encouraged corporations to fire workers who tried to create unions, even though such an action was illegal. They calculated that it was worth paying the relatively small fines and back wages when the case was finally decided after the exhaustion of their delaying tactics, if unions could be defeated in the meantime. They also attempted to decertify unions that already had been established. In addition, the ongoing movement of unionized factories out of Northern states to the South and lower-wage foreign destinations made workers more hesitant to ask for large wage increases. This wide-ranging corporate attack, from the labor board to the factory gates, and the consequent loss of union power, is one of the major reasons for the decline in income for average workers during the 1970s (Bluestone and Harrison 1982).

DEFEATS FOR THE CORPORATE COMMUNITY?

The Nixon administration initiated two major pieces of regulatory legislation, the National Environmental Protection Act of 1969 and the Occupational Safety and Health Act of 1970, which came to be viewed by the corporate community as setbacks just a few years later. The new revisionists therefore claim that the enactment of these laws was a defeat for the corporate community (e.g., Vogel 1989). One revisionist even claims that these laws were adopted as a result of "direct actions and lobbying campaigns against business" (Phillips-Fein 2009, p. 153). It is therefore essential to analyze the origins of this legislation to see what actually happened.

The Origins of the Environmental Protection Agency

The Environmental Protection Agency had its origins in the wildlife and conservation organizations that corporate moderates first created during the Progressive Era (Gonzalez 2001). They were supplemented and made more policy relevant in the 1950s due to the corporate community's growing concern with overpopulation and the pressure on scarce natural resources that might develop. In keeping with the recommendations of a Truman-appointed presidential commission chaired by the head of CBS, the Ford Foundation and Rockefeller philanthropies provided several million dollars in start-up funding for the first and most prominent environmental think tank, Resources for the Future, which broke new ground by incorporating market economics into thinking about conservation and resources (Collier and Horowitz 1976, pp. 304–306; Robinson 1993). Basically, its economists demonstrated that resource substitution could be managed through the price system and that it was a myth to claim there is a trade-off between jobs and environmental regulation. They also noted that there was money to be made in cleaning up the air and water. Their work reassured corporate moderates that most environmental initiatives were completely compatible with corporate capitalism, contrary to the angry outcries against environmentalism by ultraconservatives (Alpert and Markusen 1980).

The Ford Foundation next granted $7 million over a three-year period in the early 1960s to develop ecology programs at seventeen universities around the country, thereby providing the informational base and personnel infrastructure for efforts to control pesticides and industrial waste. At the same time, several foundations, including the Ford Foundation, put millions of dollars into the land-purchase programs of the Nature Conservancy and the National Audubon Society (Robinson 1993). They also encouraged environmental education and citizen action through donations to municipal conservation commissions and the nationwide Conservation Foundation, the latter founded by the Rockefeller family as a combined think tank and policy-discussion group. Laurence Rockefeller, who had taken the lead within his family on environmental issues, played a prominent role in Johnson's 1965 Task Force on Natural Beauty, which drew heavily on reports from projects in which he was involved (Collier and Horowitz 1976, pp. 384–387). Although a more militant wing of younger environmentalists soon emerged, the fact remains that much of the early grassroots movement was encouraged and legitimated by the major foundations of which the corporate moderates were trustees (Mitchell 1991).

The top environmental appointees in the Nixon administration came from this network of environmental policy-planning groups, starting with Russell Train, the son of a naval officer, and an army officer himself during World War II. A graduate of Princeton and Columbia Law School, Train founded the Wildlife Leadership

Foundation in 1959, became the vice president of the World Wildlife Fund from 1961 to 1965, and served as its president from 1965 until he joined the Nixon administration in 1969, eventually becoming chair of the new White House Council on Environmental Quality. Train and his coworkers then formulated the legislation that became the Environmental Protection Agency. The EPA's first administrator was a corporate lawyer, William Ruckelshaus, who graduated from Harvard Law School and returned home to join his family's law firm, which also led to his involvement in Republican politics in Indiana. Train then succeeded Ruckelshaus, thereby completing his move from the policy-planning network to a top government position in textbook fashion. By all accounts, corporate moderates were supporters of this series of events. They also served as sponsors of the first Earth Day, in March 1970.

The Occupational Safety and Health Act

The original version of the Occupational Safety and Health Act, which led to the establishment of the Occupational Safety and Health Administration (OSHA) to regulate all work sites, was proposed by the Johnson administration in 1968. However, the bill did not make it to the floor of either house in the face of strong opposition by both the NAM and the US Chamber of Commerce. Still, the corporate community was "divided" on the issue, which suggests that the corporate moderates were not completely opposed to the idea at the time (Vogel 1989, p. 84). Based on the original opposition by ultraconservatives, it is surprising that the entire corporate community nonetheless supported the Nixon administration when it introduced similar legislation in 1969 as part of its efforts to win electoral support from workers. It is also noteworthy that the administration put its proposal forward without any urging from organized labor or environmentalists.

Ironically, the corporate community's support did not lead to immediate passage of the bill because the unions and the environmental movement insisted that the agency be part of the Department of Labor, not the independent agency Nixon advocated. The environmental-labor coalition also called for higher standards and tougher enforcement procedures than Nixon envisioned. These two demands, which most non-Southern Democrats supported, led the corporate community and the conservative coalition to block the bill. After nearly two years of arguing back and forth, a compromise was reached: the agency would be in the Department of Labor, but a separate three-person commission would enforce the regulations.

As for the standards, they were essentially the ones developed in previous decades by corporate moderates through their long-standing and interlocked nonprofit organizations for dealing with safety and health issues. Called the "compensation-safety apparatus" in one detailed study of injury, illness, and death in American workplaces, this subset of the larger corporate policy-planning network includes the National Safety Council, the National Council on Compensation Insurance, and the American National Standards Institute, among several (Berman 1978, chapter 4). More specifically, almost two hundred standards were requested from the American National Standards Institute by the Department of Labor in 1969, which then adopted 180 of them as its own before passage of the safety and health act. When the OSHA legislation finally passed, the privately determined standards "were taken over intact under Section 6(a) of the OSHA law" (Berman 1978, p. 79). For those instances in which other private organizations had developed more stringent regulations, as was the case for airborne contaminants, OSHA adopted the American National Standards Institute's weaker standards.

Neither business nor labor was enthusiastic about the final bill because it did not include all that either of them wanted, but neither opposed the bill, and it passed easily in both houses. There was little indication that the corporate community saw the agency as the regulatory monster it was later said to be (Noble 1986).

THE NIXON ADMINISTRATION AS A CORPORATE SUCCESS STORY

Despite the economic problems that persisted throughout the first Nixon administration, those four years were extremely successful ones for the corporate moderates in terms of policies and politics. Their labor lawyers and industrial relations vice presidents played a key role in the appointment of conservatives to the National Labor Relations Board, which then made decisions that aided in the project to weaken unions. Pressures from the corporate moderates also encouraged the Department of Labor to reshape the craft unions' apprenticeship programs by expanding their size and taking over the power to select new applicants, thereby bringing about some racial integration and weakening the construction unions. In the case of the Construction Users Anti-Inflation Roundtable, it helped to set up a government advisory board to limit wages in the industry, and the percentage of unionized construction work fell from 80 percent in 1968 to 60 percent in 1975 (Quadagno 1994, pp. 78–85).

In addition, corporate moderates either suggested or supported all of the measures that Nixon tried in his attempt to control inflation, and they approved of his decision to close the gold window at the Treasury Department. The forcefulness of the Business Council in calling for a wage-price freeze is particularly noteworthy in this regard, especially in light of later claims by one revisionist that this "august group" in general "remained aloof from political engagement" (Phillips-Fein 2009, p. 166). Its assertiveness also contradicts the idea that the corporate community was not very organized or assertive until the Business Roundtable was formed (Hacker and Pierson 2010; Vogel 1989). Nor did the CED's *Report of Activities in 1971* mince words in expressing its pleasure with Nixon's decisions on these issues, and it took some of the credit as well. The opening sentence in the report claimed, "1971 was the year in which important CED recommendations were translated into national policy"; it then quoted a liberal newspaper, the *Boston Globe,* saying that the CED's recommendations for dealing with inflation in 1970 "laid the groundwork for the Nixon economic controls." The same paragraph also noted that the CED's 1971 report on monetary policy in relation to Europe "urged that currency revaluation be accompanied by removal of the import surcharge" and added that Eberle had been appointed the President's Special Representative for Trade Negotiation to carry out this policy (Committee for Economic Development 1972b, p. 3).

At the same time, the corporate moderates supported a variety of social welfare measures to deal with discontent and social disruption at the lower levels of society, some of which were passed by Congress, some not. Corporate moderates also advocated the federalization of benefits for low-income families through expanded social welfare programs with a work component. They endorsed the concept of an "earned income tax credit," which eventually emerged as the consensus program to support social stability without disrupting low-wage labor markets. Corporate moderates also supported occupational safety and health as long as the government adopted standards already created by private corporate-sponsored organizations, and they supplied many of the ideas for Nixon's environmental initiatives through their numerous policy-planning and discussion organizations related to environmental issues. It is simultaneously an understatement and overkill to point out that the wistful romantics are wrong about the origins of the EPA and OSHA.

After strong lobbying by urban real estate interests, even more cities became eligible for Model Cities funding during the Nixon administration, and a growing portion of the Department of Housing and Urban Development's budget was spent on nearly a thousand urban renewal projects that had not been completed. The remaining Model Cities money was shifted from social service programs for the poor to "hardware" for the "most affluent communities," which were primarily white (Frieden and Kaplan 1975, pp. 259, 261, 264–265). Some of the money was spent on tennis court complexes in high-income neighborhoods and the extension of municipal golf courses. In effect, HUD became a conduit for money for the growth coalitions. It was a return to the role of the original Housing and Home Finance Agency, which remained HUD's biggest agency throughout the efforts in the 1960s to create new programs for low-income communities.

The conservative coalition formed more frequently than it ever had during the first Nixon administration and won a large percentage of its challenges, including 75 percent of the time in the Senate in 1971–1972. Among the coalition's victories on domestic legislation in Nixon's first term was a long list of cuts or alterations in Johnson's Great Society programs, most of them advocated by Nixon and bitterly opposed by the liberal-labor alliance: reducing funds for the Job Corps and closing most of its offices, giving governors a veto over Legal Services programs, reducing Office of Economic Opportunity funding by $292.1 million, limiting federal authority to reduce school desegregation, and defeating the Family Assistance Plan (Manley 1973, pp. 240–241). What remained of the War on Poverty was divided up and tucked away within existing departments (Quadagno 1994, p. 175).

Successes that can be attributed to the liberal-labor alliance were few and far between. Unemployment compensation was extended for an additional twenty-six weeks, the food stamp program was expanded, and a liberal filibuster killed strong anti-busing legislation passed by the conservative coalition in the House. In addition, the liberal-labor alliance won the support of moderates in blocking the appointments of two Southerners with segregationist pasts to the Supreme Court, and led the way in limiting the ground war in Vietnam (Manley 1973, p. 241; Roof 2011, chapter 4).

In terms of the lives of ordinary Americans, the most significant gains concerned improvements in Social Security benefits, which were increased by 15 percent in 1969, 10 percent in 1971, and 20 percent in 1972. In 1972 Congress legislated automatic cost-of-living increases in Social Security benefits that would begin in 1975. In connection with the large increase in benefits between 1969 and 1972, the automatic cost-of-living adjustments ensured that most elderly Americans could live the remainder of their lives above the poverty line, a dramatic change from just a few years earlier. In addition, Congress put benefits for low-income blind, disabled, and elderly people into a new program, Supplemental Security Income, which was funded out of general revenues and administered by the Social Security Administration (Altman 2005, p. 211; Bernstein and Brodshaug 1988, p. 34).

Although liberals in Congress enthusiastically supported all of these changes and additions to Social Security, they were in good part due to the initiative of Nixon and congressional Republicans, who wanted to hold on to the support of retired voters. This sudden solicitude for Social Security beneficiaries on the part of Republicans provides a genuine example of how the competition for voters in the electoral arena can allow average citizens to have an impact on government. At the same time, these changes were acceptable to corporate moderates. More generally, the contrast between the corporate moderates' support for government insurance programs and their complete opposition to unions could not be more dramatic, continuing the pattern that began in 1935. Meanwhile, the Chamber of Commerce found itself betwixt and between during the first Nixon administration. It heartily approved of and lobbied for the various cuts in the War on Poverty programs, but it opposed the benefit changes in Social Security.

The general success of Nixon's mix of fiscal, monetary, and labor policies in aiding the rich and their corporations is revealed by the fact that the decline in income inequality from 1962 to 1968 ended in 1969, just as the new offensive against construction unions began, taking the Gini coefficient from 0.318 in 1968 to 0.335 by 1973, the highest it had been since 1951. At the same time, the effective tax rate on the top 1 percent of income earners was about what it was in 1967, 26.3 percent, most likely because inflation had moved even more of the highest incomes into the very top tax bracket.

As for union density, the combined efforts of the Construction Users Anti-Inflation Roundtable and the Department of Labor contributed to its ongoing slide from 27.9 in 1968 to 23.5 percent in 1973, despite the continuing growth of public-employee unions in the face of the varied efforts by the corporate community to obstruct them (Mayer 2004, p. 22, table A1; Miller and Canak 1995b, p. 19, table 1). Taken together, the rise in inequality and the decline in union density are consistent with findings from a carefully controlled quantitative comparison of income inequality and union strength between 1973 and 2004, which concluded that one-third of the increase in income inequality after 1973 was due to the attack on unions (Western and Rosenfeld 2011).

Rather than suffering setbacks during the Nixon administration, as the new revisionists claim, the corporate moderates were supportive and influential on economic, labor, and social welfare issues. Government spending programs that were increasingly redirected to the middle class and conservative states, along with increases in Social Security benefits and food stamps, are not evidence for liberal-labor power. Nevertheless, the fact remains that the leaders of the Construction Users Anti-Inflation Roundtable and other members of the corporate community were not satisfied with their progress on labor issues. They claimed wages were still too high and that labor unions were responsible for inflation. They also began to criticize the increase in government regulations they had looked at more benignly just a few years earlier, and to be concerned about the foreign competition that a previous generation of corporate moderates confidently encouraged as part of their effort to revive capitalism in Europe and Japan. While still supportive of social spending, they feared that it might get out of hand.

At the same time that Nixon was putting together his 1972 reelection campaign, which triumphed in the face of an unemployment rate that was 5.5 percent in September and 5.6 percent in October, the corporate moderates were trying to figure out how to have even more impact in the near future. The world was changing, so they were changing, too. Many were moving in a rightward direction, which created new divisions within their ranks.

Chapter Ten

The Rise of the Business Roundtable and Tension within the CED, 1973–1976

Encouraged by their success in shaping the National Labor Relations Board and in combating the construction unions, the hard-liners among the corporate moderates decided to transform the Labor Law Study Group and Construction Users Anti-Inflation Roundtable into committees within a more general business organization. The Business Roundtable was incorporated in October 1972, announced in mid-November, and began putting together an administrative structure by early 1973, just as President Nixon's second term began. A few months later the Business Roundtable came to include the March Group, a gathering of forty chief executive leaders and their Washington representatives, who were working on ways to influence Congress and sway the electorate (Gross 1995, pp. 234–235).

The Business Roundtable's leadership came from the Links Group, an informal gathering of thirty-five to forty CEOs, most of them in charge of the companies that sponsored the original efforts of the LLRG, the anti-inflation roundtable, and the March Group. This leadership cadre derived its name from its meeting place, the exclusive Links Club in downtown New York, which served as "the New York rendezvous of the national corporate establishment," according to sociologist E. Digby Baltzell (1964, p. 371), a pioneering researcher on the linkages between the social upper class and the corporate community.

Blough became the roundtable's founding chair, but W. Beverly Murphy, who retired as the CEO of Campbell Soup a year or so earlier, replaced him a few months before it was formally incorporated. Blough and another CED trustee, Frederick Borch of General Electric, were designated as vice chairmen to assist Murphy. In addition, three of the other seven members on the original executive committee were CED trustees. Two months later, the Business Roundtable had a letterhead listing thirty-five founders, twenty-two of whom were members of the Business Council. In addition, twelve were trustees of the CED, and four were trustees of the NAM, which suggests that the organization spanned the policy breadth of the corporate community. Once the Business Roundtable was operational in mid-1973, the retired triumvirate of Murphy, Blough, and Borch was replaced by John Harper of Alcoa, the CED trustee who had made his strong views on unions and government regulation of markets and prices sharply known in CED policy statements on inflation in 1970 and 1972.

The Business Roundtable differed in two major ways from the CED. First, it was limited to the CEOs of large corporations. It thereby excluded those CED trustees who were leaders of smaller companies, vice presidents at large companies, or economic consultants. Second, its members took a direct role in lobbying because they apparently believed they could no longer entrust this task to their hired lobbyists and the employees of the various business associations. However, too much can be made of direct lobbying by the CEOs because they often took their top lawyers with them when they visited with members of Congress. They also hired a major corporate law firm to direct a lobbying campaign in 1975 and a large public relations firm to help with another lobbying campaign in 1978 (Green and Buchsbaum 1980, chapter 3).

I leave it as an open question for now as to whether direct lobbying was necessary and more effective, as claimed by those who later wrote with awe about the ruthless efficiency of the new Business Roundtable (Vogel 1989). Moreover, it is unlikely that the conservative coalition, still alive and well at the time the Business Roundtable began its personal lobbying, needed to be pressured by its corporate supporters. The role of the roundtable and its lobbying efforts are discussed further later in this and subsequent chapters. For now, the decision to do personal lobbying is at least symbolically interesting. It suggests that the CEOs were concerned enough about recent events to make a clear statement that they were directly in charge of policy matters in the corporate community. They would no longer limit themselves to testifying before congressional committees or making use of lobbyists and trade association representatives to deliver their messages for them.

The renamed Labor Law Reform Committee continued to be chaired by Douglas Soutar, carrying on the effort initiated in 1965 to bring about changes in labor law and to influence appointments to the National Labor Relations Board. The Construction Users Committee, chaired by an industrial relations lawyer at General Electric, continued the lobbying and legal work started by the Construction Users Anti-Inflation Roundtable, and the Public Information Committee sustained the March Group's efforts to shape the climate of opinion concerning corporations.

THE NEW ROUNDTABLE'S MANIFESTO

The Business Roundtable began with a lengthy 1973 statement of purpose, "The Business Roundtable: The Purpose and Challenge." Its manifesto starts by claiming that inflation had been the most "persistent" and "pervasive" of all the problems that faced the United States in the previous decade, and predicts that it was "likely to be the dominant economic challenge of the Seventies." It then quotes a statement by Federal

Reserve Board chair Arthur Burns asserting that cost-push inflation "in a never ending circle is the most difficult economic issue of our time." Burns's claim is softened a few paragraphs later with the qualification that the government's fiscal and monetary policies share "some of the blame" because they create demand inflation, and it is noted that food prices were "advancing rapidly," but the concentration is nonetheless on "the cost of labor" because "runaway unit labor costs will make economic stability impossible." It then explains that "a limited recovery from low profit margins" would necessitate that increased labor costs "would have to be quickly transmitted to the public through higher price costs" (Business Roundtable 1973, pp. 1–3). Put more directly, the power of organized labor was at the heart of the inflation problem, and government was at fault for aiding unions. Government interference in capital-labor relations, couched in terms of interference in the market and bureaucratic overregulation, was the primary object of the roundtable's lobbying over the next eight years.

The manifesto contained many suggestions. For example, Business Roundtable leaders wanted to repeal the prevailing wage rules in Davis-Bacon and to block future increases in the minimum wage. They claimed that restrictive work practices were cutting into the rate of growth in productivity. Despite the shortcomings of the productivity index, and the fact that it began its decline for unknown reasons as early as 1966, the Business Roundtable and the Business Council were soon utilizing the theme of declining productivity in a nationwide campaign: "America. It Only Works As Well As You Do." The advertising campaign was carried out in conjunction with the Advertising Council to convince people that they had to work harder and take more pride in their work. After focus groups revealed that people had no idea what was meant by the concept of "productivity" and were put off by any implications of a "speed-up" at work, the campaign was built around the theme of taking pride in work. "Would you sign your work?" asked the ads, which featured many different types of workers, from cooks to hard hats. The ads appeared in a wide array of media outlets from television to magazines to billboards to bus stations in the mid-1970s (Zaretksy 2007, pp. 131–133).

Echoing Weiss and Harper's criticisms of government in the 1970 and 1972 CED inflation reports, the Business Roundtable founders were especially annoyed by what they believed to be a rise in the use of food stamps by strikers. Although the House had rejected attempts to ban the practice in both 1971 and 1972, the Business Roundtable nonetheless claimed it violated the intent of the law for the relatively few families of strikers that actually qualified for support. While noting that it could not put a dollar figure on the amount of support food stamps provided to strikers, the manifesto cited the same case studies by industrial relations experts at the Wharton School that Weiss cited in his comment in the 1972 CED inflation report in claiming that the amounts were substantial enough to add to inflation.

Although the manifesto was written with a tone of urgency, the roundtable's first two years were taken up primarily with hiring staff, setting an agenda, and coordinating the work of its committees. Its top leaders continued their usual contacts with elected officials through the Business Council, the CED, and their company lobbyists. Even so, one key Business Roundtable leader stayed in close touch with his friend Gerald R. Ford, a Republican congressional leader from Michigan, after he became vice president in 1973. Then, when Ford became president in 1974, the roundtable also worked behind the scenes to influence his administration. For example, in a memo written for the files on September 18, 1974, Soutar summarized a last-minute effort, with Blough "strongly behind it," and "cleared" by Harper, to send a letter to Ford's CEA chair, Allan Greenspan, a libertarian who worked as a business economist selling advice to corporations before his appointment. The revealing letter expressed the roundtable's conclusions on basic economic issues (Soutar 1974).

All of the memo's five substantive points involved labor costs, starting with the claim that automatic cost-of-living adjustments were taken "too much for granted" and were compounding the economy's problems. Soutar used the letter to compare total labor costs and the consumer price index to show that "real wages in the total cost sense have increased not declined, especially when the tax-free aspects of fringes are included." Finally, the letter claimed that total labor costs "are the #1 cause of inflation. (Even if debatable)" (Soutar 1974). The phrase "even if debatable" in the previous sentence, in the context of the Business Roundtable's manifesto and the other items in Soutar's memorandum, demonstrates that the corporate moderates were primarily interested in blaming organized labor for all of the economy's problems.

DECLINE AND THEN CONFLICT IN THE CED

The creation of the Business Roundtable marked the beginning of a decline in independence and importance for the CED, which had to adapt to the roundtable's existence and deal with criticism by the hard-line CED trustees who founded it. The first immediate organizational impact for the CED was the decision by Emilio Collado of Exxon (recall that Standard Oil of New Jersey became Exxon in 1972) to ask Marvin Bower's consulting firm, McKinsey and Co., to do a study of the CED.

Collado (1973) discussed his own summary of the first installment of McKinsey and Co.'s report to trustees at a meeting in October 1973, which was called to distribute copies of it. He said the consultants liked the CED "process," as the multi-step procedure for creating policy statements was called. But they nonetheless recommended that it be carried out more quickly so that reports could be timelier. McKinsey also suggested shorter reports and more trustee involvement in their shaping. The concern about trustee involvement was a response to complaints by some trustees that the staff had too much input into the substance of reports. It was a complaint that would be heard frequently over the next four years from those trustees who did not like some of the policy recommendations. However, the criticisms of the staff, and of outside consultants from think tanks, were usually an indirect way for the hard-line trustees to argue with their moderate colleagues through the creation of scapegoats, who could be blamed for ideas they did not like. By blaming the hired hands, a standard tactic in all policy-discussion groups, the hard-liners provided a graceful way for the moderates to shift their views on specific issues.

The CED president and the CED staff also began to worry about finances because they realized they would have to compete with the Business Roundtable for support from the corporate community (Hurwitz 1990, p. 21). This might be especially problematic in the case of the six large companies that by then contributed $30,000 a year (AT&T, Exxon, Ford, General Electric, General Motors, and IBM), which is $155,460 a year in 2012 dollars (Collado 1972). Then, too, several directors of these companies, which were allowed to name two trustees each to the CED in exchange for their large dues, served as trustees for foundations from which the CED received grants for major research projects.

THE CED TIGHTENS GOVERNANCE BUT LEANS LIBERAL

CED chair Collado took another step to tighten governance in the CED in early 1974 by creating a small oversight committee to work closely with the president and to monitor staff relationships more closely. Franklin Lindsay, the president of Itek Corporation, an up-and-coming information technology firm that sold satellite reconnaissance cameras and similar equipment to the government, served as chair. Before taking over at Itek, Lindsay had a wide-ranging career as an OSS officer in World War II, a program officer at the Ford Foundation, and an associate at McKinsey and Co. (Lewis 2002). He was joined on the oversight committee by Edmund B. Fitzgerald, the chair of Cutler-Hammer, and Charles Scanlon, the CED's treasurer and a vice president at Bankers Trust in New York.

According to Lindsay (1992), the oversight committee was set up because some of the hard-line trustees thought that a few leaders within the Research and Policy Committee were too liberal. In particular, they were concerned about the views of its chair, Philip M. Klutznick. A centimillionaire who had spent his lifetime working on housing and real estate issues, first in government and then as a highly successful developer of housing tracts and shopping malls in the Chicago area, Klutznick originally became involved with the CED through his service as a member of the Commission on Money and Credit that it sponsored from 1958 to 1961. After two years as an assistant to Adlai Stevenson, the American ambassador to the United Nations in the early Kennedy administration, Klutznick became a CED trustee in 1963. Five years later, as the CED began to shift in a more liberal direction, Klutznick became a vice chair of the Research and Policy Committee, then its co-chair in 1970, and then its chair in 1972. He had been an enthusiastic supporter of Stevenson for president in 1952 and 1956, and he was a large donor to Democratic Party candidates, so he was definitely an atypical CED trustee. To allay the concerns of the restive trustees, the oversight committee made Marvin Bower the co-chair of the Research and Policy Committee (Lindsay 1992).

Meanwhile, and of more immediate concern, Collado and the rest of the CED leadership—especially the informal "cabinet" of Collado, Franklin, Klutznick, and Neal—became increasingly worried about the continuing recession. Unemployment had climbed from 5.5 percent when Ford became president in August 1974 to 8.1 percent by the beginning of 1975. But Ford, who shared the ultraconservatives' economic outlook, insisted from early October to mid-December of 1974 that the administration had to prove it was serious about stopping inflation in order to reorient everyone's thinking, even to the point of advocating a surcharge on incomes over $15,000. He had the enthusiastic support of his two main economic advisors, CEA chair Greenspan, and the secretary of the treasury, William Simon, a Wall Street financier who held strong antigovernment beliefs similar to Greenspan's. In addition to asking for a surcharge, Ford requested cuts in government spending.

After three months of economic decline, Ford warned a gathering of the Business Council on December 11, "if there are any among you who want me to take a 180-degree turn from fighting inflation to recessionary pump priming, they will be disappointed," but he also added that "we are in a recession" (Greene 1995, p. 73). Shortly thereafter, a majority of Ford's economic advisors warned him that the recession had to be confronted directly; his press secretary soon described the forthcoming plan as a "179-degree turn" (Mieczkowski 2005, pp. 130–131).

As a result of the CED's disagreement with the new administration, its concern with finding ways to counter the recession was at the top of the agenda when its executive committee met in early January 1975. The five trustees in attendance were Collado, Klutznick, Neal, Howard Petersen of Philadelphia Fidelity Trust, and John L. Burns, an engineer who managed his own investment firm and served as the voluntary president of the Boys Clubs of America after stints as the president of Cities Services and RCA. They were joined by six of the CED's academic advisors as well as the *New York Times* economics columnist, Leonard Silk, who earned a PhD in economics from Duke University in the late 1940s and was a frequent participant in CED deliberations throughout the 1970s.

After discussing and approving a draft statement, "Economic Policies for Inflation and Recession," prepared by Schiff, the committee took an unusual step that turned out to be highly controversial. According to Neal's retrospective account, "the trustee executives" who were present "insisted its [CED's] voice be raised in protest and with advice about how to overcome double-digit rates of unemployment and inflation." Since the CED's bylaws stated that any new program statement had to be based on a previous statement, and none was at the ready, "the most expeditious procedure was to commission an official public address on the situation and give it wide circulation." This executive-committee initiative began the next day with a speech at a luncheon for fourteen members of the Research and Policy Committee and several guests, including the presidents of the Conference Board and the National Audubon Society (Neal 1981, p. 45).

Klutznick, as co-chair of the Research and Policy Committee, was asked to give the address, titled "Attacking the Double-Trouble of Inflation and Recession." He began by expressing dismay that the Ford administration, which Klutznick referred to as "the engineer in control," was running the engines in reverse. It clung to a restrictive fiscal policy at a time when agricultural surpluses had been depleted and the era of cheap energy had come to an end due to OPEC (the Organization for the Petroleum Exporting Countries), while at the same time encouraging the Fed to keep interest rates high. Still, Klutznick found it liberating that closing the gold window meant the country would "no longer have to take the medicine of higher unemployment to remedy our balance of payments deficits." Instead, he thought there was need for a fiscal stimulus of $25 billion, which was about the size of the big 1964 tax cut when inflation is taken into account. To offset the decline in real wages due to food and gas prices, which hit lower-income workers the hardest, taxes should be lowered through a 3 percent tax credit for the first $15,000 of wages. However, he wanted the tax credit couched within "an explicit declaration of intent" by Congress that "the tax cut is being made as part of a social compact among business, labor and government to restrain future inflation." In exchange, labor would limit wage increases, "whether in existing contracts or otherwise," to 4 percent, which meant he was asking for an unprecedented suspension of guaranteed cost-of-living raises (Klutznick 1975a, pp. 4, 11, 14–15).

As for businesses, he called for them to pull back from any price hikes made in anticipation of future inflation or price controls: "Sellers large and small should dehydrate their prices. Businesses should remove from prices the water that has been pumped in to flood the next round of price control" (Klutznick 1975a, p. 15). In return, government should promise business that there would be no further price controls. In effect, Klutznick and the CED's executive committee were advocating a version of incomes policy using tax incentives to replace Nixon's earlier imposition of wage and price controls.

In addition to the social compact, Klutznick's statement called for "selective credit allocation and emergency sources of liquidity for essential industries," which meant that the government might have to provide loans, or loan guarantees, for the housing industry and small businesses, along with support for variable-rate mortgages, instead of lowering interest rates generally, which might fuel inflation (Klutznick 1975a, p. 11). He further thought that money for public-service jobs should be concentrated on the federal level to insure that the money was spent in areas where it was actually needed. Even with its implicit challenge to the sanctity of cost-of-living clauses in union contracts, it was the most liberal speech that a high official in the CED ever made, before or after, going well beyond what had been recommended in statements approved by the Research and Policy Committee.

The nine-paragraph story in the *New York Times* the next day, with the headline "$20-Billion Tax Cut Urged by Private Economic Unit," repeated Klutznick's call for an "explicit declaration" that the measure should be "part of a social compact among business, labor and government to restrain future inflation," as well as his colorful phrase about dehydrating prices by removing "the water that was pumped in to float the next round of price control," and ended with the important proviso that "this should be done in exchange for a guarantee that price controls will not be reimposed" (*New York Times* 1975, p. 14). Seventeen days later, Hubert Humphrey, back in the Senate as of the 1970 election and the chair of the Joint Economic Committee, put Klutznick's speech into the *Congressional Record.* In late February, Klutznick testified to the Joint Economic Committee itself.

Although Harper was in hearty agreement with the idea of large tax cuts at this juncture, a position he expressed on behalf of the Business Roundtable after Ford finally announced a tax-cut proposal in mid-January, he called Neal to convey his disagreement with other aspects of Klutznick's speech. "Basically, what John objects to is the allegation that business has deliberately raised prices as a hedge against imposition of price controls," Neal explained in a memorandum to Klutznick and Schiff on March 6. "He challenges us to prove that in recent times prices were deliberately raised in anticipation of price controls." In addition to telephoning Neal, Harper wrote that he had asked the office at the Business Roundtable "to send a copy of a paper prepared on wage and price controls which I think will interest you." Klutznick replied to Neal's memo on March 12, expressing the "hope you have satisfied John if it is possible to satisfy him on this subject. Do you think I should write him? My guess is I should not" (Harper 1975; Klutznick 1975b; Neal 1975e).

CONFLICT OVER A NEW INFLATION STATEMENT

Klutznick's luncheon speech in January convinced other hard-liners besides Harper that the likely recommendations from a newly appointed subcommittee to deal with the issue of inflation might not be to their liking. As a result, the subcommittee's deliberations and draft reports became additional bones of contention in a confrontation that determined whether the CED would continue in a mildly liberal direction or take a turn to the right. Making the situation all the more delicate, the chair in charge of the new subcommittee, John R. Coleman, was a rare CED trustee in that he was both an MIT-trained labor economist and the president of Haverford College, after working for the Ford Foundation and the Federal Reserve Bank of Philadelphia for many years. In the early 1960s he had been the star of a television course on economics sponsored by the CED, the Ford Foundation, and eighty-five corporations—because he was "a brilliant economist with a 'telegenic' personality" (Schriftgiesser 1967, p. 201). By 1974, though, he was somewhat suspect to corporate moderates after spending his 1973 presidential sabbatical from Haverford working briefly in a series of blue-collar jobs in an effort to understand how average workers lived, an experience he recounted in *Blue-Collar Journal: A College President's Sabbatical* (1974), which expressed considerable sympathy for the difficulties blue-collar workers face.

Five trustees who had served on earlier inflation subcommittees, including Harper and Frazar Wilde, as well as several trustees who had not served on any previous inflation subcommittees, joined Coleman on the subcommittee. Barry Bosworth, a Keynesian economist at the University of California, Berkeley, who accepted a position at The Brookings Institution after he was hired for the CED project, led a threesome of outside experts. Schiff, the CED's chief economist, served as project director.

The depth of the disagreements in the CED over how to deal with inflation was signaled in a letter that Bower wrote to Coleman two weeks after Klutznick's speech to the Research and Policy Committee. His cordial but blunt note to Coleman, with copies to Neal and Klutznick, said that he intended to be present for as many subcommittee meetings as possible, even though he was not an appointed member, and then asked "whether CED should continue to be a proponent of Keynesian doctrine" (Bower 1975). For his own part, he thought it might be time to replace Keynesianism with the theories of the 1974 Nobel Laureate in economics, Friedrich Hayek, one of the founders of the free-market school of economics. An Austrian émigré who taught at the London School of

Economics (1931–1950), the University of Chicago (1950–1962), and the University of Freiburg (1962–1968) before retiring at age sixty-nine, Hayek had decided in the 1920s that any form of liberal welfare state was almost as dangerous as a socialist society. He thought liberal welfare states restricted the freedom of a sociologically diverse citizenry to hold different individual values and limited efficiency and incentives (Hayek 1944).

Bower attached a recent speech by Hayek, "Government Deficits and Inflation," reprinted in the *Daily Telegraph* in London. It began with the strong assertion that "the responsibility for current world wide inflation, I am sorry to say, rests wholly and squarely with the economists, or at least with that great majority of my fellow economists who have embraced the teachings of Keynes." The problems were all the "economic consequences of Lord Keynes," a reference to the title of one of Keynes's earlier books, *The Economic Consequences of the Peace* (1919), which criticized the post–World War I peace treaty as economic suicide. Keynesian policies, he claimed, simply make things worse in the long run (Bower 1975).

Bower was out of town for the subcommittee meeting of January 29, but four other Keynesian critics who were not on the subcommittee attended it, starting with Fletcher Byrom, the president of Koppers, the 223rd largest company in the country at the time, and soon to be a major presence in the CED. A close friend of Harper's, who had suggested him as a CED trustee in 1970, Byrom and Harper were both part of the then tightly knit complex of companies in Pittsburgh that were founded and owned by the Mellon family since the 1880s. Joining Byrom as insurgent guests at the meeting were Weiss, the vice chair of General Electric; James Q. Riordan, a senior vice president for finance at Mobil Oil; and R. Stewart Rauch, the chair of the Philadelphia Savings Fund.

Economist Robert Nathan, by far the most liberal of the CED trustees, who gave his friends "Back to Hoover" buttons in reference to Ford's policies, also appeared as a nonmember of the subcommittee. Nathan first came to the attention of corporate leaders when he was in charge of planning for the War Production Board during World War II. After the war, he started his own economic consulting firm, Robert R. Nathan and Associates, which deployed its handful of expert employees in a wide range of developing countries. In the late 1950s he was elected the president of Americans for Democratic Action, the most prominent liberal advocacy and lobbying organization of the postwar era. He participated in the CED-sponsored Commission on Money and Credit in the late 1950s and became a CED trustee in the early 1960s through the sponsorship of Fred Lazarus of Federated Department Stores (Nathan 1995).

Following the subcommittee meeting that included the trustees who were not members, Neal wrote all four of them and Bower with an invitation to join the subcommittee. Byrom, Nathan, Riordan, and Weiss accepted it. Shortly thereafter, Bosworth sent members of the subcommittee the first of three confidential background reports on the issues that needed to be discussed, and attached three recent research papers by other experts. His report stressed that the effects of both inflation and unemployment are complex; in the case of inflation, the effects vary depending on its causes. For example, the inflation after 1972, generated by large increases in food and energy prices, ran up prices on everyone, but its worst effects were on low-income workers because it differentially raised the costs of necessities. In the case of increasing unemployment, the obvious impacts are on those who lose their jobs, but he also pointed out that unemployment reduces demand, which reduces the incentive for companies to invest. As a result of recession-induced decline in investment, there might be inflationary effects when spending increased again, due to a lack of productive capacity (Bosworth 1975a).

While the inflation subcommittee was working its way through Bosworth's analysis, other corporate leaders were hearing a very different viewpoint from Hayek, who told a forum at the American Enterprise Institute that it was necessary to restore market equilibrium through a period of recession and unemployment. But he also "stressed he did not recommend putting the economy through the wringer of a severe deflation." This message also went out through the spring issue of the institute's newsletter (American Enterprise Institute 1975, p. 1).

MAY 1975: A CED SYMPOSIUM ON THE ECONOMY

As tensions boiled inside the CED and the Ford administration tried to reverse the skyrocketing unemployment, the CED held a symposium in New York in May that provided a Keynesian assessment of the current situation, just as unemployment reached the 9 percent mark. In the process, it reinforced several of the points Klutznick made in his speech to CED trustees in early January. It featured a frequent CED economic advisor, Charles Schultze of The Brookings Institution, who unexpectedly became the chair of the CEA twenty months later due to Jimmy Carter's victory in the 1976 elections.

After receiving a PhD in economics at the University of Maryland in the late 1950s while employed on the staff of the CEA, Schultze taught at Indiana University for two years before returning to the Washington area and writing a supplementary report for the CED in 1959 on "Prices, Costs, and Output for the Postwar Decade: 1947–1957." He became an assistant director of the budget under President Kennedy and director of the budget from 1965 to 1967 under Johnson. He joined The Brookings Institution when he left government in 1968 and organized its yearly report on the state of the economy. After 1968 he was an advisor on several CED policy statements and served on its Research Advisory Board.

William Franklin, the retired chair of Caterpillar Tractor and at the time a director of Exxon and chair of the CED board of trustees, introduced the symposium and then posed a question for Schultze: should the CED be making different recommendations than it usually would to deal with the recession that began in 1974? Schultze took a circuitous route in his answer but in the end said that the sudden downturn in the economy was due to a huge decline in consumer demand and had little or nothing to do with Nixon's economic policies, however misguided they may have been. In fact, by late 1973 inflation was moderating and wages were gaining, and there was only a $2 billion deficit in the middle of that year. Instead of blaming the Nixon administration or unions, he pointed out that the American economy had been hit by three inflationary shocks that acted like major new taxes on consumers, draining purchasing power and causing the worst economic downturn in thirty years during 1974 and early 1975, with output 11 percent below what it could have been if there had not been a 9 percent unemployment rate.

To begin with, farm prices had risen sharply due to bad harvests around the world, along with a $1.25 billion ($6.5 billion in 2012 dollars) grain and soybean sale of American reserves to the Soviet Union in 1972 and 1973, taking extra billions out of consumers' pockets. Then the prices of nonpetroleum raw materials shot up as well, taking many more billions from consumers. Most dramatically, the six-month Arab oil embargo beginning in October 1973 quadrupled the price of oil, sending $36 billion of consumer purchasing power to oil-producing countries, only $5 billion of which made it back to American commercial and investment banks for loans and investments. As if that were not enough, the resulting inflation pushed individuals and corporations into higher tax brackets, taking another $55–60 billion out of the consumer and investment streams. Due to the major decline in demand caused by this combination of factors, employers began to lay workers off, which jumped the unemployment rate from 4.6 percent in October 1973 to 8.1 percent by January 1975.

Put frankly, the problems facing the economy were hardly the mystery to Keynesian economists that they were claimed to be, and Schultze thought it was foolish for the Federal Reserve Board to fight inflation under these circumstances. He then suggested a way to deal with both unemployment and inflation that had parallels with Klutznick's recent recommendations. The corporate community should forge an understanding with organized labor, an idea that very few corporate moderates of any stripe were willing to entertain by that point. In exchange for restraints on wage demands by unions, he suggested there should be a reduction in payroll taxes because they hit low-income earners the hardest (Committee for Economic Development 1975).

CONTINUING CONFLICT IN THE CED OVER INFLATION

Arguing in much the same vein as Schultze at the May symposium, and in contrast to Hayek, Bosworth began his August 1975 discussion paper by saying it is not true "that inflation results almost entirely from too much demand relative to supply and unemployment from too little," which also contradicted Harper's dissenting comments to CED inflation recommendations in 1970 and 1972. Bosworth asserted that the 1970–1971 inflation was due to catch-up, not high demand, and that the recovery of 1973 was disrupted by the rise in the cost of food and raw materials in the first three quarters of that year and the oil embargo at the end of the year. In his September 1975 report for the subcommittee, Bosworth added that industries in which there are barriers to entry are reluctant to lower prices, citing high tech as an example. He also noted that the existence of unions contributes to the lack of flexibility in prices because of their insistence on wage increases and their resistance to wage cuts (Bosworth 1975a, p. 1; 1975b).

Harper did not appreciate Bosworth's discussion papers or the comments by the Keynesian-oriented advisors present at subcommittee meetings. He made his displeasure known to Neal, who then wrote Klutznick yet again on September 24 to report that Harper had "expressed great concern about our inflation project because of the influence of Brookings, Lekachman [a very liberal Keynesian of the day], and Schiff (incomes policy)." Neal thought Harper was "calmed down now" because he trusted Coleman and "signed up for the November R & P [Research and Policy] meeting." But he also noted that Harper thought the CED "should use more American Enterprise Institute people" even though "we have [Murray] Weidenbaum [who had worked in the Treasury Department in the Nixon administration] on the project now" (Neal 1975d). In a similar fashion, a relatively new trustee, Jerome Van Gorkom, the president of the Trans Union Corporation, which provided consumer-credit information to businesses, wrote Neal around the same time to complain that there were no monetary economists at the first three subcommittee meetings. He added that he thought some members of the CED staff were "anti-monetarist" (van Gorkom 1975).

It turned out that Harper was not at all satisfied. After the subcommittee's November meeting, Neal sent a letter to Klutznick and Petersen reporting that Harper opposed the inflation report: "As things now stand, he thinks the report makes no contribution; he would oppose our issuing it, and said that if it is published *there will be an exodus from CED* [my italics]. Harper said Bosworth is Brookings, Brookings is anti-business, business has stopped supporting it, and why can't we get a project director from the American Enterprise Institute." Neal added that "we balanced with the AEI economists to the best of our ability (McCracken, Weidenbaum), and explained to him that Bosworth was not Brookings but the University of California when we hired him and that Jack Coleman was a real pro in the field." Neal ended with the comment that "Harper bases his opposition on off-the-cuff 'anti-business' statements noted by his advisers, not on the monetarist thesis" (Neal 1975c).

Nor was Harper alone in criticizing Bosworth. After happening to see Klutznick at the Commonwealth Club in Chicago and taking the opportunity to bend his ear about Bosworth, Gordon Corey, the vice chair of Commonwealth Edison, the large utility company in Chicago, wrote Klutznick a brief follow-up letter that gave him the occasion to attach a copy of a letter he had sent to Bosworth challenging his claim at a subcommittee luncheon about the reasonableness of most government regulation. Klutznick replied that Bosworth "is a bright young man [he was thirty-three at the time] and as such is occasionally a little loose with his language." Klutznick also said "he has tremendous possibilities, but as Al [Neal] and I know, he needs careful attention as he matures," adding in regard to regulatory issues that "he and others have a tendency to get involved in areas that are not really their specialty" (Corey 1975; Klutznick 1975c). Klutznick then took the opportunity to bring Corey up to date on the inflation subcommittee in general, reporting that Coleman had "cancelled his December meeting of the subcommittee in order to do a complete rewrite as a result of the [previous] meeting." He concluded, "I think you will find that the report is reaching a more balanced and solid level," but it turned out that the process would drag on for another nine months (Klutznick 1975c).

The tensions reflected in the CED files accord with Bosworth's (1992) later recollections of his involvement in the project. Although he originally enjoyed the back-and-forth of subcommittee discussions, he recalled that they became increasingly uncivil and that the criticisms became more personal, including the insulting accusation that he was a Communist. From Bosworth's perspective, the argument was over using an incomes policy or unemployment to tame inflation, with the main "blow-up" coming at a meeting of the subcommittee with the Research and Policy Committee, in which several trustees spoke harshly of the incomes-oriented policy statement that he, Coleman, and Schiff had drafted. Given the apparent backing for the report by most trustees on the subcommittee, Bosworth thought that Coleman felt "sandbagged" by the response at the Research and Policy Committee meeting by trustees who had not participated in the discussion. Bosworth recalled Harper as verbally attacking him on a personal level but said his colleague Byrom was tolerant in his objections. Either way, Bosworth subsequently concluded that conservatives dislike any form of direct government involvement in wage-price issues, which they label as socialism and Communism (Bosworth 1992).

ADDED TENSIONS OVER A TENTATIVE PROJECT ON PLANNING

Still another issue generated concerns on the part of the most conservative CED trustees in the spring of 1975—a new initiative by the leaders of the Research and Policy Committee to do a series of studies on government planning under the title "National Economic Planning Project." Reacting to the widespread discussion of planning by liberals, labor leaders, and a few business leaders at the time, the tentative CED project began with a three-page letter from the Itek CEO, Lindsay, by then the vice chair of the Research and Policy Committee, to Klutznick on April 8. Lindsay's carefully worded proposal argued that "the CED should now actively study the full range of planning methods, policies, and devices that might be used—for clearly there are both good and very bad ways that it might come about." He wanted the CED to recommend "those approaches to planning that are most compatible with the US economy and its own special public/private character; and which can be most effective in achieving national objectives while making the best use of the private market mechanism for both capital and products" (Lindsay 1975, p. 2).

In making his case, Lindsay mentioned that a new group—headed by Wassily Leontief, a Nobel Laureate in economics at MIT; Leonard Woodcock, the president of the UAW; and Robert Roosa, a Wall Street investment banker—was drafting legislation for national economic planning. "The weakness of that group's specific proposal," he continued, "is that it immediately jumps from a broad conclusion on the inadequacies of present policies to an organizational solution of creating a national planning commission reporting direct to the President." As a result, "the key problem of how such a planning agency should function is completely neglected." Returning to his proposal for a CED study, Lindsay concluded, "If we were to do nothing else but point out the pitfalls of certain kinds of planning before they are adopted, we would be making a very valuable contribution" (Lindsay 1975, pp. 2–3).

Lindsay's proposal seemed to be consistent with the type of projects that the Committee for Economic Development had often undertaken. As Neal put it a year later, the CED in effect wanted to make the best of things if planning was on the country's agenda: "We want to be sure that whatever we come up with fits American institutions and philosophy" (Rosen 1976, p. 36). However, the more conservative trustees did not see it that way. For example, Fitzgerald (1975), one of three vice chairmen at the time and a member of the oversight committee Collado appointed in 1974, warned Neal that there would be a "trustees' revolt" if "the purpose of the proposed new study is misunderstood" to mean greater government involvement in the economy.

The specific proposal from the Initiative Committee for National Economic Planning that Lindsay was referring to in his letter was sketched in outline form in the summer of 1974, when Leontief entered into discussions with Woodcock. Shortly thereafter, a small drafting group brought together by Leontief and Woodcock adopted the name Initiative Committee for National Economic Planning at the suggestion of John Kenneth Galbraith, still operating to the left of most contemporary Keynesians because of his interest in planning and his belief that defense industries should be nationalized. Leontief, Woodcock, and Galbraith were joined in the small group that launched the proposal by CED trustee Robert Nathan and the former CED and CEA economist Walter Heller.

Comparing the planning proposal to a revival of the National Resources Planning Board from the early 1940s, the main idea was to establish a planning board within the White House that would have the power to ask for and compile economic information from a wider range of public and private sources than were usually tapped, which could then be analyzed to suggest a list of specific proposals that might provide guidelines and goals within a five-to-ten-year time horizon. The founding statement emphasized that most decisions would continue to be made through the market, and it specifically named General Electric, General Motors, and General Foods in noting that the government would not try to tell corporations what to do. However, in the process of gathering information and projecting goals for the future, the would-be National Economic Planning Council was supposed to have far more impact than the CEA, which members of the Initiative Committee saw as limited to a narrow range of information and to a few Keynesian recommendations about fiscal and monetary policy. The proposal gained visibility and legitimacy through endorsements from about seventy well-known public figures in politics, science, academia, and business, including a small number of highly visible corporate leaders. Two CED trustees were among the supporters: W. Michael Blumenthal, the CEO of Bendix; and Philip Sporn, the retired president of American Electric Power (*Challenge* 1975).

Abram Chayes, a prominent liberal law professor at Harvard, turned the basic ideas in the Initiative Committee's statement into a legislative draft. Some of the Initiative Committee's ideas then appeared in a bill introduced into the Senate in early May by Humphrey and Jacob Javits, the moderate Republican from New York. "But the bill that was finally written is far more moderate than the proposal originally drafted by the Initiative Committee," according to a report in *Dun's Review*, a business magazine of that era. The article noted that Humphrey and Javits were "acutely conscious of business discomfort about planning," so they "rejected the Initiative Committee's call for specific targets for auto, electric generator and even frozen-food production, along with its insistence that a planning board 'try to induce the relevant industries to act accordingly.'" Humphrey and Javits also ignored suggestions to call for "guidance of capital flows" and "selective credit controls" (Rosen 1976, pp. 36–37).

Basically, Humphrey and Javits's Balanced National Growth and Planning Act called for a new Office of Economic Planning to be lodged in the White House and for a Joint Committee on Economic Planning in Congress to receive and discuss the reports (Akard 1996, pp. 107–108). Adding fuel to the fire within the CED, trustees Klutznick, Blumenthal of Bendix, Stanley Marcus of Neiman-Marcus, and William May, the chair of American Can, were listed as supporters of this more moderate plan in an opinion piece by the well-known liberal historian, Arthur Schlesinger Jr., which appeared in the *Wall Street Journal* (1975). In addition, and even more annoying to the hard-line faction within the CED, Neal was mentioned as a supporter in Schlesinger's article, which led Neal to request soon thereafter that his name be removed from future public statements by supporters of the plan.

The Initiative Committee's statement and the Humphrey-Javits bill received respectful treatment in the *New York Times* and *Business Week*, but they led to a large outcry in most of the business press, as well as rejection by most economists, who thought that the coordination of economic policy would be impossible at best and a thin entering wedge for more centralized planning at worst. In addition, the great majority in the corporate community was completely opposed to any form of planning. This point was firmly established in a book by Leonard Silk, the *New York Times* economics reporter, and David Vogel, a political scientist at the University of California, Berkeley, who wrote as observers at several wide-ranging discussions by top-level executives at the Conference Board in 1974 and 1975. The 360 executives who attended one or more of the sessions, with thirty-five to fifty-five present at any given meeting, provided a "fair cross-section of the country's business-leadership group" at the time; they were primarily "chief executives of American-owned and headquartered corporations" (Silk and Vogel 1976, pp. 10, 35, 38). According to Silk and Vogel's estimate, 90 percent were strongly opposed to any form of government planning; they regarded even the mildest form of government analysis and forecasting over a five-year period as a starting point for more government control of the economy.

It cannot be determined with certainty just how many of these corporate executives were trustees of the Committee for Economic Development because Silk and Vogel understandably assured them of anonymity. However, sixteen of the fifty-seven companies they thank for the "anonymous views expressed by conferees" also had one or more top officers who were CED trustees. They included two from Exxon and IBM and one each from Bethlehem Steel, General Foods, Koppers, United Airlines, and Westinghouse Electric (Silk and Vogel 1976, pp. 249–251).

TRANSITION AND REEVALUATION AT THE CED

As the tensions mounted over the inflation subcommittee and the new planning project during the spring of 1975, Neal quietly told Collado, Franklin, and Klutznick that he had had enough. He wanted their permission to retire in March 1976, at age sixty-three, a year earlier than he had originally anticipated. There is virtually no mention of Neal's request for an early retirement in the CED files I had access to, although Neal's September 24th letter to Klutznick about Harper suggested his frustration with the CED hard-liners. It ended with the comment, "I hope my successor has a better experience than I with the conservative wing!" (Neal 1975d). Two retired staff members who worked with Neal at the time said he had grown weary of trying to balance the tensions within the organization, which reached a turning point for him due to suggestions for reorganizing the CED in the final portion of the McKinsey study, delivered in the spring of 1975 (Hurwitz 2001; Schiff 1990a).

According to one retired staff member, who was interviewed as part of the McKinsey study, "It was clear that the McKinsey team didn't have a clue about CED or how it worked and had little interest in learning." The report was tabled at a meeting of the executive committee, "but the damage was done" as far as Neal wanting to stay on any longer (Hurwitz 2011). After his decision to retire early, Neal worked with Collado, Franklin, and Klutznick in picking his successor, making many of the early contacts with potential candidates. He discussed the position in June with his eventual successor, Robert C. Holland, a member of the Federal Reserve Board (Neal 1975b).

An economist with much the same background as Neal's, Holland joined the Federal Reserve Bank of Chicago in 1949 after receiving an MA in finance from the Wharton School of Business, then moved to the Federal Reserve in Washington after earning a PhD in economics at Wharton in 1959. He worked in the Division of Research and Statistics and as an advisor to the board before being appointed to it by Nixon in mid-1973. Holland made his support for strong monetary medicine clear a year earlier when he told *Business Week* that the Federal Reserve Board had to bear "a very heavy share of the burden of fighting inflation, for the very practical reason that no other public policy tool seems capable now of doing more of the job" (*Business Week* 1974, p. 34).

According to Holland (1992), he was approached about taking the position by Franklin, the retired Caterpillar Tractor CEO and current CED chair, who was on the board of the Federal Reserve Bank of Chicago when Holland worked there. Franklin, Lindsay, and Byrom then provided Holland with a clear indication of what they wanted the CED to do. After Holland agreed to take the reins as of March 1976, the executive committee began a process of reevaluation in mid-October 1975 that carried the transformation of the CED a step further. One of the few bankers among the trustees, Donald Platten, the chair of Chemical Bank in New York, sent a letter to fellow trustees saying that he had been authorized by the executive committee to seek out frank critiques of the functioning of the organization.

The first reply arrived five days later from the vice chair of US Steel, R. Heath Larry, who had been appointed a trustee three years earlier at the request of his company to replace one of its retiring trustees. Larry also was a member of the inflation subcommittee that was still meeting and arguing. He raised questions about the continuing existence of the CED by wondering if there were too many business organizations doing the same tasks, and therefore draining executive time and corporate financial resources (Larry 1975). Several others wrote letters in which they complained that the trustees no longer controlled the organization. This refrain led Franklin, writing as the chair of the trustees and a member of the executive committee, to rebut these claims on November 3, asserting that the executive committee and the program committee made all the key decisions, not the staff (Franklin 1975).

Despite Franklin's rejoinder, Weiss, the highly conservative trustee from GE, wrote Platten a week later repeating many of the same criticisms expressed in earlier letters, adding that he sensed "an unfavorable drift in dedicated interest in CED by some of our major corporations" (Weiss 1975). He also objected to the participation of academic and government economists in the writing of reports, but thought they should still be invited to participate in subcommittee discussions. Similar critical letters from top leaders at Sears and BF Goodrich were addressed to Neal during the same week, with the letter from a BF Goodrich vice president adding that top management had decided to give its CED contribution to the American Enterprise Institute (Ashe 1975).

Three days before the letter from BF Goodrich was sent, Neal (1975a, p. 2) had written a letter to Platten saying among other things that CED had operated on a "level budget" for the previous several years in the face of "rapidly increasing operating costs" and had been forced to make reductions in its 1975 budget due to lack of funds. As some of the staff feared when the Business Roundtable was first launched three years earlier, the CED was facing a funding squeeze by an unknown number of its corporate sponsors.

GENERAL ANGER IN THE CORPORATE COMMUNITY

The eight three-hour discussions at the Conference Board in 1974 and 1975 attended by Silk and Vogel revealed that hostility toward government planning was only one dimension of a general anger toward government and the general public that coursed through the corporate community. Some of the top executives may have been playing to the grandstands because they knew that Silk and Vogel might write an article or book about the meetings, as evidenced by the fact that many of them gave copies of their prepared remarks to the authors. However, what they said as the discussions unfolded was frank enough that Silk and Vogel seem to be right when they conclude, "we do not think our attendance inhibited the full and natural flow of discussion" (Silk and Vogel 1976, p. 40).

For example, the corporate leaders did not think the federal government was as responsive as it should have been to their opinions. "The have-nots are gaining steadily more political power to distribute the wealth downward," complained one executive. Some wondered whether democracy and capitalism are compatible. "Can we still afford one man, one vote? We are tumbling on the brink," one of them said. "One man, one vote has undermined the power of business in all capitalist countries since World War II," said another. Several viewed recessions as a saving grace because they helped to keep the expectations of employees in check. "People need to recognize that a job is the most important thing they can have." "We should use this recession to get the public to better understand how our economic system works." "It would be better if the recession were allowed to weaken more than it will, so that we would have a sense of sobriety" (Silk and Vogel 1976, pp. 50, 64, 75).

In the context of rising inflation, high unemployment, and tensions with OPEC, the comments by these corporate leaders suggest that 1973 through 1976 were crisis years in the collective mind of the corporate community. But before that mind-set is discussed in relation to any actual changes in corporate dominance, it is useful to see what was happening by way of policy outcomes in the battles between the Ford administration and the new "Watergate Congress" elected in November 1974.

PRESIDENT FORD VERSUS CONGRESS

While top executives were expressing their anger during Conference Board discussions and CED trustees were arguing about future economic policies, other members of the corporate community were preparing to face the enlarged Democratic majorities that were swept into Congress, just as the tide seemed to be turning permanently in a Republican direction in white America. Democrats from outside the South had an even larger delegation in the House (211) than they had enjoyed in 1965 (194), and their representation in the Senate was up to forty-nine, just three fewer than it was in 1965.

Although corporate lobbyists and conservative pundits reacted with loud outcries about the possible dangers the new Congress presented for the country, the conservative coalition still had the potential to muster 236 votes in the House and 57 in the Senate, far more than were needed to stop new liberal-labor legislation. However, there remained the possibility that not all of those potential votes would materialize on every issue of concern to the corporate community. The conservative coalition's estimated operational size in the House was only 216, two short of a majority, so controversial votes were likely to be extremely close. As for the Senate, the conservatives were fairly certain of 47 votes, more than enough to sustain a filibuster or uphold Ford's likely vetoes of any new liberal-labor initiatives (Shelley 1983, pp. 152, 154).

The direst predictions were offered in a speech in January 1975 to the US Chamber of Commerce by Bryce Harlow, a longtime and highly visible Washington lobbyist for Procter & Gamble. Harlow's experience in government also made him a key link between business, the White House, and conservatives in Congress. Harlow was the son of a highly successful Oklahoma businessman, and his comments to the chamber are of special interest because his claims, such as "we had to prevent business from being rolled up and put in a trash can by that Congress," are used by social scientists as evidence of how terrified business was because of the Democratic landslide in 1974 (Hacker and Pierson 2010, p. 117; Vogel 1989, p. 194).

Harlow came to Washington in 1938 to work on an MA thesis about the Ways and Means Committee, joined the committee's staff in 1939, and went from there to the Armed Services press office during World War II, writing speeches for Eisenhower and other generals. He moved back and forth between congressional staff positions and a vice presidency in his father's publishing company between 1946 and 1950, and became a Republican in 1950 to support Eisenhower. He then joined Eisenhower's White House staff in 1953 as a congressional liaison and speech writer, making use of his long-standing connections with Southern Democrats to arrange "secret meetings between Eisenhower, House speaker Sam Rayburn, and Senate Majority Leader Lyndon Johnson" (Burke and Thompson 2000, p. 56).

After Kennedy won the White House, Harlow became the head of the Washington Office for Procter & Gamble through his White House liaison work with Eisenhower's second secretary of defense, Neil McElroy, a top officer at Procter & Gamble and a CED trustee from the early 1960s until his death in 1972. Harlow began his new job just as conflicts over regulatory issues concerning the use of dangerous chemicals in industry were about to heat up, including battles over the company's use of alkyl benzene sulfonate (ABS) in its cleaning agents. During the next few years, Harlow became known as the dean of the "Washington representatives," as these high-level corporate go-betweens called themselves. He served on the governing board of the Business-Government Relations Council, a corporate lobbying group he helped to found in 1966 along with lobbyists from US Steel, GE, and Goodyear. He also kept Eisenhower and Nixon, with whom he first worked in 1947 as a staffer for the House Armed Services Committee, in touch with each other and with what was going on politically in Washington. In addition, he carried messages to Eisenhower from members of Congress seeking favors. In 1969 he returned to the White House for a year as an assistant to the president, after which he went back to Procter & Gamble for three years and then rejoined the White House for the final time in 1973–1974 (Burke and Thompson 2000, pp. 150–151, 155–159).

Harlow's speech to the Chamber of Commerce, which he actually gave several times in different venues during 1975, included many colorful statements about the monumental obstacles facing conservatives, starting with the opening comment, "I intend to give you no good news whatever." But a reading of Harlow's speeches from the 1960s onward reveals that his main message was always a crisis scenario that was in effect a way to motivate conservative lobbyists. In the new 1975 horror story, Harlow claimed corporate fortunes had suffered what "geologists call a diastrophism—a revolutionary, seismic recasting of forces," and already the nature of his remarks is apparent. "Stripped of nonessentials, the essence of the matter is that, unless business can force itself to shape up, and very quickly, it is in for the most abusive, most disruptive, most disheartening season since the earliest New Deal days forty years ago.... It's awfully hard to sing bass when you've just been made a soprano—which is to say, our old ways just won't hack it anymore." There had been a "massive leftward lurch" that gave the Democrats "overwhelming, crushing control" (Harlow 1975, pp. 1–3).

The social scientists who use Harlow's scare words as evidence for the dangers facing a frightened business community at this juncture only focus on the first half of his usual message that year. After sizing up vote counts in various committees that seemed stacked overwhelmingly against conservatives, he turned to "ground zero—the crux of the matter over the next couple of years," explaining how conservatives could stop the liberal-labor alliance in its tracks. Vetoes by President Ford could be sustained by the 126 solidly conservative Republican votes in the House if they were joined by twenty-five of the thirty conservative Democrats, who were mostly Southerners, as he also noted, "so if the old patterns hold the votes should be there to man the President's barricade" (Harlow 1975, pp. 7–8).

As for the Senate, by his overly stringent standards there were twenty-six conservative Republicans who were likely to be joined by at least ten conservative Southern Democrats, "again just enough to uphold the President now and again even in the Senate." In all honesty, there was no great danger of new liberal initiatives becoming law if the conservative coalition stayed together. But it might take some work to bring it together, or so corporate lobbyists liked to think, because the conservatives "will not rally automatically to the President." It would therefore be "largely up to this anarchic business aggregation that we so fondly call a community to ensure that these critical votes are there—largely for us to make it possible for the President to be assertive in the first instance, and for his Congressional soul mates to cling to principle once the President has shown the way" (Harlow 1975, p. 8).

The alleged need for lobbyists to save the day gave Harlow's hair-raising speech its rationale. It was a pep talk meant to rouse the troops into action, not a statement to be taken on its face by political analysts. The following punch lines reveal his motivations very clearly: "This I know from years past—if all of us can somehow be made to care enough to coalesce the enormous strength business has all across the country, we will do just fine." And then the grand finale: "So let's get to it now, here and across the country, simply because we know we have to, and not await the legislative blowtorch which hour by hour is turning closer to our posterior" (Harlow 1975, p. 9).

As it turned out, the liberal and moderate Democrats in Congress apparently understood the power constellation in much the same way as Harlow did. They decided they could not win over enough moderate Republicans on new initiatives to overcome the large contingent of conservative Democrats who would support the conservative coalition in upholding Ford's vetoes. They therefore announced they would wait until after the 1976 presidential elections to put forward most of their agenda. Perhaps needless to add, the Humphrey-Javits Balanced National Growth and Planning Act went nowhere for the next two years.

However, at the urging of organized labor, supporters of the liberal-labor alliance did manage to push a bill through the House and Senate that would allow common-situs picketing in the construction industry, a high-level priority for union leaders since the Supreme Court banned such activity as an illegal secondary boycott in 1951. The new legislation included compromises with John Dunlop, a Harvard professor and prominent labor mediator serving as Ford's secretary of labor. The two sides agreed on a ten-day notice of union intentions to picket and a thirty-day limit on how long the picketing could last. After the liberal-labor alliance overcame a Senate filibuster with a cloture vote, Ford broke his promise to sign the compromise bill due to enormous lobbying pressure from a united corporate community, including the Business Roundtable and the construction industry's trade association. He claimed that he had changed his mind about signing the bill because it might lead to greater conflict in the construction industry, but he was more concerned about corporate support and the challenge for the Republican presidential nomination in 1976 by former California governor Ronald Reagan. Dunlop, who had worked for several years to craft a management-labor accord in construction that could tame inflation, resigned shortly after the veto (Greene 1995, pp. 96–98).

Even so, liberal Democrats did have the satisfaction of taking the lead on issues that appealed to the spending coalition within the party, and to some of the few remaining moderate Republicans in Congress. They were able to make the tax cuts Ford finally advocated larger than he wanted them to be, which drew no protest from the corporate moderates at the CED. They also angered Ford, but did not suffer his veto, by rejecting his proposed spending cuts for 1975 and 1976. In addition, they were able to extend unemployment benefits once again. Liberal Democrats also led the way in eliminating funding for the Vietnam War in 1975, although by this point they had the support of some machine Democrats, Southern Democrats, and moderate Republicans because most elected officials wanted to put the war behind them. Liberals also received some of the credit for the expansion of the earned income tax credit (EITC) through doubling the level of income necessary before it was phrased out. However, as noted in the discussion of Nixon's Family Assistance Plan in Chapter 9, both the corporate community and the conservative coalition supported the EITC as the best of the alternatives available to them for income maintenance.

Despite its several victories and partial victories on income-related issues, the liberal-labor alliance had to endure sixty-six vetoes by Ford over a period of twenty-nine months, fifty-four of which were upheld by core members of the conservative coalition, including his veto of the common-situs picketing bill. Democrats therefore spent much of their time preparing for future battles by developing procedural reforms that might make new legislation possible in spite of the conservative coalition. These proposals had been prepared for House members by the staff of the Democratic Study Group, the liberal caucus created in 1959, which had experienced a gradual growth in its size and analytical capabilities (Roof 2011, pp. 136–139, 144).

The Democratic caucus first decided that the party's new Steering and Policy Committee, not the party members on the Ways and Means Committee, would make future committee assignments. It also agreed that committee chairs would be selected by a majority vote within the Democratic caucus, not by their years of seniority. Under the new rules, members of the caucus could call for a vote if they wanted to challenge the automatic ascension of a senior member to the chair or replace an aging chair. All of these changes had been discussed with fear and trembling as part of Harlow's exhortations to the Chamber of Commerce.

Once its new rules were in place, the House Democrats caused a major media stir by displacing three longtime committee chairs from the South, Edward Poage of Texas, who used his position as head of the Agricultural Committee to keep subsidy payments flowing into agribusiness; F. Edward Hebert of Louisiana, who used his top post on the Armed Services Committee to deliver defense contracts to companies in the South and keep military bases open; and Wright Patman of Texas, a populist who used his position on the Banking and Currency Committee to make investigations of big New York banks and fling jeremiads at the Federal Reserve System. It seemed as if a more general shake-up might be on the horizon, but no senior Democratic chair was again challenged until 1985 (*Congressional Quarterly* 1987, p. 108).

Liberals in the Senate were able to make a change in the rules on filibusters, which had allowed a determined (usually Southern) minority to block legislation since the 1830s. In 1917, in the first in a series of small changes, senators agreed that two-thirds of the senators present and voting could end a filibuster. The conservative coalition had rolled back that change somewhat in 1949 by requiring two-thirds of all Senate members to support the end of debate, not simply two-thirds of those present and voting. In 1959 the liberals and moderates had been able to restore the rule that held between 1917 and 1949. After failed attempts at further change in the 1960s, liberal senators proposed in early 1975 that the threshold for cutting off debate should be lowered to three-fifths of those present and voting. However, the conservative coalition would only agree to a change that lowered the barrier to three-fifths of the Senate as a whole. Liberal-labor successes did not increase, but obstruction became even more frequent as an unexpected result (Binder and Smith 1997, pp. 181–182; Roof 2011, p. 130).

While all the procedural changes and vetoes were taking center stage, the Business Roundtable made its first major attempt to influence Congress by coordinating an effort to block liberal amendments to the antitrust laws. The proposed changes would allow state attorneys general more leeway to sue corporations for damages for violations that cost consumers large sums of money. Roundtable members, claiming that the amendments would permit large unwarranted claims that could bankrupt companies, urged senators friendly to them to delay and even filibuster (Shanahan 1975, 1976b). They then introduced a compromise acceptable to large corporations. "In the end," conclude a pair of researchers from Ralph Nader's Public Citizen organization, who did several interviews related to the case, the Business Roundtable "was able to get excised from the original bill the provisions it considered most offensive" (Green and Buchsbaum 1980, p. 132).

All in all, the legislative outcomes for 1975–1976 were far from a disaster for the corporate community. The corporate community as a whole supported tax cuts, and the corporate moderates were comfortable with deficit spending and the extension on unemployment benefits. Liberal efforts to ease the rules on common-situs picketing were blocked, major changes in the antitrust laws were eliminated, and any liberal-labor attempts at substantive reform had been postponed. Leaders in the corporate community may have felt annoyed, frustrated, and powerless, as evidenced by their fulminations at the sessions sponsored by the Conference Board, but they and their allies in the conservative coalition were still the dominant force in Washington.

THE CHANGING OF THE GUARD AT THE CED

The years 1976 and 1977 saw a changing of the guard at the top of the CED. When Holland took over as president in March 1976, he traveled extensively for the first few months to meet with CED trustees and learn firsthand of their goals for the organization. Lindsay replaced Klutznick as chair of the Research and Policy Committee two months later, just after the focus of his planning initiative was changed to "improving the long-term performance of the economy." Byrom became the acting chair in 1977, at about the time he was being elevated to chair of the board at Koppers. He also served on the boards of Mellon National Bank, the Continental Group, Ralston Purina, North America Phillips, and American Smelting and Refining.

The Inflation Report Finally Appears

The CED's contentious report on inflation, *Fighting Inflation and Promoting Growth*, finally materialized in mid-August 1976, after a record number of subcommittee meetings—fourteen—with the help of a supplementary grant from the Lilly Endowment (Committee for Economic Development 1976a). The subcommittee also ended up with an expanded advisory committee that included thirteen members, among them such well-known Keynesian economists as Otto Eckstein, Arthur Okun, and Robert Solow, who all served on the Council of Economic Advisors during the Kennedy or Johnson administrations and as consultants on earlier CED inflation reports. There were also two conservative economists, Murray Weidenbaum of Washington University and Arnold Weber of Carnegie Mellon University, along with two business economists, one the chief economist in the corporate planning department at Exxon, the other an assistant economist at Morgan Guaranty Trust.

The report concluded that there are multiple sources of inflation, such as excess demand, supply shortages, and adjustments in the exchange rate, not simply union demands for higher wages and/or too much government spending. As a consequence of the many-faceted nature of inflation, no single policy could deal with it, and the process of taming it had to be long and slow. Coleman, the beleaguered subcommittee chair, told the *New York Times* that all of these conclusions reflected advances in corporate leaders' understanding of inflation. However, and perhaps more revealing, there was no mention in the report of any of the recommendations in Klutznick's January 1975 speech concerning a new social compact involving business, labor, and government.

The *New York Times* account of the report found only one recommendation worth highlighting—a call for government action whenever unemployment reached 5 percent. Instead, its story concentrated on the fact that there had been disagreements over the report's contents and that it appeared many months later than originally anticipated. The article may have reflected what many conservative corporate executives were saying off the record when it claimed that the report "appears to be especially critical of the [Ford] Administration, particularly since many of its recommendations echo the emerging themes of Jimmy Carter's campaign." A CED spokesperson countered that the report was "aimed at the gentleman who presides in the Oval Office, whoever he may be," and added "many of us wish we could have released the report earlier" (Crittenden 1976b, p. 41).

To say there were disagreements within the CED concerning the report is a major understatement. As if to symbolize the new direction the CED was taking, six hard-liners among the trustees voted against its publication, starting with subcommittee members Byrom of Koppers, Riordan of Mobil Oil, and van Gorkom of Trans

Union. They were joined by three members of the Research and Policy Committee: Fitzgerald of Cutler-Hammer; Jervis Babb, the retired chair of Lever Brothers; and Charles P. Bowen Jr., the retired chair of Booz, Allen and Hamilton, a management consulting firm. As for the comments and reservations, most came from a handful of strong opponents of any government controls, although two liberal trustees, both economists, also commented a few times, with one noting that the United States "has never even tried a carefully conceived incomes policy" (Committee for Economic Development 1976a, p. 92).

Harper made sixteen of the forty-eight comments, with Weiss of GE and Larry of US Steel each making six. Harper also joined with other conservatives on ten of their comments, putting him at the center of the opposition clique once again. Most of the comments were brief, claiming there was a lack of evidence for a particular assertion or denying the validity of a specific statement, but the more sustained comments added up to a complete monetarist analysis that rejected any form of government controls and blamed government and organized labor for all the problems of inflation.

As was in the case for the two previous inflation reports, the opposition view was best exemplified in the comments by Harper, which were usually joined by top executives from Heinz, Wyandotte Chemicals, and Mobil Oil. Rejecting the idea that inflation can be triggered by several different kinds of shocks to the system, Harper claimed it is an "underlying, ongoing monetary phenomenon initiated by federal budget deficits"; therefore, a combination of "excessive government spending and the printing of money to finance the deficit remains, as always, the fundamental cause of the inflation process." More emphatically, he asserted, "there is no recorded instance in all of history in any country in the world where inflation was not caused by excessive increases in money supply relative to output" (Committee for Economic Development 1976a, pp. 82–83, 87).

Harper also stated the Business Roundtable view of the current economic situation very clearly when he argued that "labor's share of national income has trended upward steadily over the years and now constitutes three-fourths of the total pie," which he used as evidence to refute the claim that business is powerful: "If big business has the power to dominate the economy, as its critics allege, such power is not reflected in any public figures." He also claimed that prices are more flexible than liberal economists claim, not "administered," a fact that is masked because corporations cannot announce price reductions due to their fear of new government regulations. Specifically, companies "have become increasingly unwilling to reduce book prices of their products when faced with the threat or prospects of controls imposed by a misguided Congress" (Committee for Economic Development 1976a, p. 85).

In effect, the industrialists' concern with blocking government involvement in pricing decisions and eliminating unions led them to find monetary economics a far more attractive solution for their major concerns at that juncture than even a limited commercial Keynesianism. More generally, monetarism's concentration on the money supply, and on the need to endure slumps to bring the economy back to equilibrium, made more sense to them in terms of the power issues they confronted in their daily corporate lives than did the Keynesian prescriptions they had adopted when they feared low demand and the potential power of the liberal-labor alliance. They also appreci-ated the fact that a monetary remedy to inflation through high interest rates could be applied by a quasi-independent government agency, the Federal Reserve Board, within which the corporate community had, to say the least, great influence. Fiscal policy, in contrast, had to be enacted by a Congress in which the liberal-labor alliance might be able to delay legislation and gain some concessions in the process.

As media coverage of the CED's belated inflation report quickly faded, Holland circulated an in-house report on September 7, based on his summer of interviewing, on how the trustees envisioned the future. It told of his plans to institute an annual survey to ask trustees what they thought were the important issues, to increase the size of the Washington staff to have more legislative impact, and to invite government officials to sit in as guests at meetings of various subcommittees, with assurances that they would not be identified or quoted (Holland 1992). His suggested changes were then highlighted at a New York luncheon two days later.

Two weeks after the luncheon, this in-house report was the main agenda at a special meeting of the reconstituted executive committee, with Byrom and Holland directing the discussion. The minutes of the meeting reveal the new directions that were envisioned, starting with a renewed effort to obtain more input from trustees and to take more care in selecting the appropriate subcommittee chairs and project directors. For the staff members present, the message in these two recommendations must have been very clear. The remaining eleven objectives varied in their generality. Among several things, there would be a sustained effort to establish working relationships with the other policy-discussion organizations that have been mentioned throughout the book, including the Conference Board, the Business Roundtable, the National Association of Manufacturers, the American Enterprise Institute, and The Brookings Institution. The minutes noted the need for more emphasis on short program statements, regional meetings that would bring more trustees into discussions, and new fundraising strate-gies (Committee for Economic Development 1976b).

Despite the nearly three years of internal conflict in the CED, it is noteworthy that there were no hints of it in the press, other than the brief comments in the *New York Times* related to the inflation report, until a story appeared in the *Wall Street Journal* on December 17, 1976, with a headline reading "Rehabilitation Project: Once-Mighty CED Panel of Executives Seeks a Revival, Offers Advice to Carter." It quoted trustee James Q. Riordan, the senior vice president for finance at Mobil Oil, who voted against the 1976 inflation statement and joined most of Harper's dissents, as saying that "in the early days, the trustees were men who saw a need for some more government interven-tion, but now some of the trustees believe the intervention has gone far enough." The story also quoted "an anonymous academic economist who once advised the CED" as saying it had "lost its purpose" and "doesn't have the sense to go out of business." However, Holland told the reporter that any differences within the organization were short-term problems, and he added that he preferred to concentrate on specific long-term issues to reduce ideological differences (*Wall Street Journal* 1976, p. 38).

Still, for all of Holland's efforts to put tensions over the inflation recommendations to rest, they lingered. In response to a fund-raising letter from CED treasurer Richard

Shinn, the CEO of Metropolitan Life, written four months after the report appeared, Larry of US Steel replied, "I have very serious concern about the future plans of CED. Several of its recent pronouncements were utterly useless; and made no real contribution." He concluded, "I hate to suggest dissolution," then added that "I'm not really comfortable with CED, enough at least, to consider raising its ante—at this point on the calendar" (Larry 1976). Larry resigned from the CED a year later when he became the president of the National Association of Manufacturers.

A year after the inflation report appeared, Collado (1977) wrote a note to his fellow trustees saying that the inflation statement put "too much emphasis on controls," and he blamed its mistakes on "a poor compromise between the views of trustees and a stubborn chair [meaning economist John Coleman] and project director [Schiff, the CED's chief economist since 1969]." Fitzgerald (1996), reflecting on the tense year of 1976 twenty years later, had views similar to those of Collado, recalling Schiff as the only staff person who tried to press his views on trustees. Collado's analysis also is consistent with Bosworth's (1992) later reflection that he, Coleman, and Schiff had probably pushed the trustees further than they wanted to go, leading to an "explosion." He thought that his lack of experience at that point in dealing with corporate executives probably caused him to be too insensitive to their primary concerns.

Similarly, Harper brought up the inflation report in his reply to a request for suggestions in July 1977 on what subjects the CED should be studying in the next year or two. He began by saying, "I think without any question a very high priority should be given to a study of the regulating system in this country and its effects on American business." He also wrote, "Another item of equally high priority is the prospect for the economy if the present government policies of holding down capital accumulations are continued." Then he added, "I have not given much detailed study to the recent CED publications. I must confess that I was so completely turned off by the inflation paper in which I participated and which I thought was a total disaster that I have given very little time to the subject since that time" (Harper 1977).

A RETROSPECTIVE LOOK AT THE DECLINE OF TURMOIL

As the 1976 elections approached, the majority of American citizens and the key power figures in the corporate community were in far different places than they had been just six or seven years before. First and foremost, the civil rights movement gradually declined after it attained two of its most important goals, civil rights and voting rights in the South, even though African Americans still faced many obstacles. Although there still were (and are) large gaps in wealth, income, and education between black and white Americans, the civil rights victories meant that many of the movement's members and leaders, along with long-standing middle-class African Americans and a growing number of black scholarship students, could take advantage of the gains that had been made. They did so by enrolling in college and then obtaining white-collar, professional, and high management positions (Collins 1997; Zweigenhaft and Domhoff 2003; 2011, chapter 6).

Moreover, there had been no major inner-city riots since 1968, so planning to improve downtown land values was moving forward through such people magnets as university expansions, medical centers, convention centers, music halls, and museums, which could provide substitutes for the movement of factories to the South and the Third World, and of office buildings and high-income housing to the suburbs. With ample federal funds, mayors and growth coalitions were prepared by this point to deal with the kind of large social disruptions that had taken them by surprise in the 1960s. They could do so with immediate and overwhelming force by deploying the well-armed Special Weapons and Tactics (SWAT) teams that had been developed in two hundred cities across the country (Kraska and Kaeppler 1997, p. 6, figure 1).

The Vietnam War was finally over and the military draft had ended, which meant young adult males could pursue their educational and career aspirations without fear of facing injury or death in Southeast Asia. The frustrated anti-war Left, which had more impact on the conduct of the war from 1967 to 1969 than it realized, as revealed in the deliberations of Johnson's wise men and changes in public opinion about the war, fragmented at its most successful moment. Then it was finished off by government harassment and repression over the next two or three years (Cunningham 2004). There had been no student demonstrations of any size since the massive spontaneous response to the Cambodian invasion in the spring of 1970, which at first appeared to be the beginning of a new anti-war movement. It disappeared during the summer months and did not revive when students returned to school in the fall.

The feminists and the most activist environmentalists, who used a wide range of nonviolent disruptive tactics from the mid-1960s to early 1970s to gain entrée into corporate offices and legislative chambers for themselves and their ideas, were being accepted into graduate schools or working through channels, except in the case of the highly confrontational antinuclear movement, which focused its energies on blocking entrances, occupying potential construction sites, and filing legal challenges. In particular, the women who fought for expanded rights went to law school, medical school, and business school in far greater numbers than at any time in the past—and eventually would rise to high positions in business, politics, and federal agencies (Zweigenhaft and Domhoff 2006; 2011, chapter 2).

In addition to the gradual decline of the various social movements due to the complex combination of their successes, internal failures, and governmental harassment, the backlash against the successes of these movements by white middle-income Americans reshaped the electorate from the early 1960s onward. Liberals hoped that the white votes for George Wallace in the North in the 1964 primaries were a temporary aberration that would be overcome by economic self-interest, but the Democrats' loss of one-fourth of their white presidential voters between 1964 and 1968, and more of them in 1972, showed that the white pushback was only growing larger in the face of concern with new civil rights initiatives, affirmative action, school integration, and busing.

The right turn in the electorate was facilitated by the rise of what was by then a religious right. In the South, religious fervor was merged with racial resentments because the federal government rejected the claim that the dozens of newly created segregated schools should be granted tax exemptions because they were proclaimed to be Christian.

Now the government's attempts to end segregation could be framed as an attack on religious freedom (Crespino 2008). Outside the South, the general rise of the religious right was shaped in part by the negative reactions of conservatives within the mainstream Protestant denominations to the involvement of their ministers and some of their fellow parishioners in the civil rights movement, including their participation in many of the marches in the early 1960s. Support for the anti-war and feminist movements by Social Gospel Protestants generated further conflict. Most of all, the charged issue of abortion energized the religious movement that arose in the 1970s (Quadagno and Rohlinger 2009; Rohlinger 2002). Vehement opposition to women's right to choose became the major bridge between conservative Protestants and the Catholic Church, which provided much of the original financial and organizational support for the anti-abortion movement (Tribe 1990). Money raised through direct mailings and financial backing from a handful of ultraconservative super-rich families and their foundations facilitated these efforts (Diamond 1995; Phillips-Fein 2009).

Working within the new political climate of the early 1970s, the resistance organized by the Construction Users Anti-Inflation Roundtable and the Business Roundtable put the building trades unions on the defensive. This resistance received a large assist from the Nixon administration through its changes in apprenticeship programs and its integration of construction sites financed by federal contracts. As a result, an estimated 40 percent of new construction jobs were nonunion by 1975 (Levitan and Cooper 1984, p. 120). More generally, the National Labor Relations Board's anti-union decisions after 1971 made it even more difficult to organize or maintain unions, which opened the way for outsourcing and "off shoring" to low-wage Third World countries. In addition, the number of court rulings against union discrimination rose from fewer than ten a year to over twenty, and were destined to reach a peak of seventy cases in 1980, usually with drastic financial penalties for the unions (Frymer 2008, pp. 88–92). Although strong unions were still winning good contracts in the first half of the 1970s, overall membership fluctuated at between 18 and 19 million between 1968 and 1973, and union density declined from 27.9 percent to 23.5 percent (Mayer 2004, p. 22, table A1). The fall-off would have been even greater if not for the continuing growth of the public-sector unions, which gained over one million members and reached a union density of 38 percent in 1974 (Miller and Canak 1995b, p. 19, table 1).

The interruption of the Republican march to majority status by the Watergate scandals and Nixon's resignation in disgrace enlarged the Democratic majority in Congress in 1975–1976, which generated major concerns for many corporate executives and their hired lobbyists. But the liberal-labor alliance was unable to pass any liberal initiatives due to the efforts of the conservative coalition and Ford's extensive use of his veto power. Despite this, the spending coalition within the Democratic Party was able to enact larger tax cuts than Ford recommended and blocked most of his spending cuts. The Office of Economic Opportunity was abolished in 1973, but the liberal-labor alliance had been able to save most jobs programs by agreeing to merge them into one program as part of the Comprehensive Education and Training Act (Quadagno 1994, p. 84). Ironically, organized labor became a stronger presence within the Democratic Party just at the time that conservative forces were regaining their strength. Liberal and labor organizations continued to lobby together even while their voting base eroded (Roof 2011, chapter 5).

As for the US Chamber of Commerce, it took a stand on sixteen issues between 1973 and 1976 that managed to pass both houses, taking the winning side on eleven of them. It lost on increases in Social Security benefits and an increase in the minimum wage. It also unsuccessfully opposed a 1973 bill allowing highway trust finds to be used for nonhighway programs, a 1975 bill for the temporary regulation of oil prices, and a 1976 bill to regulate solid waste disposal. All in all, ultraconservatives in the corporate community had little to complain about by the end of the Ford administration.

Meanwhile, the corporate community in general, for all its worrying and grumbling at meetings of the Conference Board and the Business Roundtable, was even more united than it had been in the past, and it was politically mobilized in a very conservative direction. Despite the exposure of illegal corporate campaign contributions, illegal bribes to foreign governments, several scandals involving oil leaks and chemical spills, and challenges to developers by public-interest law firms, Congress rejected legislation to prohibit bribes of foreign government officials by American corporations, approved an Alaskan pipeline sought by the oil companies, and gave local growth coalitions full control of federal subsidies for cities, now repackaged as Urban Development Action Grants.

Reacting to the campaign-finance scandals, Congress passed reforms that called for full disclosure of donors and limits on the size of individual contributions. But with the help of an unlikely ruling by the Federal Elections Commission, it also opened the door to large donations from corporate political action committees (PACs), which were allowed to use company funds to solicit donations for candidates from stockholders, executives, administrative employees, and their families (Alexander 1976, pp. 157–159). Corporate PACs had very little impact in 1976, but they played a role in the 1980s, perhaps especially at the congressional level (Alexander 1979, chapter 10; Clawson, Neustadtl, and Weller 1998).

By 1976 the Business Roundtable was clearly at the center of the corporate-financed policy-planning network in terms of interlocking directors, with thirty-three of the forty-five members of its policy committee also members of the Business Council; in addition, the members of those two groups had numerous directorship and funding links to all the prominent foundations and think tanks of that era (Colwell 1993). Although the Business Roundtable and Business Council shared many members, the division of labor was clear. "We leave the advocacy to the Business Roundtable," the chair of the Business Council told a journalist (Shoup 1980, p. 168).

Based on the findings on the blocking power of the conservative coalition in the mid-1970s, it is doubtful that the Business Roundtable deserves much of the credit it is given for its impact on Congress. However, it did provide greater coordination for corporate lobbyists, and it was able to put extra pressure on Ford to veto legislation it did not like, thanks to its ability to mobilize support for rival Republican presidential candidates if necessary. Due to the roundtable's inclusion of trustees from both the CED and NAM, its creation should be understood as evidence for a greater unity in the corporate community, which also made possible stronger links to the conservative coalition. At the same time, the Business Roundtable had the ability to put fear of electoral retaliation into the minds of centrist Democrats newly elected from previously Republican districts. As for the Committee for Economic Development, it was being taken over and moved to a secondary position in the policy-planning network by trustees who were much more conservative than the centrists and liberals who were stepping down from active roles.

After the former governor of Georgia, Jimmy Carter, a born-again Christian evangelical, defeated Ford for the presidency by fifty-seven electoral votes, thanks in good part to his victories in every Southern state except Virginia, the corporate-conservative alliance faced Democratic control of both the White House and Congress for the first time since 1968. But in terms of organizational strength and policy initiatives, the corporate community, in harness with the conservative coalition, was poised to brush past Democratic control and take full advantage of Middle America's rightward trend. As if to signal their determination, the Business Roundtable and the CED had statements calling for tax reductions ready to hand Carter as he was about to take office. A *New York Times* article described the Business Roundtable proposal as "remarkably similar" to a proposal presented to Carter by his transition staff (Shanahan 1976a, p. A1). The CED report appeared a week later and made similar recommendations (Committee for Economic Development 1976c; Crittenden 1976a).

Chapter Eleven

Corporate Triumphs during the Carter Administration

Jimmy Carter came to the White House as a relative unknown, presenting himself as a soft-spoken and humble born-again Christian from Plains, Georgia, with such a modest social standing that his mother told a journalist, "He makes us sound so poor you want to get out a hat and take up a collection" (Shoup 1980, p. 22). In fact, Carter was raised on a large farm that had been in the family for five generations. After graduation from the Naval Academy and a seven-year career as a submarine officer, he returned home shortly after his father's death in 1952 and began to expand the family's landholdings, employing several hundred field hands, while running the family's general store and warehouses as well. He and his family had an estimated net worth of $5 million in 1975, which is about $21.3 million in 2012 dollars (Pessen 1984, pp. 51–52, 132–134).

During his ten years as what he described as a "peanut farmer," Carter also served on the boards of schools, hospitals, and libraries, then won election to the state senate in the early 1960s, which brought him into contact with potential financial backers in Atlanta. He lost his first bid for governor in 1966, and then won a four-year term in 1970, with strong financial support from Atlanta corporate leaders. By 1972 Carter had decided to run for national office, either president or vice president, which led him to hire a policy expert, Stuart Eizenstat, a graduate of Harvard Law School and a corporate lawyer in Atlanta. As part of the process, he began to demonstrate that he was knowledgeable about foreign affairs by taking numerous trips to other countries to tell their leaders about trade and investment opportunities involving Georgia corporations, most notably Coca-Cola, which provided him with a company airplane for these trips and paid a large part of the expenses (Biven 2002, p. 16).

A year later, Carter was asked to join a new policy-discussion organization, the Trilateral Commission, which had representatives from Western Europe and Japan as well as the United States. Carter later told one of his aides, "those Trilateral

Commission meetings for me [which occurred during the years 1973–1975] were like classes in foreign policy—reading papers produced on every conceivable subject, hearing experienced leaders debate international issues and problems" (Biven 2002, p. 18).

To increase his national visibility, Carter contacted the chair of the Democratic Party, Robert Strauss, a Texas corporate lawyer well known as a consummate Washington insider, to volunteer to campaign in 1974 for Democratic congressional candidates. Strauss responded by making Carter the chair of the Democratic Congressional Campaign Committee, which gave him the opportunity to raise money and campaign for Democrats throughout the country. Carter also had Eizenstat develop issue papers that might be useful to these candidates. Eizenstat, who had spent a year on the White House staff in 1967 after graduating from law school, received help from experts at The Brookings Institution that Carter knew through the Trilateral Commission.

Carter ran for president in the context of a mild economic recovery from what had turned out to be the most severe decline since the early 1930s. Unemployment had climbed as high as 9 percent in the aftermath of the fifteen-month recession that officially ended in March 1975, but a lingering high unemployment rate of 7.8 percent made jobs the number-one issue on people's minds in 1976. As a result, Carter's biggest promise throughout the campaign was to lower unemployment to the 4 percent range by the end of his first term. He also called for a jobs program through the private sector, as well as for 800,000 summer jobs and an increase in government-financed jobs from 300,000 to 600,000 (Biven 2002, pp. 28–29, 36).

At the same time, Carter insisted that his expansionary fiscal and monetary policies would lead to an eventual balancing of the budget. He did so by adopting the CED's balancing budget concept, including its terminology. "Social needs and the need for economic stabilization," his position paper claimed, "may require from time to time the unbalancing of the budget," but it quickly added, "we should strive toward budget balance, *within an environment of full employment,* over the long term." He then concluded that "*I therefore call for balanced budgets over the business cycle,*" which in his telling could be achieved by 1979 (Biven 2002, p. 34, italics in the original).

CARTER'S KEY APPOINTMENTS, FOREIGN AND DOMESTIC

Once in office, many of Carter's appointments reflected the national connections that he and his choice for vice president, liberal Minnesota senator Walter Mondale, had established through their shared involvement in the Trilateral Commission. The secretary of state, Cyrus Vance, one of the "wise men" who advised Johnson to de-escalate the Vietnam War in 1968, was a member, as was the secretary of defense, Harold Brown, a prominent physicist and the president of the California Institute of Technology, who also sat on several corporate boards. The secretary of the treasury, W. Michael Blumenthal, the president of Bendix Corporation, was a member of the Trilateral Commission as well as a trustee of the Committee for Economic Development. The national security advisor, Zbigniew Brzezinski, a professor of international relations at Columbia, was the executive director of the Trilateral Commission and wrote several speeches for Carter during the presidential campaign. More generally, the early Carter administration included twenty appointees who were members of the Trilateral Commission; four were trustees of the CED, and five were employed by The Brookings Institution (Shoup 1980, p. 51).

Carter's main economic advisors on both domestic and foreign issues also came from the Trilateral/Brookings/CED nexus. Secretary of the Treasury Blumenthal coordinated both domestic and foreign economic policy, but the basic work on domestic economic policy was carried out by the new CEA chair, Charles Schultze, the Brookings employee and frequent advisor to the CED. Schultze in turn had the assistance of the two other CEA appointees, William Nordhaus, a Yale economics professor and CED advisor, and Lyle Gramley, a senior staff economist for the Federal Reserve Board in Washington.

Carter's international economic advisors were members of the Trilateral Commission and frequent advisors to CED subcommittees on international economic policies: Richard Copper, Trilateral Commission and CED; Fred Bergsten, Trilateral Commission, CED, and The Brookings Institution; Henry Owens, Trilateral Commission and Brookings; and Anthony Solomon, the undersecretary of the treasury for monetary affairs, an economist who became a millionaire through selling his start-up food company to General Foods and spent the rest of his career in public service. The liberal-labor alliance had its representation on domestic policy through economist Ray Marshall, a professor at the University of Texas, who served as secretary of labor.

THE CARTER AGENDA

One of the first orders of business for the new Carter administration was the development of the kind of economic package that had eluded most presidents in the past, one that was supposed to simultaneously create more jobs and control inflation. It started with a stimulus package that included a one-time tax rebate of $50 per person, but that idea was withdrawn in the spring of 1977 when the economy seemed to be on a strong upward path. The plan also called for the public-works programs and summer jobs for low-income youth promised during the campaign.

Carter's economic advisors claimed that inflation would not be a major problem during 1977 because agricultural production was back to normal levels and oil was flowing again. Still, the new administration developed an anti-inflation policy meant to avoid the high human and economic costs of raising interest rates in case inflation flared up again. As Schultze wrote to Carter in forwarding the plan approved by the Economic Policy Group, "The human and social costs of this approach [raising interest rates] are prohibitive"; it would therefore be necessary to explain this fact very carefully in order to "undo the nonsense that emanated out of Washington in recent years which tried to sell high unemployment (achieved by hawkish fiscal-monetary policies) as a panacea for inflation" (Biven 2002, p. 128).

In making this point, Schultze was drawing in part on a new concept at the time, "core inflation," which excludes foods and raw materials from the mix of products that are used to track inflation because their prices are so volatile. The notion of core inflation provides a much better indication of the long-term direction of inflation or deflation, but at the time it was also in effect an index of wages increases. As economist Carl Biven (2002, p. 129) explains, "Since labor costs contributed about 70 percent of production costs in the 1970s, the underlying rate [of inflation] can also be thought of as measured by labor costs." This implies, of course, that any decline in inflation, aside from decreases in the prices of oil and agricultural products, would be a matter of controlling labor costs.

Carter's anti-inflation policy of necessity included a series of proposals to deal with high energy costs, the most important of which, heartily endorsed by the Business Roundtable/Business Council/CED nexus, was to decontrol oil prices and let market pricing cut oil consumption. Carter's plan also called for faster development of synfuels, and there were plans to reduce inflation through improving worker productivity and cutting unnecessary government regulations, by then the corporate community's favorite remedies for inflation (Biven 2002, p. 155). The Carter team's economic goals were closely tied to projected improvements in the international economy that were supposed to follow from joint expansionary efforts led by Germany and Japan, a recommendation from the Trilateral Commission known as the "locomotive strategy." To that end, Vice President Mondale, along with economic advisors Bergsten and Cooper, all of them acquainted with their European counterparts through the Trilateral Commission, visited Germany and Japan shortly after Carter was inaugurated (Biven 2002, p. 96).

Impressive as the Carter administration's plans appeared to be, they actually did not have much to offer beyond the hope that there would be a revival of the international economy and no supply shocks on food or raw materials. In case those hopes did not materialize, there was also a recommendation for "suggested" wage-price guidelines for capital-labor agreements, which consisted of delivering private messages of restraint to corporate executives and labor leaders. This backup plan was added to the package because Carter's economic advisors decided it would be impossible to convince corporations and unions to reach cooperative arrangements on their own. To prepare for any use of government suasion to dampen inflation, the Carter administration revived the remnants of Nixon's Council on Wages and Prices to do studies that monitored wage and price levels. None other than Barry Bosworth of Brookings was its director, but it had no power. As a last resort if inflation spun out of control, Carter said he would make use of voluntary wage and price controls, if the Council on Wages and Prices recommended them, although the Business Roundtable made clear that it did not like the idea.

Negotiations with Congress over the Carter stimulus and inflation-control package were complicated from the outset by Carter's unexpected decision to eliminate nineteen water-development projects, which had been long sought and carefully negotiated by senior legislators for their local growth coalitions. Ignoring the power of local landed interests, Carter claimed that the projects were a combination of wasteful pork barrel spending and environmentally unsound engineering. He further added the obvious point that some of the projects benefited only a handful of landowners, which was of course why the legislation was proposed. In making this decision, Carter challenged the spending coalition among the congressional Democrats, which had a strong interest in increasing land values, whether for agricultural interests in the South or for developers in all regions of the country. Senator Long of Louisiana retaliated by holding up Carter's overall program in the Senate Finance Committee for several months (Biven 2002, pp. 80–81).

The stimulus package that passed in May included tax cuts for individuals, tax credits for employers, and a jobs program. It had the support of the Business Roundtable, but with important changes that its leaders advocated. When Reginald Jones, the CEO of GE, testified before the Ways and Means Committee on behalf of the roundtable, he disagreed with Carter by arguing that the tax cuts should be permanent, not temporary: "There is so much slack in the economy right now that we believe a fairly sizable program of permanent tax cuts and job-oriented action programs would not cause unmanageable inflation or deficits, rather would strengthen the economy against future inflation and future deficits" (Biven 2002, p. 87). In the end, there were permanent cuts, as Jones advocated. In addition, the conservative coalition, with strong support from liberal Democrats, extended the life of the earned income tax credit (EITC), increasing the benefits slightly and making them available to workers with somewhat higher incomes. The program also became permanent for the first time (Howard 1997, p. 144).

As for the inflation predictions, whether by the administration or Jones, they proved to be very inaccurate. Their analyses were illusory because core inflation was 6.0 to 6.5 percent higher than they anticipated, a fact that was masked by declining food prices. Moreover, food prices soon shot up again, by 14 percent in the first six months of 1977. However, there were no inflationary impacts from demands by organized labor. In fact, real wages did not keep up with inflation in 1977 (Biven 2002, pp. 134–135).

THE END OF LIBERAL-LABOR INFLUENCE IN CONGRESS

The liberal-labor agenda for 1977–1978 was very different from the one put forward by Carter. It called for an increase in the minimum wage and the creation of a long-delayed Office of Consumer Representation, along with a government commitment to reduce unemployment through an enhanced version of the original Full Employment Act of the mid-1940s. Most ambitious of all, the liberal-labor alliance wanted to revive the legislation on common-situs picketing that Ford had vetoed in 1975 and pass reforms in the National Labor Relations Act that would stop employers from delaying representation elections and in other ways defying orders from the labor board. Of the five most important issues on the agenda, only one, the minimum wage proposal, met with any success, and it was severely watered down.

Raising the Minimum Wage

In early 1977 a pro-labor House Democrat introduced a bill that would raise the minimum wage from $2.30 to $3.35 on January 1, 1978. Organized labor proposed a slightly smaller increase, to $3.00, but with a provision that the minimum wage should be indexed to inflation. The Carter administration supported labor's proposal for indexation but wanted a three-stage increase that would not reach $3.35 until 1981. The corporate community and the conservative coalition took a much more stringent view. The four-step increase they finally accepted, and that Congress passed, began at $2.65 on January 1, 1978, and reached its maximum of $3.35 per hour in January 1981 (Biven 2002, pp. 214–215). There was no provision for indexing, which meant that the $3.35 hourly minimum in 1981 was below the $3.69 that would have been necessary to maintain the purchasing power of $2.65 in early 1978. Nevertheless, the four-step increase proved to be the last one until 1987, which is of course another reason why the income distribution became even more unequal in the 1980s.

Another Defeat on Common-Situs Picketing

Carter and all of his main advisors supported the unions' agenda for changes in labor law and thought it should be brought forward in one package to maximize the chances for success. However, union legislative strategists insisted that common-situs picketing could pass easily on its own because virtually the same Congress had supported it so strongly in 1975. After making the bill slightly stronger than the one Ford vetoed, union leaders focused most of their lobbying on the Senate, assuming the bill would face its greatest opposition there.

A united corporate community, guided by a group called the National Action Committee on Secondary Boycotts, put a very large effort into the House in an effort to stop the bill even before it reached the Senate. It framed the issue as one in which union bosses were trying to gain even higher wages for overpaid construction workers, and then targeted undecided or hesitant representatives, especially those who had been elected for the first time in 1974 or 1976. As the vote neared, the liberal-labor alliance fell back to a more moderate bill similar to the one vetoed by Ford, but even this retreat and a few other compromises could not save the bill from a 217–205 defeat. Despite a large contingent of Northern Democrats in the House and a Democrat in the White House, labor was unable to overcome the efforts of the corporate community (Eccles 1977; Levitan and Cooper 1984, pp. 121–122).

Legislation for an Office of Consumer Representation

Consumer advocates within the liberal-labor alliance renewed their slowly growing forty-year effort to bring about more government involvement in protecting consumers by launching an all-out lobbying effort for an Office of Consumer Representation in 1969 (Glickman 2009, chapter 9). The powers of the proposed agency would be limited to research, consultation, and posing direct questions to regulatory agencies and executive departments about new regulations that might adversely affect consumers. It also could ask relevant courts to review regulatory decisions, but it would have no regulatory or enforcement powers itself (Arieff 1978). Basically, it would monitor the actions of other government regulatory agencies, give them advice, and make what they were doing known to the president, Congress, and the public (Schwartz 1979, p. 46).

The lobbying campaign was spearheaded by Ralph Nader, who became the focal point of consumer action when he revealed the safety problems of a small General Motors automobile, the Chevrolet Corvair, at congressional hearings in 1965. In addition to Nader, long-standing pro-consumer groups, such as the Consumer's Union and the Consumer Federation of America, played a role in shaping the legislation. President Johnson's former White House advisor on consumer affairs, Esther Peterson, a labor organizer and activist from the 1930s through the 1950s, was highly involved in creating the legislation as well, and later was appointed by Carter as his special assistant to lobby for the bill. At the outset the plan was even supported by ninety-five corporations, including Atlantic Richfield, Connecticut General Life, and Mobil Oil (Schwartz 1979, pp. 47–48).

Despite the limited size and powers of the proposed agency, and the support from those ninety-five corporations, it was strongly opposed by one of the many coalitions of lobbyists that were regularly deployed at the time by the corporate community (Hall 1969). Named the Consumer Issues Working Group, and including dozens of large corporations pulled together by Bryce Harlow of Procter & Gamble and his counterpart at Armstrong Cork, the coalition ignored the modest nature of the proposal. It claimed that the legislation would lead to a large and expensive bureaucracy, generate too much red tape, and hamper product innovation. Its campaign became a model for the ultraconservatives' use of "conservative populism" to undercut liberalism, accomplished "by defining the consumer movement and the countervailing power of government regulation as the establishment and by denying their own lofty perch in that very establishment" (Glickman 2009, p. 285). The problem was portrayed as the result of know-it-all experts who implied through their calls for extensive government oversight that ordinary people could not think for themselves.

The first version of the bill breezed through the Senate by a vote of 74–4 in 1970, which seemed to augur well for its eventual passage, but conservatives on the Rules Committee kept it from a floor vote in the House. Then the House supported the bill by large majorities in 1971 and 1973. However, members of the Consumer Issues Working Group were able to convince Southern Democrats in the Senate that the bill would be harmful to the corporate community, which led to successful filibusters in both years. Next, the bill passed the Senate with over a two-thirds majority in the 1975–1976 Congress, but it won by only nine votes in a House that had given it large majorities a few years earlier. Due to the close vote in the House, it was clear that a veto by President Ford would be upheld, so the liberal Democrats in the Senate did not bother to ask the House for a conference committee to iron out small differences (Akard 1992, p. 603).

When the bill was reintroduced into Congress with the strong support of President Carter in early 1977, the bulk of the corporate community challenged it as a bureaucratic monstrosity even more vigorously than in the past, with Business Roundtable leaders serving as informal advisors and funders for the Consumer Interest Working Group. Roundtable members claimed the proposal for a new agency was another example of needless burdensome delay and paperwork that would increase production costs for business, inflation for consumers, and expenses for government. There were no longer any corporate supporters for the legislation by this point.

With the Consumer Issues Working Group apparently gaining support in key House committees, advocates for the Office of Consumer Representation expressed willingness to compromise on a few issues. However, it also became clear to consumer advocates that several of the Democrats who previously voted for the bill did so because they knew that Ford would veto the bill if it passed, thereby avoiding unnecessary conflicts with consumer interests. Facing a likely defeat, Nader and Peterson appealed to grassroots supporters to send nickels to members of Congress to remind them that the agency would only cost each taxpayer five cents a year. They also ran ads in favor of the act in the home districts of those House members who seemed to be on the fence. But the bill lost in early 1978 by a large margin, 227–189, which put an end to the nine-year effort to pass it (Schwartz 1979, p. 54).

The House vote in 1978 not only revealed the ongoing power of the conservative coalition on issues of great concern to it but also showed that many of the moderate suburban-based Democrats swept into office by the anti-Watergate tide in 1974 were not prepared to resist strong lobbying efforts by a united business coalition. Of the nineteen representatives who switched their vote from 1975, twelve were moderate Democrats (Arieff 1978, p. 323).

The Labor Law Reform Act

With virtually all members of the corporate community breaking labor laws with impunity throughout the first seven years of the 1970s, and using a variety of tactics to delay up or down votes on union recognition, organized labor wanted several procedural changes in the laws that ensured and protected workers' rights. In particular, it wanted to (1) expand the size of the National Labor Relations Board from five to seven members to deal with a backlog of 19,000 cases, (2) introduce procedures that would lead to certification votes only a few weeks after labor organizers filed petitions asking for them, (3) provide stronger penalties against companies that fired activist employees, (4) increase the back payments owed to workers fired for union activities, and (5) prohibit companies that violated the law from bidding on government contracts. The final bill had President Carter's endorsement after lengthy negotiations with union leaders in which he insisted that their challenge to right-to-work laws (by then on the books in twenty states) be dropped because his advisors were sure it would sink the other reforms. He also insisted that new owners of a business should not have to honor an existing union contract (Fink 1998, p. 245).

For the purposes of this campaign, the corporate community created the National Action Committee on Labor Law Reform, with a vice president for industrial relations from Bethlehem Steel directing the lobbying team. The Council on a Union-Free Environment, founded in 1977 by the National Association of Manufacturers in anticipation of the effort by unions to reform labor legislation, aided the effort. Although the bill covered only 20 percent of American businesses, the corporate campaign stressed the dangers of the legislation for small businesses (Akard 1992, p. 605). Due to this emphasis on the plight of small business, social scientists later paid a great deal of attention to the efforts of the National Federation of Independent Business, the organization that they mistakenly see as the representative of the smallest of small businesses (Hacker and Pierson 2010, p. 119; Vogel 1989, p. 199).

In stark contrast to its image, however, the National Federation of Independent Business is best understood as an ultraconservative political lobby, a spin-off from the US Chamber of Commerce. In fact, it began as a small business itself, created in 1943 by a former Chamber of Commerce employee who became a political entrepreneur in order to make profits on membership fees while lobbying for conservative policy preferences (Zeigler 1961, pp. 31–32). The organization switched to a nonprofit status in the late 1960s, with another former Chamber of Commerce employee as its president. However, it continued to be based on annual memberships sold to small businesses by several hundred traveling sales representatives, working strictly on commission. Unlike standard voluntary associations, there were no general meetings or votes for officers, and membership turnover was very large each year (White 1983).

Business owners who signed up with the National Federation of Independent Businesses received membership stickers for their store windows, a newsletter with suggestions for small businesses, and periodic surveys on a wide range of issues. Called "mandates" to give them more apparent heft, the surveys were slanted to evoke conservative responses, the results of which were compiled at national headquarters and mailed to state and national legislators. Comparisons of the results of these surveys, which typically were returned by only about 20 percent of the members, with those from national surveys suggest that the ultraconservative claims made on the basis of the mandates were not representative of small business owners, who mostly share the attitudes of their ethnic group and/or local community (Hamilton 1975, chapters 2 and 7; Kazee, Lipsky, and Martin 2008). Moreover, only a small percentage of the federation's paid-up members had enough employees to be subject to the proposed reforms.

There was one moment of drama shortly before Congress took up the legislation because of differences within the Business Roundtable on whether or not to join the coalition. Several companies that were said to have good relationships with their unions, along with some companies that had small or harmless unions, did not want to become involved. In the end, the roundtable's policy committee voted 19–11 to enter the fray on the antireform side, but the fact that there had been an argument and that the vote was made public gave the Business Roundtable some legitimacy with corporate critics. The split vote nurtured the liberal-labor hope that at least some corporate moderates might be as flexible on this labor issue as they were on Social Security and civil rights. It also led some ultraconservatives to complain about corporate moderates in private interviews. An anonymous employee of the National Federation of Independent Businesses criticized the Business Roundtable for "sucking eggs with the president." Another anonymous Chamber of Commerce lobbyist told the same interviewer, "We view the Roundtable a little bit as lacking guts and selling out." The chair of NL Industries (formerly National Lead Company) defended the Business Roundtable with the comment that "the organization tries to deal rather pragmatically with what is possible," and he viewed any danger of alienating the Chamber of Commerce and NAM as "an acceptable loss" in pursuing roundtable goals (Green and Buchsbaum 1980, p. 103).

The campaign by the National Action Committee on Labor Law Reform was large and extensive, and it included a very expensive effort to influence public opinion. Business-oriented journalists also claimed that organized labor's resistance to the Carter administration's inflation guidelines might make some members of Congress less favorable toward the legislation. But in spite of all these efforts by the corporate community, the bill passed the House by a large margin, 257–163, in early October. Nor did the efforts of organized business or any alleged senatorial hostility toward labor for opposing inflation guidelines keep the Senate's Human Resources Committee from approving the bill by a 13–2 vote in late January 1978. However, the bill was then delayed for four months while the Senate debated the Panama Canal treaty, which was higher on Carter's list of priorities than labor law reform. Even with this extra time for the National Action Committee for Labor Law Reform to lobby senators and influence public opinion, it could not keep fifty-eight senators from going on record to end a filibuster that was undertaken by the hard core of the conservative coalition (Roof 2011, pp. 157–162).

Despite its ability to achieve strong majorities in both the House and the Senate, the liberal-labor alliance could not overcome the filibuster sustained by most Republicans, virtually all Southern Democrats, and Democratic senators from the right-to-work states of Nebraska and Nevada. They were bolstered in their efforts by the full support of Business Roundtable lawyers, who provided sixty-five time-consuming amendments and an Employee Bill of Rights that were introduced for debate. Along the way, organized labor offered further compromises, exempting even more businesses, but the filibuster still could not be broken. The bill was recommitted to the Senate Committee on Human Resources for further review in late June, never to emerge again. The corporate community won, but it did so with a minority vote by the conservative coalition in the Senate. This fact is often overlooked by those who say that organized labor lost political power in the 1970s, as political scientists Taylor Dark (2001, pp. 111–113) and Tracy Roof (2011, p. 161) rightly underscore. In fact, the liberal-labor alliance won 58 percent of the vote in the House and 59 percent in the Senate, which would be more than enough in a society in which the majority rules.

However, it is not at all certain that the enactment of the Labor Law Reform Act would have helped organized labor in its attempt to reverse the decline in private-sector union density because it "still would have had to undergo the same judicial and agency review that so effectively gutted the legislative intent of the NLRA" (Fink 1998, p. 241). Nor was it clear that union organizers could overcome employer resistance at the company gates. Racial divisions among workers, the continuing movement of factories to the South and overseas, and anti-union industrial relations firms might have been too much to overcome.

The Humphrey-Hawkins Act

The final liberal-labor initiative brought to a vote in 1978, the Full Employment and Balanced Growth Act, best known at the time as the Humphrey-Hawkins bill, was an amalgam of two earlier liberal bills. Augustus Hawkins, an African American from Los Angeles, first elected to the House in 1963, formulated the initial version in 1974. It provided government jobs for the unemployed on projects created by local planning councils; the jobs would be available at the prevailing local wage rate for those who could not find work in the private sector. The second ingredient was the Humphrey-Javits bill that built on parts of the proposal for an Office of Economic Planning, which had been launched in 1975 by the Initiative Committee for National Economic Planning.

The new bill, drafted in early 1976, called for officials at the national, state, and local levels to work together to create a plan that would provide full employment at the prevailing local wage for all those not accommodated by private employers. As might be expected, the Chamber of Commerce, NAM, and the Business Roundtable opposed the bill. After withering congressional testimony against it by economic experts in May, moderate Democrats delayed even a committee vote because support for the bill might hurt Democrats in the upcoming national elections. The expert critics included Charles Schultze while he was still at Brookings, whose testimony was considered to be "the most effective" by political scientist Margaret Weir (1993, p. 138) in her study of politics and jobs. Schultze expressed his agreement with the general goals of the legislation but opposed it because of his belief that government employment should be used only as a countercyclical measure to combat high unemployment. He also strongly warned against the inflationary impact of hiring unemployed workers at the prevailing wage in a district or state (Akard 1996, pp. 113–114).

The slightly redrawn version of the Humphrey-Hawkins bill debated in Congress in the summer months of 1978 was not formally "defeated" in that it was signed into law in late October. However, it was amended to the point that it embodied the policies of the corporate policy-planning network and the conservative coalition more than it did those of the liberal-labor alliance. The sponsors had to accept additional policy goals as equally important to reducing unemployment, starting with the stipulation that the Federal Reserve Board should try to minimize inflation. It also said the Fed had to begin any efforts toward increasing employment by expanding the money supply, one of the key prescriptions of the free-market monetary economists. As part of this emphasis on the money supply, the Fed had to send reports to Congress twice a year that stated its monetary policy. Then, too, the executive branch was instructed to aim for balanced budgets, which generate a downward pressure on demand when the economy slips (Akard 1996, pp. 122–123).

One nonbinding goal related to employment remained in the bill: by 1983 the unemployment rate should be 3 percent for adults over age twenty and 4 percent for individuals ages sixteen to twenty. Efforts to create jobs through private enterprise were to be made if the goal was not reached, followed if necessary by government programs (a "reservoir of public employment") limited to low-skill jobs so they did not compete with private-sector jobs. These employment goals were soon ignored, and nothing came of them. In the end, the bill was devoid of substance from a liberal-labor perspective, offering only hope for the distant future.

THE RIGHT TURN ON TAX REFORMS

With the economy growing in 1977 despite the agricultural shortages and inflationary problems, and with no signs of any moderation in inflation, the Carter administration developed plans in early 1978 for tax reforms. In doing so it was acting on Carter's repeated refrain during the presidential campaign that the American tax system was "a disgrace to the human race." He also may have felt impelled to act because the approval ratings on his handling of the economy fell from 47 percent to 24 percent between mid-1977 and early 1978. His original proposal, never officially released, was meant to stimulate the economy through lowering taxes on middle- and lower-income taxpayers, but it also raised taxes on capital gains and cut out some business tax breaks, including a provision that deferred taxes on corporate income earned in other countries. Alerted to the contents of the proposal, the corporate community began a lobbying campaign against it.

In good part due to concerns about declining business profits, which corporate leaders expressed directly to Blumenthal and Schultze as well as to the media, and knowing that corporate lobbyists were gaining support for their alternatives in Congress, the Carter proposal was altered to include cuts in corporate taxes from 48 percent to 44 percent. The reforms relating to capital gains and tax loopholes were dropped. After a compromise bill passed in the House that gave corporations most of what they wanted, the Senate increased the overall tax cuts from $16.3 billion to $29.1 billion; 85 percent of the individual cuts went to those making over $15,000 a year ($52,900 in 2012 dollars), and the corporate tax rate was cut from 48 percent to 45 percent. Rather than increasing the tax on capital gains, as Carter originally intended, the maximum effective tax rate on capital gains was cut from 49 to 28 percent, which contributed greatly to the after-tax incomes of the top 0.5 percent. (Akard 1996, pp. 126–129).

THE RIGHT TURN ON INFLATION

As the legislative battles over the failed liberal-labor initiatives and the Revenue Act of 1978 gradually faded from view, the problem of inflation came to the forefront once again. Although unexpected declines in oil prices in 1977 and early 1978, along with the deregulation of natural gas prices, held inflation to 6.5 percent in 1977 and 7.7 percent in 1978, another round of crop failures and likely OPEC increases in oil prices created a new threat. Making inflation worries worse, Carter agreed at a summit meeting in July 1978 to deregulate the price of domestically produced oil by the middle of 1979, because America's artificially low prices were exporting inflationary pressures to Europe. In exchange, Germany and Japan agreed to support new stimulus measures (Biven 2002, p. 153).

At this point the Carter administration tried to implement its liberal plan to deal with inflation, but with no success. The starting point would be a cap on wage-and-benefit packages at 7 percent and on price hikes at 5.75 percent. The difference of 1.25 percentage points between the wage and price increases was supposed to be canceled out by presumed gains in productivity rates. However, critics quickly pointed out that there was no evidence for such productivity gains at that time. To make the new plan more attractive to wage and salary employees, especially those with cost-of-living clauses in their union contracts, it included the promise of tax rebates for any inflation over 7 percent per year. This proposal was much the same as the tax reduction for low-income workers advocated by Klutznick on behalf of the CED leadership in 1975. According to The Brookings Institution economists who suggested this "tax incentive plan," it would serve as a kind of government insurance policy, guaranteeing that workers' real incomes would be protected (Biven 2002, p. 189). It was attractive to Carter's economic advisors because it embodied the spirit of a social compact with labor, which Keynesian economists and liberal CED trustees had been trying to fashion since the wage-price spiral began in the late 1960s.

In addition to this positive inducement for employees, there was a mortal threat to businesses if they could not certify that they had stayed within the wage and price guidelines: they would not be eligible to bid for government contracts. As for the government, it would do its part by reducing budget deficits through spending cutbacks, a promise Carter's economic advisors hoped would make the plan more attractive to the many business groups that had been calling for decreases in government spending. However, the package was not acceptable to any of the key participants. Most corporate leaders and all members of the conservative coalition opposed it as involving too much government interference in the market, and most unions preferred to stick with the cost-of-living adjustments that were built into 60 percent of their collectively bargained contracts.

Union leaders were especially wary because they were convinced that all previous rounds of wage-price guidelines and controls, and especially those under Nixon, limited wages more than they did prices. They were not willing to discuss wage-price guidelines until they saw evidence of price restraint by corporations and signs that prices in general were holding steady.

Organized labor also resisted because there was no evidence that its wage demands were the cause of the renewed inflation, as Carter's economic advisors also concluded in a background memo they sent to him at about this time. The return of rapid inflation was more likely due to the new supply shocks in agriculture and petroleum, along with a rise in housing prices (Biven 2002, pp. 191–195). However, the supply-side inflation did trigger cost-of-living adjustments for many workers, to the great annoyance of corporate leaders, who thought that everyone should contribute to the common sacrifice that would be needed to stop inflation.

Although workers were right that they had not gained in real wages, and moreover had experienced a gradual decline since 1969–1971, it was also true that corporations had not increased their profits. At the same time, the long-standing corporate desire to reduce dependence on foreign oil by using more coal and nuclear power was thwarted by environmentalists, who claimed that coal-burning was polluting the air, and by the highly disruptive antinuclear activists, who shut down construction sites and filed successful lawsuits by emphasizing the deadly consequences of nuclear accidents and the inability to store spent nuclear fuel rods in a safe manner. Making matters far worse, OPEC's price increase in January 1979, which doubled the previous price, had an even more inflationary effect than the quadrupling of oil prices in 1973–1974 because the United States was much more reliant on imported oil than it had been just six years earlier. Taken together, the OPEC price rise and the partial deregulation of oil prices led to a 32 percent rise in oil prices in the first four months of 1979. Facing the likelihood of double-digit inflation for the years 1979 and 1980, and with his inflation-control proposals going nowhere, Carter decided he had no choice except to pressure the Fed to cause interest rates to rise. In so doing, he was adopting the hawkish "nonsense" that Schultze had decried in a memo just two years earlier. As Schultze said later, using a metaphor favored by many economists, "We just don't know how to get rid of inflation without putting the country through the wringer" (Hargrove and Morley 1984, p. 492).

Moreover, Carter's handpicked chair for the Federal Reserve Board, G. William Miller—the CEO of Textron, the 89th-largest industrial company in the country, and a member of the Business Council and the Business Roundtable—resisted the president's new approach. Miller, who was also the chair of the Conference Board and the National Alliance of Businessmen, supported increases in both the federal funds rate (the rate that banks charge each other for short-term loans, usually overnight) and the discount rate (the rate the Fed charges banks for loans) during his first year in office, which led to increases in commercial interest rates. However, he did not think there should be a sole concentration on inflation above all else. Instead, he and other members of the board called attention to the positive news that the economy was in its fifth year of recovery from the 1973–1974 recession and was growing at a rate of 8 to 10 percent a year (Biven 2002, pp. 142–143).

Shortly thereafter, an opportunity to change directions at the Fed developed when Blumenthal resigned as secretary of the treasury in August 1979. Miller left the Fed to replace Blumenthal, which created an opening as Fed chair for a hard-line inflation hawk. In came Paul Volcker, the former Chase Manhattan executive and Nixon undersecretary of the treasury for International Monetary Affairs, who was by then the president of the Federal Reserve Bank of New York and a member of the Trilateral Commission. Volcker immediately announced that he would try to control inflation by tightening the supply of money, which had been expanding for a variety of reasons, such as the greater liquidity of mutual funds and the increasing use of credit cards. Although reigning in the money supply has the same effect as the indirect actions that raise interest rates, Volcker argued that it was a better way to deal with inflation because, he argued, the average person understood that inflation involved too much money at a time when there were not enough goods to buy.

Monetary economists interpreted Volcker's decision as evidence that he had become an advocate of monetary theory, which he neither confirmed nor denied, but to others a concentration on the money supply seemed to be a clever political maneuver. For example, one of the members of Carter's CEA, Lyle Gramley, believed from the outset, due to his previous experience working for the Fed, that Volcker's policies were politically motivated. He based his opinion on research by economists showing that manipulating the federal funds rate could control the growth in the money stock with considerable precision. He then noted that Volcker "was well aware of this, and ninety-eight percent of the reason for going in this direction [i.e., attempts at direct control of the money supply] was a cover." "He felt," Gramley continued, "and perhaps quite justifiably, that the central bank could not take responsibility for setting interest rates when interest rates might have to go as high as they did, in order to stop inflation" (Biven 2002, p. 315n18).

Although Schultze initially opposed Volcker's plan because controlling the money supply is not easy to do and can lead to volatility in interest rates, he later decided that the new policy was ideal from a political point of view because people would be less likely to blame either Carter or the Fed for the decline in the economy. The analysis he provided to fellow economist Carl Biven in 1991, long after any of this mattered to anyone but academicians, is astute enough, and such a strong case that a political bamboozlement had been carried out, that it seems well worth a lengthy quotation:

> Either consciously or unconsciously, Volcker was absolutely dead right on the politics of it. In order to do what had to be done to stop and reverse inflation, the Fed had to jack interest rates up to unprecedented heights. Now if the Fed had gone about doing it in the way it used to do things, every month picking the federal funds target, then, in the eyes of the public, the Fed would have been driving those rates up. And the genius of what Volcker did, during the period when you had to get the public used to this, was to adopt a system which came to the same thing, but in which he said we are not raising interest rates, we are just setting a non-inflationary path for the money supply, and the markets are raising the interest rates. It enabled the Fed to do politically, during that transition period, what it couldn't have done in a more direct way. (Biven 2002, p. 242)

Nor was this a new realization by Schultze. Eight years earlier he told two economists interviewing him for a book on the continuity of policy advice by the CEA over the decades that he was "morally certain" that Volcker had political motives for donning the monetary mantle (Hargrove and Morley 1984, p. 486). And in the late 1980s he told a conference on the Carter administration that "no democratically elected president can or would" take the overt steps that were needed to stop inflation by increasing unemployment from 6 percent to 10 percent (Biven 2002, p. 244). It took a relatively independent central bank to halt the inflationary spiral in a way that was acceptable to the corporate community, that is, without large increases in high-end taxes and government controls on wages and prices.

Although it is likely that Gramley and Schultze are right in their political analysis, it was not simply political chicanery at work. Congress had passed a concurrent resolution in 1975 that required the Federal Reserve to "report to Congress its objectives for annual growth of the money supply," and it formalized this directive as one of its conservative amendments to the Humphrey-Hawkins Act one year before Volcker swung into action (Biven 2002, p. 242). Just as Volcker provided Carter and the Fed with political cover, so, too, Congress provided Volcker with legislative legitimacy.

However, over and beyond the political dimension of Volcker's actions, it was also based on an unstated "sociological" assumption about the potential for social unrest. After years of domestic tranquility, the corporate community and the Carter administration intuitively understood that high unemployment would not lead to social disruption. There would be complaints and rallies, but there would be no major strikes, widespread sit-ins, physical destruction of private property, violent confrontations with SWAT teams and riot police, or votes for liberal Democrats. In short, there were no longer any risks to inducing high unemployment.

With fear of Volcker and the Fed in the air, organized labor agreed to a "national accord" on inflation in September 1979. It took the form of a Tripartite Pay Advisory Board, with representatives from labor, business, and the general public. Its charge was to advise the Council on Wages and Prices on the likely limits on noninflationary wage increases. When the board came to the conclusion that wage increases in the 7.5 to 9.5 percent range were reasonable, the White House grumbled, saying that was no ceiling at all, but it was in fact well below the 1979 inflation rate of 13.0 percent (Biven 2002, p. 194). Meanwhile, as rate hikes continued and unemployment rose, Carter's chances for reelection were further damaged. At about the same time, in August 1980, the Business Roundtable called for the dismantling of the Council on Wages and Prices, signaling that the corporate community was backing Volcker in the exclusive use of high interest rates to dampen demand, increase unemployment, and bring down inflation.

BALANCED CHANGES ON SOCIAL SECURITY IN 1978 AND 1980

Shortly after Social Security benefits reached a level at which they were alleviating poverty among the elderly and making it possible for a widowed parent to raise children in at least modest circumstances, the program began to have financial problems. The large increase in inflation after 1973 caused prices to rise faster than wages, which distorted benefit formulas in ways that are too technical to be discussed here (see Altman 2005, p. 216, on the lack of funds, and Chapter 12 in this volume for an explanation of why the fund had financial problems). This totally unprecedented situation was compounded by the fact that the recent indexing of Social Security benefits made it impossible to cut monthly benefits through inflation, as had been the case in the past. In addition, more people than expected were leaving the workforce through successful claims for disability benefits (Kingson 1984, p. 134). This combination of events caused pensions and benefits to rise faster than payroll tax payments, resulting in a decline in the small cushion in the Social Security Trust Fund. In 1975, Social Security actuaries warned that the funds could be gone by 1979.

Congress dealt with the problem in 1977 in a bipartisan way that raised the maximum income that could be taxed for Social Security purposes and increased payroll taxes equally on employers and employees. (Nevertheless, the outcome did involve slight long-term cutbacks in benefits.) Actuaries then reassured the general public in the annual trustees' report that the amendments "restore the financial soundness of the cash benefit program throughout the remainder of this century and into the early years of the next one" (Bernstein and Brodshaug 1988, pp. 34–35). However, the second round of oil shocks soon proved them wrong. The ensuing economic turmoil once again threw the projected relationship between payroll tax collections and cost-of-living increases out of balance. Further adjustments therefore were seen as necessary so the fund would not be exhausted in 1983 (Altman 2005, p. 222; Kingson 1984, pp. 136–138).

By this juncture, however, ultraconservatives inside and outside the government thought that changes in the political climate, along with the Republican gains in the 1978 elections, made it possible to define the new problem as a major crisis, not the temporary shortfall projected by centrist and liberal experts. Moreover, they could take advantage of the fact that "Social Security was also becoming a more noticeable portion of the federal budget because it was included as part of the unified federal budget," which was adopted during the Nixon administration at the urging of a report by the Committee for Economic Development (1966b) and a blue-ribbon presidential commission appointed by President Johnson (Kingson 1984, p. 133). Now it could be claimed that Social Security was both a big part of the budget and another reason to worry about future government debt, even though it was funded by payroll taxes, not federal income and excise taxes.

It was in these altered circumstances that the ultraconservative think tanks used the actuarial assessments from 1977 to claim that experts were either covering up the deep problems in the system or else did not know what they were talking about. They published reports that readily gained dramatic coverage in the media, in part because any "crisis" attracts readers and viewers, and in part because the media tries to report all sides of an issue. For example, the ultraconservative reports talked of "bankruptcy," even though the worst-case scenario involved shortfalls of 4 percent to 10 percent without any increases in payroll taxes, and even though bankruptcy was impossible because payroll taxes always would continue to flow into the Social Security Trust Fund. The seemingly inviolate nature of the trust fund established by Congress in 1939 was now ignored or forgotten (Estes 1983; Myles 1981). Taking advantage of the ultraconservative media campaign, congressional conservatives made a further change in Social Security in 1980 by reducing disability benefits on the grounds that they were overly generous (Bernstein and Brodshaug 1988, pp. 34–35).

THE CED COMPLETES ITS RIGHT TURN

Although the Business Roundtable had the most visible role in representing the corporate community to the Carter administration, the CED continued to be an important source of perspective, specific policy advice, and congressional access for the corporate moderates, and thus an excellent window into their evolving viewpoint. This section therefore shows how the CED completed its right turn and helped prepare the way for the Reagan agenda. It then provides a close look at how the CED formulated a new inflation report that trustees and staff brought to the attention of both appointed and elected officials through face-to-face meetings and testimony to Congress.

The rightward shift by the CED in 1976 and 1977 was accelerated when Fletcher Byrom, its acting chair for the previous two years and chair of Carter's Export Council, was elected in 1978 to the first of three two-year terms. At the same time, he served on the policy committee of the Business Roundtable, providing a major tie between the two groups. However, the strong links between the CED and the Business Roundtable also can be seen in the roundtable's top leadership in 1978; its chair and its three vice chairs, who were high-level officers at General Motors, General Electric, Exxon, and Goodyear, were trustees of the CED as well.

The success of the new leadership in repositioning the CED within the corporate policy-planning network is documented in Byrom's 1978 letter to the CEOs and public relations vice presidents at AT&T, Ford Motor, and General Motors. It discusses the outcome of his meeting with a "small group of executive officers of leading US corporations." The meeting, he wrote, "was especially helpful in sharpening our sense of CED's special role within the spectrum of major national business-related organizations." He went on to explain where the CED stood in relation to several organizations, making it possible to minimize overlap in functions: "The group was encouraged to learn of new efforts by CED to coordinate its work with that of the Business Roundtable, the Conference Board, the American Enterprise Institute, and others, thus minimizing duplication and overlap." More specifically, the CED would help turn the ideas of scholars into useful principles for shaping public policy, but only on a few issues: "CED can be especially effective, it was felt, in synthesizing the ideas of scholars and converting them into practical principles that can provide guidance for public policy on a selected number of key issues" (Byrom 1978, p. 1). As Robert Holland (1992) succinctly put it, Byrom had created a "niche" for the CED between the Business Roundtable and the AEI.

The CED also augmented its usefulness to the corporate community by hiring two new staff members. The first, Kenneth Duberstein, originally came to Washington for two years as an intern and staff member in the office of Senator Jacob Javits upon graduating from Franklin and Marshall College in 1965. After earning an MA degree at American University in 1967 while working for Javits, he returned to Franklin and Marshall as an administrative assistant to the president for three years. He then took a position in the Government Services Administration in 1970 as its deputy director for congressional liaison, which led to a position as director of congressional and intergovernmental affairs in the Department of Labor during the Nixon and Ford administrations. In 1977 he began work at the CED as its vice president and director of business-government relations. His duties included "presenting CED ideas to individual senators and representatives, Congressional committee staffs, and officials of executive department and agencies," but he was not registered as a lobbyist (Duberstein 1980). Frank Schiff described him as the CED's "non-lobbying lobbyist" (Schiff 1994). According to Edmund Fitzgerald of Cutler-Hammer, Duberstein was too sophisticated to leave his "fingerprints on anything" (Fitzgerald 1996).

Staff liaisons such as Duberstein play an important role as middlemen between the corporate policy-discussion organizations and Congress because they have expertise in human relations and knowledge of how Congress operates. They are usually younger than the CEOs and congressional leaders, coming to prominence when older lobbyists, who are usually advisors to political candidates as well, become their sponsors. William Timmons, a longtime Republican lobbyist and campaign advisor who later served as Reagan's deputy director for campaign operations, recommended Duberstein for his CED position. As if to demonstrate the dense network of ties among corporate go-betweens, Timmons had created his own consulting firm, Timmons and Co., after working with Bryce Harlow as a lobbyist for many years at Procter & Gamble and serving in the Ford administration. He also did lobbying for the Business Roundtable (Phillips-Fein 2009, p. 248).

Being employed by the CED or other policy organizations, in turn, provides a further career boost for the staffer. Duberstein's case is of special interest because in 1981 he was appointed to Reagan's White House staff as its liaison to Congress and became the White House chief of staff in 1988 after joining Timmons and Co. for two years in 1984. Following his year as White House chief of staff, he returned to Timmons and Co. as its president, and eventually started his own advisory firm, the Duberstein Group. As of 2012 he was or had been a director of Boeing, ConocoPhillips, and the St. Paul Companies, as well as a trustee of the Council on Foreign Relations, John Hopkins University, and the Kennedy Center for the Performing Arts.

The second new employee, Kenneth McLennan, was a conservative economist who worked primarily on policy reports. As he said in an interview in 1995, he was hired to "keep an eye" on Frank Schiff—that is, as a ballast to a staff member who was too strongly identified in the eyes of the CED leadership with the Keynesian position and incomes policy (McLennan 1995).

CED staffers prepared the groundwork for informal lobbying by CED trustees and economists through conversations with their counterparts employed as congressional staff members. Put another way, there were usually two intermediaries between corporate leaders and elected officials, but both were in very close and detailed communication on policy issues with their "principals," as the people of power are called in this network. The value of the liaison role Duberstein and McLennan played in the case of CED trustees can be seen in a note to the CED president from William Eberle, the former president of American Standard who served as the US trade representative for Nixon and Ford from 1971 to 1975. In 1978–1979, when he chaired a subcommittee on reining in government regulation, Eberle praised the two new staff members "not only in helping to complete the project on disciplining the government in the market economy, but they were and are of inestimable help in working The Hill. I just could not let it go by without saying what an excellent job they had done" (Committee for Economic Development 1979; Eberle 1979).

More generally, seventy-four of the 208 CED trustees appeared before at least one congressional committee between 1978 and 1980, as shown by my study of the index of *Congressional Information Services*. Forty-two testified in one of the three years, twenty-three testified in two of the three, and nine appeared in all three. Although a wide range of topics was discussed, most of their testimony concerned regulation, inflation, productivity, and other domestic issues on which the CED had written reports. The following example of ongoing CED involvement in lobbying the federal government is one of several that could be provided based on CED archives.

Fighting Inflation: A New CED Report

A new report on inflation, *Fighting Inflation and Rebuilding a Sound Economy* (Committee for Economic Development 1980a), reveals how the CED worked behind the scenes to influence government as well as how its thinking had evolved on this contentious issue. The report was written under the direction of trustee Reuben Mettler, the chair of TRW, a major defense contractor that was the 68th-largest corporation in 1980. Mettler was on the policy committee of the Business Roundtable and active in the National Alliance of Businessmen, and he soon would be a strong Reagan supporter. He was joined on the subcommittee by two of the people who had been critical of the CED's direction between 1974 and 1976, Fitzgerald of Cutler-Hammer and Charles Scanlon of General Motors. The subcommittee included Collado, the Exxon executive, along with Frazar Wilde, the retired chair of Connecticut General Life. The sole liberal trustee on the subcommittee, economist Robert Nathan, had sold his consulting firm to his employees in 1978 and gone into semi-retirement at age sixty-nine. The firm's gross revenues for 1977 were only $5 million, which gives an idea of how small it was compared to those of other CED trustees (Rowe 1978).

The four main economic advisors to the subcommittee, who did much of the talking and arguing at meetings, provided striking contrasts. Martin Feldstein, a professor of economics at Harvard and the president of the National Bureau of Economic Research, was an outspoken conservative who later served as the chair of Reagan's Council of Economic Advisors from 1982 to 1984. He was joined on the subcommittee by the more liberal-leaning Thomas C. Schelling, a professor of political economy at the Kennedy School of Government at Harvard; George L. Perry, a Keynesian economist at The Brookings Institution; and Gardner Ackley, the chair of the CEA in the Johnson administration. The advisory subcommittee also included an economist employed by Mettler at TRW as an assistant treasurer for international affairs. Duberstein and McLennan, the key communication links to Congress on this report, were the CED staff advisors, with McLennan's more liberal counterpart, Schiff, serving as the project director.

The flavor of the discussions and the general drift of the committee's thinking can be seen in the transcript for a meeting of the subcommittee on April 24, 1980, in which Mettler and Itek CEO Lindsay were the only corporate leaders present, along with the economists advising the committee and three CED employees, Holland, Schiff, and McLennan. After Perry said that the draft statement put too much emphasis on overcoming productivity bottlenecks as a means of reducing inflation, Feldstein in effect agreed when he said that too many business executives were arguing that tax cuts would lead to increased production and thereby reduce both inflation and unemployment. Feldstein then criticized supply-side economics from a conventional conservative perspective, while at the same time implying that high interest rates and the resulting high unemployment were the only way to control inflation.

Feldstein's comments led to the following blunt exchange between him and Schiff, which Feldstein concluded by warning that the CED had to be careful that it did not become part of the problem: Mr. Schiff: "Let me ask. Are you saying that the answer is a period of high and protracted unemployment?" Mr. Feldstein: "It may be." Mr. Schiff: "That is the only answer?" Mr. Feldstein: "It may be. Certainly, if the CED says the opposite, that makes it harder." After further general discussion, Feldstein suggested that the CED had to back Volcker in staying the course with high interest rates until the inflationary spiral was broken. A few minutes later, Perry put the choices starkly when he said that there were two groups of policy analysts, those who thought a period of high interest rates was necessary for as long as was needed and those who thought that the government could not follow that option for long enough. But he also made it clear that he thought an incomes policy had several advantages (Committee for Economic Development 1980b, pp. 13, 77).

At this point Mettler spoke for the first time, and he did so in the name of the business community, making it clear that he and his fellow CEOs favored high interest rates to cut demand: "I think there is widespread support for persistent, steady demand management in the business community. There is strong support there." A few minutes later, as the meeting was coming to an end, Mettler returned to the topic of demand management, mentioning the Business Roundtable because its members wanted to reduce government spending as a percentage of GNP as part of controlling inflation. He also mentioned the long-standing differences among the various business associations, which he connected with the size of the corporations that supported them: "Taking the [Business] Roundtable, the Roundtable is a group of large companies; there are differences between the Roundtable and NAM and the Chamber; there are differences between large companies and small ones that are quite clear" (Committee for Economic Development 1980b, pp. 82, 120).

When the subcommittee met again on June 17, Holland reported that he had shown the draft report to "some key bi-partisan figures in Congress" and that "we got back strongly encouraging language from all of them, saying, given the way things are sliding in Washington, if you would make this kind of declaration it would help us develop what we think is a responsible policy—so please, if your trustees come forward on this, we would like very much to have the help." Holland, by then a member of the Congress Leadership Group, which consisted primarily of corporate representatives in Washington, said he also had checked with other business organizations but mentioned only the Business Roundtable, reporting that the CED draft was "consistent" with the more specific document the roundtable would be issuing. Mettler then added that the new draft was "quite different than the one you saw earlier," with a stronger emphasis "on demand restraint and on not relaxing at the first sign of some recovery" (Committee for Economic Development 1980b, pp. 4–5, 9–10).

As the discussion unfolded, some participants wanted tax reductions, but others thought tax cuts might counteract the emphasis on reducing inflation through restricting demand. At that point Rand Araskog, the newly appointed CEO of ITT Industries,

No. 11 on the *Fortune* 500 list in 1980, stated his desire to circumscribe government spending through tax cuts, whatever their effects on short-term demand management. His comments reflect the deeper concern of many corporate officials, who wanted to limit the power of the government whatever the economic costs: "I understand the concern about proposing a tax cut. But I think to get the emphasis on federal reduction of expenditure you need it. There is just too great a tendency for the federal government to keep spending and as a result of that I think this tax cut can be beneficial in terms of forcing that issue" (Committee for Economic Development 1980b, pp. 29–30).

Ackley, who by 1980 probably had been thinking about wage-price stability longer than anyone in the United States, based on over thirty-six years of experience, then said that an incomes policy based on tax incentives was a better answer than strict demand management. In this instance he meant that taxes should be lowered for unionized workers whose wage hikes did not exceed preset limits. However, he added that he knew the CED was "not ready to support such a policy." His suggestion elicited no follow-up comments, but Feldstein went on to say that he liked the new draft because the CED would be "clearly on record as putting primary emphasis on reducing inflation and recognizing that that is going to require a period of sustained slack." Euphemisms about "slack" aside, conservatives decided to put people out of work in order to cut inflation rather than follow a more pro-worker path such as that suggested by Ackley (Committee for Economic Development 1980b, pp. 46, 48).

Just before the discussion ended, Mettler told the group that he had spent "a lot of time in the last three or four months with politicians and with Congressmen on both the Republican and Democratic side of the House and the Senate." Holland repeated that members of Congress and people inside the administration thought the document would be helpful, adding that Volcker said so as well (Committee for Economic Development 1980b, pp. 64, 66). In addition to meeting with politicians, Mettler made a statement to the Republican Party's platform committee that was written by Holland, based in good part on the CED inflation draft. The closeness of the corporate community, the policy-planning network, and the government could not be more clear than in the case of Mettler.

The final report called for reductions in government regulations, the use of cost-benefit analysis for deciding whether to issue new regulations, the use of market pricing to control energy use and increase production, a series of tax credits for corporations designed to improve productivity and investment, a reexamination of full indexation of income payments (with Social Security as one big target), and, most of all, "firm restraint in fiscal and monetary policies in order to reduce the inflation rate." The CED's leaders realized these policies would lead to another recession, but they argued that inflation was a greater danger in the long run than a short-term recession. The blunt comments by Feldstein in his exchange with Schiff, which suggested that the Fed would have to persist with high interest rates, even though many people would lose their jobs, were stated in a more indirect way in the report: "A major risk is that recession will lead to an abandonment of the battle against inflation. This could happen if observed reductions in the inflation rate, combined with growing concern over the social and economic effects of the recession, should lead to relaxation of the degree of demand restraint needed to overcome inflation in the long run. Such a policy would be very shortsighted" (Committee for Economic Development 1980a, p. 4).

Once the report was available, it became the basis for a major lobbying campaign aimed at members of Congress, although once again it was not labeled as such. For the most part, the campaign took the form of meeting informally with elected officials and giving them or their staff copies of the report. However, it also included testimony to congressional committees.

THE CARTER ERA AS A COMPLETE CORPORATE TRIUMPH

The corporate agenda triumphed completely during the Carter administration, as one pair of romantic revisionists also notes (Hacker and Pierson 2010). Tax rates were reduced yet again for the wealthy and corporations, and energy prices were deregulated. The liberal-labor program was pared back in the case of an increase in minimum wages and rendered harmless in the case of the Humphrey-Hawkins Act. Common-situs picketing, the Office of Consumer Representation, and the Labor Law Reform Act were rejected completely. The liberal-labor alliance tended to blame Carter's moderation and lack of pressure on Congress for its losses, but the defeats were at the hands of the corporate community and the conservative coalition. In the case of the Labor Law Reform Act, it is clear that the Carter administration fully supported it, and solid majorities of Democrats voted for it in both legislative chambers, but the liberal-labor alliance lost to the determined core of the conservative coalition in the Senate, which was backed by the entire corporate community.

The policy defeats and compromises suffered by the liberal-labor alliance in 1977 and 1978 marked the end of any systematic influence on Congress for the liberal-labor alliance, which seemed to be on the verge of success on several occasions in the postwar era, and was regularly portrayed as a powerhouse in the *Wall Street Journal* and business magazines. Overall union density hovered between 21.6 percent and 22.3 percent during the Carter years, but as political scientist Michael Goldfield (1987, p. 15) concludes, "The aggregate figures actually hide an absolute decline in union membership in the private sector in the 1960s and 1970s," which is what mattered the most to corporate leaders. Union density in the private sector dropped from 25.1 percent in 1976 to 20.6 percent in 1980, so the rout was clearly accelerating (Miller and Canak 1995b, p. 19, table 1).

As the failures of the liberal-labor alliance on major issues suggest, the conservative coalition mobilized very frequently during the Carter years (490 times in the House, 503 times in the Senate) and usually won, especially after the 1978 elections added three Republicans to the Senate and fifteen to the House. It had a 58 percent success rate in the House and 63 percent success rate in the Senate in 1977–1978, and a success rate of 71 percent in both the House and Senate in 1979–1980 (Shelley 1983, pp. 34, 38). The electoral gains in 1978 were at least in part made possible by right-wing Christian activists concerned about one or another hot-button social issue, especially abortion, school prayer, pornography, homosexuality, and gun control (Himmelstein 1990).

As for the US Chamber of Commerce, it was still on the losing side six out of nine times, despite the dominance of the conservative coalition, usually because it opposed conservative coalition victories that in its view did not go far enough. It did not want any regulation of strip mining, thought the relaxation of standards in the Clean Air Act was not enough, and found the reforms on price controls on natural gas too timid. The chamber also opposed the modest increase in the minimum wage and an increase in payroll taxes. And yet, the outcomes of these legislative battles were catalogued as defeats for the corporate community as a whole by at least one political scientist because of the chamber's opposition, reinforcing the false claim that business in the United States often loses on key issues (Smith 2000).

The changes in the CED's policy stance over the course of the 1970s, and by inference among most moderates in the corporate community, can be seen in a comparison of CED statements from the early and late 1970s, *The Social Responsibility of Business Organizations* (1971b) and *Redefining Government's Role in the Market System* (1979). Since 43 percent of the members of the Research and Policy Committee in 1971 were still on it in 1979, with all but one of those continuing members voting to support both statements, it is likely that the differences in the two statements reflected changing sentiments, not a turnover in committee personnel (Frederick 1981, p. 26).

As might be expected, both statements were based on several bedrock principles held to firmly by all American business leaders whatever the year and whatever the economic circumstances, such as the importance of profits for both economic and social progress, a strong preference for market solutions, a belief that the public sector should be subordinate to the private sector, and a concern that "government involvement, once underway, can easily expand to a level that hampers the efficiency of markets," as business school professor William Frederick notes in his comparison of the two reports. However, he continues, "the contrast between the two documents could hardly be greater. A spirit of social concern and an emphasis upon social equity suffuses CED's 1971 statement while CED's 1979 statement speaks mainly of the importance of the efficiency of markets" (Frederick 1981, pp. 22–23). More generally, the emphasis in the early 1970s on business participation in policy matters out of enlightened self-interest was abandoned and the nature of the business-government collaboration was limited to economic issues by 1979, with no mention of a partnership to solve social problems.

The change is also notable in what was not said in the 1980 inflation report, *Fighting Inflation and Rebuilding a Sound Economy.* There was no mention of what was a major concern in the 1970 version, *Further Weapons against Inflation,* namely, a need for lower interest rates and higher federal expenditures to solve "the urgent problems of our cities, education, poverty and welfare, health care, and the environment"; nor is there any mention of the fact that unemployment was "likely to be substantially greater than the American people would or should tolerate" (Committee for Economic Development 1970a, pp. 11, 17). Instead, there was concern with the overall economy, and with the degree to which government officials had the fortitude to do what was necessary to be sure inflation was defeated, by keeping interest rates high in the face of the rising unemployment they would create.

Despite the overwhelming success experienced by the corporate community, its leaders were not satisfied because the economy was suffering from both high inflation (due to the large increases in agricultural and petroleum prices) and high unemployment (due to the high interest rates engineered by the Fed). Even worse from the corporate point of view, profits still had not returned to the postwar historical highs they reached in the first six years of the 1960s (Ruess 2009).

In the context of high inflation and high unemployment, a combination that had not been solvable with the policy tools acceptable to the corporate community, Ronald Reagan asked Americans during his 1980 campaign if they were better off than they had been four years ago. When voters emerged from the polling booths to tell exit interviewers whom they voted for and what issues were of greatest concern to them, a large number of white Middle American voters—soon to be called "Reagan Democrats"—emphasized that they blamed the Democrats for the decline in real wages due to inflation and the rising unemployment that were foremost in their minds. They voted for Reagan because of his optimistic program to restore the economy, they said, not because of the foreign policy and hot-button social issues that energized the fundamentalist Christian activists and voters who helped him win the nomination (Himmelstein and McCrae 1984; Johnson and Taney 1982). Still, the fact that Carter had refused to sign legislation legitimating the Southern segregationist academies as tax-exempt religious schools may have played a role in his loss of every Southern state except his home state of Georgia (Quadagno and Rohlinger 2009).

Below the presidential level, however, the religious right's media attacks and grassroots campaigns contributed to the Democrats' loss of twelve seats in the Senate, including those of liberals from Idaho, Iowa, and South Dakota, which put Republicans in control of one of the two houses in Congress for the first time since 1954. The Democrats also lost thirty-four seats in the House, which gave the conservative coalition a strong majority. It thus became easier for the corporate-conservative alliance and the conservative coalition to pursue their overlapping agendas without concern for compromise with the minority of congressional members who were supporters of the liberal-labor alliance.

Chapter Twelve

The Reagan Culmination, 1981–1984

The Reagan administration is often portrayed as an ultraconservative takeover in terms of both ideas and personnel. It is further claimed that the corporate moderates were reluctant to support Reagan, as evidenced by the fact that many of them gave their initial financial support to others who ran for the Republican nomination, such as Nixon's former secretary of the treasury, John Connelly, or George H. W. Bush, a former member of the House, the director of the CIA in 1976 and 1977, and a member of the Trilateral Commission (e.g., Phillips-Fein 2009, pp. 238–239). But corporate leaders always have different personal favorites early in the primary season, and in fact almost all corporate leaders were for Reagan for president, except for the usual handful of Democratic supporters. This was especially the case after he reassured them that he was not an extremist on issues of concern to them by selecting Bush, the son of a Wall Street investment banker and a Texas oilman in his own right, as his running mate.

In contrast to the image some portray of the Reagan administration as dominated by ultraconservatives and opposed by corporate moderates, corporate moderates supported Reagan's candidacy with campaign donations, served on his task forces, and were highly influential within his administration. They advocated highly conservative policies on some issues because they had been moving to the right on those issues since the late 1960s. However, they were not as conservative on all issues as their ultraconservative corporate counterparts, so one important piece of evidence for their continuing power concerns the issues on which they were able to fend off the ultraconservatives or quickly reverse legislative changes the ultraconservatives were able to pass between 1981 and 1983.

To begin with, 85 percent of the CED trustees who made campaign contributions supported Reagan, sometimes after giving to other Republican candidates as well. Only 5 percent gave exclusively to Carter; the other 10 percent gave to presidential candidates in both parties and to Republican John Anderson, who ran as a centrist third-party candidate. CED trustee support for Republicans was equally strong at the congressional level; 90 percent of them gave to at least one Republican in Senate or House races, and 15 percent gave to five or more Republican candidates. Most of the very few Democrats supported by CED trustees came from the South, although Bill Bradley, the moderate Democratic senator from New Jersey, received donations from 10 percent of them during the primaries. Significantly, the CED trustees who most frequently testified before Congress in the 1978 to 1980 period were also the most likely to support Reagan. Twenty-five of the thirty-two who testified three or more times before Reagan took office gave to at least five Republican candidates at the presidential or congressional level, in addition to making contributions to Reagan.

After the elections, many of Reagan's major campaign advisors joined the President's Economic Policy Advisory Board. It met with Reagan six times during the first year, reinforcing the directions he was already taking. Although most of the committee members were economists from the Hoover Institution and the American Enterprise Institute, the committee was chaired by George Shultz, who had been named president of the multinational Bechtel Construction Company shortly after he left the Treasury Department in 1974 and became a CED trustee soon thereafter. Paul McCracken from Nixon's CEA was part of the group. So was Herbert Stein, formerly of the CED and Nixon's CEA, although Martin Anderson (1990, p. 267), Reagan's libertarian policy advisor, claims that Stein's suggestions were roundly rejected as too liberal by the rest of the board. The advisory board also included Walter Wriston, the Business Roundtable leader at the time and president of Citibank in New York.

As had been the case for the Eisenhower, Nixon, and Carter administrations, Reagan's first secretary of the treasury was a CED trustee. Donald Regan, the chair of Merrill Lynch, had taken part in the production of the CED's 1980 report on inflation, was a member of the policy committee of the Business Roundtable, and was a member of the Council on Foreign Relations. President Reagan's first appointee as secretary of state, former army general and White House advisor Alexander Haig, who lasted for only a few months, was president of United Technologies; a director of Chase Manhattan Bank, Crown Cork and Seal, Texas Instruments, and ConAgra; and a member of the Council on Foreign Relations. Shultz, by that time a director of J. P. Morgan Bank and the Council on Foreign Relations as well as president of Bechtel Corporation and a CED trustee, replaced Haig and served for the next six years. The secretary of defense, corporate lawyer Caspar Weinberger, was a vice president and general counsel of the Bechtel Corporation, a director of PepsiCo and Quaker Oats, a member of the Trilateral Commission, and the secretary of health, education, and welfare in the Nixon years.

Most other top officials in the new administration also came from the corporate community or the policy-planning network. In addition to Haig, Shultz, and Regan, eight top-level appointments at the State Department were members of the Council on Foreign Relations, including the director of the CIA, the secretary of commerce, the special trade advisor, and the deputy secretary of defense. More generally, thirty-one of the administration's appointees, advisors, and consultants were members of the Council on Foreign Relations; twenty-five were associated with the American Enterprise Institute; and twelve were members of the Trilateral Commission (Jenkins and Shumate 1985; Sklar and Lawrence 1981).

In keeping with the pattern set by several previous administrations, including those of Nixon and Carter, the chair of the CEA was a longtime CED advisor, but this time a very conservative one—Murray Weidenbaum, who was also a consultant to the Business Roundtable. He was joined on the CEA by two members of the CED's Research Advisory Board: Martin Feldstein, the Harvard professor, who was also the president of the National Bureau of Economic Research; and William Poole, a professor at Brown University, a former employee of the Federal Reserve Board, and a strong monetarist.

Although there was no one grand design guiding the Reagan administration's policy initiatives, six widely shared themes emerged that were carried out with varying degrees of success: (1) an all-out attack on unions; (2) the use of high interest rates to tame inflation; (3) massive tax cuts for the well-to-do and corporations; (4) major reductions in projected increases in social spending, including for the highly popular Social Security program; (5) very large increases in military spending; and (6) cuts in government regulations that were said to be costly to business and expensive for the government to carry out. Although the cuts in social spending for low-income and unemployed people were minor as a percentage of the overall budget, they were enough to cripple the agencies that provided those living in or near poverty with a wide range of social and housing services.

CED trustees testified to Congress numerous times on specific issues related to this general agenda. Thirty trustees testified three or more times to congressional committees between 1981 and 1986. Staff member McLennan testified three times as well. With Duberstein working as an assistant on the White House staff, his liaison role between the CED and Congress was taken over by Nathaniel Semple, a staff aide for Republicans in the House since 1972, including the previous seven years working for the Republican members of the Education and Labor Committee. He was also the son of a conservative CED trustee, Robert Semple, by then the retired chair of BASF Wyandotte, a chemical company.

FINISHING OFF INDUSTRIAL UNIONS

Reagan's all-out attack on organized labor began very dramatically when he fired the striking members of PATCO, the air traffic controllers' union, who were not allowed by law to strike. Although Reagan tried to arrange a very generous settlement with the adamant and frustrated union, which had supported him for the presidency after years of relative failure under Democratic presidents, the union leaders demanded even more. Reagan then felt he had no other recourse, and the legend of his determination to set an example by breaking the union began to develop (McCartin 2011).

Reagan's decree had an immediate dramatic impact, leading to a quick decline in actions by public-sector unions, although they were able to hold on in most areas of the country (McCartin 2011, pp. 338–350). Taking advantage of a 1938 Supreme Court ruling declaring that companies had the right to hire "permanent replacements" for workers who went on strike for "economic reasons," corporations were emboldened to make even more use of union-busting consulting firms that offered replacement workers.

The consulting firms also became more confrontational in dealing with strikers, using video cameras and other high-tech devices as part of their intimidating surveillance efforts. One firm, Vance International, founded by President Gerald Ford's former son-in-law, had its own heavily armored SWAT team (Goldfield 1987, pp. 189–195; Smith 2003, pp. 119, 121–123).

With high unemployment rates, the movement of production overseas, and corporate challenges in the workplace decimating unions, Reagan applied the final blow by appointing a series of ultraconservatives to the National Labor Relations Board. The appointment process was drawn-out and contentious because the low-key ultraconservatives suggested by Douglas Soutar on behalf of the Business Roundtable were not considered conservative enough by some Reagan advisors. After tumultuous confirmation hearings and the exchange of personal insults among the ultraconservative appointees, the board made extremely conservative decisions even while experiencing turnover and tension. In the process, it reversed several pro-labor decisions by the Democratic majority during the Kennedy, Johnson, and Carter administrations (Gross 1995, pp. 246–265).

With the help of several Supreme Court decisions, many of the statutory guarantees of protection against employers that had been granted to workers by the National Labor Relations Act in exchange for labor peace were taken away. There was little chance of possible labor insurgencies. Decisions made by the board during the first Reagan administration and the two previous postwar Republican administrations also created a long list of prohibitions on actions by unions and their organizers. By 1985 a law that was originally meant to facilitate unionization and collective bargaining as a moderate way to handle class conflict had been turned into an anti-union employer protection law (McCammon 1990, 1994; McCammon and Kane 1997). The only solace for organized labor was that it fended off repeated efforts by the conservative coalition to eliminate the Davis-Bacon Act and to restrict union involvement in politics (Roof 2011, pp. 190–191).

HIGH INTEREST RATES AND HIGH UNEMPLOYMENT

With Reagan's full public support, the Federal Reserve Board sent the federal funds rate to a peak of 20 percent in June 1981, up from 11.2 percent in 1979. The prime rate—the rate banks charge their best corporate customers—reached 21.5 percent at the same time. Then, just as the Mexican government began to teeter on the brink of financial disaster because it could not service its loans from American banks, the Fed quickly eased its policy. It is also possible that any further delays in lowering interest rates would have forced Citibank into bankruptcy because of its risky loans throughout Latin America. Citibank then stretched out the loans ("extend and pretend," "delay and pray," as these negotiations were called) with the hope that the cash-strapped countries would be able to resume their payments. While all this was going on and thereafter, the unemployment rate relentlessly climbed to 10.1 percent in September 1982, peaked at 10.8 percent in November and December, and stayed above 10 percent until July

1983, when it came down to 9.4 percent. The inflation rate tumbled from 13.5 percent in 1981 to 3.2 percent in 1983.

TAX CUTS AND SPENDING CUTS

Drawing on proposals by congressional Republicans in the late 1970s, Reagan's original platform called for individual income tax cuts of 10 percent a year for three years ("10-10-10"), which added up to a 27 percent reduction. Once in office, however, his closest economic advisors, including former CEA chair Alan Greenspan and former undersecretary of the treasury Charls Walker, told him that it would be best to introduce the tax cuts more slowly in order to avoid massive deficits. To their surprise, he replied, "I don't care," which led Walker to report that he and his colleagues "almost fell out of their chairs" (Brownlee 2004, p. 148). Not only did Reagan want everyone to have immediate tax cuts, with the hope that he might solidify a permanent Republican realignment, but he was also out to make increases in social spending more difficult. As he explained in a national address in February 1981, "Well, we can lecture our children about extravagance until we run out of voice and breath. Or we can cure their extravagance simply by reducing their allowance" (Brownlee 2004, p. 149). The tax bill also had other features that put long-term limits on the ability of the federal government to raise revenues, such as lower gift and estate taxes. Most of all, it indexed tax brackets to inflation, which meant that the government could no longer raise increased revenues due to the movement of taxpayers into higher tax brackets because of inflation.

As part of the final compromise with Congress, Reagan agreed to a 5 percent tax decrease in the first year and 10 percent in each of the next two years, which meant that the overall cut was reduced to 25 percent, but that still added up to a massive revenue reduction for the federal government. The package included reductions in the effective tax rate on the top 1 percent of income earners from 29.8 percent to 24.8 percent by 1983, thereby saving each of them over $25,000 a year ($57,750 in 2012 dollars) (Baker 2007, pp. 66–67). According to the most enthusiastic of the ultraconservatives, known as the "supply siders," much of the increasing debt created by the presumably temporary budget deficits would be paid off by the expanding tax revenues that would result from renewed economic growth.

Corporations received their tax reductions through a "10-5-3" package fashioned by an umbrella group of corporate lobbyists that had been meeting regularly since 1975. The phrase meant that real estate could be completely depreciated in ten years, even while its value was growing, which made the buying and selling of properties even more attractive; most industrial equipment could be written off in five years, which pleased the big corporations; and trucks could be written off in just three years, a bonanza for trucking, local delivery, and retail businesses. Led by Walker, with representatives from the Business Roundtable, NAM, US Chamber of Commerce, and the National Federation of Independent Business, the umbrella group served as the intermediary between the corporate chieftains and the leaders of the conservative coalition. It also offered strategic leaks to the media and leaned on wavering moderate and liberal Democrats who were afraid of being swept away in the 1982 elections (Akard 1992, p. 608).

As the legislative process on the tax cuts unfolded, much was made of Reagan's persuasive skills in convincing House Democrats to vote for the bill (e.g., Cannon 2000, pp. 219–220). In fact, the conservative coalition had more than enough votes to pass a program that its members had been advocating for some time. Not only had the Republicans increased their numbers from 41 to 53 in the Senate and from 158 to 192 in the House, but the conservative Democrats in both houses were now organized into caucuses that fully stated their intentions through the use of the word *conservative* in their names. The fourteen-person Conservative Democratic Caucus in the Senate (eleven from the South, two from Nebraska, and one from Arizona) gave the conservative coalition a strong majority on tax cuts, along with the ability to muster sixty votes to break a filibuster if necessary. Similarly, the forty-seven-member Conservative Democratic Forum in the House (forty-three from the South, along with one representative each from rural areas in Arizona, Maryland, Nevada, and New York) could supply Reagan with many more than the twenty-six Democratic defectors he needed to win if he had full Republican support.

To ensure their support, the Southern Democrats were offered special tax breaks for industries located in the South, including for individual recipients of royalties from big oil companies. There was a moment of hesitation and uncertainty when the more zealous Reaganites wanted to balance the new sweeteners for Southern Democrats with reductions in the breaks for corporations, but the corporate lobbying group, backed by phone calls from many CEOs, stood its ground. In the end, the urban growth coalitions and the corporate community received their depreciation allowances.

As might be expected based on Reagan's negative view of government, the tax reductions in the Economic Recovery Tax Act of 1981 were paralleled by cuts in social spending via the Omnibus Budget Reconciliation Act. The act reduced the rate of growth in spending on many social programs, disability benefits, welfare payments, housing subsidies, food stamps, unemployment insurance, and school lunches (Mayhew 1991, table 4.1). In passing the bill, Republicans used a relatively new procedural motion, called the "budget reconciliation process." This parliamentary stratagem permitted only a "yes" or "no" vote on overall spending levels agreed to in committee once the magic word *reconciliation* was uttered, without any opportunity for amendments. In an era in which there appeared to be little or no threat of inner-city disruption, the budget cuts closed down the Community Services Administration and other neighborhood-oriented agencies because they were said to be outposts of the left. By 1985 federal funding for community development activities had diminished by $1 billion. From 1981 to 1992, federal aid to cities was cut by 60 percent.

Most dramatically, appropriations for subsidized housing programs fell by more than 80 percent in the years after the budget act permitting reconciliation passed in 1974, thereby accelerating the contraction in the supply of affordable housing that began in the early 1970s with earlier reductions in this program. In 1968, 29 percent of new housing was due to federal subsidies, but it was down to 14 percent in 1972, and then all but ended between 1981 and 1985, when funds were slashed from $26.1 billion to

$2.1 billion. Furthermore, low-income families had to pay 30 percent of their incomes toward housing, up from 25 percent (Quadagno 1994, p. 114). As a direct result of these changes, African Americans were further ghettoized in crowded housing. There was also an exponential increase in homelessness for everyone with low incomes, which caused more inner-city tensions, angered downtown merchants, and put new financial strains on private charitable agencies and city governments (see Rosenthal 1994 for the processes through which ultraconservatives created homelessness in the United States).

CUTTING BACK ON SOCIAL SECURITY

As dramatic and impactful as cuts in social benefits were for those with low-paying jobs, or no employment or housing, the most informative events related to social spending unfolded around an attempt to make major reductions in Social Security benefits. This process revealed that the corporate moderates who had long supported the gradual expansion of this program were now determined to limit it. It also showed that the liberal-labor alliance was able to hold on to most of the improvements in Social Security benefits when it made concessions and played its cards well.

With the clock still ticking on the Social Security Trust Fund due to the continuing high inflation in the early 1980s, the solvency of Social Security became a major issue. As was the case just two years earlier, relatively easy adjustments could have been made, but the corporate-conservative alliance mounted a large-scale scare campaign. Although national surveys soon reported that most people, and especially those under thirty-five, believed that the system would be bankrupt by the time they were eligible to receive benefits, they also made clear they wanted to preserve the system through tax increases. Their fears were encouraging to those who wanted to privatize Social Security, but the fact that most people wanted to preserve the current system was encouraging for the program's supporters (Bernstein and Brodshaug 1988, p. 42).

The CED contributed to the crisis atmosphere with a report entitled *Reforming Retirement Policies*, which claimed "a retirement disaster is on the way early in the twenty-first century." Using projections that assumed a declining birth rate and an increasing number of retired workers, the CED warned that the rate of growth in the labor force might decline and that older workers would become a "burden" on "future generations," ignoring the burden that Social Security removes from families that would have to support their elderly parents. In addition, the presumed shrinkage in the growth of the workforce, which was in fact being countered by millions of Latin American and Asian immigrants in the 1970s, supposedly meant that older workers who remained productive might have to continue working for the sake of the economy. The CED report therefore concluded that the retirement age should be gradually raised two months a year until it reached age sixty-eight in the year 2000. It also called for changes in the formula used to determine cost of living increases, which were said to "overcompensate" for inflation (Committee for Economic Development 1981, pp. 3–5).

Once again, the CED did extensive non-lobbying lobbying in relation to its report. One retrospective CED document (N.D.), put together in the late 1980s for a manuscript a CED staff member was working on, reported that trustees and staff discussed it with every member of the Senate Finance Committee as well as with every member of the House Ways and Means Committee when it appeared. Although Duberstein was by then on the White House staff as a deputy assistant for the president for legislative affairs, he encouraged the distribution of the CED report. On February 11, 1981, he wrote a note to a member of the CED's public relations staff saying that "the report will come in handy" and in the process urged that if "the other Ken, Dr. McLennan, would only hurry with the retirement statement, we might be able to do something positive about Social Security (while assuring the integrity of the program, of course)" (Duberstein 1981).

At this point, the Reagan administration overplayed its hand. In doing so it drew on suggestions from a Social Security Task Force set up during the campaign, which was chaired by an economist at the Hoover Institution and consisted primarily of free-market economists at several universities. Starting with this report, the director of the Office of Management and Budget, David Stockman, a former Republican member of the House from Michigan, created a draconian plan in early May 1981 that would produce twice as much savings as was actually needed through a variety of benefit cuts (Altman 2005, p. 231; Kingson 1984, pp. 140–141). The result was a barrage of criticism aimed at the White House, including some from Republicans, who feared that such drastic changes might put them in danger of losing their congressional seats in 1982. The proposed policies also solidified and energized Save Our Security, a liberal-labor-elderly leadership group formed in 1979, which spoke for a coalition of nearly one hundred liberal, labor, and senior citizens organizations. Wilbur Cohen, whose involvement in Social Security by then stretched back forty-seven years, including his strategic role in the passage of Medicare, served as the Save Our Security chair.

The ambitious White House plan was withdrawn before it was formally presented to Congress. But the bad publicity it received short-circuited the efforts to cut Social Security that were moving forward quietly in the House under the direction of Southern Democrat Jake Pickle of Texas, the chair of the Social Security Subcommittee of the Ways and Means Committee. Pickle's plan would have dealt with the short-term budgeting problems by means of a six-month delay in the next cost of living adjustment (COLA) and with the elimination of long-term shortfalls by increasing the retirement age to sixty-eight between 1990 and 2000, both of which were consistent with the CED's recommendations. His plan also would have eliminated minimum benefits and payments to college children of deceased beneficiaries. Due to the outcry caused by the Reagan plan, Pickle had to settle in 1981 for a cutback in payments to the 775,000 children of deceased beneficiaries who were twenty-two years old and still in college. The average reductions of $259 a month for these students saved $700 million the first year (less than 1 percent of the Social Security payments in 1982).

Faced with a potential political backlash, the White House suggested to Thomas ("Tip") O'Neill, a Boston Democrat and the Speaker of the House, that the president and Congress should jointly appoint a bipartisan Commission on Social Security to examine the issues and make recommendations. The plan called for Reagan to select three Republicans and two Democrats, with the Republican leader of the Senate suggesting three Republicans and (with the advice of the Senate Minority Leader) two Democrats. In addition, O'Neill would add three Democrats and (with the advice of the Republican Minority Leader) two Republicans. This formula led to an 8–7 majority for the Republicans, but the more important point is that conservatives outnumbered liberals 10–5 because two of the Democrats appointed by Reagan were very conservative. The first of these nominal Democrats—former oilman and chemical executive Alexander Trowbridge, Johnson's secretary of commerce for the last year of his term—was the president of NAM. The second, a small-town banker from Louisiana, Joe Waggonner, had been an informal leader among Southern Democrats in the House from 1961 until his retirement in 1979.

For the chair, Reagan selected business economist Alan Greenspan, who had been Ford's CEA chair in 1975. Reagan also appointed the president of Prudential Life, Robert Beck, who was a member of the CED's Research and Policy Committee, the chair of the Business Roundtable's task force on Social Security, and a trustee of both the Conference Board and the Business Council. In a meeting with CED president Holland two years earlier, Beck told Holland of his interest in the CED Social Security project and said he wanted "to keep the two projects [i.e., the CED and Business Roundtable projects] coordinated insofar as feasible." Holland asked Beck "to name a staff man that we could invite to all our retirement meetings, and Beck said Mr. James Swenson," who worked on corporate pension plans for Prudential. Holland then instructed McLennan to call Swenson and become acquainted with him, and told Duberstein to send Swenson the relevant CED materials on retirement (Holland 1979). Based on Beck's corporate stature and policy-group connections, it can be safely inferred that he represented the general CED and Business Roundtable views on Social Security.

Reagan's final appointment was a business woman, Mary Falvey Fuller, who earned a BA from Cornell and an MBA from Harvard, took her first job at her family's Falvey Automobiles, Inc., and then worked for McKinsey and Co., Citibank, and Blyth Eastman Dillon before becoming the vice president for finance with the Shaklee Corporation in 1981. She had legitimacy on the Social Security issue as a member of a 1979 Advisory Council on Social Security. Her business executive husband, Craig Fuller, was a White House aide who had been in charge of organizing business support during Reagan's presidential campaign.

The Republican congressional representatives included three moderates: Senator Robert Dole, chair of the Senate Finance Committee; John Heinz, chair of the Senate Special Committee on Aging; and Barber Conable, a member of the Ways and Means Committee. There were also two Republican ultraconservatives: Senator William Armstrong, chair of the Senate Finance Committee's Subcommittee on Social Security; and William Archer of Texas, the ranking Republican member of the House Ways and Means Committee's Subcommittee on Social Security. Both Armstrong and Archer were outspoken opponents of the Social Security program.

The Democratic appointees started with two emblematic elected Democrats. Senator Patrick Moynihan, a CED advisor in the late 1960s and one of the drafters of Nixon's Family Assistance Plan, had been elected to the Senate from New York in 1976. Representative Claude Pepper, who first served in Congress as a liberal senator from Florida from 1936 to 1951, had been a member of the House from a Miami district since 1963. The third and fourth Democrats were a former House member from Michigan, Martha Keyes, who had been the assistant secretary of health and human services during the Carter administration, and Lane Kirkland, the president of the AFL-CIO after decades as one of Meany's top assistants.

Perhaps most significant of all, the fifth Democratic appointee was Robert M. Ball, the executive director for the Advisory Committee on Social Security in 1947 and a key strategist in the fight for Medicare. Still highly respected for his patience and ability to forge compromises, he immediately became the de facto leader for the other four liberal Democrats, who knew that he spoke for O'Neill on Social Security issues. Ball was in almost daily touch with O'Neill and consulted regularly with the leaders of Save Our Security, AARP, the National Council of Senior Citizens, and dozens of individuals, so that there would be no surprises for any of them, thereby making it possible to alter the Democrats' bargaining stance rapidly as the process moved forward (Ball 2010, pp. 12–13; Bernstein and Brodshaug 1988, p. 39). (Trowbridge and Waggonner, although nominal Democrats, did not attend the frequent meetings held by the other five Democrats to discuss strategy.) Overall, the balance of forces represented a classic matchup between the corporate-conservative and liberal-labor alliances.

The commission met seven times before the elections, heard testimony, and discussed numerous issues. For the most part, the commissioners did no serious bargaining during this period because the main unstated goal of the Republicans was to keep Social Security out of the next midterm election. However, the commission did agree to set Medicare aside, which greatly simplified the problems, despite repeated objections by Beck, who wanted to deal with both issues at the same time so that major cuts could be made in benefits. It also ruled out, with an unexpected assist from ultraconservative Waggonner, a quasi-privatization plan put forward by a prominent young Stanford economist (see Ball 2010, pp. 20, 27, for the information on Beck and Waggonner). More generally, it agreed to leave the basic structure of the system as it was and then to work from the most pessimistic projections concerning the short run and more moderate projections about the long run. Within that context, it also agreed that it had to close a short-run deficit of between $150 billion and $200 billion and make up for a gap of about 1.8 percent over the seventy-five-year period between 1983 and 2056. The Democrats doubted that any meaningful projections could be made over such a long time period, but they accepted them as part of their plan to restore confidence in the stability of the system (Bernstein and Brodshaug 1988, pp. 41–43).

Despite the Republicans' hope that the establishment of the commission would render the Social Security issue less visible until after the elections, the Democrats made the earlier Republican attempt to cut Social Security a major campaign issue in 1982. They did so by deploying Pepper, who was eighty-two years old and widely known to senior citizens as "Mr. Social Security," to give fiery speeches in favor of Democratic candidates in a large number of House districts. Although the ongoing recession was the Republicans' most serious electoral problem, some Republicans believed that the Social Security overreach contributed to the near loss of the Senate majority and a decline of twenty-six seats in the House, which in turn made it more likely that they would seek compromise on the issue.

The commission met for three consecutive days shortly after the elections and made substantial progress toward a bargain. The five liberal Democrats then decided to offer a three-month delay in the COLA, but there was no further give on the Republican side. At this point a key Reagan aide of a moderate stripe held secret discussions with Ball that signaled that Reagan and at least some members of his staff wanted to make a deal. Then, just when it seemed unlikely that any agreements could be reached, Dole wrote an op-ed column for the *New York Times* in early January 1983, stating in effect that the crisis was solvable "through a combination of relatively modest steps" (Altman 2005, pp. 245–246). This public signal led to a discussion between Moynihan and Dole on the Senate floor, and then a suggestion from Dole that a small group of commissioners (Dole, Conable, Greenspan, Moynihan, and Ball) begin a series of private meetings. The meetings soon involved Reagan's White House chief of staff, James Baker, and then two of his assistants, Richard Darman and Duberstein, along with Stockman from the Office of Management and Budget.

Duberstein's role in the process is often overlooked because he said little, but as Ball asserted in a telephone interview in 1990, he was important because he was a likable person who had good relations with both Democrats and Republicans in Congress and was committed to bringing about an agreement. In particular, he had a close connection to Daniel Rostenkowski, a machine Democrat from Chicago who chaired the Ways and Means Committee. Ball later made similar claims about Duberstein's role in a posthumously published insider account of how the negotiations unfolded (Ball 1990; 2010, p. 36).

With Reagan's approval ratings lower than Carter's at a comparable point in his administration, the White House was faced with a deadline for reporting the likely large deficits that would occur in the unified budget due to the large tax cuts. Reagan and his aides therefore became even more eager to find a compromise. The final bargain started with the six-month delay in the COLA originally advocated by the Reagan administration and Representative Pickle of Texas, which added up to about a 2 percent cut in benefits in the long haul and savings in the short run that cut one-fourth of the gap. In return, the Republicans agreed to tax those retirees in higher income brackets on up to half of their Social Security benefits, a significant concession. However, it could be spun by the Republicans as a cut in benefits rather than a tax increase, which made it symbolically acceptable. The Republicans also agreed to move forward to 1984 a payroll tax increase that had been scheduled for 1999. In addition, they agreed to extend coverage to new federal employees and to the small percentage of employees in nonprofit organizations that were not yet covered, which would help to build up a substantial reserve in a short time. There were a few smaller changes as well, some quite technical, but most of the savings and new revenues came from the large changes just mentioned (Ball 2010, pp. 46–52; Bernstein and Brodshaug 1988, pp. 50–55).

By agreeing to the acceleration in payroll tax payments, the Republicans in effect agreed to something that had been anathema to them before, a large reserve fund that would ensure the full stability of Social Security for fifty to seventy-five years. This time, though, it was left unmentioned that such reserves could be used to fund ongoing government operations until the Treasury bonds purchased by the Social Security Trust Fund with the new taxes came due in future decades (see Altman 2005, p. 135, for an excellent discussion of the inviolable legal status of these trust assets). According to Robert Hormats (2007, p. 241), a former State Department official and a retired vice chair of Goldman Sachs, the large reserve fund provided the federal government with "a surplus it could draw on to cover increases in the regular operating deficit." He then added, "And American leaders did not hesitate to raid those funds on a regular basis, relieving the pressures on the president and Congress to slash the deficit." More specifically, the payroll tax could be used to partially cover tax cuts for the wealthy and increases in the defense budget.

In spite of the general agreement forged between the five Democrats and the Republican moderates on the major issues, there was nonetheless resistance to the overall deal by six conservative members of the commission. The fact that the three business representatives (Beck, Fuller, and Trowbridge) were part of this dissident group was of great concern to the White House staff. It arranged a personal meeting for Beck with Reagan, which led to his decision to join the majority. Beck then convinced Fuller and Trowbridge to join the compromise, which left retired Southern Democrat Waggonner, Senator Armstrong, and Representative Archer on the losing end of a 12–3 vote to accept the report (see Altman 2005, p. 248, on Beck's meeting with Reagan; and Ball 2010, p. 50, for Beck's influence with the other business representatives). To complete the compromise, the commission left it up to Congress to fill the remaining one-third of the long-run gap through one of two options. The conservative members, including the two conservative Democrats, suggested that the retirement age should be raised from sixty-five to sixty-seven through monthly increments that would begin in 2000. The five liberal Democrats proposed that the gap should be filled through gradual tax increases that would begin in 2010 if they were needed. With the 1982 elections safely over, the conservative coalition accepted the general compromise offered by the commission. Then it opted to increase the retirement age starting in 2000 rather than leave it to a future Congress to decide if taxes actually needed to be raised in 2010. This preemptive decision once again reveals conservatives' deep-seated desire to limit any government support for social benefits as much as possible.

Both Republicans and Democrats declared victory and breathed a sigh of relief, but the CED leaders stated publicly that they were disappointed in the results, which they had tried to influence through meetings with Greenspan, Dole, and other key participants as well as with staff members of the relevant Senate and House committees. In the aftermath, they expressed their dissatisfaction in a 1984 CED report, *Social Security: From Crisis to Crisis?* (1984), which repeated the CED's 1981 recommendations. They complained that the cuts were too small and cautious, leaving too small a margin of safety. Ball called the new CED report "quite irresponsible" and predicted large surpluses by 1988, while claiming that the CED was "looking for any excuse to push their proposals for further benefit cuts" (Associated Press 1984, p. 16). According to Ball, the corporate executives he knew were willing to support Social Security at a minimum level of payments, but they did not want to see any expansion in it because of their general antigovernment ideology and their resulting preference for private pension plans (Ball 1990).

Ball turned out to be more than correct in predicting large surpluses. According to testimony before Moynihan's Senate Subcommittee on Social Security and Family Policy in 1988, the trust fund was taking in $109.4 million per day by that year and had grown to almost $100 billion in just four years (Moynihan 1988). By 2010 the Social Security Trust Fund had $2.6 trillion in Treasury notes, enough to pay benefits for at least three decades. However, ultraconservatives continued to claim that Social Security was in crisis because the Social Security Administration did not have any actual money in the bank, only the "IOUs" from the Treasury Department, thereby ignoring the fully protected legal standing of the trust funds, or perhaps hoping that the Supreme Court would take their side if the issue came to a court fight. In the eyes of liberal economists, the issue that really concerns the conservatives is that federal taxes might have to be raised, including income taxes on the well-to-do, when the time comes for the Social Security Trust Fund to collect on its Treasury bonds (e.g., Baker 2001; Baker and Weisbrot 1999).

Still, the fact remains that the corporate community and the Reagan administration did not win all that they hoped to on Social Security in the early 1980s. True, benefits were trimmed significantly through delaying the COLA and increasing the retirement age, and the money collected for the trust fund was used to pay for part of the large budget deficits over the next thirty years. But the liberal-labor alliance was able to restore public confidence in the system and give it legitimacy for the next fifteen to twenty years in the face of a predominantly conservative Congress eager to make larger reductions or privatize the whole system. It was also able to make some changes that benefited women and brought all employees of the federal government and nonprofit organizations into the system. The overall result accurately reflects the comparative power of the two rival coalitions as the corporate-conservatives consistently pushed national policy in a rightward direction.

THE RISE IN DEFENSE SPENDING

Reagan's proposals for large increases in defense spending represented the resolution of a major argument among rival foreign policy groups within the corporate policy-planning network concerning Soviet strategy in the Third World and the wisdom of continuing a policy of détente. The disagreements first emerged in a serious way during the Ford administration over CIA estimates of Soviet intentions and military strength that were considered too benign by the foreign-policy hawks. Their complaints led to the appointment of an assessment group more to their liking, which proceeded to make estimates of the growth in Soviet military spending that later proved to be wildly off the mark. As part of this argument, in early 1976 the hawks created a new incarnation of the Committee on the Present Danger, reviving the name first utilized by foreign policy analysts when they called for an arms buildup in 1950. The argument widened in the face of apparent Soviet support for insurgencies in Africa, which was followed by a popular uprising against the American-backed Shah of Iran in early 1979 and the Soviet invasion of Afghanistan later in the same year in an attempt to prop up its puppet government.

As an early member of the Committee on the Present Danger, Reagan already had positioned himself as a strong anti-Communist hawk during the Carter years. He gained further foreign-policy visibility and legitimacy on the right in 1977 by leading the unsuccessful attempt to block the Panama Canal treaty crafted by international-ists in both parties, which ceded sovereignty and gradual control over the canal to the government of Panama over a twenty-year period. In calling for increases in defense spending, Reagan had far more in mind than maintaining the stalemate with the Soviet Union. Robert Hormats, the former vice chair at Goldman Sachs, provides evidence that Reagan saw a military buildup as a way to force the Soviet Union to spend its way into bankruptcy. The president did not think the Soviets could keep up with the arms race while trying to defend the Afghanistan government and other pro-Soviet regimes that the United States was helping to undermine (Hormats 2007, pp. 235–236).

Reagan also was acting in the context of a renewed consensus in the foreign policy establishment that emerged during events in Afghanistan and Iran. This new consen-sus was symbolized and in part brought about by a large-scale effort by the Council on Foreign Relations to mediate the dispute over the extent of the Soviet Union's threat to US interests. After convening several narrower discussion groups and study groups, in the fall of 1980 it created a special Commission on US-Soviet Relations that included representatives of both the Soviets-can-be-worked-with and the Soviets-are-expansionists-and-dangerous views. The discussants had served in Republican and Democratic administrations. The commission was chaired by Henry Grunwald, the editor-in-chief of Time, Inc., and included W. Michael Blumenthal, the former secre-tary of the treasury, as well as Paul Nitze, a State Department advisor to Dean Acheson in the Truman administration and one of the leaders in the new Committee on the Present Danger. There were two congressional members: William Cohen, a moderate Republican senator from Maine; and Millicent Fenwick, a moderate Republican in the House of Representatives from New Jersey. Helmut Sonnenfeldt of The Brookings Institution, who had served as a State Department counselor under Henry Kissinger from 1974 to 1977, drafted a thirty-one-page report based on the discussions. It was distributed free of charge with money from a Ford Foundation grant and was widely publicized in newspapers and magazines.

The participants agreed that the Soviets were a "vastly more formidable foe" than had been thought a decade earlier and that their intentions were relentlessly hostile to Western interests. The report called for an even bigger defense buildup than either presidential candidate had advocated in the 1980 campaign. *Time* (1981) described the commission's recommendations as "tough-minded." The *New York Times* noted that "the panel went beyond Mr. Reagan's proposed rearmament policy" by calling for military outlays to reach 6.0 percent of the gross national product compared to his plan to go to 5.6 percent (*New York Times* 1981, p. 10). The commission itself said, "First priority must go to improving existing forces" and called for "some form of compulsory military service" (Council on Foreign Relations 1981). It is therefore a mistake to attribute Reagan's large increase in defense spending to ultraconservatives alone.

The increases in defense spending, which eventually reached the level called for by the CFR commission, when combined with the large cuts in income taxes and the continued federal aid to state governments, added up to a very large Keynesian demand stimulus, even though Reagan and his advisors did not see them in this way. In all, the Reagan administration increased defense spending by $36 billion in inflation-adjusted dollars. The growth in defense spending accounted for 15–20 percent of the employment gains from 1983 through 1985, which is strong evidence that it was functioning as a Keynesian stimulus (Wirls 1992, pp. 46–50, 224).

CUTTING BACK ON REGULATIONS

Corporations that did a large amount of shipping via the highly regulated trucking and railroad industries triggered a growing chorus of complaints about government regulatory agencies in the early 1970s. Their concerns were augmented by the problems created for the tightly regulated airlines industry by rising fuel costs after OPEC price hikes (Robyn 1987). Successful deregulation of the airlines and trucking industries soon occurred through bipartisan efforts in Congress that included liberal Democrats and had the support of the Carter administration (Biven 2002, pp. 217–228). Although these efforts were later hailed as successes in terms of creating greater efficiencies and lower prices, some did undercut unions and put downward pressure on the wages of their lower-level employees, thereby contributing to greater income inequality (Baker 2007, p. 39; Peoples 1998).

For all the bipartisanship on deregulating specific sectors of business, tensions arose concerning the new form of regulation represented by the Environmental Protection Agency and the Occupational Health and Safety Administration. They were said to be different in that they regulated general business practices for the good of the general public, not simply specific industries that originally had benefited in one way or another from being regulated. By the late 1970s the corporate community blamed all forms of regulation for inflation, low productivity gains, and most other economic ills (Tolchin and Tolchin 1983).

The Reagan administration's effort to deregulate business in general began with a task force on regulatory reform housed in the office of Vice President Bush and staffed by economist James C. Miller III, an opponent of regulation formerly employed at the American Enterprise Institute. The task force was fortified by a presidential executive order saying that cost-benefit analyses had to be carried out for new regulations and then approved by the Office of Management and Budget before they could be put into effect. The task force immediately abolished the remnants of the Council on Wage and Price Policy and ended price controls on oil nine months before they were due to expire.

The economic rationale for the new offensive against regulation was based primarily on a study carried out at the Center for the Study of American Business at Washington University under the direction of Weidenbaum, the frequent CED consultant and the chair of Reagan's CEA (DeFina and Weidenbaum 1978). The study estimated that regulation would cost the economy about $100 billion in 1979, but the government's Congressional Research Service criticized the Weidenbaum study for major flaws (Allen 1978). Basically, the center's report overstated costs by including the budgets of regulatory agencies, relied on self-report data provided by corporations, and included basic reporting tasks such as filing income and payroll taxes. Most of all, it failed to consider benefits as well as costs, such as the economic savings from eliminating the corrosive effects of acid rain and the reduction in medical costs from ensuring safe drinking water, inspecting food, and making certain that new medications are safe.

Appointees who were openly hostile to the missions of regulatory agencies and supportive of industry objectives were put in charge. The Department of Interior and the Environmental Protection Agency (EPA) serve as two prototypical examples. The secretary of the interior, James G. Watt, previously headed an ultraconservative public-interest law firm, backed by landowning, cattle-raising, and mine-owning interests in the Rocky Mountain states. He sparked fierce opposition from environmentalists when he immediately opened more government land for grazing, lumbering, and mining, including land in national parks. He also annoyed oil company executives by attempting to auction off leases for shoreline and offshore sites for exploration at a time when they were dealing with an oil glut. He was forced out of office in late 1983 after making personally offensive remarks about the members of one of his advisory committees. Anne Gorsuch, the head of the EPA, a former lawyer for Mountain Bell Telephone and then a state legislator in Colorado, acted in a similar fashion, producing much the same reaction. She cut the agency's budget by 22 percent in the first year, relaxed clean-air standards, and appointed executives from industries regulated by the EPA to key posts. In 1982 she defied Congress by refusing to provide documents concerning an accusation that the agency mishandled funds for cleaning up toxic waste. She resigned in early 1983 when the White House gave up on its efforts to claim executive privilege for the documents.

Although the Reagan appointees at the Department of the Interior and the EPA did not last long, their efforts were successful in slowing the environmental movement while at the same time heightening tensions with moderate Republicans (Baker 2007, p. 81). More generally, the Reagan administration failed in its most ambitious goals for deregulation because it alienated the leaders of key congressional committees and lost court battles initiated by public-interest groups supported by consumer and environmental activists. Most of its successes came through cutting budgets and reducing inspection staffs.

RESISTANCE AND CORRECTIONS BY MODERATE CONSERVATIVES

Although the corporate community was unified in supporting many of the Reagan administration's initiatives, disagreements between the corporate moderates and ultraconservatives soon arose on a few issues once they had completely vanquished the liberal-labor alliance. As sociologist Patrick Akard (1992, p. 611) concluded, "The only question was which conservative faction would rule." As events unfolded, the corporate moderates stopped some ultraconservative initiatives, overturned others, or made the corrections they felt necessary through nongovernmental initiatives. As conservative as the early 1980s were, they were not as conservative as the ultraconservatives wanted them to be.

Limiting Funding Cuts for the Export-Import Bank

One of the first setbacks suffered by the ultraconservative budget cutters concerned their attempt to make very large reductions in the money available to the government's Export-Import Bank, which had been loaning money to foreign borrowers at bargain rates in a program supported by corporate moderates since the 1930s to boost American exports. Seven large firms, Boeing, Combustion Engineering, General Electric, Lockheed, McDonnell Douglas, Western Electric, and Westinghouse, whose overseas deals accounted for two-thirds of Export-Import Bank loans, were the major beneficiaries in the late 1970s. These and other corporations, brought together through the National Foreign Trade Council and other trade associations, began an intensive lobbying campaign within both the White House and Congress. The 25 percent cut proposed by the Reagan administration was reduced to 9 percent by Congress and was eliminated entirely in the second and third years of Reagan's presidency (McQuaid 1982, pp. 316–318).

Corporate Moderates Back Tax Increases

The large tax cuts in 1981 led to deficits and a growing debt that were so large that everyone but the most ultra of ultraconservatives became concerned. Both the Business Council and the Business Roundtable soon recommended tax increases. The result was the Tax Equity and Fiscal Responsibility Act of 1982, which reduced some personal deductions and business depreciation allowances and raised various excise taxes (Akard 1992, p. 611; Campagna 1994, pp. 71–72). Liberals and ultraconservatives liked to point out, with appropriate glee or disgust, that the various tax increases added up to the largest tax increase in history, but Reagan still ended up with most of what he originally hoped for and the large deficits continued. A year later, a tax of five cents a gallon on gasoline, which had little or no impact on high-income earners, provided further revenues.

Provisioning Low-Income Neighborhoods

The drastic cuts in social spending programs were a major blow to the infrastructure of nonprofit organizations that corporate moderates and their foundations slowly constructed in inner-city neighborhoods during the 1960s and 1970s. Although the corporate moderates financed and encouraged these private efforts, the vast majority of the financial support for most of the programs, and especially housing, came from the federal government before Reagan was elected.

With the Ford Foundation once again taking the lead, the corporate moderates modified their approach in the face of the new circumstances by putting more effort into their plans for public-private partnerships in urban areas. They also worked to secure funding sources for a new form of financial intermediary, local initiatives support corporations (LISCs), to raise money for community development corporations from governments, foundations, and private gifts. In effect, the LISCs served as the nonprofit equivalents of the for-profit investment companies on Wall Street. Coincidentally, the first of many local and regional LISCs was launched on a trial basis in 1979 with $4.5 million from the Ford Foundation and $4.8 million from six corporate sponsors (Peirce and Steinbach 1987, p. 74). In the aftermath of the Reagan budget cuts, a somewhat similar nonprofit financial intermediary, the Enterprise Foundation, founded by a major real estate developer, joined the original LISC three years later. The Ford Foundation then added its support to the Enterprise Foundation, giving it just over $9 million between 1982 and 1991 (Liou and Stroh 1998, p. 583).

Once the LISCs and the Enterprise Foundation were in place, the Ford Foundation created a "community development partnership strategy" in 1983, which drew on the concept of public-private partnerships and other ideas championed in a report from the CED's large-scale project on urban areas, funded in good part by the Ford Foundation. This 1978 report, *An Approach to Federal Urban Policy*, was prepared by a subcommittee on Revitalizing America's Cities, which consisted primarily of insurance and banking executives, with the assistance of six economists and urban policy experts. It advocated an increased role for private capital in solving urban problems, criticized local governments for being inefficient, and urged cities to model themselves after business firms by becoming more entrepreneurial through public-private partnerships. Further information on public-private partnerships was provided in a later report, accompanied by a book edited by CED staff members that summarized the key ideas and presented seven case studies (Committee for Economic Development 1978, 1982; Fosler and Berger 1982).

Basically, the Ford Foundation and the CED called for the pooling of resources from the private sector, foundations, government agencies, and nonprofit institutions to support renewed efforts to revitalize neighborhoods. Their allies in inner-city nonprofit networks then lobbied for giving wealthy individuals tax credits for LISC donations, which they hoped would open the floodgates for funding the community development corporations. As one account notes, "Politically, the intermediaries claim no small role in winning new tax credits for low-income housing in the 1986 Tax Reform Act" (Peirce and Steinbach 1987, p. 74).

Inner-city housing groups in Cleveland, backed by the top executives of Standard Oil of Ohio, took the central role on this issue (Tittle 1992, pp. 239–240). Most importantly, it was the Cleveland Housing Network, working with both the Cleveland LISC and the Enterprise Foundation, that in 1984 pioneered in offering tax write-offs to finance low-income housing, borrowing the idea from an Indiana insurance company. Although the Cleveland leaders first thought of the tax break as a way to gain the support of wealthy individuals, the real breakthrough came through a last-minute suggestion by one of their employees that corporations should be included in this new tax-deduction amendment (Guthrie and McQuarrie 2005).

The use of corporate tax breaks turned out to be an ideal solution from the point of view of both moderates and ultraconservatives in the corporate community for providing at least some social provisions for low-income neighborhoods through public-private partnerships. Ultraconservatives were pleased because tax breaks reduce the direct role of the federal government and encourage initiatives by the private sector. Corporate moderates liked the idea because the family, corporate, and community foundations they established in previous decades could continue to deliver needed resources to the inner city at no cost to themselves and simultaneously minimize a direct role by local government agencies. In effect, the arrangement enhanced the potential for a private government of nonprofit organizations controlled by the foundations and corporations, with community development corporations playing the role of go-betweens. Moreover, this approach made social services less expensive because the employees for nonprofits were paid less than the unionized social workers and other well-educated professionals who used to be employed by city and county governments.

Retaining Affirmative Action and Reaffirming Diversity

Ultraconservative Republicans and members of the religious right were zealously opposed to any form of affirmative action, which they tried to dismantle through successful efforts to hobble the Equal Employment Opportunity Commission and unsuccessful efforts to make changes in the law. However, by then the corporate community had adapted to the pressures generated by African Americans, Latinos, Asian Americans, and women since the 1960s by incorporating a growing number of women and people of color into executive positions. In fact, they had decided that "diversity," as the diluted version of affirmative action came to be called after a Supreme Court ruling in 1978, was on balance a good policy for many reasons. It provided public-affairs liaisons to nearby African American and Latino communities; salespeople to attract new customers from the growing black, Latino, and Asian American middle classes; bilingual executives who might work in company facilities in other countries; and in general a larger talent pool to draw from (Zweigenhaft and Domhoff 2011, pp. 111–114). Corporations therefore resisted the ultraconservatives' efforts to dismantle their diversity programs, with the editors at *Business Week* and *Fortune* supporting their position. In 1985 a NAM committee opposed a Reagan administration proposal to weaken the Office of Federal Contract Compliance (Delton 2009, pp. 278–279; Zweigenhaft and Domhoff 2011, chapter 6).

LOOKING BACKWARD AND FORWARD FROM 1984

The Reagan administration was the culmination of a rightward shift in the corporate community that sought to counter the collective bargaining power of unions, any government involvement in the control of inflation through wage-price policies, and the rise in government social spending. Political journalist Thomas Edsall provided a pithy overview of key aspects of this one-sided class war as the first four years of Reagan's reign were drawing to a close:

> Perhaps one of the most substantial achievements of the policy changes in the Reagan administration has been to consistently weaken the governmental base of support provided organized labor in its dealing with management—through sharp reductions in unemployment insurance, through the complete elimination of the public service job program, through the weakening of the Occupational Safety and Health Administration, and through appointments of persons hostile to organized labor both to the National Labor Relations Board and to the Department of Labor. (Edsall 1984, pp. 228–229)

The attempt to control inflation through high interest rates had high costs for some sectors of the economy. It made domestic manufacturing goods too expensive to compete against imports from Western Europe and Japan, thereby encouraging more industrial firms to move their production overseas and then import the finished product back into the United States. In effect, it was a policy of deindustrialization. The Reagan policies also depressed the housing industry due to the high mortgage rates they created.

Despite the heavy costs of this version of class warfare in terms of recession, deindustrialization, and tough times for the housing industry, Reagan administration officials insisted it was necessary in order to break the back of inflation, claiming credit for the decline in inflation from 13.6 percent in 1980 to 4.3 percent in 1984. However, as a study by researchers at the centrist Urban Institute concluded, one-third to one-half of the decline was first due to unexpected decreases in world prices for food and oil, along with a decrease in the price of imports to the United States due to the high value of the dollar, which was caused in good part by the high interest rates (Stone and Sawhill 1984, p. 2). The rest of the decline was due to the high unemployment rates and demand compression induced by the high interest rates, a project already under way with the enthusiastic support of corporate moderates before Reagan was elected.

In all, the fight against inflation cost the US economy $1 trillion in lost productivity. The standard use of tight fiscal policy and a looser monetary policy would have done almost as well and not hurt the export and housing industries nearly as much (Stone and Sawhill 1984, p. 4). The cold hard discipline of monetary policy, dispensed by people who call themselves "libertarians" and express great contempt for liberals and Keynesians, had arrived with a vengeance, along with Nobel Prizes for many of the economists who were among the champions of austere discipline (Krugman 1994).

Despite the economic costs of Reagan's policies, most corporate leaders found the recession of 1981–1982 to be worthwhile, according to a survey in the spring of 1982. In the face of the huge number of small-business bankruptcies, the loss of manufacturing jobs to foreign countries, and high unemployment due to the Carter-Volcker-Reagan monetary policies, "a majority of the 800 executives at large and medium-sized companies" said that the recession was good for the country; they believed this because of its sobering effect on the liberal-labor alliance in general and on workers seeking wage increases in particular (Vogel 1989, p. 256). They also believed that the humbling of unions would mean that automatic cost-of-living adjustments would no longer feed into core inflation when commodity prices rose very suddenly due to food shortages or oil embargoes. On this score they proved to be very right. Later research showed that increases in commodity prices impacted core inflation in the 1960s and 1970s, but not afterward (Krugman 2011b; 2012a, pp. 154–155).

Nor did the tax cuts lead to greater investment. Secretary of the Treasury Donald Regan, who spoke strongly in favor of the tax reductions, also urged businesses to make plans for the investments in new facilities, machinery, and research that would be necessary to reduce unemployment. He reminded the corporate community that it would face "its biggest challenge" since World War II, "how to carry out this program once you're free of the fetters that you've been decrying for so many years" (McQuaid 1982, p. 321). But with interest rates high and demand low, companies did not do much investing after all. Instead, many used the money for takeovers, such as a proposed Mobil Oil takeover of the equally large Conoco (formerly Continental Oil Company). When that merger did not pass muster with the government's antitrust division, Conoco ended up as part of Du Pont. When Mobil then tried to take over a relatively small oil company in Ohio called Marathon, it fought back, so US Steel gobbled up Marathon instead (McQuaid 1982, p. 322). More generally, a study of expenditures by the corporations that received the biggest breaks between 1981 and 1983 showed that most used their new tax savings "to increase dividends, expand cash reserves, fund mergers or acquisitions, raise executive pay, or increase advertising budgets" (Peschek 1987, p. 200).

Nor did the high growth rates assured by the supply-side ultraconservatives materialize: the economy's general growth rate was only 2.9 percent from the 1979 peak of the economy to the 1990 peak, which was lower than the 3.2 percent in the 1970s (Baker 2007, p. 67). However, ultraconservatives were able to disagree with this conclusion because they made their calculations about growth rates from the low point in the economy in 1981, after high interest rates had brought the economy to its knees. Using this highly unorthodox measure, which is rejected by all mainstream economists, liberal and conservative, Reagan's libertarian policy advisor claimed that Reagan had unleashed the largest economic upswing in American history (Anderson 1990, pp. 175–176). According to figures cited by Reagan's most detailed and perceptive biographer, the real income of every economic strata increased during the 1980s, albeit more for the rich than the poor, but the nation's overall wealth grew by only 8 percent after the recession ended, compared to 31 percent between 1975 and 1980 (Cannon 2000, pp. 744, 746).

The gradual replacement of traditional Southern Democrats with even more conservative Southern Republicans made the conservative coalition less visible, even though traditional conservative dominance had been strengthened by these changes because the new Southern elected officials voted much like Northern Republicans on all issues. Still, the continuing importance of the remaining white Southern Democrats in the Reagan years is demonstrated by the fact that the conservative coalition formed 75 times in the House and 104 times in the Senate in 1981, not simply on the tax and budget issues. It won 88 percent of the time in the House and 95 percent in the Senate, cutting back on food stamps, resisting attempts to reduce tobacco price supports, decreasing federal monies for abortion, limiting the use of busing for desegregation, and putting restraints on the federally financed Legal Services programs, which had been providing legal help to low-income people since the mid-1960s (Shelley 1983, p. 158). It appeared slightly less often in the next decade, but it always won 79 to 90 percent of the time (*Congressional Quarterly* 1992, p. 3845). As recently as 1996, with conservative white Southern Democrats accounting for fewer than thirty votes in the House, the conservative coalition formed on 11.7 percent of the congressional votes and was successful 98.9 percent of the time. The Southern Democratic votes were essential to thirty-three of the fifty-one conservative successes by offsetting the defections by the handful of moderate Republicans remaining in the House at the time (*Congressional Quarterly* 1996).

The three power indicators all registered gains for the corporate rich in the first Reagan administration. Income inequality among employed urban males rose from 0.366 in 1980 to 0.397 in 1984 and 0.401 in 1985, the highest it had been since 1942 (Kopczuk, Saez, and Song 2010). Although union density in the public sector held about even at 35.8 percent, union density in the private sector fell from 20.6 percent in 1980 to 15.5 percent in 1985, and the drop in the number of trade unionists in the private sector was dramatic. From a high point of nearly 17 million members in 1970, the number had fallen gradually to 16.2 million in 1975 and to 15.3 million in 1980; by 1984 the number was only 11.6 million, a 32 percent decline (Miller and Canak 1995b, p. 19, table 1). As for the effective tax rate on the top 1 percent, it was down to 22.1 percent by 1986, only a half-percent more than what it was in 1940 (Brownlee 2000, p. 61).

Contemplating the scene at the end of Reagan's first term, especially with the defeats and trends of the previous forty-six years in mind, it is hard to imagine how anyone could think by 1985 that anybody but the owners and managers of large income-producing properties dominated the United States. However, many theorists in the social sciences continued to believe otherwise. The successes of business between 1975 and 1988 were claimed to be just another swing in the fluctuating fortunes of business over the decades (Vogel 1989). Besides, a study of the successes and failures of the Chamber of Commerce from 1953 to 1992 concluded that business usually lost when public opinion favored liberal-labor legislation (Smith 2000).

Still others wrote, based on studies of specific issue areas, that there was no evidence of a cohesive corporate community, just a variety of traditional "interest groups," including one with heavy labor representation (Heinz, Laumann, Nelson, and Salisbury 1993; Laumann and Knoke 1987; McFarland 2004). Moreover, environmentalists, consumer activists, and many other liberal interest groups, which focused on postmaterialist values rather than the old bread-and-butter issues, added up to a "new liberalism" that was a "rising power" in Washington (Berry 1999).

Chapter Thirteen

The Road to the Great Recession

By 1985, following President Reagan's successful bid for a second term, the main trends in the march to greater inequality in the United States were firmly in place. The Republicans' successes in limiting unions led to more victories for their party in the electoral arena, followed by more tax cuts for the well-to-do, the continuing decline in the value of the minimum wage, and the deregulation of the financial sector. Industrial corporations moved most high-wage blue-collar jobs to the Southern states, Mexico, Southeast Asia, and China, which furthered union decline and greater income inequality. Financial deregulation led to greater risk-taking by Wall Street both at home and in foreign markets. By the late 1990s the United States once again had a boom-and-bust economy of the kind that existed before the New Deal. When consumer demand declined rapidly after the housing bubble burst in 2007–2008, the country fell into a Great Recession, from which it had not fully recovered by the end of 2012. At the same time, despite the tensions and dramas generated by the end of the Cold War, the horrors of 9/11, the deaths and traumatic brain injuries that resulted from the invasions of Afghanistan and Iraq, and the ups and downs of the economy, corporate dominance inexorably grew.

In the process, the corporate community continued its collective journey to a more conservative stance. The Business Roundtable and the Business Council remained at the center of the corporate network, but the CED drifted to the margins in terms of its impact. By 2012 the CED's board of trustees had more top officers from foundations, universities, and sundry advisory firms than it did from major corporations, and most of the representatives from the very largest corporations were retired CEOs or vice presidents, a clear indication of the CED's fall in stature. It was best known for its ongoing attempts to improve educational performance in schools and its steadfast support for campaign finance reform.

By contrast, the Business Roundtable took the lead in bringing about the legislation that made it possible to send more jobs to low-wage countries and complete the humbling of American industrial unions. It began by organizing the grassroots pressure and forceful lobbying for the corporate community's victory in 1994 on the North American Free Trade Agreement (NAFTA), which created a Canada–United States–Mexico free trade zone (Dreiling 2001). Then it successfully lobbied Congress in 2000 to give China the legal status called "permanent normal trade relations," which made it possible to ship jobs to an undemocratic nation in which workers have to work for a small fraction of what their counterparts in the United States had been paid up until that time. For both of the trade agreements, the Business Roundtable organized the corporate community on a state-by-state basis and contacted most members of Congress. In the process, it overcame the initial majority opposition to both pieces of legislation on the part of the public and Congress, as well as the efforts of the liberal-labor alliance to block it (Dreiling and Darves 2011).

FURTHER UNION DECLINE, LOWER TAXES FOR THE RICH

Union density in the public sector held about even post-1984, standing at 37 percent in 2011, but the overall percentage of wage and salary workers in unions declined to 11.8 percent, reflecting the continuing disappearance of unionism in the private sector in the face of the employer onslaught; the figure went down to 6.9 percent (Bureau of Labor Statistics 2012). By 2012 there were twenty-four right-to-work states—twelve in the South, five in the Great Plains, five in the Rocky Mountain region, and two in the Midwest—due to successful campaigns in Idaho in 1986, Oklahoma in 2001, and Indiana and Michigan in 2012. There was virtually nothing left of the industrial unions that had provided campaign donations, campaign workers, and votes to pro-labor political candidates in the postwar era. The task of bringing likely Democratic voters to the polls fell increasingly to the members of public employee, service, and communication unions.

The relentless drive to lower taxes for high-income individuals and corporations, which was made possible by the decline of the unions and the growing strength of the conservative coalition, resumed in 1986 with the passage of the Tax Reform Act. The initial draft floated by the Treasury Department lowered general tax rates for individuals and corporations while at the same time removing most loopholes and tax breaks, but it went through numerous changes before it finally reached Congress. In the end, the top individual rate fell from 50 to 28 percent, an even steeper decline than the one from 70 percent to 50 percent due to Reagan's 1981 tax legislation. Contrary to original intentions, the 1986 legislation also retained mortgage deductions for both first and second homes. In contrast, the tax rate on capital gains was raised from 20 to 28 percent, following the reform principle that all income should be treated the same, whatever its source (Brownlee 2004, p. 174). As a concession to Democrats, six million low-income individuals no longer had to pay income taxes due to higher personal exemptions, and the Earned Income Tax Credit was increased, which compensated for the fact that higher payroll taxes were enacted in 1983.

At the same time, the top corporate tax rates dropped from 46 to 34 percent, although most corporate sectors lost their tax breaks as part of the deal, including the investment tax credit (Martin 1996, p. 399). However, last-minute efforts by Vice President George H. W. Bush and Regan's successor as secretary of the treasury, James Baker, a corporate lawyer from Houston, saved the long-standing depletion allowance that allows oil and gas companies to take a tax deduction on their exploration and drilling efforts. Still, according to Brownlee (2004, pp. 176–177), the Tax Reform Act of 1986 was "the most dramatic transformation of federal tax policy since World War II" and was "decidedly progressive" in the main, although he also notes that the effective federal tax rate on the top 1 percent of families (counting both income and payroll taxes) fell slightly, from 31.8 percent in 1980 to 28.9 percent in 1991.

The reforms did nothing to deal with the yearly budget deficits and rising debt caused by the large 1981 tax cuts and the increases in defense spending. Forced to choose between raising taxes and making drastic spending cuts, in 1990 President George H. W. Bush reluctantly agreed to raise the gas tax by a few cents and the top marginal tax rate on individual incomes from 28 to 31 percent as part of a budget compromise with congressional Democrats. The compromise included a large increase in the Earned Income Tax Credit and reductions in social spending over a five-year period. Three years later, President Bill Clinton disappointed his middle-income voters by reneging on his 1992 campaign promise to lower their taxes, but he did persuade the Democrats in Congress, with no votes from Republicans in either chamber, to raise the top marginal tax rate to 39.6 percent and make another substantial increase in the Earned Income Tax Credit (Brownlee 2004, pp. 191, 194). When the increased revenues from the Clinton tax hikes were combined with slightly slower growth in federal spending and much higher tax collections on capital gains due to the stock market bubble of the late 1990s, the yearly budget deficit that had been decried by conservatives for decades suddenly vanished. The federal debt, a bludgeon of doom and obligation that conservatives had used to silence any talk of increased social spending, was projected to disappear within a mere decade (Baker 2007, p. 169). Moreover, the stock market bubble brought unemployment down to 4 percent or just below it for the last month of 1999 and ten of the twelve months in the year 2000, the first time that level had been reached since January 1970.

As most Democrats and Republicans breathed an apparent sigh of relief that government debts finally had been mastered, Republican presidential candidate George W. Bush used the improved prospects for government revenue as a reason to promise large personal tax cuts if elected in 2000. Following his victory in the Supreme Court despite losing the nationwide popular vote count (and the highly disputed popular vote in Florida that gave him the edge in the Electoral College, as sampling by newspapers subsequently revealed), Bush's call for a tax cut was supported in congressional testimony by the chair of the Federal Reserve Board, Alan Greenspan. Greenspan, the former chair of Ford's CEA and Reagan's commission to fix Social Security, warned that the disappearance of the debt might make it more difficult for the Fed to influence interest rates through the purchase or sale of Treasury bonds; besides, he added, the government might be "forced to buy up private assets, such as corporate bonds or shares of stock" (Baker 2007, p. 169).

Over the next several years, the Bush tax cuts gradually reduced income taxes for most Americans, but they benefited upper-income Americans the most by lowering the rates on the top tax bracket from 39.6 to 35 percent and by dropping rates on dividends, interest, and capital gains to 15 percent. By 2007 the effective tax rate on the top 1 percent of households, counting both income and payroll taxes, was down to 20.6 percent from 28.9 percent in 1991 (*New York Times* 2012a). The Bush tax cuts also raised the amount of wealth that could be exempted from inheritance taxes, which reached $5.1 million in 2012, with anything over that amount taxed at a maximum rate of 35 percent.

The success of the corporate-conservative alliance in reducing tax payments for those with higher incomes, while at the same time shifting some of the tax burden to those at the middle of the income ladder, is most clearly demonstrated in an analysis of the percentage of people's incomes going to federal income, payroll, and estate taxes between 1960 and 2004. There were large declines for the top 0.1 percent, from 60 percent to 33.6 percent, and for the top 1 percent, from 44.4 percent to 30.4 percent, with most of that drop coming after 1975. For the well-off 10 percent, the percentage remained roughly the same (28 percent), but for those in the vast middle, between the 20th and 90th percentiles, who paid between 16 percent and 26 percent, it increased a point or two, which helped compensate the Treasury for the taxes lost from the top levels. For the bottom 20 percent, the share of their incomes going to federal taxes declined from 14.1 percent to 10.5 percent (Leonhardt 2012).

The effective tax rates on corporations varied greatly, depending on how many loopholes they could create and how much of their profits they could shelter overseas (Kang and Ngo 2011). By 2006 many of the corporate tax loopholes eliminated by the Tax Reform Act of 1986 had been restored (Chamberlain 2006). Twenty-six large companies, including Boeing, General Electric, DuPont, and Verizon, paid no taxes at all between 2008 and 2011 (Citizens for Tax Justice 2012). The effective tax rate on corporations in general was 23 percent in 2011, well below the official top rate of 35 percent (Duhigg and Kocieniewski 2012; *New York Times* 2012b).

While taxes on wealthy individuals and corporations were being cut in the name of stimulating the economy, the unemployment rate was rising, just as it did with the advent of the Eisenhower, Nixon, and Reagan administrations (Bartels 2010). It was 5.7 percent at the end of President Bush's first year in office and 6 percent at the end of his second year, and then rose to 6.3 percent in June 2003 before ending the year at 5.7 percent. It varied between 4 percent and 6 percent until his last few months in office, reaching 6.5 percent in October 2009 and 7.3 percent in the month he left office. Neither the several tax cuts nor war spending had much impact on the unemployment rate or the stagnating wages of the great majority of those who remained employed.

FINANCIAL DEREGULATION AND ITS DRASTIC CONSEQUENCES

The drive toward financial deregulation made possible by the increasing dominance of the corporate-conservative alliance gradually became the most important economic legacy of the Reagan years, eventually driving the economy off the cliff in a frenzy of risky boom and bust. The deregulation that began in the 1970s, which increased efficiency and lowered costs in some business sectors, had a drastically different outcome in the financial sector for a very simple reason. Banks are subject to sudden losses of their assets ("bank runs") due to the fact that they make their profits by lending more money than they can pay back to their depositors at any given moment (Krugman 2012a, chapter 4). Ignoring this basic axiom, which led to periodic bank runs and financial collapses until the Banking Act of 1933 was enacted, banks, savings and loans (S&Ls), investment banks, and brokerage firms successfully lobbied for a series of small step-by-step changes between 1980 and 1999 that led to the financial implosion in 2008 after the housing bubble began losing air in 2007, taking consumer demand down with it (Baker 2009).

This long saga began with the high interest rates of the late 1970s, which caused major financial problems for the thousands of locally owned S&Ls, because they had ceilings on the interest rates they could offer to depositors and were restricted to making mortgage loans in their local areas. As people moved their money into the new higher-paying money market accounts that Wall Street was just beginning to offer, the S&Ls' lobbying association clamored for changes in federal banking laws. These changes allowed them to compete with the new "shadow banks," that is, with financial institutions that were not regulated by the federal government, even though they were now functioning as banks by taking in deposits and allowing people to write checks and borrow money based on those deposits (Krugman 2012a, pp. 63, 111, 114–115).

Faced with major problems in a sector of the financial community with widespread popularity and deep local roots in growth coalitions, Congress passed legislation in 1980 that gradually phased out the S&Ls' interest-rate ceilings while at the same time lowering their capital requirements (the percentage of their deposits they had to keep in reserve to protect against bank runs). Congress also freed the S&Ls from the geographical boundaries that had restricted their lending areas. Most of all, the legislation raised the limit on their federal deposit insurance from $40,000 to $100,000, which was turned into a money-making opportunity by brokerage firms by offering investors risk-free $100,000 investment packets that could be deposited in many different S&Ls across the country (Kleinknecht 2009, pp. 116–117). In turn, S&Ls were given a heads-they-win, tails-taxpayers-lose opportunity to make riskier loans with government backing. Roosevelt's 1933 warning that deposit insurance would guarantee "bad banks as well as good banks" was soon supported with a vengeance (Cannon 2000, p. 740).

Even with all the new congressional dispensations, eight hundred S&Ls did not meet the minimum net worth requirement and were subject to shutdown by 1982. But the secretary of the treasury, Donald Regan, pressured the Republican that had been appointed to direct the Federal Home Loan Bank Board (the regulator for S&Ls) to make changes in the board's accounting practices. He thereby made the troubled S&Ls look more solvent than they actually were. With Regan's urging, Congress passed a new law in 1982 that eliminated a requirement that S&Ls could only make loans on housing, which made them similar to commercial banks. It also repealed the requirement that S&Ls had to have at least four hundred local owners to be granted a charter. As a result of these changes, many S&Ls ventured into exotic loans, and some of them came to be owned by individual developers, who could then make loans to themselves for their own projects (Kleinknecht 2009, pp. 117–118).

Reagan and Regan saw the 1982 law as a major step in their mission to deregulate the financial sector, but the head of the Federal Deposit Insurance Corporation, who was a White House advisor during the Ford administration, knew it was a recipe for disaster: "The Reagan administration turned these people loose. Frankly, I thought it was crazy" (Cannon 2000, p. 742). When the head of the Federal Home Loan Bank Board resisted Regan's efforts to give more regulatory breaks to the S&Ls, which by 1983 were in even more trouble due to bad loans, he was shunned by the rest of the Reagan administration as a "re-regulator." He was asked to resign, but refused to do so. "The administration was so ideologically blinded," he later said, "that it couldn't understand the difference between thrift deregulation and airline deregulation. I'm not a rocket scientist, but I understood that" (Cannon 2000, p. 744).

As problems continued to mount, no high official in the Treasury Department was willing to admit that hundreds of S&Ls would have to be shut down at taxpayers' expense. When a leading financial expert asked a Treasury official in 1986 when he was "going to admit the size" of the problem, he replied, "not on my watch" (Cannon 2000, p. 744). The admission was postponed until after the 1988 elections, which meant that a bailout that would have cost an estimated $25 billion in 1983, and $100 billion in 1986, ended up costing the federal government $131 billion by 1999, with almost 60 percent of the money going to Texas alone (Cannon 2000, p. 744; Krugman 2012b).

The debacle in the S&L industry was only a prelude to what happened with traditional commercial banks. Undeterred by the S&Ls' increasing troubles between 1980 and 1983, Regan pressed ahead with his efforts to repeal all New Deal financial regulations. He introduced legislation in 1983 to abolish the Glass-Steagall provisions in the Banking Act of 1933, which separated commercial banking and investment banking into separate business activities that could not be carried out by any one company. His bill passed the Senate by an 89–5 margin, but the Democrats in the House stopped it by not letting it out of committee.

The campaign to eliminate Glass-Steagall then shifted to the Republican-dominated Federal Reserve Board, which voted in 1986 to allow commercial banks to engage in investment banking and stock sales, if they did not provide more than 5 percent of their revenues. They did so based on the rationale that the law only said the commercial banks could not "primarily engage" in underwriting and stock sales. In 1987 the Fed approved a request from the major New York commercial banks to underwrite municipal bonds and mortgage bonds, another encroachment into the realm of investment banking. With these de facto breaches of the Glass-Steagall walls in place, the Reagan administration again asked Congress to repeal the entire law, but was blocked once again in the House. The Fed came to the rescue in 1989 by doubling its 5 percent exception for commercial banks, and in 1996 it upped the exception to 25 percent, effectively putting an end to Glass-Steagall (Kleinknecht 2009, pp. 120–121). But there was one more wall to be leveled before Glass-Steagall was fully gone. In 1998 Citicorp, the holding company for Citibank, purchased Travelers Insurance, which owned two big investment-banking firms. "But there was one small problem," as economist Paul Krugman (2012a, p. 85) recounts as part of his explanation for the meltdown in 2008:

"the merger was illegal." As Clinton sang the praises of new legislation that would legalize the end of Glass-Steagall, Congress quickly passed the bill.

With commercial banks increasingly deregulated, and shadow banks still unregulated, the stage was set for a new era of free-wheeling finance, just as the Fed lowered interest rates in 2001 to counteract the collapse of the stock market bubble that had revved up the economy in the late 1990s. In the process of lowering interest rates to the lowest levels in fifty years, the Fed enlarged a housing bubble that had been developing gradually since 1997 (Baker 2007, p. 187). Both respectable and fly-by-night mortgage companies, many of them indirectly owned or secretly bankrolled by commercial and investment banks, began providing low-interest mortgages and equity lines to speculators, who were buying properties with the hope of profitable resales. Quick in-and-out sales were encouraged by several legislative changes in 1997 that lowered the tax rate on capital gains realized through housing sales (Henchman 2008). Eventually individuals with low incomes and/or poor credit ratings were drawn into the process with low-interest start-up loans. Wall Street then bought this combination of "good" and "bad" mortgages and bundled them into mortgage-backed securities, claiming they were as likely to bring in a steady flow of income as any other security.

When the housing bubble began leaking air in 2007, and popped in 2008, thereby leading to a dramatic cutback in consumer spending, the new financial house of cards was exposed for what it was, a rerun of the late 1920s, when bankers took large gambles and helped bring down the economy for years to come. As the financial system imploded in 2008 and the Great Recession deepened, two of the largest investment banks, Goldman Sachs and Morgan Stanley, were miraculously converted into commercial banks over a weekend, thereby giving them federal deposit insurance to help stem the tide. Soon thereafter, Congress provided a potential bailout of $700 billion for the financial sector in general, but not for the homeowners who owed more than their houses were now worth, unlike what happened in the early New Deal, when the Home Owners' Loan Act rescued homeowners. In December 2011 the Fed was forced to disclose its behind-the-scenes support for banks during the crisis, a staggering $7.7 trillion, eleven times as much as the congressional bailout. Six of the biggest banks alone received $460 billion from the Fed, but small lenders and banks in other countries were propped up as well (Spitzer 2011).

TOP INCOMES, POVERTY, AND FOOD STAMPS

Due to the decline in union power in the workplace, the continuing loss of high-paying jobs at home as more companies moved production overseas, and the decline in the purchasing power of the minimum wage by a little over 35 percent since its high point in 1968, along with the many tax cuts and loopholes for those with high incomes, the income distribution became ever more unequal (Bartels 2010). At the same time, members of the financial sector took home an even larger portion of total yearly income, accelerating an upward trend that began in the late 1940s (Philippon 2012, figures 1 and 2). More generally, the share of income going to the top 1 percent rose from 12.8 percent in 1982 to 23.1 percent in 2007 (Wolff 2010). The top 1 percent's share declined to 18.1 percent in 2009 because it could not cash in on capital gains due to the big fall in stock prices, but in 2010 its income "grew by 11.6 percent, while bottom 99 percent incomes grew by only 0.2 percent. Hence, the top 1 percent [those earning $352,000 and above] captured 93 percent of the income gains in the first year of recovery" (Saez 2012, p. 4). In New York City, the home of Wall Street and many large corporations, the top 1 percent's share was up to 32.5 percent (Newman 2012). While the top 1 percent was making its comeback, the median family lost 7.7 percent of its income and 38.8 percent of its net worth, mostly through the drop in housing prices, in the same three-year period (Applebaum 2012; Baker 2012).

For those who were unemployed and destitute, welfare payments were insufficient even when they were provided, because they had been dramatically reduced in 1996 as a result of Clinton's 1992 campaign promise to "end welfare as we know it." Then Clinton's plan was made more draconian by the Republicans' insistence that his provisions for child care and health insurance for those on welfare had to be eliminated (Quadagno and Rohlinger 2009). Sixteen states cut their welfare rolls between 2007 and 2012, and diverted their federal grants to other programs (DeParle 2012). Most states also eliminated their extended unemployment benefits in 2012, with 95,000 people in California losing unemployment checks in May alone (Dewan 2012).

The relaxation and extension of eligibility rules for food stamps, along with the Earned Income Tax Credit, were the only saving graces for the 46.5 million people who lived in poverty in 2012, about 15 percent of the adult population (Seefeldt, Abner, Bolinger, Xu, and Graham 2012; *Wall Street Journal* 2012). But many jobless food-stamp recipients were so strapped for cash to pay utility bills and buy necessities that they had to sell some of their food stamps for fifty cents on the dollar to those slightly better off than themselves, which resulted in further stratification at the bottom of the income ladder, perhaps more aptly described by then as a pecking ladder (DeParle 2012).

THE VIEW FROM 2012

Although the Great Recession officially ended in June 2009, the United States remained in a depression, defined by Keynes in 1930 as a "chronic condition of subnormal activity for a considerable period without any marked tendency either towards recovery or towards complete collapse," for another three years (Krugman 2012a, p. x). During that time the country suffered a loss of $3 trillion in economic growth that could never be recovered. It also experienced an unemployment rate that peaked at 10 percent in October 2009 (four months after the recession formally ended) and stayed above 9 percent for all but one of the next twenty-three months, followed by eleven months above 8 percent. In early 2009 the Obama administration had underestimated the depth of the crisis and then sent Congress an anemic stimulus package that its economists knew was too small (Scheiber 2011). The Republicans then resisted every attempt at doing more.

Armed with the filibuster in the Senate and a majority in the House, the Republicans did agree at the last minute to a bargain that preserved most of the Bush-era tax cuts and staved off self-imposed draconian reductions in government spending that were meant to force Democrats and Republicans to make just the sort of deal they finally made. In exchange, the Democrats achieved the extension of unemployment benefits for one year and of the Earned Income Tax Credit, the child tax credit, and education tax credits for five years. Although the compromise was hailed as a Democratic victory because it saved the economy from a potential slide into another recession and helped individuals and families with low incomes, the corporate rich and highly paid professionals preserved most of their gains from the George W. Bush era, even though the tax on earned income was raised from 35 to 39.6 percent on earned income over $400,000 ($450,000 for a married couple), and from 15 to 20 percent on dividends and capital gains for those with incomes over $400,000. Moreover, and of far greater importance to the corporate rich than to professionals, up to $5 million in yearly gifts and inheritable estates were exempted from taxation (and the $5 million was indexed for inflation). The tax on anything over that amount was only raised from 35 to 40 percent, which meant that family fortunes could be passed on to children largely intact even without the use of esoteric trust arrangements and other traditional tax-avoidance strategies. In addition to the personal benefits for the corporate rich, their general strategy of constricting revenues for discretionary domestic social spending was reinforced, and Wall Street received an $11-billion-a-year windfall through the extension of the "active financing exemption," which allows financial companies to defer taxes on profits made (or surreptitiously moved) overseas.

Whatever the foreseeable future may bring, whether mild reforms by an enlarged and refurbished liberal-labor alliance or a continuing assault on Social Security benefits, veterans' benefits, discretionary spending, and government regulation by a well-fortified corporate-conservative alliance, it appears very likely that the corporate rich will continue to reign. The years from 1976 to 2012 marked nothing less than the triumph of the corporate rich after its four previous decades of hotly contested battles with a liberal-labor alliance that was weakened by racial discrimination, religious disagreements, and numerous other divisive social issues.

References

Akard, Patrick. 1992. "Corporate mobilization and political power: The transformaton of US economic policy in the 1970s." *American Sociological Review* 57:597–615.

———. 1996. "The political origins of 'supply-side' economic policy: The Humphrey-Hawkins Bill and the Revenue Act of 1978." *Political Power and Social Theory* 10:95–148.

Alba, Richard. 1973. "A graph-theoretic definition of a sociometric clique." *Journal of Mathematical Sociology* 3:113–126.

Alba, Richard, and Gwen Moore. 1978. "Elite social circles." *Sociological Methods and Research* 7:167–188.

Alexander, Herbert E. 1971. *Financing the election: 1968.* Lexington, MA: Heath Lexington Books.

———. 1976. *Financing politics: Money, elections, and political reform.* Washington, DC: Congressional Quarterly Press.

———. 1979. *Financing the 1976 election.* Washington, DC: Congressional Quarterly Press.

Allen, Julius. 1978. *Costs and benefits of federal regulation: An overview.* Washington, DC: Congressional Research Service.

Alpert, Irvine, and Ann Markusen. 1980. "Think tanks and capitalist policy." Pp. 173–197 in *Power structure research,* edited by G. W. Domhoff. Beverly Hills, CA: Sage.

Altman, Nancy. 2005. *The battle for Social Security: From FDR's vision to Bush's gamble.* New York: John Wiley and Sons.

American Enterprise Institute. 1975. "Nobel Laureate Hayek guest at AEI discussion." *AEI Notes,* p. 3.

Anderson, Martin. 1990. *Revolution: The Reagan legacy.* Stanford, CA: Hoover Institution Press.

Applebaum, Binyamin. 2012. "For US families, net worth falls to 1990s levels." *New York Times,* June 12, p. A1.

Arieff, Irwin. 1978. "Carter dealt major defeat on consumer bill." *Congressional Quarterly,* February 11, pp. 323–325.

Arsenault, Raymond. 2006. *Freedom rider: 1961 and the struggle for racial justice.* New York: Oxford University Press.

Ashe, A. J. 1975. "Letter to Alfred Neal, November 17." *Committee for Economic Development Archives, President's Trustee Files: Ashe.* Washington, DC: Committee for Economic Development.

Associated Press. 1984. "Business leaders urge cuts in Social Security." *San Francisco Chronicle,* February 16, p. 16.

Bailey, Stephen K. 1950. *Congress makes a law: The story behind the Employment Act of 1946.* New York: Columbia University Press.

Baker, Dean. 2001. "Defaulting on the Social Security Trust Fund bonds: Winner and losers." Washington, DC: Center for Economic and Political Research.

———. 2007. *The United States since 1980.* New York: Cambridge University Press.

———. 2009. *Plunder and blunder: The rise and fall of the bubble economy.* Sausalito, CA: PoliPoint Press.

———. 2012. "Why middle class has taken a big hit." CNN.com, June 13, http://edition.cnn.com/2012/06/13/opinion/baker-family-worth/index.html.

Baker, Dean, and Mark Weisbrot. 1999. *Social Security: The phony crisis.* Chicago: University of Chicago Press.

Ball, Robert. 1990. Telephone interview with G. William Domhoff, August 7.

———. 2010. *What really happened: The Greenspan Commission.* New York: Century Foundation Press.

Baltzell, E. Digby. 1964. *The Protestant establishment: Aristocracy and caste in America.* New York: Random House.

Bank, Steven. 2010. *From sword to shield: The transformation of the corporate income tax, 1861 to present.* New York: Oxford University Press.

Bank, Steven, Kirk Stark, and Joseph Thorndike. 2008. *War and taxes.* Washington, DC: Urban Institute Press.

Barber, William. 1975. "The Kennedy Years: Purposeful pedagogy." Pp. 135–192 in *Exhortation and control: The search for a wage-price policy 1945–1971,* edited by C. Goodwin. Washington, DC: Brookings Institution.

Bartels, Larry M. 2010. *Unequal democracy: The political economy of the new Guilded Age.* Princeton, NJ: Princeton University Press.

Bauer, Raymond, Ithiel de Sola Pool, and Lewis Dexter. 1963. *American business and public policy: The politics of foreign trade.* New York: Atherton Press.

Berkowitz, Edward. 1987. "The first Advisory Council and the 1939 amendments." Pp. 55–78 in *Social Security after fifty: Success and failures,* edited by E. Berkowitz. New York: Greenwood Press.

———. 2003. *Robert Ball and the politics of Social Security.* Madison: University of Wisconsin Press.

———. 2006. *Something happened: A political and cultural overview of the Seventies.* New York: Columbia University Press.

Berman, Daniel. 1978. *Death on the job: Occupational health and safety struggles in the United States.* New York: Monthly Review Press.

Bernstein, Barton. 1965. "The removal of War Production Board controls on business, 1944–1946." *Business History Review* 39:243–260.

———. 1967a. "Clash of interests: The postwar battle between the Office of Price Administration and the Department of Agriculture." *Agricultural History* 41:45–58.

———. 1967b. "The debate on industrial reconversion: The protection of oligopoly and military control of the economy." *American Journal of Economics and Sociology* 26:159–172.

Bernstein, Irving. 1996. *Guns or butter: The presidency of Lyndon Johnson.* New York: Oxford University Press.

Bernstein, Merton, and Joan Brodshaug. 1988. *Social Security: The system that works.* New York: Basic Books.

Berry, Jeffrey M. 1999. *The new liberalism: The rising power of citizen groups.* Washington, DC: Brookings Institution.

Binder, Sarah, and Steven Smith. 1997. *Politics or principle? Filibustering in the United States Senate.* Washington, DC: Brookings Institution.

Biven, W. Carl. 2002. *Jimmy Carter's economy: Policy in an age of limits.* Chapel Hill: University of North Carolina Press.

Blough, Roger. 1968/1972. "The case for limiting steel imports (*Los Angeles Times,* September 20, 1968)." Pp. 427–431 in *Issues in business and society,* edited by G. Steiner. New York: Random House.

Bluestone, Barry, and Bennett Harrison. 1982. *The deindustrialization of America: Plant closings, community abandonment, and the dismantling of basic industry.* New York: Basic Books.

Blum, John. 1967. *From the Morgenthau diaries: Years of war, 1941–1945.* Boston: Houghton Mifflin.

———. 1976. *V was for Victory.* New York: Harcourt Brace Jovanovich.

Bonacich, Phillip. 1972. "Technique for analyzing overlapping memberships." In *Sociological Methodology,* edited by H. Costner. San Francisco: Jossey-Bass.

Bonacich, Phillip, and G. William Domhoff. 1981. "Latent classes and group membership." *Social Networks* 3:175–196.

Bonafede, Dom. 1965. "Our sideline congressmen." *New York Herald Tribune,* p. 1.

Bosworth, Barry. 1975a. "Some notes for the meeting of the Subcommittee for the New Inflation, February." Philip M. Klutznick Papers, Box 203, Folder 8. Chicago: University of Chicago Regenstein Library.

———. 1975b. "Some notes for the meeting of the Subcommittee for the New Inflation, September." Philip M. Klutznick Papers, Box 204, Folder 4. Chicago: University of Chicago Regenstein Library.

———. 1992. Telephone interview with G. William Domhoff, September 30.

Bower, Marvin. 1975. "Letter to John Coleman, January 22." Philip M. Klutznick Papers, Box 203, Folder 7. Chicago: University of Chicago Regenstein Library.

Boyle, Kevin. 1995. *The UAW and the heyday of American liberalism.* Ithaca, NY: Cornell University Press.

———. 1998. "Little more than ashes: The UAW and American reform in the 1960s." Pp. 217–238 in *Organized labor and American politics, 1894–1994: The labor-liberal alliance,* edited by K. Boyle. Albany: State University of New York Press.

Brady, David, and Charles Bullock. 1980. "Is there a conservative coalition in the House?" *Journal of Politics* 42:549–559.

Brinkley, Alan. 1995. *The end of reform: New Deal liberalism in recession and war.* New York: Knopf.

Brown, Michael K. 1999. *Race, money, and the American welfare state.* Ithaca, NY: Cornell University Press.

Brownlee, W. Elliot. 2000. "Historical perspective on US tax policy toward the rich." Pp. 29–73 in *Does Atlas shrug? The economic consequences of taxing the rich,* edited by J. Slemrod. Cambridge, MA: Harvard University Press.

———. 2004. *Federal taxation in America: A short history.* New York: Cambridge University Press.

Brownlow, Louis. 1958. *A passion for anonymity: The autobiography of Louis Brownlow,* vol. 2. Chicago: University of Chicago Press.

Bureau of Labor Statistics. 2012. "Union membership 2011 USDL-12-0094: Bureau of Labor Statistics." Washington, DC: Department of Labor.

Burke, Bob, and Ralph Thompson. 2000. *Bryce Harlow: Mr. Integrity.* Oklahoma City: Oklahoma Heritage Association.

Burman, Leonard. 1999. *The labyrinth of capital gains tax policy: A guide for the perplexed.* Washington, DC: Brookings Institution.

Burris, Val. 1992. "Elite policy-planning networks in the United States." *Research in Politics and Society* 4:111–134.

———. 2008. "The interlock structure of the policy-planning network and the right turn in US state policy." *Research in Political Sociology* 17:3–42.

Business Roundtable. 1973. "The Business Roundtable: The purpose and the challenge." *Business Roundtable.* Washington, DC: Laborers' International Union of North America.

Business Week. 1974. "The Fed braces for a political storm." *Business Week,* May 11, p. 34.

Byrom, Fletcher. 1978. "Letter to CED Trustees, August 23." *Committee for Economic Development Archives, President's Trustee Files: Byrom.* Washington, DC: Committtee for Economic Development.

Campagna, Anthony. 1994. *The economy in the Reagan years: The economic consequences of the Reagan administrations.* Westport, CT: Greenwood Press.

Campbell, Alec. 2004. "The invisible welfare state: Establishing the phenomenon of twentieth century veterans' benefits." *Journal of Political and Military Sociology* 32:249–267.

———. 2010. "The sociopolitical origins of the American Legion." *Theoretical Sociology* 39:1–24.

Campbell, Christina. 1962. *The Farm Bureau and the New Deal.* Urbana: University of Illinois Press.

Campbell, Levin. 1946. *The Industry-Ordnance Team.* New York: Harcourt Brace.

Cannon, Lou. 2000. *President Reagan: The role of a lifetime.* New York: Public Affairs Press.

Carliner, Michael. 1998. "Development of Federal Homeownership Policy." *Housing Policy Debate* 9:299–321.

Carmines, Edward G., and James A. Stimson. 1989. *Issue evolution: Race and the transformation of American politics.* Princeton, NJ: Princeton University Press.

Carosso, Vincent. 1970. *Investment banking in America.* Cambridge, MA: Harvard University Press.

Carter, Dan. 2000. *The politics of rage: George Wallace, the origins of the new conservatism, and the transformation of American politics.* Baton Rouge: Louisiana State University Press.

Catton, Bruce. 1948. *The war lords of Washington.* New York: Harcourt Brace.

Challenge. 1975. "For a national economic planning system: The Initiative Committee for National Economic Planning." *Challenge,* March–April, pp. 51–52, 64.

Chamberlain, Andrew. 2006. "Twenty years later: The Tax Reform Act of 1986." Tax Foundation blog, www.taxfoundation.org/blog/show/1951.html.

Champagne, Anthony, Douglas Harris, James Riddlesperger, and Garrison Nelson. 2009. *The Austin/Boston connection: Five decades of House Democratic leadership, 1937–1989.* College Station: Texas A&M Press.

Citizens for Tax Justice. 2012. "Big no-tax corps just keep on dodging." www.ctj.org/.

Clausen, Aage R. 1973. *How congressmen decide: A policy focus.* New York: St. Martin's Press.

Clawson, Dan, Alan Neustadtl, and Mark Weller. 1998. *Dollars and votes: How business campaign contributions subvert democracy.* Philadelphia: Temple University Press.

Clawson, Marion. 1981. *New Deal planning: The National Resource Planning Board.* Baltimore: Johns Hopkins University Press.

Cochrane, James. 1975. "The Johnson Administration: Moral suasion goes to war." Pp. 193–293 in *Exhortation and control: The search for a wage-price policy 1945–1971,* edited by C. Goodwin. Washington, DC: Brookings Institution.

Coleman, John R. 1974. *Blue-collar journal: A college president's sabbatical.* Philadelphia: Lippincott.

Collado, Emilio. 1972. "Letter to John Sagan, July 14." *Committee for Economic Development Archives, President's Trustee Files: Collado.* Washington, DC: Committee for Economic Development.

———. 1973. "Speech to Trustees, October 30." *Committee for Economic Development Archives, President's Trustee Files: Collado.* Washington, DC: Committee for Economic Development.

———. 1977. "Memorandum to Trustees, No Date." *Committee for Economic Development Archives, President's Trustee Files: Collado.* Washington, DC: Committee for Economic Development.

Collier, Peter, and David Horowitz. 1976. *The Rockefellers: An American dynasty.* New York: Holt, Rinehart, and Winston.

Collins, Robert M. 1981. *The business response to Keynes, 1929–1964.* New York: Columbia University Press.

———. 2000. *More: The politics of economic growth in postwar America.* New York: Oxford University Press.

Collins, Sharon M. 1997. *Black corporate executives: The making and breaking of a black middle class.* Philadelphia: Temple University Press.

Colwell, Mary Anna. 1993. *Private foundations and public policy: The political role of philanthropy.* New York: Garland.

Committee for Economic Development. 1944a. *A postwar federal tax plan for high employment.* New York: Committee for Economic Development.

———. 1944b. *Report of activities: After two years,* Vol. Report No. 1–2. New York: Committee for Economic Development.

———. 1945a. *American industry looks ahead.* New York: Committee for Economic Development.

———. 1945b. "CED statements in circulation." *CED News,* September, p. 13.

———. 1945c. *International trade, foreign investment, and domestic employment.* New York: Committee for Economic Development.

———. 1945d. *The Bretton Woods proposals: A statement on national policy.* New York: Committee for Economic Development.

———. 1945e. *Toward more production, more jobs, and more freedom.* New York: Committee for Economic Development.

———. 1947a. *An American program of European economic cooperation.* New York: Committee for Economic Development.

———. 1947b. *Taxes and the budget: A program for prosperity in a free economy.* New York: Committee for Economic Development.

———. 1948. *Monetary and fiscal policy for greater economic stability.* New York: Committee for Economic Development.

———. 1953. *Britain's economic problem and its meaning for America.* New York: Committee for Economic Development.

———. 1954. *United States tariff policy.* New York: Committee for Economic Development.

———. 1957. *Soviet progress vs. American enterprise: A report of a confidential briefing session held at the fifteenth anniversary meeting of the Committee for Economic Development.* New York: Committee for Economic Development.

———. 1958a. *Anti-recession policy for 1958.* New York: Committee for Economic Development.

———. 1958b. *Defense against inflation: Policies for price stability in a growing economy.* New York: Committee for Economic Development.

———. 1958c. *The problem of national security; Some economic and administrative aspects.* New York: Committee for Economic Development.

———. 1959. *Paying for better schools.* New York: Committee for Economic Development.

———. 1960a. *Guiding metropolitan growth.* New York: Committee for Economic Development.

———. 1960b. *National objectives and the balance of payments problem.* New York: Committee for Economic Development.

———. 1961a. *Cooperation for progress in Latin America.* New York: Committee for Economic Development.

———. 1961b. *Distressed areas in a growing economy.* New York: Committee for Economic Development.

———. 1961c. *Growth and taxes: Steps for 1961.* New York: Committee for Economic Development.

———. 1961d. *The public interest in national labor policy.* New York: Committee for Economic Development.

———. 1962a. *A new trade policy for the United States.* New York: Committee for Economic Development.

———. 1962b. *Reducing tax rates for production and growth.* New York: Committee for Economic Development.

———. 1964. *Union powers and union functions: Toward a better balance.* New York: Committee for Economic Development.

———. 1965a. *East-West trade: A common policy for the West.* New York: Committee for Economic Development.

———. 1965b. *Raising low incomes through improved education.* New York: Committee for Economic Development.

———. 1966a. *A better balance in federal taxes on business.* New York: Committee for Economic Development.

———. 1966b. *Budgeting for national objectives.* New York: Committee for Economic Development.

———. 1966c. *CED in 1965: A report of activities.* New York: Committee for Economic Development.

———. 1966d. *The dollar and the world monetary system.* New York: Committee for Economic Development.

———. 1968a. *Financing a better election system.* New York: Committee for Economic Development.

———. 1968b. *Innovation in education.* New York: Committee for Economic Development.

———. 1968c. *The national economy and the Vietnam War.* New York: Committee for Economic Development.

———. 1969a. *CED in 1968: Economic resources and social demands.* New York: Committee for Economic Development.

———. 1969b. *Fiscal and monetary policies for steady economic growth.* New York: Committee for Economic Development.

———. 1970a. *Further weapons against inflation.* New York: Committee for Economic Development.

———. 1970b. *Improving the welfare system.* New York: Committee for Economic Development.

———. 1971a. *Leadership for effective social and economic policies: Report of activities 1970.* New York: Committee for Economic Development.

———. 1971b. *The social responsibility of business organizations.* New York: Committee for Economic Development.

———. 1971c. *The United States and the European community: Policies for a changing world economy.* New York: Committee for Economic Development.

———. 1972a. *High employment without inflation.* New York: Committee for Economic Development.

———. 1972b. *Report of activities in 1971.* New York: Committee for Economic Development.

———. 1973. *Building a national health-care system: A statement on national policy.* New York: Committee for Economic Development.

———. 1975. *Progress toward recovery of the economy: CED Symposium.* New York: Committee for Economic Development.

———. 1976a. *Fighting inflation and promoting growth.* New York: Committee for Economic Development.

———. 1976b. "Minutes of the special executive committee meeting, September 20." *Committee for Economic Development Archives.* New York: Committee for Economic Development.

———. 1976c. *The economy in 1977–78: Strategy for an enduring expansion.* New York: Committee for Economic Development.

———. 1978. *An approach to federal urban policy.* New York: Committee for Economic Development.

———. 1979. *Redefining government's role in the market system: A statement on national policy.* New York: Committee for Economic Development.

———. 1980a. *Fighting inflation and rebuilding a sound economy.* New York: Committee for Economic Development.

———. 1980b. "Transcript/subcommittee on inflation." *Committee for Economic Development Archives, Transcript Library.* New York: Committee for Economic Development.

———. 1981. *Reforming retirement policies.* New York: Committee for Economic Development.

———. 1982. *Public-private partnership: An opportunity for urban communities.* New York: Committee for Economic Development.

———. 1984. *Social Security: From crisis to crisis?* New York: Committee for Economic Development.

———. N.D. "CED Impact: Reforming retirement policies and Social Security." *Hurwitz Papers.* Washington, DC: Committee for Economic Development.

Commons, John. 1934. *Myself.* New York: Macmillan.

Congressional Quarterly. 1987. *Power in Congress: Who has it, how they got it, how they use it.* Washington, DC: Congressional Quarterly.

———. 1992. "Southern Democrats may score if fading alliance dissolves." *Congressional Quarterly,* pp. 3845–3848.

———. 1996. "Will the rise of 'blue dogs' revive the partisan right?" *Congressional Quarterly,* December 21, pp. 3436–3438.

Corey, Gordon. 1975. "Letter to Philip M. Klutznick, November 17." Philip M. Klutznick Papers, Box 204, Folder 7. Chicago: University of Chicago Regenstein Library.

Council on Foreign Relations. 1981. *The Soviet threat: A perspective for the 1980s.* New York: Council on Foreign Relations.

Crespino, Joseph. 2008. "Civil rights and the religious right." Pp. 90–105 in *Rightward bound: Making America conservative in the 1970s,* edited by B. Schulman and J. Zelizer. Cambridge, MA: Harvard University Press.

Crittenden, Ann. 1976a. "Business group in favor of tax cut." *New York Times,* December 17, p. A1.

———. 1976b. "Business unit asks 5% jobless ceiling." *New York Times,* August 12, pp. 41, 45.

Cunningham, David. 2004. *There's something happening here: The New Left, the Klan, and FBI counterintelligence.* Berkeley: University of California Press.

Dahlberg, Robert. 1984. "Review of 'Closing the gold window: Domestic politcs and the end of Bretton Woods.'" *Political Science Quarterly* 99:585–586.

Dark, Taylor. 2001. *The unions and the Democrats: An enduring alliance.* Ithaca, NY: Cornell University Press.

David, Donald. 1961. "Confidential Attachment to Letter from Alfred Neal to William Benton, June 2, 'Reactions to CED proposals.'" William F. Benton Papers, Box 262, Folder 3. Chicago: University of Chicago Regenstein Library.

Davidson, Chandler, Tanya Dunlap, Gale Kenny, and Benjamin Wise. 2004. "Republican ballot security programs: Vote protection or minority vote suppression—or both?" Washington, DC: Center for Voting Rights and Protection.

DeFina, Robert, and Murray Weidenbaum. 1978. *The taxpayer and government regulation.* St. Louis: Center for the Study of American Business.

DeLong, J. Bradford. 2012. "Re-Capturing the Friedmans, May 1." *Project syndicate: A world of ideas,* www.project-syndicate.org/commentary/re-capturing-the-friedmans.

Delton, Jennifer. 2009. *Racial integration in corporate America, 1940–1990.* New York: Cambridge University Press.

Dennison, Henry, Lincoln Filene, Ralph Flanders, and Morris Leeds. 1938. *Toward full employment.* New York: McGraw-Hill.

DeParle, Jason. 2012. "Welfare limits left poor adrift as recession hit." *New York Times,* April 8, p. A1.

Dewan, Shaila. 2012. "US winds down longer benefits for the jobless." *New York Times,* May 29, p. A1.

Diamond, Sara. 1995. *Roads to dominion: Right wing movements and political power in the United States.* New York: Guilford Press.

Dixon, Marc. 2007. "Limiting labor: Business political mobilization and union setback in the states." *Journal of Policy History* 19:313–344.

———. 2010. "Union threat, countermovement organization, and labor policy in the states, 1944–1960." *Social Problems* 57:157–174.

Domhoff, G. William. 1978. *Who really rules? New Haven and community power re-examined.* New Brunswick, NJ: Transaction Books.

———. 1987. "Where do government experts come from? The CEA and the policy-planning network." Pp. 189–200 in *Power elites and organizations,* edited by G. W. Domhoff and T. Dye. Beverly Hills, CA: Sage.

———. 1990. *The power elite and the state: How policy is made in America.* Hawthorne, NY: Aldine de Gruyter.

———. 1996. *State autonomy or class dominance? Case studies on policy making in America.* Hawthorne, NY: Aldine de Gruyter.

———. 1998. *Who rules America? Power and politics in the year 2000.* Mountain View, CA: Mayfield.

———. 2010. *Who rules America? Challenges to corporate and class dominance.* New York: McGraw-Hill.

———. 2013. *Who rules America? The triumph of the corporate rich.* New York: McGraw-Hill.

Domhoff, G. William, and Michael J. Webber. 2011. *Class and power in the New Deal: Corporate moderates, Southern Democrats, and the liberal-labor coalition.* Palo Alto, CA: Stanford University Press.

Downes, Brian. 1970. "A critical re-examination of the social and political characteristics of riot cities." *Social Science Quarterly* 51:349–360.

Dreiling, Michael. 2001. *Solidarity and contention: The politics of class and sustainability in the NAFTA conflict.* New York: Garland.

Dreiling, Michael, and Derek Darves. 2011. "Coporate unity in American trade policy: A network analysis of corporate-dyad political action." *American Journal of Sociology* 116:1514–1563.

Duberstein, Kenneth. 1980. "Resume, Kenneth Duberstein." *Committee for Economic Development Archives, President's Staff Files: Duberstein.* Washington, DC: Committee for Economic Development.

———. 1981. "Memo to Sol Hurwitz, February 11." *Committee for Economic Development Archives, President's Staff Files: Duberstein.* Washington, DC: Committee for Economic Development.

Dubofsky, Melvyn, and Warren R. van Tine. 1977. *John L. Lewis: A biography.* New York: Quadrangle/New York Times Book Co.

Duhigg, Charles, and David Kocieniewski. 2012. "How Apple sidesteps billions in taxes." *New York Times,* April 29, p. A1.

Eakins, David. 1969. "Business planners and America's postwar expansion." Pp. 143–171 in *Corporations and the Cold War,* edited by D. Horowitz. New York: Monthly Review Press.

Eberle, William. 1979. "Memo to Robert Holland, July 31." *Committee for Economic Development Archives, President's Trustee Files: Eberle.* Washington, DC: Committee for Economic Development.

Eccles, Mary. 1977. "House rejects labor-backed picketing bill." *Congressional Quarterly,* March 26, pp. 521–524.

Edsall, Thomas B. 1984. *The new politics of inequality.* New York: W. W. Norton.

Edsall, Thomas B., and Mary D. Edsall. 1992. *Chain reaction: The impact of race, rights, and taxes on American politics.* New York: W. W. Norton.

Estes, Carroll. 1983. "Social Security: The social construction of a crisis." *Milkbank Memorial Fund Quarterly* 61:445–461.

Farhang, Sean, and Ira Katznelson. 2005. "The Southern imposition: Congress and labor in the New Deal and Fair Deal." *Studies in American Political Development* 19:1–30.

Feild, John. 1967. "Oral history interview, January 16." John G. Feild Personal Papers. Boston: John F. Kennedy Presidential Library and Museum.

Fennelly, John. 1965. *Memoirs of a bureaucrat: A personal story of the War Production Board.* Chicago: October House.

Fink, Gary. 1998. "Labor law reform and the end of the postwar era." Pp. 239–257 in *Organized labor and American politics, 1894–1994: The labor-liberal alliance,* edited by K. Boyle. Albany: State University of New York Press.

Fisher, Robert. 1994. *Let the people decide: Neighborhood organizing in America.* New York: Twayne.

Fitzgerald, Edmund B. 1975. "Letter to Alfred C. Neal, June 2." *Committee for Economic Development Archives, President's Trustee Files: Fitzgerald.* Washington, DC: Committee for Economic Development.

———. 1996. Personal interview with G. William Domhoff, September 27. Nashville, TN.

Fones-Wolf, Elizabeth. 1994. *Selling free enterprise: The business assault on labor and liberalism, 1945–1960.* Urbana: University of Illinois Press.

Ford Foundation. 1961. *Annual report.* New York: Ford Foundation.

———. 1966. *Annual report.* New York: Ford Foundation.

———. 1972. *Annual report.* New York: Ford Foundation.

Fosdick, Raymond. 1952. *The story of the Rockefeller Foundation.* New York: Harper and Brothers.

Fosler, R. Scott, and R. A. Berger. 1982. "Public-private partnerships in American cities: Seven case studies." Lexington, MA: Lexington Books.

Franklin, William. 1975. "Letter to Trustees, November 3." *Committee for Economic Development Archives, President's Trustee Files: Franklin.* Washington, DC: Committee for Economic Development.

Fraser, Steven. 1991. *Labor will rule: Sidney Hillman and the rise of American labor.* New York: Free Press.

Frederick, William. 1981. "Free market vs. social responsibility: Decision time at the CED." *California Management Review* 23:20–28.

Freidel, Frank. 1973. *Franklin D. Roosevelt: Launching the New Deal.* Boston: Little, Brown.

Friedberg, Aaron. 2000. *In the shadow of the garrison state: America's anti-statism and its cold war grand strategy.* Princeton, NJ: Princeton University Press.

Frieden, Bernard, and Marshall Kaplan. 1975. *The politics of neglect: Urban aid from Model Cities to revenue sharing.* Cambridge, MA: MIT Press.

Frydl, Kathleen. 2009. *The GI Bill.* New York: Cambridge University Press.

Frymer, Paul. 2008. *Black and blue: African Americans, the labor movement, and the decline of the Democratic party.* Princeton, NJ: Princeton University Press.

Fuccillo, Vincent. 1969. "The Committee for Economic Development: A study of a corporate sponsor-participant policy research interest group." PhD diss., Political Science, New York University, New York.

Gall, Gilbert. 1988. *The politics of right to work: The labor federations as special interests, 1943–1979.* New York: Greenwood Press.

Gibbons, William. 1989. *The US government and the Vietnam War: Executive and legislative roles and relationships. Part III: January–July, 1965,* Vol. 3. Princeton, NJ: Princeton University Press.

———. 1995. *The US government and the Vietnam War: Executive and legislative roles and relationships; Part IV: July 1965–January 1968,* Vol. 4. Princeton, NJ: Princeton University Press.

Glickman, Lawrence. 2009. *Buying power: A history of consumer activism in America.* Chicago: University of Chicago Press.

Goertzel, Ted. 1985. "Militarism as a sociological problem." *Research in Political Sociology* 1:119–139.

Goldfield, Michael. 1987. *The decline of organized labor in the United States.* Chicago: University of Chicago Press.

Goldin, Claudia, and Robert Margo. 1992. "The Great Compression: The wage structure in the United States at mid-century." *Quarterly Journal of Economics* 107:1–34.

Golland, David. 2011. *Constructing affirmative action: The struggle for equal employment opportunity.* Lexington: University Press of Kentucky.

Gonzalez, George. 2001. *Corporate power and the environment: The political economy of US environmental policy.* Lanham, MD: Rowman and Littlefield.

———. 2005. *The politics of air pollution.* Albany: State University of New York Press.

Gordon, R. Scott. 1975. "The Eisenhower administration: The doctrine of shared responsibility." Pp. 95–134 in *Exhortation and control: The search for a wage-price policy 1945–1971,* edited by C. Goodwin. Washington, DC: Brookings Institution.

Gotham, Kevin Fox. 2000. "Racialization and the state: The Housing Act of 1934 and the creation of the Federal Housing Administration." *Sociological Perspectives* 43: 291–317.

———. 2002. *Race, real estate, and uneven development.* Albany: State University of New York Press.

Graham, Hugh. 1984. *The uncertain trumpet: Federal education policy in the Kennedy and Johnson years.* Chapel Hill: University of North Carolina Press.

———. 1990. *The civil rights era: Origins and development of national policy, 1960–1972.* New York: Oxford University Press.

Green, Marguerite. 1956. *The National Civic Federation and the American Federation of Labor, 1900–1925.* Washington, DC: Catholic University of America Press.

Green, Mark, and Andrew Buchsbaum. 1980. *The corporate lobbies: Political profiles of the Business Roundtable and the Chamber of Commerce.* Washington, DC: Public Citizen.

Greene, John. 1995. *The presidency of Gerald R. Ford.* Lawrence: University Press of Kansas.

Griffith, Robert. 1982. "Dwight D. Eisenhower and the corporate commonwealth." *American Historical Review* 87:87–122.

Gross, James A. 1981. *The reshaping of the National Labor Relations Board.* Albany: State University of New York Press.

———. 1995. *Broken promise: The subversion of US labor relations policy.* Philadelphia: Temple University Press.

Grossman, Jordan. 2007. "Lyndon Johnson's unfinished legacy: The 1964 State of the Union address and the 'War on Poverty.'" *CUREJ—College Undergraduate Research Electronic Journal,* repository.upenn.edu/cg:PDF download.

Groves, Harold. 1944. *Production, jobs, and taxes: Postwar revision of the federal tax system to help achieve higher production and more jobs.* New York: McGraw-Hill.

Guthrie, Douglas, and Michael McQuarrie. 2005. "Privatization and low-income housing in the United States since 1986." Pp. 15–51 in *Research in political sociology: Politics, class, and the corporation,* vol. 14, edited by H. Prechel. Oxford: Elsevier.

Haar, Charles. 1975. *Between the idea and the reality: A study of the origins, fate, and legacy of the Model Cities Program.* Boston: Little, Brown.

Hacker, Jacob, and Paul Pierson. 2010. *Winner-take-all politics: How Washington made the rich richer—and turned its back on the middle class.* New York: Simon and Schuster.

Hall, Donald. 1969. *Cooperative lobbying.* Tucson: University of Arizona Press.

Halpern, Robert. 1995. *Rebuilding the inner city: A history of neighborhood initiatives to address poverty in the United States.* New York: Columbia University Press.

Hamilton, Richard. 1975. *Restraining myths: Critical studies of US social structure and politics.* New York: Sage.

Hargrove, Erwin, and Samuel Morley. 1984. *The president and the Council of Economic Advisers: Interviews with CEA chairmen.* Boulder, CO: Westview.

Harlow, Bryce. 1975. "Remarks by Bryce N. Harlow at the Chamber of Commerce of the United States, Washington, DC, January 22." Bryce Harlow Papers, Carl Albert Center, University of Oklahoma, Norman. www.ou.edu/special/albertctr/archives/harlow.htm.

Harper, John. 1975. "Letter to Alfred Neal, March 5." Philip M. Klutznick Papers, Box 204, Folder 1. Chicago: University of Chicago Regenstein Library.

———. 1977. "Reply to questionnaire on 'subjects suggested for CED study.'" *Committee for Economic Development Archives, President's Trustee Files: Harper.* Washington, DC: Committee for Economic Development.

Hayek, Frederick von. 1944. *The road to serfdom.* Chicago: University of Chicago Press.

Heinz, John P., Edward O. Laumann, Robert L. Nelson, and Robert H. Salisbury. 1993. *The hollow core: Private interests in national policy making.* Cambridge, MA: Harvard University Press.

Heller, Walter. 1957. "CED's stabilizing budget policy after ten years." *American Economic Review* 42:634–651.

Henchman, Joseph. 2008. "Did 1997 capital gains tax exclusion for housing contribute to economic crisis?" Tax Policy blog at Tax Foundation, September 25, www.taxfoundation .org/blog/show/23659.html.

Hess, Jerry. 1972. "Oral history interview with Dr. Edwin G. Nourse." Edwin G. Nourse Papers. Independence, MO: Harry S. Truman Library and Museum.

Hetzel, Robert, and Ralph Leach. 2001. "The Treasury-Fed Accord: A new narrative account." *Federal Reserve Bank of Richmond Economic Quarterly* 87:33–55.

Himmelberg, Robert. 1976/1993. *The origins of the National Recovery Administration.* New York: Fordham University Press.

Himmelstein, Jerome L. 1990. "To the right: The transformation of American conservatism." Berkeley: University of California Press.

Himmelstein, Jerome, and James McCrae. 1984. "Social conservatism, new Republicans, and the 1980 election." *Public Opinion Quarterly* 48.

Hogan, Michael. 1987. *The Marshall Plan: America, Britain, and the reconstruction of Western Europe, 1947–1952.* New York: Cambridge University Press.

Holl, Richard. 2005. *From the boardroom to the war room: America's corporate liberals and FDR's preparedness program.* Rochester, NY: University of Rochester Press.

Holland, Robert. 1979. "Memo to CED Staff on Beck, October 22." *Committee for Economic Development Archives, President's Trustee Files: Beck File.* Washington, DC: Committee for Economic Development.

———. 1992. Telephone Interview with G. William Domhoff, September 29.

Hooks, Gregory. 1991. *Forging the Military-Industrial Complex: World War II's battle of the Potomac.* Urbana: University of Illinois Press.

Hoopes, Townsend. 1969. *The limits of intervention: An inside account of how the Johnson policy of escalation in Vietnam was reversed.* New York: D. McKay.

Hormats, Robert. 2007. *The price of liberty: Paying for America's wars.* New York: Times Books.

Howard, Christopher. 1997. *The hidden welfare state: Tax expenditures and social policy in the United States.* Princeton, NJ: Princeton University Press.

Hunter, Floyd. 1959. *Top leadership, USA.* Chapel Hill: University of North Carolina Press.

Hurwitz, Sol. 1989. "Interview with Alfred C. Neal, February 2." *Committee for Economic Development Archives.* Washington, DC: Committee for Economic Development.

———. 1990. "Beyond the bottom line: The impact of the Committee for Economic Development, 1942–1992." *Committee for Economic Development Archives,* Unpublished manuscript. Washington, DC: Committee for Economic Development.

———. 2001. Interview with G. William Domhoff, October 19. Rye, NY.

———. 2011. E-mail communication with G. William Domhoff, June 6.

Huthmacher, J. Joseph. 1973. *Trial by war and depression: 1917–1941.* Boston: Allyn and Bacon.

Isaacson, Walter, and Evan Thomas. 1986. *The wise men: Six friends and the world they made.* New York: Simon and Schuster.

Jacobs, David, and Marc Dixon. 2006. "The politics of labor-management relations: Detecting the conditions that affect change in right-to-work laws." *Social Problems* 53:118–137.

———. 2010. "Political partisanship, race, and union strength from 1970 to 2000: A pooled time-series analysis." *Social Science Research* 39:1059–1072.

Jacobs, Travis. 2004. *Dwight D. Eisenhower and the founding of the American Assembly.* New York: American Assembly.

Jacoby, Sanford. 1997. *Modern manors: Welfare capitalism since the New Deal.* Princeton, NJ: Princeton University Press.

Jenkins, J. Craig, and Teri Shumate. 1985. "Cowboy capitalists and the rise of the 'new right': An analysis of contributors to conservative policy formation organizations." *Social Problems* 33:130–145.

Johnson, Lyndon. 1965. "Annual message to the Congress on the state of the union." *The American Presidency Project.* Santa Barbara: University of California. www.presidency .ucsb.edu/ws/index.php?pid=26907#ixzz1h7ysZOUG.

Johnson, Stephen. 1976. "How the West was won: Last shootout for the Yankee-Cowboy theory." *Insurgent Sociologist* 6:61–93.

Johnson, Stephen, and Joseph Taney. 1982. "The Christian Right and the 1980 presidential election." *Journal for the Scientific Study of Religion* 21:123–131.

Jones, Jesse. 1951. *Fifty billion dollars: My thirteen years with the RFC, 1932–1945.* New York: Macmillan.

Jost, John T., and Jim Sedanius. 2004. *Political psychology: The key readings.* New York: Psychology Press.

Kang, Samuel, and Tuan Ngo. 2011. "Corporate America untaxed: Tax avoidance on the rise." Greenlining Institute, Berkeley, CA, www.greenlining.org.

Katznelson, Ira, Kim Geiger, and Daniel Kryder. 1993. "Limiting liberalism: The Southern veto in Congress, 1933–1950." *Political Science Quarterly* 108:283–306.

Kaufman, Richard. 1970. *The war profiteers.* New York: Bobbs Merrill.

Kazee, Nicole, Michael Lipsky, and Cathie Jo Martin. 2008. "Outside the big box: Who speaks for small business?" *Boston Review,* July/August, http://bostonreview.net/BR33.4/kazee.php.

Kelly, Erin, and Frank Dobbin. 2001. "How affirmative action became diversity management: Employer responses to antidiscrimination law, 1961–1996." Pp. 87–117 in *Color lines: Affirmative action, immigration, and civil rights options for America,* edited by J. Skrentny. Chicago: University of Chicago Press.

Keynes, John Maynard. 1919. *The economic consequences of the peace.* London: Macmillan.

Kimeldorf, Howard. 2013. "Worker replacement costs and unionization: Origins of the American labor movement." Unpublished manuscript, Department of Sociology, University of Michigan.

Kingson, Eric. 1984. "Financing Social Security: Agenda-setting and the enactment of the 1983 amendments to the Social Security Act." *Policy Studies Journal* 13:131–155.

Kleinknecht, William. 2009. *The man who sold the world: Ronald Reagan and the betrayal of ordinary Americans.* New York: Basic Books.

Klutznick, Philip M. 1975a. "Attacking the double-trouble of inflation and recession: Statement by Philip M. Klutznick at Luncheon of the Research and Policy Policy." Philip M. Klutznick Papers, Box 203, Folder 7. Chicago: University of Chicago Regenstein Library.

———. 1975b. "Letter to Alfred Neal, March 12." Philip M. Klutznick Papers, Box 204, Folder 1. Chicago: University of Chicago Regenstein Library.

———. 1975c. "Letter to Gordon Corey, November 25." Philip M. Klutznick Papers, Box 204, Folder 7. Chicago: University of Chicago Regenstein Library.

Knapp, Daniel, and Kenneth Polk. 1971. *Scouting the war on poverty.* Boston: Heath Lexington.

Kopczuk, Wojciech, Emmanuel Saez, and Jae Song. 2010. "Earnings inequality and mobility in the United States: Evidence from social security data since 1937." *Quarterly Journal of Economics,* pp. 81–128.

Kraska, Peter, and Victor Kaeppler. 1997. "Militarizing American police: The rise and normalization of paramilitary units." *Social Problems* 44:1–18.

Krugman, Paul. 1994. *Peddling prosperity: Economic sense and nonsense in the age of diminished expectations.* New York: W. W. Norton.

———. 2007. *The conscience of a liberal.* New York: W. W. Norton.

———. 2011a. "An insurance company with an army." *New York Times,* April 27, http://krugman.blogs.nytimes.com/2011/04/27/an-insurance-company-with-an-army/.

———. 2011b. "The Un-COLA era." *New York Times,* February 1, http://krugman.blogs.nytimes.com/2011/02/01/the-un-cola-era/.

———. 2012a. *End this depression now!* New York: W. W. Norton.

———. 2012b. "What a real external bank bailout looks like." *The conscience of a liberal,* June 17, http://krugman.blogs.nytimes.com/2012/06/17/what-a-real-external-bank-bailout-looks-like/.

Lagemann, Ellen. 1989. *The politics of knowledge: The Carnegie Corporation, philanthropy, and public policy.* Middletown, CT: Wesleyan University Press.

Lakoff, George. 1996. *Moral politics: What conservatives know that liberals don't.* Chicago: University of Chicago Press.

Larry, R. Heath. 1975. "Letter to Donald Platten, October 22." *Committee for Economic Development Archives, President's Trustee Files: Larry.* Washington, DC: Committee for Economic Development.

———. 1976. "Letter to Richard Shinn, December 28." *Committee for Economic Development Archives, President's Trustee Files: Larry.* Washington, DC: Committee for Economic Development.

Laumann, Edward, and David Knoke. 1987. *The organizational state.* Madison: University of Wisconsin Press.

Leonhardt, David. 2012. "Coming soon: Tax 'Armageddon.'" *New York Times,* April 15, pp. SR1, SR15–16.

Leuchtenburg, William. 1963. *Franklin D. Roosevelt and the New Deal, 1932–1940.* New York: Harper and Row.

Levitan, Sar, and Martha Cooper. 1984. *Business lobbies: The public good and the bottom line.* Baltimore: Johns Hopkins University Press.

Lewis, Jonathan. 2002. *Spy capitalism: ITEK and the CIA.* New Haven, CT: Yale University Press.

Lindsay, Franklin. 1975. "Letter to Philip M. Klutznick, April 8." Philip M. Klutznick Papers, Box 204, Folder 2. Chicago: University of Chicago Regenstein Library.

———. 1992. Intereview with G. William Domhoff, September 24. Palo Alto, CA.

Liou, Thomas Y., and Robert C. Stroh. 1998. "Community development intermediary systems in the United States: Origins, evolution, and functions." *Housing Policy Debate* 9: 575–594.

Littlewood, Thomas. 2004. *Soldiers back home: The American Legion in Illinois.* Carbondale: Southern Illinois University Press.

Logan, John, and Harvey Molotch. 1987/2007. *Urban fortunes: The political economy of place.* Berkeley: University of California Press.

Magat, Richard. 1979. *The Ford Foundation at work: Philanthropic choices, methods, and styles.* New York: Plenum Press.

Manley, John F. 1970. *The politics of finance: The House Committee on ways and means.* Boston: Little, Brown.

———. 1973. "The conservative coalition in congress." *American Behavioral Scientist* 17:223–247.

Manza, Jeff. 1995. "Policy experts and political change during the New Deal." PhD diss., Sociology, University of California, Berkeley.

Marchi, Neil. 1975. "The first Nixon administration: Prelude to controls." Pp. 295–352 in *Exhortation and control: The search for a wage-price policy, 1945–1971,* edited by C. Goodwin. Washington, DC: Brookings Institution.

Mariolis, Peter. 1975. "Interlocking directorates and control of corporations." *Social Sciences Quarterly* 56:425–439.

Marmor, Theodore. 2000. *The politics of medicare.* Hawthorne, NY: Aldine de Gruyter.

Marris, Peter, and Martin Rein. 1982. *Dilemmas of social reform: Poverty and community action in the United States.* Chicago: University of Chicago Press.

Martin, Cathie Jo. 1996. "American business and the taxing state: Alliances for growth in the postwar period." In *Funding the modern American state, 1941–1995,* edited by W. E. Brownlee. New York: Cambridge University Press.

Matusow, Allen. 1998. *Nixon's economy.* Lawrence: University Press of Kansas.

Mauss, Marcel. 1924/1969. *The gift: Forms and functions of exchange in archaic societies.* London: Cohen and West.

Mayer, Gerald. 2004. *Union membership trends in the United States.* Congressional Research Service, http://digitalcommons.ilr.cornell.edu/key_workplace/174.

Mayhew, David. 1991. *Divided we govern: Party control, lawmaking, and investigations, 1946–1990.* New Haven, CT: Yale University Press.

McAdam, Doug. 1982. *Political process and the development of Black insurgency, 1930–1970.* Chicago: University of Chicago Press.

McAdams, Alan. 1964. *Power and politics in labor legislation.* New York: Columbia University Press.

McCammon, Holly J. 1990. "Legal limits on labor militancy: US labor law and the right to strike since the New Deal." *Social Problems* 37:206–229.

———. 1994. "Disorganizing and reorganizing conflict: Outcomes of the state's legal regulation of the strike since the Wagner Act." *Social Forces* 72:1011–1049.

McCammon, Holly J., and Melinda D. Kane. 1997. "Shaping judicial law in the post–World War II period: When is labor's legal mobilization successful?" *Sociological Inquiry* 67:275–298.

McCartin, Joseph. 2011. *Collision course: Ronald Reagan, the air traffic controllers, and the strike that changed America.* New York: Oxford University Press.

McFarland, Andrew. 2004. *Neopluralism: The evolution of political process theory.* Lawrence: University Press of Kansas.

McLellan, David, and Charles Woodhouse. 1960. "The business elite and foreign policy." *Western Political Quarterly* 13:172–190.

McLennan, Kenneth. 1995. Personal interview with G. William Domhoff, March 27. Washington, DC.

McQuaid, Kim. 1976. "The Business Advisory Council in the Department of Commerce, 1933–1961." *Research in Economic History* 1:171–197.

———. 1979. "The frustration of corporate revival in the early New Deal." *Historian* 41:682–704.

———. 1982. *Big business and presidential power from FDR to Reagan.* New York: Morrow.

Melone, Albert. 1977. *Lawyers, public policy, and interest group politics.* Washington, DC: University Press of America.

Mieczkowski, Yanek. 2005. *Gerald Ford and the challenges of the 1970s.* Lexington: University Press of Kentucky.

Miller, Berkeley, and William Canak. 1995a. "Laws as a cause and consequence of public employee unionism." *Industrial Relations Research Association Series,* pp. 346–357.

————. 1995b. "There should be no blanket guarantee: Employers' reactions to public employee unionism, 1965–1975." *Journal of Collective Negotiations in the Public Sector* 24:17–35.

Miller, Norman. 1970. "The machine Democrats." *Washington Monthly,* pp. 70–73.

Millett, John. 1954. *The Army Service Forces: The organization and role of the Army Service Forces.* Washington, DC: Department of the Army.

Mills, C. Wright. 1948. *The new men of power: America's labor leaders.* New York: Harcourt, Brace.

Mintz, Beth, and Michael Schwartz. 1981. "Interlocking Directorates and Interest Group Formation." *American Sociological Review* 46:851–869.

————. 1985. *The power structure of American business.* Chicago: University of Chicago Press.

Mitchell, Robert. 1991. "From conservation to environmental movement: The development of the modern environmental lobbies." Pp. 81–113 in *Governmental and environmental politics,* edited by M. Lacey. Baltimore: Johns Hopkins University Press.

Mizruchi, Mark. 1982. *The American corporate network, 1904–1974.* Beverly Hills, CA: Sage.

————. 1983. "Relations among large American corporations, 1904–1974." *Social Science History* 7:165–182.

Molotch, Harvey. 1972. *Managed integration: Dilemmas of doing good in the city.* Berkeley: University of California Press.

Moore, William. 1998. "The determinants and effects of right-to-work laws: A review of the recent literature." *Journal of Labor Research* 19:445–469.

Morgenstern, Oskar. 1963. *On the accuracy of economic observations.* Princeton, NJ: Princeton University Press.

Moss, David. 1996. *Socializing security: Progressive era economists and the origins of American social policy.* Cambridge, MA: Harvard University Press.

Moynihan, Daniel. 1973. *The politics of a guaranteed income: The Nixon administration and the Family Assistance Plan.* New York: Random House.

————. 1988. "Conspirators, trillions, limos in the night." *New York Times,* May 23, p. A15.

Mueller, John E. 1973. *War, presidents, and public opinion.* New York: Wiley.

————. 1984. "Reflections on the Vietnam antiwar movement and on the curious calm at the war's end." Pp. 151–157 in *Vietnam as history: Ten years after the Paris Peace Accords,* edited by P. Braestrup. Washington, DC: University Press of America.

Musgrave, Richard. 1947. "Book review." *Review of Economic Statistics* 2009:203–206.

Myles, John. 1981. "The trillion dollar misunderstanding." *Social Policy* (July–August): 25–31.

Nathan, Robert. 1995. Interview with G. William Domhoff, March 28. Alexandria, VA.

Neal, Alfred. 1975a. "Letter to Donald Platten, November 14." *Committee for Economic Development Archives, President's Trustee Files: Platten.* Washington, DC: Committee for Economic Development.

————. 1975b. "Letter to Emilio Collado, Philip M. Klutznick, and William Franklin, June 20." Philip M. Klutznick Papers, Box 204, Folder 2. Chicago: University of Chicago Regenstein Library.

————. 1975c. "Letter to Philip M. Klutznick and Howard C. Petersen, November 17." *Committee for Economic Development Archives, President's Trustee Files: Harper.* Washington, DC: Committee for Economic Development.

————. 1975d. "Letter to Philip M. Klutznick, September 24." Philip M. Klutznick Papers, Box 204, Folder 4. Chicago: University of Chicago Regenstein Library.

————. 1975e. "Memorandum to Philip M. Klutznick, Frank Schiff, Sol Hurwitz, March 6." Philip M. Klutznick Papers, Box 204, Folder 1. Chicago: University of Chicago Regenstein Library.

————. 1981. *Business power and public policy.* New York: Praeger.

New York Times. 1975. "$20-billion tax cut urged by private economic unit." January 10, p. 14.
———. 1981. "Foreign affairs council backs higher arms outlay." May 14, p. 10.
———. 2012a. "Effective income tax rates." January 18, www.nytimes.com/interactive/2012/01/18/us/effective-income-tax-rates.html.
———. 2012b. "Shrinking corporate tax rates." April 28, www.nytimes.com/interactive/2012/04/28/business/Shrinking-Corporate-Tax-Rates.html.
Newman, Philip. 2012. "City's 1% made up 1/3 of 2009 income: Study." *Queens Time Ledger,* www.timesledger.com/stories/2012/21/incomedisparity_all_2012_05_24_q.html.
Nielsen, Waldemar. 1972. *The big foundations.* New York: Columbia University Press.
Nieuwbeerta, Paul, Clem Brooks, and Jeff Manza. 2006. "Cleavage-based voting in cross-national perspective: Evidence from six countries." *Social Science Research* 35:88–128.
Nitze, Paul. 1980. "The origins of NSC-68." *International Security* 4:170–176.
Noble, Charles. 1986. *Liberalism at work: The rise and fall of OSHA.* Philadelphia: Temple University Press.
Nossiter, Bernard. 1990. *Fat years and lean: The American economy since Roosevelt.* New York: Harper and Row.
O'Connor, Alice. 1996. "Community action, urban reform, and the fight against poverty: The Ford Foundation's Gray Areas program." *Journal of Urban History* 22 (July): 586–625.
———. 1999. "The Ford Foundation and philanthropic activism in the 1960s." Pp. 169–194 in *Philanthropic foundations: New scholarship, new possibilities,* edited by E. Lagemann. Bloomington: Indiana University Press.
Okner, Benjamin. 1972. "Alternatives for transferring income to the poor: The Family Assistant Plan and universal income supplements." Pp. 348–353 in *Redistribution to the rich and the poor: The grants economics of income distribution,* edited by K. Boulding and M. Pfaff. Belmont, CA: Wadsworth.
Olson, James. 1988. *Saving capitalism: The Reconstruction Finance Corporation and the New Deal, 1933–1940.* Princeton, NJ: Princeton University Press.
Page, Benjamin, and Robert Y. Shapiro. 1992. *The rational public: Fifty years of trends in Americans' policy preferences.* Chicago: University of Chicago Press.
Parrish, Michael E. 1970. *Securities regulation and the New Deal.* New Haven, CT: Yale University Press.
Pastor, Robert. 1980. *Congress and the politics of US foreign economic policy, 1929–1976.* Berkeley: University of California Press.
Patterson, James T. 1967/1981. *Congressional conservatism and the New Deal: The growth of the conservative coalition in Congress, 1933–1939.* Lexington: University of Kentucky Press.
Paul, Randolph. 1954. *Taxation in the United States.* Boston: Little, Brown.
Pearson, Drew, and Jack Anderson. 1968. *The case against Congress: A compelling indictment of corruption on Capitol Hill.* New York: Simon and Schuster.
Pedriana, Nicholas, and Robin Stryker. 2004. "The strength of a weak agency: Enforcement of Title VII of the 1964 Civil Rights Act and the expansion of state capacity, 1965–1971." *American Journal of Sociology* 110:709–760.
Peirce, Neil R., and Carol F. Steinbach. 1987. *Corrective capitalism: The rise of American community development corporations.* New York: Ford Foundation.
Peoples, James. 1998. "Deregulation and the labor market." *Journal of Economic Perspectives* 12:111–112.
Peschek, Joseph. 1987. *Policy-planning organizations: Elite agendas and America's rightward turn.* Philadelphia: Temple University Press.

Pessen, Edward. 1984. *The log cabin myth: The social backgrounds of the presidents.* New Haven, CT: Yale University Press.

Philippon, Thomas. 2012. "Has the US finance industry become less efficient? On the theory and measurement of financial intermediation." New York: Stern School of Business, New York University.

Phillips-Fein, Kim. 2009. *Invisible hands: The making of the conservative movement from the New Deal to Reagan.* New York: W. W. Norton.

Piven, Frances, and Richard Cloward. 1971/1993. *Regulating the poor: The functions of public welfare.* New York: Vintage Books.

Piven, Frances, Lorraine Minnite, and Margaret Groarke. 2009. *Keeping down the black vote: Race and the demobilization of American voters.* New York: New Press.

Poen, Monte. 1979. *Harry S. Truman versus the medical lobby: The genesis of Medicare.* Columbia: University of Missouri Press.

Potter, Wendell. 2010. *Deadly spin: An insurance company insider speaks out on how corporate PR is killing health care and deceiving Americans.* New York: Bloomsbury Press.

Preeg, Ernest. 1970. *Traders and diplomats: An analysis of the Kennedy round of negotiations under the General Agreement on Tariffs and Trade.* Washington, DC: Brookings Institution.

President's Advisory Committee. 1953. *The president's advisory committee on government housing policies and programs.* Washington, DC: US Goverment Printing Office.

Quadagno, Jill S. 1988. *The transformation of old age security: Class and politics in the American welfare state.* Chicago: University of Chicago Press.

———. 1990. "Race, class, and gender in the US welfare state: Nixon's failed Family Assistance Plan." *American Sociological Review* 55:11–28.

———. 1994. *The color of welfare: How racism undermined the war on poverty.* New York: Oxford University Press.

———. 2005. *One nation, uninsured: Why the US has no national health insurance.* New York: Oxford University Press.

———. 2011. "Interest-group influence on the Patient Protection and Affordability Act of 2010: Winners and losers in the health care reform debate." *Journal of Health Politics, Policy, and Law* 36:449–453.

Quadagno, Jill S., and Deana Rohlinger. 2009. "Religious conservatives in US welfare state politics." Pp. 236–266 in *Religion, class coalitions, and welfare states,* edited by K. Kersbergen and P. Manow. Cambridge: Cambridge University Press.

Reagan, Patrick. 1999. *Designing a new America: The origins of New Deal planning, 1890–1943.* Amherst: University of Massachusetts Press.

Roberts, Alasdair. 1994. "Demonstrating neutrality: The Rockefeller philanthropies and the evolution of public administration, 1927–1936." *Public Administration Review,* pp. 221–228.

Robinson, Marshall. 1993. "The Ford Foundation: Sowing the seeds of a revolution." *Environment,* pp. 10–20.

Robyn, Dorothy. 1987. *Braking the special interests: Trucking deregulation and the politics of policy reform.* Chicago: University of Chicago Press.

Rohlinger, Deana. 2002. "Framing the abortion debate: Organizational resources, media strategies, and movement-countermovement dynamics." *Sociological Quarterly* 43:479–507.

Roof, Tracy. 2011. *American labor, Congress, and the welfare state, 1935–2010.* Baltimore: Johns Hopkins University Press.

Rosen, Gerald. 1976. "A Plan for the US Economy?" *Dun's Review* (March): 35–37.

Rosenthal, Rob. 1994. *Homeless in paradise: A map of the terrain.* Philadelphia: Temple University Press.

Ross, David. 1969. *Preparing for Ulysses: Politics and veterans during World War II.* New York: Columbia University Press.

Ross, Robert. 1967. "Dimensions and patterns of relating among interest groups at the Congressional level of government." PhD diss., Political Science, Michigan State University, East Lansing.

Rossi, Peter, and Robert Dentler. 1961. *The politics of urban renewal.* New York: Free Press.

Rossiter, Clinton. 1955. *Conservatism in America.* New York: Alfred A. Knopf.

Rowe, Charles. 1978. "Nathan giving up presidency of firm." *Washington Post,* September 5, p. 8.

Ruess, Alejandro. 2009. "That 70s crisis." *Dollars and Sense,* November/December, www.dollarsandsense.org/archives/2009/1109reuss.html.

Saez, Emmanuel. 2012. "Striking it richer: The evolution of top incomes in the United States updated with 2009 and 2010 estimates." Berkeley: Department of Economics, University of California.

Salzman, Harold, and G. William Domhoff. 1980. "The corporate community and government: Do they interlock?" Pp. 227–254 in *Power structure research,* edited by G. W. Domhoff. Beverly Hills, CA: Sage.

———. 1983. "Nonprofit organizations and the corporate community." *Social Science History* 7:205–216.

Sanders, Heywood. 1987. "The politics of development in middle-sized cities: Getting from New Haven to Kalamazoo." Pp. 182–198 in *The politics of urban development,* edited by C. Stone and H. Sanders. Lawrence: University Press of Kansas.

Sanders, Jerry. 1983. *Peddlers of crisis: The Committee on the Present Danger and the politics of containment.* Boston: South End Press.

Scheiber, Noam. 2011. *The escape artists: How Obama's team fumbled the recovery.* New York: Simon and Schuster.

Schiff, Frank. 1990a. Personal Interview with G. William Domhoff, August 9. Berkeley Springs, WV.

———. 1990b. Telephone interview with G. William Domhoff, June 4.

———. 1994. Telephone interview with G. William Domhoff, October 10.

Schlesinger, Arthur. 1958. *The coming of the New Deal.* Boston: Houghton Mifflin.

———. 1965. *A thousand days: John F. Kennedy in the White House.* Boston: Houghton Mifflin.

———. 1975. "Laissez-faire, planning and reality." *Wall Street Journal,* p. 10.

Schriftgiesser, Karl. 1960. *Business comes of age.* New York: Harper and Row.

———. 1967. *Business and public policy.* Englewood Cliffs, NJ: Prentice-Hall.

Schwartz, George. 1979. "The successful fight against a federal consumer protection agency." *MSU Business Topics* 27:45–56.

Schwarz, Jordan. 1981. *The speculator: Bernard M. Baruch in Washington, 1917–1965.* Chapel Hill: University of North Carolina Press.

Seefeldt, Kristin, Gordon Abner, Joe Bolinger, Lanlan Xu, and John Graham. 2012. "At risk: America's poor during and after the Great Recession." Bloomingon: School of Public and Environmental Affairs, Indiana University.

Shanahan, Eileen. 1975. "Antitrust bill stopped by a business lobby." *New York Times,* November 16, pp. A1, 74.

———. 1976a. "Carter gets 2 plans for tax reductions and creation of jobs." *New York Times,* December 10, p. A1.

———. 1976b. "Ford now opposes damage-suit law." *New York Times,* March 17, pp. 59, 66.

Shelley, Mack C. 1983. *The permanent majority: The conservative coalition in the United States Congress.* Tuscaloosa: University of Alabama Press.

Shoup, Laurence. 1974. "Shaping the national interest: The Council on Foreign Relations, the Department of State, and the origins of the postwar world." PhD diss., History, Northwestern University, Evanston.

———. 1977. "The Council on Foreign Relations and American policy in Southeast Asia, 1940–1973." *Insurgent Sociologist* 7:19–30.

———. 1980. *The Carter presidency, and beyond: Power and politics in the 1980s.* Palo Alto, CA: Ramparts Press.

Silk, Leonard, and David Vogel. 1976. *Ethics and profits: The crisis of confidence in American business.* New York: Simon and Schuster.

Sinclair, Barbara. 1982. *Congressional realignment, 1925–1978.* Austin: University of Texas Press.

Sklar, Holly, and Robert Lawrence. 1981. *Who's who in the Reagan administration.* Boston: South End.

Smith, Jean. 2007. *FDR.* New York: Random House.

Smith, Mark A. 2000. *American business and political power.* Chicago: University of Chicago Press.

Smith, Robert M. 2003. *From blackjacks to briefcases: A history of commercialized strikebreaking and unionbusting in the United States.* Athens: Ohio University Press.

Sonquist, John, and Thomas Koenig. 1975. "Interlocking directorates in the top US corporations." *Insurgent Sociologist* 5:196–229.

Soutar, Douglas. 1974. "RE: Business Roundtable letter to Greenspan, September 18." *Douglas Soutar Papers.* Ithaca, NY: Institute of Industrial and Labor Relations, Cornell University.

———. 1996. Telephone interview with G. William Domhoff.

Spitzer, Elliot. 2011. "A secret scandal: The government and the big banks deceived the public about their $7 trillion secret loan program." *Slate,* November 30, http://org2 .democracyinaction.org/dia/track.jsp?v=2&c=gEdCFRb8ov%2BYF4XPHE3Pvb65% 2B5DK4eo8.

Stein, Herbert. 1969. *The fiscal revolution in America.* Chicago: University of Chicago Press.

Stewart, James. 2011. "Questioning the dogma of tax rates." *New York Times,* August 20, p. B1.

Stone, Charles, and Isabell Sawhill. 1984. *Economic policy in the Reagan years.* Washington, DC: Urban Institute Press.

Sugrue, Thomas. 2001. "Breaking through: The troubled origins of affirmative action in the workplace." Pp. 31–52 in *Color lines: Affirmative action, immigration, and civil rights options for America,* edited by J. Skrentny. Chicago: University of Chicago Press.

———. 2008. *Sweet land of liberty: The forgotten struggle for civil rights in the North.* New York: Random House.

Sutton, Francis, Seymour Harris, Carl Kaysen, and James Tobin. 1956. *The American business creed.* Cambridge, MA: Harvard University Press.

Swenson, Peter. 2002. *Capitalists against markets: The making of labor markets and welfare states in the United States and Sweden.* New York: Oxford University Press.

Thieblot, Armand, and Ronald Cowin. 1972. *Welfare and strikers: The use of public funds to support strikers.* Philadelphia: Industrial Research Unit, Wharton School of Finance and Commerce, University of Pennsylvania.

Thomson, J. Cameron. 1954. *Balance and flexibility in fiscal and monetary policy.* New York: Committee for Economic Development.

Time. 1958. "Business: Roger Blough." June 8.

———. 1969. "Construction: Roger's Roundtable." August 29.

———. 1981. "Tough response: Meeting the Soviet threat." May 25.

Tittle, Diana. 1992. *Rebuilding Cleveland: The Cleveland Foundation and its evolving urban strategy.* Columbus: Ohio State University Press.

Tolchin, Susan, and Martin Tolchin. 1983. *Dismantling America: The rush to deregulate.* New York: Oxford University Press.

Tomkins, Silvan. 1964. "Left and right: A basic dimension of personality and ideology." Pp. 388–411 in *The study of lives,* edited by R. W. White. New York: Atherton Press.

Tribe, Laurence H. 1990. *Abortion: The clash of absolutes.* New York: W. W. Norton.

Unekis, Joseph. 1993. "Blocking the liberal agenda in house committees: The role of the conservative coalition." *Congress and the Presidency* 20:93–99.

Useem, Michael. 1980. "Which business leaders help govern?" Pp. 199–225 in *Power Structure Research,* edited by G. W. Domhoff. Beverly Hills, CA: Sage.

———. 1984. *The inner circle: Large corporations and the rise of business political activity in the US and UK.* New York: Oxford University Press.

van Gorkom, Jerome. 1975. "Letter to Alfred Neal, September 22." Philip M. Klutznick Papers, Box 204, Folder 4. Chicago: University of Chicago Regenstein Library.

Vernon, Raymond. 1959. *The changing economic function of the central city.* New York: Committee for Economic Development.

Vogel, David. 1989. *Fluctuating fortunes: The political power of business in America.* New York: Basic Books.

von Hoffman, Alexander. 2000. "A study in contradictions: The origins and legacy of the Housing Act of 1949." *Housing Policy Debate* 11:299–326.

Waddell, Brian. 2001. *The war against the New Deal: World War II and American democracy.* DeKalb: Northern Illinois University Press.

Wala, Michael. 1994. *The Council on Foreign Relations and American foreign policy in the early Cold War.* Providence, RI: Berghahn Books.

Wall Street Journal. 1976. "Rehabilitation project: Once-mighty CED panel of executives seeks a revival, offers advice to Carter," December 17, p. 38.

———. 2012. "More than 1 in 7 use food stamps in US." Real Time Economics, March 2, http://blogs.wsj.com/economics/2012/03/02/more-than-1-in-7-use-food-stamps-in-u-s/.

Webber, Michael. 2000. *New Deal fat cats: Business, labor, and campaign finance in the 1936 presidential election.* New York: Fordham University Press.

Weinstein, James. 1968. *The corporate ideal in the liberal state.* Boston: Beacon Press.

Weir, Margaret. 1993. *Politics and jobs: The boundaries of employment policy in the United States.* Princeton, NJ: Princeton University Press.

Weischadle, David T. 1980. "The Carnegie Corporation and the shaping of American educational policy." In *Philanthropy and cultural imperialism: The foundations at home and abroad,* edited by R. F. Arnove. Boston: G. K. Hall.

Weiss, Herman. 1975. "Letter to Donald C. Platton, November 10." *Committee for Economic Development Archives, President's Trustee Files: Weiss.* Washington, DC: Committee for Economic Development.

Welsh, James. 1973. "Welfare reform born, Aug. 8, 1960, died, Oct. 4, 1972: A sad case study of the American political process." *New York Times Sunday Magazine,* January 7, pp. 14–17, 21–23.

Western, Bruce, and Jake Rosenfeld. 2011. "Unions, norms, and the rise in US wage inequality." *American Sociological Review* 76:513–537.

White, Donald. 1983. "Golden handshake: Small business big bonanza." *San Francisco Chronicle,* p. 23.

White, Harry. 1945. "Memorandum to Henry Morgenthau Jr." In *Morgenthau Diaries,* Book 828. Hyde Park, NY: Franklin D. Roosevelt Presidential Library.

Whitham, Charlie. 2010. "More than a stepchild: The Committee for Economic Development, foreign trade, and the advance of American corporate liberalism, 1942–48." London: Department of History, City University of London.

Wirls, Daniel. 1992. *Buildup: The politics of defense in the Reagan era.* Ithaca, NY: Cornell University Press.

Wolff, Edward. 2010. "Recent trends in household wealth in the US, update to 2007: Rising debt and middle class squeeze." Annandale-on-Hudson, NY: Levy Economics Institute of Bard College.

Wolkinson, Benjamin. 1973. *Blacks, unions, and the EEOC: A study in administrative futility.* Lexington, MA: D.C. Heath.

Wood, Robert. 1959. *Metropolis against itself.* New York: Committee for Economic Development.

Woodhouse, Charles, and David McLellan. 1966. "American business leaders and foreign policy: A study in perspectives." *American Journal of Economics and Sociology* 25:267–280.

Yeazell, Stephen. 1987. *From medieval group litigation to the modern class action.* New Haven, CT: Yale University Press.

Ylvisaker, Paul. 1973. "Oral history." *Ford Foundation Archives.* New York: Ford Foundation.

Zaretksy, Natasha. 2007. *No direction home: The American family and the fear of national decline, 1968–1980.* Chapel Hill: University of North Carolina Press.

Zeigler, Harmon. 1961. *The politics of small business.* Washington, DC: Public Affairs Press.

Zweigenhaft, Richard L., and G. William Domhoff. 2003. *Blacks in the white elite: Will the progress continue?* Lanham, MD: Rowman and Littlefield.

———. 2006. *Diversity in the power elite: How it happened, why it matters.* Lanham, MD: Rowman and Littlefield.

———. 2011. *The new CEOs: Women, African American, Latino, and Asian American leaders of Fortune 500 companies.* Lanham, MD: Rowman and Littlefield.

Index

About the Author

G. William Domhoff is a Distinguished Professor Emeritus and a Research Professor at the University of California, Santa Cruz, where he has taught since 1965. He is the author or coauthor of fifteen books on power, politics, and social change in America, starting with *Who Rules America?* (1967) and *The Higher Circles* (1970), along with *The Powers That Be* (1979) and *The Power Elite and the State* (1990). His most recent books are *The Leftmost City: Power and Progressive Politics in Santa Cruz* (with Richard Gendron, 2009); *Class and Power in the New Deal: Corporate Moderates, Southern Democrats, and the Liberal-Labor Coalition* (with Michael J. Webber, 2011); *The New CEOs: Women, African American, Latino, and Asian American Leaders of Fortune 500 Companies* (with Richard L. Zweigenhaft, 2011); and *Who Rules America? The Triumph of the Corporate Rich* (seventh edition, 2013).